HOW-TO

HOW-TO:
1400 BEST BOOKS
ON
DOING ALMOST EVERYTHING

*Bill Katz and
Linda Sternberg Katz*

R. R. BOWKER COMPANY
New York and London, 1985

Published by R. R. Bowker Company
205 East 42nd Street, New York, NY 10017
Copyright © 1985 by William A. Katz
All rights reserved
Printed and bound in the United States of America

Library of Congress Cataloging in Publication Data

Katz, William A., 1924–
    How-to : 1400 best books on doing almost everything.

    Includes indexes.
    1. Do-it-yourself work—Bibliography. 2. Bibliography
—Best books—Do-it-yourself work. 3. Public libraries
—Book lists. 4. Libraries, University and college—
Book lists. I. Katz, Linda Sternberg. II. Title.
Z6151.K38 1985   [TT155]   011'.7   84-24167
ISBN 0-8352-1927-5

SHORT CONTENTS

DETAILED CONTENTS

PREFACE

The purpose of this book is to annotate approximately 1,400 of the best how-to-do-it books, including some government publications, published primarily between 1980 and 1984. A few "classics" from the 1970s are also included. It is hoped that *How-To* will assist those readers who are bewildered by the number of such titles constantly being published, as well as those still in print. There is no question that how-to-do-it books are popular. The *New York Times Book Review* editors acknowledged this when they added a special section devoted to these titles to the review's weekly listings of best-sellers.

A companion book, *Self-Help: 1400 Best Books on Personal Growth*, published by R. R. Bowker, should be used with the present work.

How-To is geared for use not only in public libraries, but also in school and academic libraries. It may be used to help individuals find specific titles and also to identify books that the library may wish to purchase or obtain on interlibrary loan. Laypersons, too, will find help here in selecting books for their home libraries. Booksellers will also find this work valuable for making decisions about which titles to stock.

Although there is no satisfactory definition of the ubiquitous how-to-do-it book, the scope is fairly well defined and identified. The focus is on guides, manuals, and general treatises that *help the individual carry out an action, usually with materials of one sort or another.* No one, for example, would confuse a guide to building a patio with a guide to exploring the personality of an introvert. The problem, of course, is that the boundaries refuse to be fixed. It is one thing to include sports and games, but can one honestly say that chess or bridge belong in the how-to category? Well, yes—at least for the purpose of this guide and according to the Dewey Decimal Classification system, which includes "indoor games of skill" along with "games of chance" and "athletic and outdoor sports and games" in the mid-790s. When in doubt, Dewey generally has been followed to establish the lines of scope.

Decisions about what to include or exclude were at our discretion, based on examination of the books, conversations and correspondence with librarians and publishers, and, where possible, standard bibliographies in the field. No one will agree entirely with our choices, or the space devoted to various subject areas. Still, an effort has been made to meet the demands and needs of the general public and libraries serving that public.

It is important to stress that this is a selective list. The materials have been judged by us to be the best now available for the average person looking for a specific how-to-do-it book. The purpose is to offer librarians, booksellers, and everyday readers a trustworthy guide. Here and there a few less-than-perfect books are included, and this is so noted in the individual annotations. The reason is twofold. First and foremost, the book may have been a best-seller, and it seems fitting to at least note its presence. Of course, many best-sellers are more than suitable, but others do not pass the relevancy or quality tests. Second, some are included simply because there is nothing else in the field. This is rare, for the real problem is not finding books in subject areas, but selecting the best ones.

The criteria for inclusion are multiple. The book must be written for the layperson and must be in language well within the grasp of the average reader. At the same time, every effort has been made to include a generous selection of titles for various education and interest levels within a given subject area. Technical titles are usually not included, although sporadically one is listed because there is nothing else available, or because it is the best in the field.

The author or compiler of the specific title must be authoritative. Usually they are experts in the field. Where this is not the case, an effort was made to test whether the derivative materials are accurate. At any rate, with exceptions noted above, only books of superior reference value are included.

The book should be current. This is more or less ensured by the 1980–1984 publication data criterion, although, of course, this in itself is not always a sure test. Each work has been examined to see if the information is up-to-date, and not simply reprinted from an earlier title. Here and there some older books are included because they remain the best in the field and are not dated.

The format should be such that the book may be used with ease. Books were examined for quality and relevance of illustrations and their proper placement in the text. Where an index is important this is noted; books lacking an index and/or exhaustive contents normally are not included.

Finally, the style of writing, the overall skill of presentation, and the sense that the book would be of real help in any how-to-do-it project or activity have been considered. Some titles that had passed the other tests failed on this count.

In addition to books, some subjects include U.S. government documents. The government has in the past, and to a lesser extent in the early 1980s, published numerous how-to-do-it pamphlets and books. The better ones are identified and briefly annotated. While it was tempting to include nonprint materials, the necessity of keeping this guide within a manageable size has precluded any reference to them.

The annotations are both descriptive and evaluative. Annotations give a brief description of content and an impression of the quality of the book, particularly as it fits into its special field of interest. It is important to re-stress that only the best titles are included, and this explains why almost all of the annotations are favorable. At the same time, an effort has been made to point out the weaknesses of an otherwise solid contribution to the subject. For example, the information may be accurate, but the illustrations only adequate.

For each title, there is a standard bibliographic entry. The price is usually the one in effect when the book was first published and is only indicative. Following the price is the Dewey Decimal Classification number, normally taken from the Online Computer Library Center (OCLC) records. In addition to an examination of the books, the OCLC record is the primary verification source. The Superintendent of Documents number is supplied for government publications. The subject headings are based on those of the Library of Congress with variations to suit the particular needs of this book.

The Detailed Contents displays the alphabetical arrangement of subject headings; there are also numerous cross-references. See also the Author Index, the Title Index, and the Subject Index.

We wish to thank the numerous librarians who so generously made suggestions, with special thanks to the staff at the Albany Public Library and the SUNY-Albany Libraries. Grateful acknowledgment, too, to Kay Callan who typed and otherwise corrected the manuscript. Also, special thanks to Julie Moore and Iris Topel at R. R. Bowker for their editorial guidance.

HOW-TO

ACROBATICS. *See* Gymnastics

ACTING. *See* Theater

ADVERTISING. *See* Show Windows

AGRICULTURE. *See* Farming; Gardening

AIRBRUSH. *See* Painting (Art)

AIRPLANES, MILITARY

Angelucci, Enzo, ed. **The Rand McNally Encyclopedia of Military Aircraft, 1914–1980.** Chicago: Rand McNally, 1981. 550p. $100 (623.74)
   The best book on the subject (excepting *Jane's All the World's Aircraft,* annual, since 1909). This offers descriptions and illustrations of over 1,700 aircraft. There are thousands of diagrams and cutaway drawings, many in color, as well as some 250 photographs. Full descriptions are given for each type of aircraft, including capsule histories. Numerous charts are used to compare and illustrate. There is no better basic reference work for anyone working with military aircraft, or, need one add, aircraft models.

AIRPLANES—PILOTING
   See also Balloons; Gliding

Baxter, Gordon. **How to Fly.** New York: Summit, 1981. 224p. $12.95 (629.13)
   Baxter, a professional writer and pilot, offers the reader some of the romance, thrills, and history of flight while giving all the basics needed to get off and back on the ground. It is a rare combination of good reading and instruction. Each step is carefully charted, from getting into the plane to the solo flight. There is a clear explanation of terminology and an even clearer one of the rules of flying. While no one can learn the art simply by reading this book, it will at least give the beginner a great deal of confidence, and certainly a feeling for the whole process. In fact, nonflyers might read it for fun.

Bramson, Alan. **Be a Better Pilot.** New York: Arco, 1980. 240p. $16.95 (629.13)
   By being "better" the author really means staying alive. The particular strength of this guide is its focus on prevention of accidents and how to get out of difficult

spots, such as a sudden downdraft or storm. Beyond that, there is a much-above-average explanation of the general principles of aeronautics by an Englishman who uses many terms heard only in the British Isles. Still, the basics of escaping death are the same anywhere.

Garrison, Paul. **Lift, Thrust & Drag: A Primer of Modern Flying.** Blue Ridge Summit, PA: TAB, 1981. 224p. pap. $8.95 (629.13)

The assumption is that the reader knows little or nothing about flying and wants to learn everything necessary to become a pilot. With that in mind, Garrison begins with basic aerodynamics and then moves logically through the various aspects of what makes up the FAA private pilot test. The book, of course, will not teach the beginner how to fly, but it does offer basic instruction in what can be learned when one is not in the pilot's seat. It would be a good book to use as a brush-up before taking the written examination.

Garrison, Peter. **Flying Airplanes: The First Hundred Hours.** New York: Doubleday, 1980. 240p. $11.95 (629.13)

The author explains basic concerns of the novice during the first hundred hours of flying, from how to get started to the probable cost of lessons. All terms are carefully defined and there are clear explanations of various aspects of the airplane and flying. From there, the author moves into a discussion of the different steps in learning to fly, from the first lesson to solo. Throughout, Garrison includes true stories, anecdotes, and various asides that give the otherwise stark manual a human, pleasant-to-read quality.

Ramsey, Dan. **Budget Flying: How to Earn Your Private Pilot License and Enjoy Flying.** New York: McGraw-Hill, 1981. 194p. $16.95 (629.13)

The author begins by giving hints on how to find a good flight instructor and how to rent a plane, plus tips on leasing or purchase. Beyond that, there are suggestions for building your own airplane. Some of the information is dated, but the background on what it takes to get a license (as well as ratings beyond the private license) is good, and the general rules concerned with securing an airplane are sound.

U.S. Department of Defense. **The Air Almanac, 1984, January–June.** Washington, DC: GPO, 1983. 472p. $10 (D213.7:984)

Essential data for anyone who is navigating an airplane. The information is updated every six months. The ephemeral and other nautical data are often used in commercial works.

U.S. Federal Aviation Administration. **Flight Training Handbook.** Washington, DC: GPO, 1980. 325p. $9 (TD4.8/5:61-21A)

An illustrated guide to the basics of flying, this takes the student from the first move into an airplane to a successful landing. In addition to basic flying procedures and maneuvers there are explanations of the airplane engine and other parts. The FAA issues a number of related publications that pilots and would-be pilots will find of value. A list is available from the FAA. *Note:* In the library, most of these will be found in the government documents section with the TD4.8 prefix.

U.S. Federal Aviation Administration. **Instrument Flying Handbook.** Washington, DC: GPO, 1980. 270p. $7.50 (TD4.8/5:61-27C)

The guide explains what is required to win an FAA instrument rating. With that, there are sections on each part of the rating. The topics covered range from basic instrumentation to radio communication. The guide assumes that the reader holds a pilot's license.

U.S. Federal Aviation Administration. **Pilot's Handbook of Aeronautical Knowledge.** Washington, DC: GPO, 1980. 260p. $11 (TD4.408:P64/5)

Anyone planning to apply for a pilot's license, as well as those who are already certified, will find this handbook of considerable value. It covers the various questions that must be answered in the certification process as well as the skills required to be demonstrated. In addition there is data on basics, from instruments to getting off and back on the ground. A section on various types of publications is of value.

ALCOHOLIC BEVERAGES. *See* Drinks; Wine

ANIMALS—FIELD GUIDES
  See also Marine Life; Nature Study; Wildlife

Audubon Society. **Field Guide Series.** New York: Knopf, 1977– . Various paging. pap. $12.50

The series, as of mid-1984, includes the following titles: *Field Guide to North American Birds: Eastern Region* (1977), *Field Guide to North American Birds: Western Region* (1977), *Field Guide to North American Butterflies* (1981), *Field Guide to North American Fishes, Whales and Dolphins* (1983), *Field Guide to North American Fossils* (1982), *Field Guide to North American Insects* (1980), *Field Guide to North American Mammals* (1980), *Field Guide to North American Mushrooms* (1981), *Field Guide to North American Reptiles and Amphibians* (1979), *Field Guide to North American Rocks and Minerals* (1979), *Field Guide to North American Seashells* (1981), *Field Guide to North American Seashore Creatures* (1981), *Field Guide to North American Trees: Eastern* (1980), *Field Guide to North American Trees: Western* (1980), *Field Guide to North American Wildflowers: Eastern* (1979), *Field Guide to North American Wildflowers: Western* (1979).

The field guides are standard in the areas covered, and among the most authoritative now available. They follow a basic pattern. Most have a "color key" consisting of color photographs of various species and types. A "habitat key," offering a detailed description of each species is also included. This series offers excellent reference material.

Burt, William. **A Field Guide to Mammals.** 3rd ed. Boston: Houghton, 1976. 289p. $14.95; pap. $8.95 (599.09)

Subtitled *Field Marks of All North American Species Found North of Mexico,* this is a member of the Peterson Field Guide series. First published in 1952, and due for a new edition shortly, it is a standard work. Approximately 400 species are discussed in detail, but the primary value of the guide is the precise information it offers on animal tracks and various other identifying features. The black-and-white illustrations are poor; the more abundant color plates are good. The guide is · sponsored by the National Audubon Society and the National Wildlife Federation.

Buschbaum, Ralph, et al. **The Audubon Society Encyclopedia of Animal Life.** New York: Potter, 1982. 606p. $45 (591)

A useful guide for the layperson. There are some 1,000 excellent black-and-white and color illustrations, including numerous close-ups. The terminology is nontechnical and descriptions are always in a readable form and the organization is easy to follow. The first five sections cover mammals, reptiles, birds, amphibians, and fish. There are 32 other categories. Each group or animal is described in a systematic way from basic characteristics to habitat and behavior. While hardly the kind of book one wants to carry about, it is an ideal encyclopedia for those who wish to know more about animal life.

Grzimek, Bernard. **Grzimek's Animal Life Encyclopedia.** New York: Van Nostrand, 1972–1975. 13 vols. $39.50 ea. (591.03)

Certainly the most famous and among the most reliable of all animal encyclopedias, this is a translation of the German original, published first in 1967. The animals are grouped together, and for each volume there is a general discussion of the group, followed by descriptions of the particular animals in their natural habitats. There are numerous illustrations, the majority in excellent color, throughout the set. The 13 volumes cover lower animals, insects, mollusks, fishes, reptiles, birds, and mammals.

Harper & Row's Complete Field Guide to North American Wildlife. Eastern Edition, ed. by Henry H. Collins, Jr. New York: Harper, 1981. 810p. $17.50; pap. $12.95 (591.97)

Western Edition, ed. by Jay E. Ransom. New York: Harper, 1981. 910p. $17.50; pap. $12.95 (591.97)

The two books cover the eastern and western sections of the United States. The Eastern edition describes and illustrates some 1,500 species, the Western edition 1,800 species. By "wildlife" the editors mean birds, mammals, reptiles, amphibians, food and game fishes, mollusks, and marine invertebrates. Each entry includes both the scientific and the common name, as well as a brief description and information on habitat. Drawings accompany many descriptions, with the color plates in the center of each book. A detailed index, which emphasizes common names, makes it easy to find the particular form of wildlife.

Murie, Claus. **A Field Guide to Animal Tracks.** 2nd ed. Boston: Houghton, 1975. 375p. $6.95; pap. $4.95 (591.5)

The classic in describing the signs animals leave in the wilderness, this is as useful today as when it was first published in 1954. Murie is a modern tracker who shows the attentive reader how to discover what animal has passed, or is near, by a careful examination of trail tracks and other marks on bushes and trees. He considers a wide variety of animals, from snakes to bears and from moles to bats. Along the way he describes the habits of the various animals and gives numerous facts and data that are as captivating as they are indicative of his understanding of the out-of-doors. The guidebook is useful for almost any part of North America.

Nowak, Ronald, and John Paradiso. **Walker's Mammals of the World.** 4th ed. Baltimore, MD: Johns Hopkins University Press, 1983. 2 vols. $65 (599)

Walker's is the standard, basic set for identification and description of the world's mammals. Often updated—it was first published in 1964—it offers a systematic arrangement of every known genus of mammal. There are concise yet good descriptions of each mammal, as well as information on its habits. For almost all genera there are photographs in natural habitats. Substantial bibliographic material is provided. This is the place to turn when all other guides fail or more information is needed.

Whitaker, John. **The Audubon Society Field Guide to North American Mammals.** New York: Knopf, 1980. 745p. pap. $11.95 (599.09)

Anyone who is trying to identify a North American (i.e., north of the Mexican border) mammal will find this guide particularly useful. The illustrations, over 180 color photographs, quickly distinguish one animal from another. There are also detailed drawings of some of the mammals. The uncomplicated text points up basic characteristics, habits of individual mammals, and other facts that inform and interest the layperson. Included are a useful index, maps, tables, and notes. The format is such that the book may be carried with ease, although it is a bit "fat."

ANTIQUES

Baker, Stanley. **Railroad Collectibles: An Illustrated Value Guide.** 2nd ed. Paducah, KY: Collector Books, 1981. 200p. pap. $8.95 (385)

Since it is virtually impossible to collect a whole train and its cars, the average collector is content with acquiring various parts of the system, as well as associated items. They are all dutifully listed here in alphabetical order, and often illustrated. Sample prices, while dated, give the collector a relative idea of value.

Bayer, Patricia, and Michael Goldman. **The Antique World Travel Guide to America: All the Best Places to Find and Buy Antiques.** New York: Doubleday, 1982. 511p. pap. $12.95 (745.1)

This is a reliable guide to about 6,000 antique dealers in the United States grouped by geographical region and then alphabetically by state and community. Hours of opening and specialties are given for most entries. Information will change, but until a new edition is published this is one of the most reliable guides of its type. In addition to dealers, the authors list major auctions, flea markets, fairs, and even museums and historic houses.

Becker, Vivienne. **Antique and Twentieth Century Jewelry: A Guide for Collectors.** New York: Van Nostrand, 1982. 301p. $24.95 (739.27)

Both a guide and an appreciative history, this book covers finer pieces of still quite wearable jewelry from the past 300 years. Items are arranged by type from cameos to stickpins, and there are numerous handsome illustrations, some in color. Each item is described quite well and in enough detail to allow the collector to determine the origin of the piece.

Bishop, Robert, et al. **Folk Art: Paintings, Sculpture & Country Objects.** Collectors' Guides to American Antiques. New York: Knopf, 1983. 478p. pap. $13.45 (745.09)

This follows the same pattern and format as the Ketchum book on chests (q.v.). There are particularly good color photographs of individual art objects and excellent advice on what to look for in determining whether the art is genuine.

Curtis, Anthony. **China.** Lyle Antiques and Their Values. New York: Putnam's, 1982. 254p. pap. $5.95 (738.07)

One of a series, this price guide offers line drawings of most of 2,000 or so priced China objects. Items are arranged in various categories and then listed in order of least expensive to most expensive. There are two sections, Western and Oriental, with breakdowns either by the company's name or by the type of ware. Prices are based on auctions, and most are in the lower to middle bracket.

Curtis, Anthony. **Dolls & Toys.** Lyle Antiques and Their Values. New York: Putnam's, 1982. 254p. pap. $5.95 (688.7)
One of a series of price guides, this is a simple, easy-to-follow approach to about 2,000 antique toys. Arrangement is by category—trains, ships, dolls, etc. Specific items are pictured, usually with a simple line drawing, followed by a short description and an estimated dollar value. The descriptions are too brief for expensive items, but most of the objects listed are in the middle range, and few collectors will need the detail required for a large investment. The handy format makes this is an ideal guide to take to an auction or to a dealer.

Curtis, Anthony. **Furniture.** Lyle Antiques and Their Values. New York: Lyle/Coward, 1982. 254p. pap. $5.95 (749.07)
One of a series, this lists prices (from least to most costly) based on auction records. Focus is on English and European furniture. Arrangement is alphabetical by furniture type and is subdivided into seventeenth- and eighteenth-century pieces and nineteenth to mid-twentieth century furniture. There are line drawings for most of the 2,000 or so items. This handy-size pocket guide will give a relative idea of an item's value although more current, more detailed guides are advised for rare, expensive pieces.

Curtis, Anthony. **Glass.** Lyle Antiques and Their Values. New York: Putnam's, 1982. 254p. $5.95 (748.2)
One of a series, this focuses on prices of mostly European glass objects (from least to most costly) based on auction records. Arrangement is alphabetical by name of object. There are line drawings for most of the items. The handy-size pocket guide will give a relative idea of an item's value, although more current, more detailed guides are advised for rare, expensive pieces.

Curtis, Anthony, ed. **The Lyle Antiques Identification Guide.** New York: Coward, 1981. 255p. pap. $4.95 (745.1)
Prepared primarily for the dealer, this is a useful guide for the dedicated collector as well. There are more than 3,000 black-and-white line drawings, which illustrate European and English antiques for almost all periods. It is a handy manual for quick recognition and dating. Arrangements are alphabetical by subject. There are numerous charts, lists, and diagrams to help readers find their way through the various periods and styles; e.g., such things as types of furniture legs and feet and china marks are found here.

Curtis, Anthony. **Metalwork.** Lyle Antiques and Their Values. New York: Putnam's, 1982. 254p. pap. $5.95 (730.07)
The emphasis in this Lyle price guide is on such collector's items as weather vanes, kettles, jugs, and other art metals. There is a line drawing for almost every object. Prices, from least to most costly, are taken from auction records.

Curtis, Anthony. **Oriental Antiques.** Lyle Antiques and Their Values. New York: Putnam's, 1982. 254p. pap. $5.95 (745.09)

One of a series of Lyle price guides, with emphasis on a wide assortment of Oriental antiques from furniture and carpets to ivory and figurines. Items are illustrated with line drawings and are briefly described. Prices, in ascending order from least to most expensive, are based on auction records.

Curtis, Anthony. **Silver.** Lyle Antiques and Their Values. New York: Putnam's, 1982. 254p. pap. $5.95 (739.2)

This Lyle price guide lists prices of mostly European silver objects (from least to most costly) based on auction records. Each item is accompanied by a line drawing. The book is divided into seventeenth to nineteenth century and nineteenth through the mid-twentieth century. Arrangement is alphabetical by name of object. The handy-size pocket guide gives a relative idea of an item's value, although more current, more detailed guides are advised for rare, expensive pieces.

Hammond, Dorothy. **Pictorial Price Guide to American Antiques.** New York: Dutton, 1977– . Irreg. 1983 ed., $12.95 (745.1)

A handy, often-updated, illustrated guide that allows the reader to easily match an antique with its price. The category arrangement is convenient, and there is a detailed index. Hammond excels at precision, i.e., there are various symbols that indicate if the price is one paid at auction or to a dealer. In addition, there is some notation of which state the price was established in, as well as an indication of the condition of the item.

Holland, Margaret. **Phaidon Guide to Silver.** Englewood Cliffs, NJ: Prentice-Hall, 1983. 256p. $12.95; pap. $6.95 (739.2)

For collectors, this is a beautifully illustrated guide to all types of silver from all periods. The author begins with the development of silverwork in the Renaissance and carries it through the nineteenth century. With that, the guide is divided by types of silver (from tableware to lighting and art works) with information on each kind of work. Silver marks, further readings, a glossary of terms, and other useful data are appended.

Hughes, Stephen. **Pop Culture Mania.** New York: McGraw-Hill, 1984. 352p. $17.95; pap. $8.95 (745.07)

Hughes sees value in "collecting 20th century Americana for fun and profit" and takes the reader on a tour of what he thinks should and should not be collected. The first part is somewhat tedious general information on collecting, much of which can be found in other books. Fortunately, the larger second section gets down to fundamentals, divided into 51 different parts. For each category, there is a general introduction and a summary of value ranges as well as tips on what to consider when purchasing an item. Just about every conceivable item, from furniture to ceramics, can be found in one of the 51 categories. Not everyone will agree on either the value or the desirability of some of these objects, but the author does offer numerous clues that will be of help to any avid pop culture collector.

Jenkins, Dorothy. **The Woman's Day Book of Antique Collectibles.** New York: St. Martin's, 1981. 239p. $19.95 (745.1)

Here the author has a definite scope for the meaning of "collectibles." They are small antiques such as fans, glass, bells, and boxes. She does not consider larger works, but within her scope the close to 40 chapters are complete and informative. Each section is accompanied by excellent photographs and, where appropriate, historical background. The guide is directed primarily to the beginning collector.

Ketchum, William C., Jr. **Chests, Cupboards, Desks and Other Pieces.** Collectors' Guides to American Antiques. New York: Knopf, 1982. 476p. pap. $13.95 (749.21)

How do you identify an antique chest, cupboard, or desk and ascertain its worth? The answer is in this guide by a contributing editor of *Antique Monthly*. This book, as with others in the series (Bishop et al., q.v.), opens with an introduction and a chapter on various collecting tools that offer a key to identification of styles and techniques. Black-and-white sketches of each type of antique, with color photographs of typical examples, appear on nearly every page. Over 300 antiques are considered over a period of about 400 years. A carefully worded text offers a basic description of the piece and enough information (materials and dimensions, place of manufacture, etc.) to allow the beginner or the expert to differentiate between the real and the fake, the variation, and the basic piece. A price guide indicates probable value. There is a glossary of terms, a bibliography, and a list of places where you may observe the various pieces.

Ketchum, William C., Jr. **Pottery & Porcelain.** Collectors' Guides to American Antiques. New York: Knopf, 1983. 478p. pap. $13.95 (738)

The entry for Ketchum's book on chests (q.v.) provides a full explanation of this series of guides. This volume follows the general pattern, with specific data on marks, dates, makers, locations, and so on. There is a good introductory section and numerous sources of potential purchases appear in the appendixes.

Kovel, Ralph, and Terry Kovel. **The Kovels' Antiques and Collectibles Price List.** New York: Crown, 1968– . Annual. 16th ed., 1983. 800p. pap. $9.95 (745.1)

This price guide now covers close to 46,000 antiques that were offered for sale the previous year. It is as reliable a guide as any published, and is quite easy to use. The prices are those reported from catalogs, auctions, antique shows, advertisements, etc. While some extremely high prices are quoted, the focus is on the middle range, i.e., antiques likely to be within the buying power of the average reader. The drawbacks are that there are only about 500 illustrations, the descriptions are so brief as to be sometimes useless unless one is an expert, and the price spread for an object may range from a few dollars to thousands without an explanation of the differences in prices. Still, as a rough guide it is the best, if only because it is so comprehensive. The same authors and publisher offer finer price breakdowns in a series that is frequently updated and usually costs $10.95 per volume. The paperbound price guides include *The Kovels' Bottle Price List; The Kovels' Illustrated Price Guide to Depression Glass & American Dinnerware; The Kovels' Illustrated Price Guide to Royal Doulton.*

Kovel, Ralph, and Terry Kovel. **The Kovels' Collectors' Source Book.** New York: Crown, 1983. 320p. $24.95; pap. $13.95 (745.1)

A useful directory for collectors, this is alphabetically arranged by type of collectible. After each entry, the authors provide information on basic publications in the field, appraisers, and auctions where the item is likely to be sold. The second part of the work is more general, including a section on basic books used to identify, price, and evaluate antiques. Other sections include restoration suppliers and buying by mail.

Kovel, Ralph, and Terry Kovel. **Kovels' Know Your Antiques.** Rev. ed. New York: Crown, 1981. 368p. $13.95 (745.1)

A general approach to antique collecting for the beginner, this is not for the specialist or near expert; the information is good, but tends to be too brief to do more than simply identify an object (almost always with an illustration, as well). No prices are given for the pieces, although occasionally ranges are indicated. It is the place to turn for a quick check to see whether a clock is an antique or a replica. It is not the best source for information on the clock. At the same time, the guide is useful for its wide coverage from pottery to needlework, from painting to furniture. Anything collected is likely to be covered here. There are also good bibliographies and the latter part of the book lists basic guides in the field from price aids to periodicals.

Kovel, Ralph, and Terry Kovel. **Kovels' Know Your Collectibles.** New York: Crown, 1982. 288p. $16.95 (745.1)

This companion to the basic *Kovels' Know Your Antiques* (q.v.) follows the same pattern of illustrations, brief descriptions, and a general introduction on collecting, avoiding fakes, etc. Each chapter covers a different subject or area, but there is no repetition of specific items found in the earlier volume. Items range from pottery and dinnerware to clocks and toys. There is a good section on paper as well as metal ephemera. The time span tends to be from mid-nineteenth century to modern, although there are exceptions. No prices are noted.

The Lyle Official Antiques Review. New York: Perigee, 1970– . Annual. 1983 ed., 670p. $24.95; pap. $14.95 (745.1)

This is the price guide for antiques and it is particularly valuable for a quick identification of items. Of the 10,000 or so items listed each year, most are relatively expensive. Antiques are mostly from continental Europe and England, with fewer ones from the United States and Canada. Figures are based on auctions held in the various countries as well as prices from a few select retail outlets. Only art (i.e., paintings and prints) is not included, and one may find everything here from furniture to automobiles. Descriptions are brief and, besides the price, include dimensions. Most items are illustrated with line drawings. The book is arranged by categories and there is a detailed index for easy access. *Note:* A run of these reviews, published now for over a decade, is a fine guide not only to prices, but to most of the world's important antiques that have come up for sale. When using for price guidance, be sure to consult the latest volume. *Also:* Earlier editions, edited by Anthony Curtis, are useful for descriptions and relative prices.

Naeve, Milo. **Identifying American Furniture: A Pictorial Guide to Styles and Terms, Colonial to Contemporary.** Nashville, TN: American Association for State and Local History, 1981. 87p. $14 (749.21)

Anyone trying to rapidly identify an American piece of furniture will find the answer here. There are some 170 black-and-white photographs of basic styles from the seventeenth to the mid-twentieth century. The book is divided into periods, with a brief introduction to each. Arrangement is ideal for quick identification. The photograph is on a left-hand page and the various elements of style are on the right. One simply locates the approximate time frame (this can be done through an excellent index), turns to the specific style section, and then compares the description and the photographs with the piece in question. The book ends with a good bibliography. While much smaller than many handbooks of this type, it is ideal to carry about for a quick notion of what one is considering. Then, if necessary, more information can be found in specialized guides.

Rush, Richard. **Selling Collectibles for Profit and Capital Gain.** New York: Harper, 1981. 288p. $14.50 (332)

Once an individual has purchased art and antiques as a hedge against inflation, how can the collectibles be sold? The answer, in considerable detail, is given by the author of the earlier *Art As an Investment* (1961). There is the usual information about working with auction houses and art dealers, and the not so usual—how to sell through newspapers and what may come out of dealing with an art museum. The information is not likely to become dated, and most of the advice is simple common sense seasoned with more than a dash of experience. Rush offers a list of various dealers and auction houses, as well as other sources (and resources) that may be of value.

Schwartz, Marvin. **Chairs, Tables, Sofas & Beds.** Collectors' Guides to American Antiques. New York: Knopf, 1982. 478p. pap. $13.95 (749.2)

This follows the same pattern and format as the Ketchum book on chests (q.v.). About 350 pieces of furniture are described that were constructed in the past four centuries. There is one item per page, and it is usually accompanied by a full-color illustration. There are prices, as well. For a fuller description of the series see the aforementioned Ketchum.

Spillman, Jane. **Glass Bottles, Lamps & Other Objects.** Collectors' Guides to American Antiques. New York: Knopf, 1983. 478p. pap. $13.95 (748.2)

Here is an expansion of the earlier Spillman book in this series on glass (q.v.) and it follows the same general pattern as the Ketchum book on chests (q.v.). There are color illustrations of the hundreds of objects, as well as full information on how to identify and date them.

Spillman, Jane. **Glass Tableware, Bowls & Vases.** Collectors' Guides to American Antiques. New York: Knopf, 1982. 478p. pap. $13.95 (748.2)

This follows the same pattern and format as the Ketchum book on chests (q.v.). The guide has a distinct advantage over the others in the series in that the time span is limited to 200 years. (The others cover some 400 years each.) This allows for more specialization. The author is the experienced curator of American glass at the Corning Museum of Glass.

Turner, Gerard. **Nineteenth-Century Scientific Instruments.** Berkeley: University of California Pr., 1983. 320p. $60 (502.8)

Ideal for the person collecting scientific instruments, this book offers photographs of each apparatus, as well as detailed explanations. Written by an Oxford Museum curator, it is divided by various functions, such as instruments that measure or are used with sound, time, light, and the like. Each is carefully described and normally put into historical context.

VonZweck, Dina. **The Woman's Day Dictionary of Glass.** Secaucus, NJ: Citadel, 1983. 161p. pap. $4.95 (748.2)

The author discusses a wide variety of collectible glass from about 1800 to the middle of the present century. The emphasis is on American products. The arrangement is by name of the glass, design, pattern, manufacturer, or other likely point of identification. Entries run from a few words to several pages, and most are accompanied by adequate black-and-white illustrations. A helpful feature is the inclusion of the approximate market cost of a given item. Considering the scope and the low price of this guide, it is surely a best buy.

The Warner Collector's Guide to. . . . New York: Random House, 1981– . Irreg. Approx. 250–300p. Approx. $10 pap.

The series includes *The Warner Collector's Guide to Pressed Glass* (1982), *Clocks* (1981), *Longarms* (1981), *Pottery and Porcelain* (1982), *Quilts* (1981), *Toys* (1981), *Dolls* (1982), *Pressed Glass* (1982), *Sterling Silver* (1982).

Written by various experts, the guides normally cover a 100–200 year period in antiques and collector's items primarily from America, with some English influence. The organization normally is by the object's various forms. Each piece is described, and there are good photographs, usually in color. The descriptive material, which includes black-and-white photographs of patterns and identification marks when needed, is precise enough to allow almost immediate identification of a piece. Prices usually are not given, except in a general way to indicate value. The pocket-size volumes are handy to carry to shows and markets.

APARTMENTS

Ardman, Harvey, and Perri Ardman. **The Complete Apartment Guide.** New York: Macmillan, 1982. 401p. $19.95; pap. $9.95 (643.2)

Carefully illustrated with fine photographs, this is a detailed guide on how to make an apartment a home. Almost every problem or question is considered, from the colors of the walls, to various approaches to furnishing, to minor and major remodeling. There is a room-by-room analysis of what may be necessary to bring the apartment up to the requirements of the particular reader. Most of the suggestions do not involve heavy cash outlays, and there are many money-saving tips. Sections on finding an apartment, legal questions, and relationships with the landlord are of more limited use.

Bradford, Barbara. **Luxury Designs for Apartment Living.** Garden City, NY: Doubleday, 1981. 344p. $24.95 (747.88)

An author of numerous books on interior decorating, Bradford readily perceives what the average reader wants to know about the subject. She has a firm grasp of both the interests and the probable incomes of her readers. The result is extremely practical advice, suitable for almost all situations whether one is renting or buying an apartment. The stress, however, is on renting, and most of the suggestions involve decoration schemes with furniture and accessories the reader may one day move to another abode. She is particularly good on the use of lighting, color, and furniture arrangement to make a room livable. There are numerous photographs with complete explanations, and here and there she gives the opinion of major designers. Actually, much of the advice is as applicable to a home as to an apartment, although the focus is on making the most of small spaces.

APPLIANCES

Bragdon, Allen. **Popular Mechanics Home Appliance Repair Manual.** New York: Hearst, 1981. 320p. $19.95 (643.6)

How to fix almost anything around the home is explained here in clear, precise steps. Each method of repair is accompanied by diagrams, checklists, detailed photographs, and other aids. The book is written so that even an incompetent should be able to handle repair and maintenance of smaller appliances from toasters to blenders. For the more ambitious and talented, there are explanations of larger units such as furnaces and solar heating systems. Then, too, there is a commonsense introduction that gives basics about such things as wiring and testing circuits. The authors appreciate the problems of less-than-mechanically minded readers and, for smaller items, clearly indicate the item by brand name. One of the best of its kind. Look for later editions.

Darak, Arthur, et al. **How to Repair and Care for Home Appliances.** Englewood Cliffs, NJ: Prentice-Hall, 1983. 184p. $22.95; pap. $12.95 (643.6)

There are two attitudes toward the average home appliance: let it run for its life span and replace it, or do everything possible to repair it and have it last forever. In the latter camp, Darak offers methods of fixing basic appliances from toasters and hair dryers to washing machines. Many of the easy-to-follow explanations are accompanied by diagrams showing where major parts fit and their functions. There is a good section on wiring and the minimum number and type of tools and supplies needed. Arrangement is by broad type of appliance, and each section shows a specific malfunction and what can be done to bring about a cure.

How Things Work in Your Home (And What to Do When They Don't). Alexandria, VA: Time-Life, 1975. 368p. $19.95 (643.7)

This differs from countless "fix-it" books because it features: (1) detailed, yet easy-to-read diagrams of just about every fixture in the average home; and (2) charts that outline the ills of machines and their cures. Whatever the problem, color-keyed drawings make it possible for you to repair the item. There are tips, too, on best approaches to home repairs, when to call a professional, and the like. While all of this requires a given amount of skill and some daring on the part of the reader, anyone who has the courage to go ahead will find all the help needed in this handy volume.

Jones, Peter. **The Electrician's Bible.** New York: Doubleday, 1982. 129p. pap. $4.95 (621.31)

While this is far from a "bible," it is a good starting point for the individual who knows little or nothing about electrical wiring, and may be quite nervous about tackling it. Jones thoroughly explains the electrical elements of an average home, and gives due attention to possibilities of danger due to ignorance. With that, he explains the basics of wiring and the tools required. This is all adequately illustrated. There are sections, too, on the maintenance of household appliances, although they are less useful. Jones offers some basic projects that are explained in detail, and they tend to be the jobs most often required about the house, e.g., how to install simple units and replace the main distribution box.

U.S. Department of Labor. **An Illustrated Guide to Electrical Safety.** Washington, DC: GPO, 1983. 184p. $5.50 (L35.6/2:3073)
    Most people are nervous about repairing electrical appliances and fixtures and dealing with wires and wiring. This guide literally explains, with illustrations, how to avoid shocks. It provides, too, advice for safety around the home and place of business.

AQUARIUMS. *See* Fish (Pets)

ARCHAEOLOGY

Sullivan, George. **Discovering Archaeology.** New York: Penguin, 1981. 273p. pap. $4.95 (930.1)
    Here, "discovering" refers to a practical how-to-do-it guide for the individual who wants to learn about digs and preservation. The focus on the day-by-day aspects of the subject is complemented by brief historical excursions. Written for the layperson, its clear explanations and good prose style make it useful for any individual of almost any age or background.

Wilson, Josleen. **The Passionate Amateur's Guide to Archaeology in the United States.** New York: Macmillan, 1981. 465p. pap. $12.95 (930.1)
    Here is a combination guide that ranges from the basics of archaeology (the first section) to a detailed description of sites and museums devoted to prehistoric America. The latter part is organized by region and by state, and full information is given about visiting hours and admission costs. While primarily a directory and travel book, it is an invaluable source of information, even for the nontraveler, about American primitive life, including early Indians.

ARCHITECTURE. *See* Homes—Building & Construction; Homes—Remodeling

ARITHMETIC. *See* Mathematics

ART—COLLECTING

Kaplan, Ellen. **Prints: A Collector's Guide.** New York: Coward, 1983. 256p. $22.95 (769)
    Beginning with a definition and an explanation of what a print is, the author considers the ins and outs of collecting for both pleasure and profit. The emphasis is definitely on business and on methods of identifying the work of a particular

artist; most of the book consists of brief sketches of twentieth-century artists and their work. (The focus is on modern prints because the author believes older ones tend to be more expensive and out of the range of most collectors.) The summaries include a representative list of the artist's work, as well as current prices. There is also an illustration of a typical print. Actually, this treatment is too cursory for the avid fan, but it at least serves to introduce the beginner to possibilities. It is not for the individual with some experience and knowledge of prints.

Rosenbaum, Lee. **The Complete Guide to Collecting Art.** New York: Knopf, 1982. 288p. $17.50 (707.5)

While collecting art is generally the province of those in upper-income brackets, it does not have to be. Here an expert explains how almost anyone can build at least a modest collection. The first requirement, of course, is an interest in art and a considerable education in art history. After that, one should go to art shows, auctions, museums, and openings to discover what one likes, dislikes, and can afford. Where the guide excels is in practical advice on how to buy art, how to determine value, what to avoid, and what to do when "taken" by someone less than honest. There are sections, too, on the advantages of art collecting as a tax aid and inflation hedge, and how to insure the art against theft and fire. All of this is written in a chatty, informative style and will be appreciated particularly by the novice.

Shapiro, Cecile, and Laurie Mason. **Fine Prints: Collecting, Buying and Selling.** New York: Harper, 1976. 256p. $10.95 (796.12)

While there are numerous books on collecting prints, this remains one of the best, at least for the amateur and beginner. True, much of the pricing information has changed, but the basic advice on how to select, evaluate, and purchase a print is as valid today as the day the book was published. The writing style is relaxed, almost conversational. The authors explain various techniques, and go through the steps necessary for the collector to master, including conservation. There are the usual glossaries—but this time in French and German as well as English—and a still-useful list of museums and dealers.

Warner, Glen. **Building a Print Collection: A Guide to Original Prints and Photographs.** New York: Van Nostrand, 1981. 192p. pap. $8.95 (769.12)

A rudimentary guide to what to look for when considering a print or a photograph for a personal collection, this book covers several basic situations. Warner believes the buyer should be more concerned with personal likes and dislikes than with monetary appreciation, but he certainly gives the latter attention. He urges the buyer to look for real bargains, that is to say, to shop around before coming to a decision. Practical advice is given on how to select a reliable dealer, on the difference between various types of print techniques, and on how to detect fakes and forgeries. There is a section, too, on selling prints.

Zigrosser, Carl, and Christa Gaehde. **A Guide to the Collecting and Care of Original Prints.** New York: Crown, 1965. 120p. $7.95 (769)

Many consider this the best introduction to prints for beginners and novices. Although now some 20 years old, the advice and the historical perspective are in no way dated. The book is particularly useful in explaining what constitutes a print and what its various states are, as well as the numerous techniques employed in print production. There is no better information in the field on how to identify an original, how to evaluate a particular work, and how to judge whether it is for the would-be purchaser. There are sections, too, on framing, care of prints, and restoration. Zigrosser knows more about prints than almost any other expert, and, fortunately, he has a witty and informative style to match his knowledge. This is the first place to turn for an introduction, and even an expert collector will find much of value.

ASTRONOMY

Chartrand, Mark. **Skyguide: A Field Guide for Amateur Astronomers.** San Marion, CA: Golden-West, 1982. 280p. $9.95; pap. $6.95 (523)

This is distinguished from other good guides in that the opening sections present a clearer-than-average method of locating particular celestial bodies and individual stars, planets, comets, etc. There are detailed maps showing what is to be found within a particular area of the sky. Each of the primary bodies is described on the left-hand page with charts, photos, and other identifying matter on the right. Compared with Muirden's *Astronomy Handbook* (q.v.), there is little distinction, both being excellent. Muirden is easier to understand, but Chartrand is almost 100 pages longer and contains some material not in Muirden.

Henbest, Nigel, and Michael Marten. **The New Astronomy.** New York: Cambridge University Pr., 1983. 240p. $24.95 (520)

While not a how-to-do-it guide, this overview of the new computer-processed astronomy deserves attention by anyone remotely interested in the subject. There is a full description of the purpose of the wide search of the sky, and a discussion of the various kinds of telescopes employed. These are extremely costly machines, well beyond the needs of the amateur. At the same time, the amateur will want to know of their existence. There are marvelous color illustrations.

King-Hele, Desmond. **Observing Earth Satellites.** New York: Van Nostrand, 1983. 184p. $16.50 (629.43)

There are now well over 5,000 man-made satellites in space. This guide shows how the amateur astronomer may track and identify at least 40 to 45 percent of the objects. What makes the guide unusual is that the spotting can be done with little more than a pair of high-powered binoculars and a thorough appreciation of mathematics. The latter qualification may limit the usefulness of this guide for many readers, but those with the patience and the necessary background will find the book fascinating. There are good illustrations.

McGraw-Hill Encyclopedia of Astronomy. New York: McGraw-Hill, 1983. 450p. $44.50 (523)

One of the best approaches to astronomy for laypersons, this represents contributions from over 100 experts (each writing in a particular area) and covers all topics of interest for anyone involved with the subject. It is particularly noteworthy for the excellent illustrations, some in color, and the thoroughness of coverage, which includes discoveries and findings to 1983. There are well-written, easy-to-follow background articles on the history of astronomy, as well as concise, clear explanations of various accepted and still problematical theories. While there is no how-to-do-it material per se, there is much of value to the individual who is considering constructing an observatory; see, for example, the detailed section on optics—necessary reading for the telescope maker. *Note:* Most of this material is found in the larger *McGraw-Hill Encyclopedia of Science and Technology* (1982) from which it was largely taken.

Mayer, Ben. **Starwatch.** New York: Perigee, 1984. 144p. $15.95; pap. $7.95 (523)

Among countless books on how to study the heavens, this is one with a difference. The difference is great enough to warrant its consideration by novice and intermediate astronomy buffs. What Mayer does is to sort out the heavens with 24 charts. Each chart locates the prominent stars, nebulae, clusters, and other objects. The individual chart is preceded by about two pages of text explaining the primary bodies to be seen within that particular area of the heavens. This division is quite simple, yet it offers a marvelous and easy-to-follow system. In addition, there are general chapters on the joys of astronomy as well as details on how to make two instruments that will help the beginner locate the stars. The illustrations are good and found throughout the guide.

Menzel, Donald, and Jay Menzel. **A Field Guide to the Stars and Planets.** 2nd ed. Boston: Houghton, 1983. 473p. $17.95; pap. $12.45 (532)

One of the Field Guide Series, this follows the pattern of others in the group. Each star and planet is clearly described and located in the heavens with indications of how it may be found. There are excellent illustrations, as well as updated monthly sky charts. The guide will be useful to both beginners and intermediate astronomers.

Muirden, James. **Astronomy Handbook.** New York: Arco, 1982. 190p. $8.95 (523)

There are numerous astronomy handbooks, but this has the advantage of being small, easy to handle, and reasonably priced. At the same time, it includes all of the basic information required by amateurs and students. (It is not for the expert.) The 13 chapters include some how-to-do-it information on such things as building telescopes, a sundial, and even a planetarium. This is not detailed enough for more complex projects, although suitable for simple things such as making a sky diary. There are clear definitions; numerous tables, charts, and diagrams; and excellent illustrations, many in color. It is one of the best of its kind because the author has a fine writing style and an appreciation for his audience.

Raymo, Chet. **365 Starry Nights: An Introduction to Astronomy for Every Night of the Year.** Englewood Cliffs, NJ: Prentice-Hall, 1982. $21.95; pap. $12.95 (523)

No telescope is needed. All that is required is a good eye and these charts. The author points out what anyone should be able to see on a given night of the year—i.e., if the atmospheric conditions are conducive to sight. As Raymo concentrates only on the larger bodies, from constellations to well-known stars, the guide allows for a simplified view of the heavens. (As such it is hardly a replacement for more concentrated guides.) Sightings may be done in any part of the United States and the southern sections of Canada. For each chart there is a brief explanation of what is in view.

Ronan, Colin. **The Practical Astronomer.** New York: Macmillan, 1981. 205p. $20 (520)

A basic guide to astronomy for the beginner and near expert, this is a well-written work by an author who is one of the leading writers in the field. Ronan organizes his work around some 60 explanations and experiments that painlessly lead the reader to a better understanding of the subject. Thanks to the organization, one need only choose a topic of interest and begin to read. Since the book does not have to be approached from chapter to chapter, it is excellent for browsing. Oversized, with numerous illustrations, many in striking color, it can be examined with pleasure.

Traister, Robert, and Susan Harris. **Astronomy & Telescopes: A Beginner's Handbook.** Blue Ridge Summit, PA: TAB, 1983. 200p. $19.95 (522.2)

The strong point of this book is the consumer reports section on how to choose a good, yet inexpensive, commercial telescope. Furthermore, there are instructions on how to build both your own telescope and a modest observatory. A useful chapter gives tips on how to photograph what you see through the telescope. Less satisfactory, although basic, are the chapters on astronomy and the solar system. Nicely balanced with illustrations and various star charts.

U.S. Department of Defense. **The Astronomical Almanac for the Year 1984.** Washington, DC: GPO, 1983. 580p. $14 (D213.8:984)

Here is data, gathered by the U.S. Naval Observatory and the British government, for both professional and amateur astronomers and space watchers. The figures are of interest to others as well, including navigators (both sea and air) and surveyors.

U.S. Department of Defense. **Stars in Your Eyes: A Guide to the Northern Skies.** Washington, DC: GPO, 1981. 24p. $3 (D103.2:St 2)

An illustrated guide that points out and explains the ten basic constellations visible in the northern skies during the summer. The illustrations support the directions for locating the stars, and there is background material on myths and legends about the constellations.

Whitney, Charles. **Whitney's Star Finder: A Field Guide to the Heavens.** Rev. ed. New York: Knopf, 1981. 128p. pap. $8.95 (523)

Here is a handy guide to almost every aspect of locating and identifying objects in the heavens. The author is as comfortable explaining how to find a star as he is discussing planets, eclipses, comets, and just about anything connected with sky watching. There are good diagrams and illustrations to support the text, and a most useful star finder guide that makes it possible to pinpoint a specific star from any location in the northern or southern hemisphere. In addition, there are lists of eclipses, phases of the moon, etc. *Note:* This is due to be updated in 1985.

ATHLETICS. *See* Games; Sports

AUTOMATION. *See* Computers

AUTOMOBILES
  See also Motorcycles

Georgano, G. V., ed. **The New Encyclopedia of Motor Cars: 1885 to the Present.** 3rd ed. New York: Dutton, 1982. 688p. $45 (629.22)

Anyone who reconditions, collects, or is otherwise interested in old cars will treasure this carefully written, nicely illustrated survey. The content truly is encyclopedic in that close to 4,500 cars from every period are dutifully identified and equally well explained in terms of their history, design, success or failure, and so on. Most are illustrated with black-and-white photographs, although a central section is reserved for color shots of about 60 classics. There is another useful feature: The editor often includes information on kits for turning a standard body into a unique automobile from almost any period. While exhaustive and the first place one would turn for the history of cars, this book does not include racing machines. *Note:* Often updated, so look for the latest edition.

Traister, Robert. **All about Electric and Hybrid Cars.** Blue Ridge Summit, PA: TAB, 1982. 303p. $16.95; pap. $9.95 (629.22)

For years, major automobile manufacturers have talked about electric cars. No need to wait. Using this guide, and admittedly considerable mechanical experience and ingenuity, one can build such a machine. About one-third of the book is devoted to information about kits that may be purchased to aid in the construction. For the less energetic there is information on small companies that now supply, although in limited numbers, such cars. The "hybrid" in the title is a reference to automobiles that have added sources of power to augment the electric drive. There are good illustrations and various charts throughout.

U.S. Department of Defense. **Principles of Automotive Vehicles.** Washington, DC: GPO, 1979. 537p. $12 (D101.11:9–8000)

An army technical and field manual, this is about as basic as one can get in describing the principles of modern automotive vehicles. As there is no emphasis on individual models, the manual is in no way dated. It sets out to explain in layperson's language the various components of automobiles—components so basic as to show little change over the years. The treatment traces the flow of power from its development in the engine to its final outlet at the wheels. Diesel as well as gasoline engines are covered. Chassis components are discussed, and there are special sections on motorcycles and trailers. The guide is heavily illustrated.

AUTOMOBILES—MAINTENANCE & REPAIR

Automotive Encyclopedia. South Holland, IL: Goodheart-Willcox, 1954–   . Biennial. 1982 ed., $16 (629.2)

A basic and easy-to-follow guide to automobiles, this serves two distinct purposes. First, it explains in great detail how an automobile operates—from the transmission to the headlights. Second, in so doing, it gives enough basic information so that one may be able to understand, if not make, simple repairs and to carry out maintenance operations. There are good sections on related matters from hydraulics to electricity, and the whole combines into what many believe to be the best introduction to the subject. Still, the reader should be reminded that for specifics, it is best to turn to a specialized guide, such as one of the Chilton manuals (q.v.).

Chilton's Auto Repair Manual. Radnor, PA: Chilton, 1940–   . Annual. 1982 ed., 1,296p. $17.95 (629.28)

While the Reader's Digest book (q.v.) is the best one for laypersons, Chilton's is a first choice for more experienced automobile fans, mechanics, and those who seek detailed information on larger jobs not covered in other manuals. (See also *Chilton's Repair & Tune-Up Guide. . . .*) Here one finds information on maintenance, troubleshooting and diagnostic advice, and analysis of each major part of the automobile from the electrical system to the transmission. There are numerous illustrations that support the basic directions. Chilton's is particularly valuable for precise data on maintenance procedures. Basic systems in all American current models are covered. (Turn to older editions for older automobiles.) The manual may be used, too, for routine matters such as checking on antifreeze requirements. The basic work is complemented by a similar title, *Chilton's Import Automotive Repair Manual,* which follows the same pattern and publication schedule, but for foreign cars.

Chilton's Guide to Consumers' Auto Repairs and Prices. Radnor, PA: Chilton, 1980. 176p. $10.95; pap. $9.95 (629.28)

Based on the more thorough, more technical *Chilton's Professional Labor Guide and Parts Manual* (1981), this gives a specific outline of what to expect a dealer or a garage to charge for a part or a specific repair. There is an itemized list of normal repairs with fair and estimated labor costs. (These, of course, may differ from area to area, but at least they give the reader a relative notion of expenses.) There are discussions on how to select a mechanic and which repairs can be done by most laypersons. Other sections consider basics such as financing a car, and what to look for in purchasing a used car.

Chilton's Repair & Tune-Up Guide. . . . [125+ guides for specific makes of cars] Radnor, PA: Chilton. Various dates, paging, prices (629.287)

The best known and in many ways the best organized and easiest to follow of all the automobile repair and tune-up guides, Chilton's is the first place to turn for this type of information. While suitable for relative beginners, much of the work described does require skill and, above all, the proper tools. Still, the volumes may be consulted by awkward car owners who simply want to understand their machines, and who may want to check repairs done by others.

Each guide follows a basic pattern, and all are comprehensive in their coverage. The explanations are detailed, and offer a step-by-step approach to every one of the hundreds of various jobs. In addition, there are numerous schematic drawings, diagrams, specification tables, photographs, etc., which make it relatively easy to follow the directions given. There is a full description of parts and the various systems. The guides all offer suggestions on how to diagnose and find the difficulty and how to solve particular problems. As of 1984 Chilton offered over 125 guides for both domestic and foreign automobiles, from BMW 1970–1982 (272p. pap. $10.95) to a VW front-wheel drive 1974–1983 (288p. pap. $10.85). The guides are updated each year and normally include models 10 to 12 years back.

In addition to the repair and tune-up guide and the auto repair manual series, Chilton publishes guides for repairing vast numbers and types of related mechanical products ranging from a group of motorcycle repair manuals to power accessories, mobile homes, and inboard engines. Almost all of these titles begin with the word *Chilton's.* They are excellent, and by and large the first place to turn for detailed, easy-to-follow, and illustrated instructions.

Fendell, Bob. **How to Make Your Car Last a Lifetime.** New York: Holt, 1981. 216p. $14.95; pap. $7.95 (629.28)

There is no reason a car should not last 10 or 20 or even 30 years according to this author, who is an expert on the subject of automobile maintenance. He explains how certain driving skills will save the driver's car from the junk heap. What to do and not to do with the engine and other vital parts is carefully explained. The value of alterations and equipment is explored, and there is a handy guide on what to look for when buying the initial new car. There is a basic explanation of how a car operates and some handy charts such as the one on the annual cost of gasoline.

Glickman, Arthur. **Mr. Badwrench: How You Can Survive the $20 Billion-a-Year Auto Repair Ripoff.** New York: Harper, 1981. 447p. $15.50; pap. $9.50 (629.28)

An expert on the bad mechanic, the author explains the various procedures employed to rip off the American public. After a thorough exposure of the auto-repair rackets, he turns to what the individual can do for self-protection. The words of wisdom are supported by extensive research, interviews, and personal experience. Not only does Glickman consider the corner or dealer garage, but he goes right to the manufacturer, where much of the rip-off begins. He also considers related areas such as automobile departments in chain stores and parts centers. The specific data are by now somewhat dated, but the problem remains much the same, and the solutions offered are as good today as the day the book was written.

Joseph, James. **The Car-Keeper's Guide.** Chicago: Contemporary, 1982. 192p. $17.50; pap. $10.95 (629.28)

The author is a bit of an optimist in his claim that most cars are sound, both in motor and in body. If one accepts this, the next step is to go out and purchase an old car and gradually bring it back to health. (His experience is based on the restoration of a 1968 automobile.) This is not advice for people with brand new automobiles, but it is for the individual who, by choice or necessity, must have a used car. The basic attack is one of restoration, that is, he believes in spending up to $100 a month on simply replacing parts and looking after the body. He indicates which parts are likely to go when, and gives advice on finding a good mechanic. This latter "catch" is a major one, for despite his words of wisdom, the fact remains that smaller communities simply may not have that type of service handy. Still, if one does have a good mechanic, it is possible to gradually build up and maintain a car that is ten years old or older.

McGraw-Hill Automotive Technology Series. New York: McGraw-Hill, 1942–   . $14.50–$17.95 (629.2)

This is a detailed, specialized series of guides for the individual with mechanical ability and at least some experience working on automobiles. The volumes follow the usual style, established by such publishers as Chilton, and they are in two or three parts. Each opens with operating principles, theories, and methods. The text then moves on to specifics, normally divided by subject or type of operation. All sections are carefully illustrated and the explanations are in logical, easy-to-follow order. Currently, these are edited by William Crouse and include *Automotive Air Conditioning; Automotive Electrical Equipment; Automotive Engines; Automotive Fuel, Lubricating and Cooling Systems;* and *Automotive Transmissions and Power Trains.* All are regularly updated, and the latest edition should be requested.

Motor's Auto Repair Manual. New York: Motor, 1937– . Annual. 1983 ed., $16.95 (629.28)

A standard work in the field, and while not as detailed as some of the Chilton guides (q.v.), this offers a good, collective overview. Automobiles in current production are considered in each annual edition. The value of the guide is that it shows the primary service operations that must be performed and it illustrates and explains basic repairs. There are useful sections concerned with tuning and maintenance. Complemented by the same publisher's *Motor's Auto Trouble Shooter* (1950– , irreg.).

Olney, Ross. Listen to Your Car: An Easy Guide to Identifying Car Troubles. New York: Walker, 1981. 80p. $9.95 (629.28)

When you hear a hum or a thud when there should be none, what is the problem? The author identifies the probable difficulty in your car. He believes "noises are the language of a car complaining about its maladies." Your car has a language of its own. Learn the language and solve its problems. This is a sound approach, and one used by most trained mechanics. It does assume, however, that you have a good ear and a basic knowledge of automotive systems. There are some basic guidelines for repair, but the primary emphasis is on diagnosis.

Reader's Digest Complete Car Care Manual. New York: Random House, 1981. 480p. $23.50 (629.28)

The best all-around general manual of its kind, at least for the layperson. Almost all minor repair work that can be done by a nonmechanic is covered. Despite the date, the manual will be useful for many years to come because it is concerned with basics that do not change that much from year to year, and the primary purpose is to give the reader enough information about automobiles to allow intelligent, reasonable care and maintenance, regardless of the car's year. For information on tuning cars produced since 1980, consult the supplement, which is found in an envelope in the book. There are six primary sections, covering what it costs to drive an automobile to how it functions to major components. The other three parts focus on maintenance, including the necessary tools and basic methods of tuning and repair. Typical times for repair are given. There is commonsense advice on what to look for in a used car, and how to road test an automobile, used or new. All of this is carefully assembled with excellent illustrations and a useful index.

Robert Bentley Complete Service Manuals. Cambridge, MA: Robert Bentley. Various dates, paging, prices (629.28)

The guides, which average about $24 each, are paperback and differ from others in that the focus is entirely on foreign cars. As of 1984 there are 9 service manuals for the Volkswagen from 1966, 3 for Audi, 5 for Toyota, and 15 for British Leyland (i.e., MG's, Jaguars, and Triumphs). The supposition is that the reader is a mechanic, or has basic skills as well as the necessary tools. Each guide is logically divided by parts of the car from the transmission and drive shaft to the engine, body, and interior. Each has an excellent section on lubrication and maintenance. Every page boasts illustrations, line drawings as well as photographs. Anyone familiar with the basic type of auto manual will be at home with these up-to-date, well-written, and carefully organized titles. They are recommended for their particular clarity and their fine, easy-to-follow directions.

Ross, James. **How to Get 50,000 More Miles Out of Your Car.** New York: St. Martin's, 1982. 255p. $13.95; pap. $7.95 (629.28)

Numerous tricks from an expert driver along with those from the mechanic's trade are outlined and explained. The idea is to make your car run and run and run—trouble free. Most of the suggestions, particularly the maintenance tips, may be carried out by the individual car owner. Here everything is explained from the function of the transmission to the necessity for waxing. The various tasks vary in difficulty, from changing the oil to repairing an engine. Where extensive treatment is necessary, Ross explains how to find a good mechanic and what to expect. There are useful directions on ways of driving to extend car life. The language is easy to follow, and there are good illustrations.

Sikorsky, Robert. **Drive It Forever: Your Key to Long Automobile Life.** New York: McGraw-Hill, 1983. 176p. $12.95; pap. $6.95 (629.28)

A man who knows how to save gas turns to telling how to save the automobile from wearing out, or at least getting it well past the 100,000 mile mark. He is concerned with several basic techniques, from driving at given speeds and in certain ways to periodic maintenance. The primary interest is in saving the engine from undue strain and wear. The author has advice on how to select oil, gasoline, and other products. While most of this is well known to experienced drivers, there are just enough tips to make it worthwhile for even the veteran car owner. A side benefit is that every mile of engine wear saved also cuts down on gas consumption.

Sikorsky, Robert. **How to Get More Miles per Gallon.** New York: St. Martin's, 1978. 111p. o.p. (629.2)

All aspects of cutting gas costs are considered in this well-written and illustrated text. The author is an expert on the subject and is able to list close to 300 ways of saving gas. Among his topics: parking methods, highway and city driving, the use of certain additives, tire pressure and care, maintenance, etc. While material on emission controls is slightly dated, most of the text is timeless in that the tips are sound no matter what model or type of car is driven.

AUTOMOBILES—PURCHASE & EVALUATION

Consumer Reports Guide to Used Cars. Boston: Little, 1983. 256p. pap. $12.95 (629.22)

The latest edition of this basic guide came out in 1983, and covers used cars manufactured from 1977 through 1982. (It is frequently updated, and one should request the latest edition. Note too that cars are covered in various issues of the nonprofit organization's magazine, Consumer Reports.) The information is about as basic and reliable as any and it should be a first stop for anyone trying to get accurate data on a used car. Each model is carefully and specifically rated with guidelines as to what to look for in the way of possible faults. As there is a systematic, similar checklist for each make of car, one may quickly see which is better for gas mileage, brakes, pickup, etc. A must for anyone trying to discover what and what not to do when buying a used car.

Darak, Arthur. **Used Cars: How to Avoid Highway Robbery.** Englewood Cliffs, NJ: Prentice-Hall, 1983. 226p. $18.95; pap. $7.95 (629.2)

Working in conjunction with a nonprofit consumer group, the author explains in detail exactly what to look for when considering the purchase of a used car. The warning signals of potential trouble are clearly and concisely indicated. There is a useful guide to the general costs of repairing a defective part or system in the prospective used car, plus specific data on individual makes and types from 1975 to the present. A fascinating feature is an explanation of cars that have the same basic engines and parts but may be far apart in price because of brand names that signify value. Both American and foreign cars are considered.

Fried, Don. **Do It Yourself Auto Inspection in 15 Easy Steps.** San Francisco (1850 Union St., Suite 927), CA: Consumer Automotive Pr., 1982. 27p. pap. $1.95 (629.2)

What steps should you take in inspecting an automobile you may wish to purchase? The basic 15 are here, and they are neither too complicated nor too superficial. Based on dozens of interviews with used-car dealers and automobile mechanics, this booklet offers good, sound information and tips. The simple, direct steps show you how to check the oil. Also included are such things as finding evidence of hidden accident damage, rust, odometer tampering, and serious leaks. There is also a section on what to look for when you test drive the car. Clear, precise illustrations are included.

Gillis, Jack. **The Car Book.** Rev. ed. New York: Dutton, 1984. 143p. pap. $7.95 (629.2)

First published in 1980, this guide to the best buys in cars is now issued annually (the author is the same one who wrote the original version). Gillis evaluates both foreign and domestic models for fuel economy based on tests by the federal Environmental Protection Agency. In addition, he has other comparative points such as maintenance costs, repair costs, and the rate of insurance for various models. New models are the focus, but there is a section on buying used cars. Possibly of most interest to consumers is the safety rating test. Here the author divides cars into subcompacts, compacts, intermediates, and large styles and then lists them in terms of their safety qualities based on crash tests developed in part from federal studies. This is by and large the most reliable of the many guides to new cars, particularly in terms of safety and repairs. Be sure to check the latest edition, although past years are useful when one is considering a used car.

Nader, Ralph. **The Lemon Book.** Ottawa, IL: Green Hill Pubs., 1980. 348p. $7.95 (629.22)

When the car you buy is a lemon, what are your rights as a consumer? They are explained by this leader of consumer justice, who advocates that everyone fight back. Specific instructions are given as to whom to contact, what steps to take, and what to expect. The book is filled with scores of examples of bad cars and numerous consumer victories. There is also a section on the simple rules to follow when buying a car, and how to drive and maintain it properly. Although this is now somewhat dated, most of the basic information remains suitable for the action-bound customer. *Note:* Several states now have "lemon laws" and these may not be included in the manual.

Ross, James. **How to Buy a Car.** Rev. ed. New York: St. Martin's, 1984. 145p. pap. $3.95 (629.2)

While *Consumer Reports Guide* . . . (q.v.) gives up-to-date information on specific makes of automobiles, the reader is given basic advice here on what to do when buying a car—any type or kind. Written by a former car salesman, the guide covers such things as how to avoid secret sales tricks, the effective negotiation of credit terms, possible pitfalls in trying to get a lower price, the ins and outs of trade-ins, and general tips on how to conserve fuel when driving. Many other objective pieces of information make this a guide for almost anyone who owns, or is considering buying, a new or secondhand car.

Sutton, Remar. **Don't Get Taken Every Time: The Insider's Guide to Buying Your Next Car.** New York: Viking, 1982. 380p. $12.95 (629.2)

Working under the assumption that the would-be car buyer is a potential victim, the author offers a manual that may ensure at least a draw if not a victory between consumer and automobile dealer. There is the usual background information on what to look for in buying a car and how to select a dealer, but the best part of the book consists of questions and answers that highlight the basic problems involved. Along the way the author gives examples of what happens when the smart (or the foolish) buyer moves into action. The guide is easy to follow and it covers most, although not all, situations. At any rate, little of the basic information is likely to date soon, and this is a guide to be consulted for many years to come.

AUTOMOBILES—RESTORATION & KITS

Brownell, Tom. **How to Restore Your Collector Car.** Osceola, WI: Motorbooks, 1984. 320p. $18.95 (629.28)

Here "collector car" means any vintage automobile, not necessarily a Rolls or such similarly expensive machines. The result is a manual that will be of interest to almost any automobile fan of any age. The author gives step-by-step instructions on the basics of restoration, and each step is accompanied by generous illustrations. The instructions are geared to basic considerations, like restoring the body paint and mechanics. (Other books are needed for specific mechanical repairs and the restoration of specific models.) There are good sections on locating a suitable car, insurance, storage, and sources of supplies.

Girdler, Allan. **Customizing Your Van.** 2nd ed. Blue Ridge Summit, PA: TAB, 1983. 247p. $16.95; pap. $10.95 (629.2)

Written for the mechanically able person who has no real experience, this is a solid introduction to turning a van into a home, or an extension of one's personality. All the information necessary is given on tools, equipment, materials, and approaches to doing everything from changing wheels to installing custom grills to painting.

Kutner, Richard, ed. **The Supercatalog of Kit Cars.** Osceola, WI: Motorbooks, 1984. 160p. pap. $9.95 (629.26)

The kit car is a new, popular form of remodeling and rebuilding machines into distinctive models such as the Auburn Speedster or the Lotus Eleven. Some 125 different full-size kit cars are featured in the guide, which has over 300 black-and-white illustrations of the cars and related details. Each kit is explained and there is a comprehensive analysis of the ease or difficulty of its assembly. Complete buying formation is given in a 32-page buyer's guide.

Lazarowich, Orest. **How to Collect and Restore Pre-WWII Cars.** Blue Ridge Summit, PA: TAB, 1981. 182p. $11.95; pap. $6.95 (629.28)

Cars produced before World War II are considered, and the author points out the ones most likely to be available for restoration. Hints on where to find the automobiles are given, but the primary purpose of the book is restoration. Here, section by section, part by part, the author guides the reader in repair. There are useful diagrams and some indifferent photographs, but between the illustrations and the text the average reader will have enough assistance. This is for the nearly expert mechanic, not the beginner.

Mills, Burt. **Auto Restoration: From Junker to Jewel.** Osceola, WI: Motorbooks, 1980. 291p. $14.95 (629.28)

Mills first explains how to locate junkers for restoration, and what to avoid. With that he moves into a clear, easy-to-follow procedure that will take the junk through many steps to the finished automobile. The book's primary value is not so much in the mechanical repairs (found in other guides), but in the loving description of how to make body and interior restorations. While the author believes that anyone with an interest in the subject may move ahead, and the book is so written, effective use of this guide does require that the reader have at least a passing knowledge of automobiles. Beyond that it is a first stop for anyone interested in the subject. Well illustrated.

Mills, Burt. **Restoring Convertibles: From Rags to Riches.** Rev. ed. Osceola, WI: Motorbooks, 1984. 239p. pap. $11.95 (629.28)

All aspects of general body and interior updating are considered in this guide to restoring convertibles. The author moves from choosing an older car for restoration—and gives tips on what to look for and models to avoid—to the actual work on the car. Specific instructions on repairing various parts of the body and upholstery are given. A separate section is devoted to the all-important "roof over your head," and there is a final chapter on painting the convertible. Illustrations are on almost every page.

BACKPACKING. *See* Camping; Hiking & Backpacking

BAKING. *See* Bread; Cooking; Desserts

BALLET. *See* Dance

BALLOONS

Waligunda, Bob, and Larry Sheehan. **The Great American Balloon Book: An Introduction to Hot Air Ballooning.** Englewood Cliffs, NJ: Prentice-Hall, 1981. 246p. $16.95; pap. $8.95 (629.13)

A competent, although not overly exciting, illustrated introduction to the sport of hot air ballooning. With basic information on balloon selection and actual flying practices, it is a solid beginning for someone contemplating going up in a balloon. The best section is the relaxed approach to the history of the sport. Almost one-half the text is made up of lists of clubs, training schools, periodical names, museums, etc.

BARBECUE. *See* Cooking—Fish & Game & Outdoor

BASEBALL

Meyer, Gladys. **Softball for Girls and Women.** New York: Scribner's, 1982. 308p. $15.95 (796.357)
   While some may object to the sexes being separated on the sports field, the fact remains that they often are, and this is a good introduction to a special kind of softball played exclusively by women. Written by a softball coach, the manual gives practical advice for every position on the team, from pitching to fielding. The rules are given, as well as explanations for various situations that seem to defy the regulations. More important, there are clear discussions, often illustrated, of how to play, from batting and pitching to fielding and running, and sections on exercise drills, team spirit, and practice time.

Reichler, Joseph, ed. **The Baseball Encyclopedia: The Complete and Official Record of Major League Baseball.** 5th ed. New York: Macmillan, 1982. 2,248p. $29.95 (796.35)
   Among fans, this is considered the ultimate baseball encyclopedia, and, as such, it is often updated. The fifth edition is a massive compilation of data, and is, as the subtitle says, the complete and official record of major league baseball. Records go back some 100 years, and will include what one man did in one game, as well as the accomplishments of stars of countless games. It is an argument stopper in that it has records of players, teams, and other facts through the 1981 world series. Over the years the editions have been improved, and it is now hard to imagine any question about baseball that cannot be answered in these pages.

Seaver, Tom, and Lee Lowenfish. **The Art of Pitching.** New York: Morrow, 1984. 224p. $15.95 (796.35)
   Thanks to numerous photographs and the author's reputation as a superior pitcher, this is a fine introduction to the art. It may be read by beginner and expert alike, and, for that matter, by just about anyone interested in or involved with baseball. The book is worth the price for the last chapter alone, which reads like a thriller in which the pitcher takes the fan at a pitch-by-pitch clip through a game. There are several sections on physical fitness, and some superior isometric exercises, which are illustrated. Seaver comes across as an exceptionally intelligent and careful player who is deeply concerned with delivering his best in each and every game. One could hardly ask for more.

Thorn, John, and Peter Palmer with David Reuther. **The Hidden Game of Baseball: A Revolutionary Approach to Baseball and Its Statistics.** New York: Doubleday, 1984. 419p. $17.95 (796.35)
   Math is demanded for an understanding of this book, and, in fact, the reader should have a good grasp of probability theory. Given those skills, one may profit

from this new approach to a statistical analysis of baseball. The authors offer a guide to comparing player abilities today with those of the past. Each method of traditionally measuring perfection is examined. Batting averages, for example, are found wanting. In their place the authors offer a system that is complicated, but takes into consideration other factors, such as runs scored and allowed. The historical approach may be enjoyed even by the reader with no mathematical inclination, but if the theory is to be applied to today's games, one must be familiar with mathematics.

Zolna, Ed, and Mike Conklin. **Mastering Softball.** Chicago: Contemporary, 1981. 90p. $12.95; pap. $5.95 (796.35)

Starting with the necessary ingredients of a good softball team—from the players' attitudes to the basic rules—the two experts discuss fundamentals, including a short history of softball. The primary explanations are concerned with such things as the difference between the fast-pitch and slow-pitch game, strategies to employ, and how to keep score and follow the rules. There is a good section on exercises and warming-up procedures. The illustrations augment the text nicely.

BASKETBALL

Isaacs, Neil, and Dick Motta. **Sports Illustrated Basketball.** New York: Harper, 1981. 110p. $8.95; pap. $5.95 (796.32)

Moving from the fundamentals of basketball to various strategies of the game, the authors cover the court in fine style. The instructions and suggestions are liberally illustrated. The text is well organized, easy to follow, and takes the reader in a logical progression from beginning to expert play. The book may be read with pleasure by both players and spectators. In fact, a final section gives tips on how the average viewer could get more out of the game.

BATHROOMS

Better Homes and Gardens Editors. **Your Baths.** Des Moines, IA: Meredith, 1983. 160p. $9.95 (643.52)

A volume in the All about Your House series, this follows the same basic pattern of brilliant illustrations, many in color, and specific advice on everything from planning a new bathroom to remodeling an old one. Every aspect is covered, from types of fixtures to water softeners and fans. If nothing else, the numerous pictures give even the most casual reader ideas on how to improve an existing bathroom.

Hollmeder, Carlton. **How to Build a Hot Tub.** New York: Sterling, 1981. 128p. $12.95; pap. $6.95 (690.8)

The title tells all, although the author makes two assumptions: (1) that the average builder has some carpenter/plumbing experience and (2) that even if working from a kit, which is suggested in some cases, the reader must be able to follow directions most carefully. Given those qualifications, this guide is ideal. Various types of tubs, for both indoor and outdoor use, are covered. There are photographs and line drawings.

Sinnes, A. Cort. **Spas & Hot Tubs: How to Plan, Install & Enjoy.** Tucson, AZ: HP Books. 1982. 160p. pap. $7.95 (728.9)

Although enthusiasm for spas and hot tubs began in California, they are now a national fad. The authors begin by defining the items (a hot tub is made of wood; a spa is made of other materials). They then explain where to purchase and how to maintain the units. Anyone with courage and an advanced knowledge of plumbing and carpentry will find the do-it-yourself section of value. The authors make their point about the joy of these baths by featuring full-color photographs of individuals enjoying a dip.

BATON TWIRLING
See also Cheerleading

Robison, Nancy. **Baton Twirling.** New York: Harvey House, 1980. 49p. $6.49 (791.6)
A children's book (for approximately grades four to eight), this may be used by adults as well. True, the early part of the work is elementary and concentrates on the history of batons, but the suggestions for staying in good condition and the explicit routines for baton twirling are suitable for any age group. All the basic routines are illustrated with excellent black-and-white photographs. There is added, although not entirely necessary, information on such things as parades and competitions.

BAZAARS. See Handicrafts

BEER. See Drinks

BEES

Gojmerac, Walter. **Bees, Beekeeping, Honey and Pollination.** Westport, CT: AVI, 1980. 192p. $19.95 (638.1)
The main focus is on the history and development of the raising of bees, as well as a detailed analysis of how the bee produces honey and fights off enemies and disease. There is a section called "The Business of Bees," but primarily the author, a professor of entomology at the University of Wisconsin, offers a meticulous, scientific document with technical information about the bee.

Mace, Herbert, and Owen Meyer. **The Complete Handbook of Bee-Keeping.** New York: Van Nostrand, 1976. 190p. pap. $8.95 (638)
By now a classic, and based on a work first published in England in 1952, this began as a basic guide for British beekeepers. Thanks to Meyer's revisions it is now as useful for Americans. The approach is twofold. The basic work is concerned with the history and the scientific aspects of bees—for example, a fine section on behavior patterns. At the same time, there is information on beekeeping as a hobby and a business, useful techniques for ensuring the health and production of the beehive, etc. It is adequately illustrated.

Meyer, Owen. **The Beekeeper's Handbook.** New York: Sterling, 1982. 253p. pap. $8.95 (638.1)
Although first published in England, this is equally useful for Americans, and is one of the best all-around guides now available on the subject. There is practical

advice on how to begin bee management and, if you are successful, how to sell the honey. In between, the author considers related matters ranging from the history and anatomy of the bee to proper beekeeping equipment. There are detailed instructions on how to start and maintain a bee business, including what to do in various emergencies or potentially dangerous situations. The book is carefully illustrated and the coverage is complete. The writing style is delightful.

Morse, Roger. **A Year in the Beeyard.** New York: Scribner's, 1983. 166p. $14.95 (638.1)

A professor of apiculture at Cornell offers an exceptionally fascinating and useful study of bees from month to month through a given year. In the process, he demonstrates what is necessary to raise bees for maximum personal and monetary profit, albeit one suspects most of his interest is on the former. Each section discusses a basic aspect of bees, beginning with the obvious questions of what they require for housing and where they may be purchased. The book concludes with the satisfying business of recovering honey. A bonus is the fine photographs found throughout the text.

U.S. Department of Agriculture. **Beekeeping in the United States.** Washington, DC: GPO, 1981. 193p. $7.50 (Al.76:335/980)

A detailed study of beekeeping, this publication gives the beginner and expert all the information necessary to start and carry on the business of keeping bees. The heart of the manual is the detailed explanation of how to establish and maintain bees. There is also information on all related areas from "bee laws" and types of pesticides to the history of the bee; contains a list of related organizations.

BETTING. *See* Gambling & Betting

BEVERAGES. *See* Drinks; Wine

BICYCLING

American Youth Hostels. **The American Bicycle Atlas.** New York: Dutton, 1981. 271p. pap. $6.25 (796.6)

For anyone going on a bike trip, this guide clearly explains the types of equipment needed, the sources of maps and travel guides, and—the heart of the book—data on close to 100 bicycle routes. These routes are arranged by region and are of various lengths and difficulty. Maps are given for each route. There is also a list of inexpensive accommodations along the way (by now, of course, prices are out of date).

Bennett, Hal. **The Complete Bicycle Commuter: The Sierra Club Guide to Wheeling to Work.** New York: Scribner's, 1982. 181p. pap. $8.95 (388.3)

The title explains the difference between this and other bike books, and the text is as good as the promise. Apparently over one-half million people get to work on bicycles. The author explains the health benefits of such a habit, and gives basic information on how anyone can join the parade. Instructions on the selection of a bike best suited for individual needs are as detailed as they are clear. Beyond that, every conceivable problem is covered, from carrying a package or suitcase to prevention of theft. There is a good section on safety and getting the maximum comfort out of a bike during bad weather.

Coles, Clarence, and Harold T. Glenn. **Glenn's Complete Bicycle Manual: Selection, Maintenance, Repair.** New York: Crown, 1973. 339p. pap. $9.95 (629.28)

Ignore the date. The information is, for the most part, timeless and the book is rightfully considered a classic by cycling enthusiasts. The primary focus is on maintenance and there are clear instructions on how to take apart and put back together a basic bike. All of this is carefully illustrated. The result is a manual that may be useful to anyone, even those without much mechanical ability. There is good advice on the selection of both American and foreign bikes, and while the prices by now are completely out of date, the method remains as valid as the day the book was published. The authors offer a time-tested formula and supporting evidence to make the decision relatively easy. There is much more, not the least of which is the style and enthusiasm of the authors. A first choice, even today, for anyone interested in the subject.

Doughty, Tom; Ed Pavelka; and Barbara George. **The Complete Book of Long-Distance and Competitive Cycling.** New York: Simon & Schuster, 1983. 380p. $17.95; pap. $8.95 (796.6)

How does one win a race on a bike? The author explains it all, beginning with information on conditioning the body, accompanied by a section on exercise and diet. Next, there is a discussion of the bike itself and what it will and will not do, as well as methods to improve it. Finally, there is the wedding of rider and vehicle and commentaries on both. While this tends to sound somewhat elementary, there are just enough unique tips to make this book a bible for the dedicated racer. As a bonus, the author offers numerous hints on weekend and extended bike tours.

Gilbert, Dave. **The American Bicycle Atlas.** New York: Dutton, 1981. 271p. pap. $6.25 (917.3)

How do you locate a good bike route? The answer is here. In fact, there are 96 possible trips from coast to coast. For each there is given the length of the tour, the type of terrain, excellent maps, notes on difficulties, and, of course, points of interest along the way. The guide begins with general information on bicycles and touring and covers such things as how to buy the right type of bike and the proper kinds of clothing.

Krausz, John, and Vera Krausz. **The Bicycling Book: Transportation, Recreation, Sport.** New York: Dial, 1982. 280p. pap. $11.95 (796.6)

Bike enthusiasts contribute to an encyclopedia of information on the use of a bike. Here the emphasis is on how to achieve the utmost satisfaction from such different experiences as bicycling a few minutes or spending several weeks on an overland tour. Experts explain the best riding techniques, what clothing to wear, how to avoid accidents, and cycling in traffic. If the reader wants to find out how to select a bike, or what to do when a dog attacks, here are the answers. There are sections on different types of bikes, from the one-wheel variety to tricycles, and considerable information on competitions. It is difficult to think of a bike subject that is not mentioned in the detailed index. There are good illustrations.

Lieb, Thom. **Everybody's Book of Bicycle Riding.** Emmaus, PA: Rodale, 1981. 324p. $12.95; pap. $9.95 (796.6)

By "everybody" the author means both beginners and intermediate riders. Lieb opens with a sales talk about the advantages of cycling, particularly in terms of keeping fit. He then offers points on how to select the best bike for a given purpose and presents various methods and techniques to ensure a fast, comfortable ride. The book winds up with a discussion of more advanced cycling, including tours and sports. The illustrations throughout are excellent, and Lieb has a pleasing style. There is even a bibliography. All in all, this is one of the best of the cycling books.

McCullagh, James. **The Complete Bicycle Fitness Book.** New York: Warner, 1984. 180p. pap. $7.95 (613.7)

The editor and publisher of *Cycling* offers the beginner the basics of cycling for fun and exercise, with emphasis on the latter. Working on the assumption that the reader knows little or nothing about the sport, he begins with suggestions on how to select the proper bike, equipment, and clothing. The background information is detailed and stresses the need for individual choice to meet individual need. With that he moves into nutrition and establishes a realistic program for weight loss and physical fitness. Specific steps are given as to the distance to travel, speed, and other elements of the sport. When it rains, or other factors interfere with bike riding, the author suggests alternatives. Well written and covering almost every aspect of cycling, this is an excellent beginner's guide.

Marino, John. **John Marino's Bicycling Book.** New York: Houghton, 1983. 239p. pap. $7.95 (796.6)

Beginning with the selection of a machine and moving into guidelines for safety this is a basic book for the individual who knows little or nothing about bikes and bicycling. There are sections on accessories, repairs, clothing, and theft-protection devices. A good part of the book concerns training for both recreation and competition. Also, there is a consideration of stationary bikes for exercise that goes into much more depth than do other books of this type. The author speaks from experience. He is the famous Los-Angeles-to-New-York rider.

Rakowski, John. **Adventure Cycling in Europe: A Practical Guide to Low Cost Bicycle Touring in 27 Countries.** Emmaus, PA: Rodale, 1981. 368p. $14.95; pap. $11.95 (914)

One of the best bicycle guides to touring Europe, this is not likely to date quickly. True, some prices will change, but the advice on what to do will remain fairly up-to-date. Of particular value: lists of organizations catering to those on bikes; map sources; passport and visa requirements; and how to cope with bad weather. Less satisfactory are the rather cursory views of the countries considered, but this is a minor matter. The focus is on how to survive and enjoy a bike trip.

Sloane, Eugene. **The All New Complete Book of Bicycling.** 3rd ed. New York: Simon & Schuster, 1981. 736p. $19.95 (629.227)

This is a gigantic book for amateurs and experts alike. It is hard to imagine any aspect of the bicycle not considered. The author gives advice on what type of machine to purchase or rent, surveys various touring trips, and discusses emergency situations. There are excellent instructions and diagrams showing the user each part of the bike and how to make repairs and carry on a regular maintenance program. The book concludes with a list of suppliers and organizations, a glossary, and a good index. The guide is revised and updated every five or six years.

BILLIARDS

Balukas, Jean. **Pocket Billiards.** New York: Atheneum, 1980. 198p. $9.95 (794.7)
   Written for the beginner, this book clearly explains the rules and the basic moves of pocket billiards. There are good diagrams and charts underlying the points. One problem, although it may prove a bonus for some, is that about two-thirds of the book is an autobiography. The author, an expert when he was a teenager, explains life on the road and what it means to have had a match with the famed Minnesota Fats. The personal notes aside, the book is one of the best for anyone seriously involved with the game.

Byrne, Robert. **Byrne's Treasury of Trick Shots in Pool and Billiards.** San Diego: Harcourt, 1982. 293p. $19.95 (794.7)
   Thanks to the good illustrations and clear explanations, this book can improve the game of almost anyone who knows the basics of pool and billiards. There are some 350 different shots explained—about three-quarters of them for pool, the rest for billiards. *Note:* The publisher is not Harcourt Brace Jovanovich, but simply Harcourt, at 1250 Sixth Ave., San Diego, CA 92101.

BINDING, BOOK. *See* Bookbinding

BIRDS
   See also Animals—Field Guides; Nature Study; Wildlife

Farrand, John, Jr., ed. **The Audubon Society Master Guide to Birding.** New York: Knopf, 1983. 3 vols. $13.95 ea. (598.07)
   Divided by types of birds, this three-volume set is the ultimate guide for bird-watchers of the United States and Canada. The writings of over 60 ornithologists are supported by the work of some 200 photographers, as well as by original paintings, drawings, maps, and silhouettes. The individual birds are described fully. The species are described by the various contributors, whose style generally is good, although here and there it gets bogged down in too much detail. There are useful tips from experts on when, where, and how to look for a particular bird. Each volume opens with a general discussion of the birds covered in that section, e.g., loons to sandpipers in the first volume; gulls to dippers in the second; and warblers to sparrows in the third. There is an index at the end of each book, and an overall index in the third volume. The editor explains that the new American Ornithologists' Union's classification system is used throughout, and there are use-ful glossaries. There is no more comprehensive set, certainly no better organized and illustrated work than this, and it can be recommended to any bird-watcher at any stage of the art. The one drawback: each of these volumes is approximately 400 pages, so too bulky to carry on most field trips.

Harrison, Kit, and George Harrison. **America's Favorite Backyard Birds.** New York: Simon & Schuster, 1983. 256p. $15.95 (598.8)

When you look out in the backyard, at least if you live in most parts of the United States, you are likely to spot a robin, a blue jay, or a nuthatch. These, and seven other common birds, are discussed in as many chapters. The life history of the bird is given, along with data concerning life habits. Written for the less-than-enthusiastic bird-watcher, this includes material on what the birds eat and how to go about feeding them on a regular basis. The drawings and photographs (some in color) add nicely to the relaxed atmosphere.

Harrison, Peter. **Seabirds: An Identification Guide.** Boston: Houghton, 1983. 448p. $29.95 (598.29)
No matter where a seabird flies, Harrison offers a description and usually a color photograph and line drawing of the bird. There are over 300 species and 1,600 birds from every corner of the globe included in this basic manual. Maps indicate precisely where the birds are likely to be found, and there is enough information given to guarantee rapid identification. No guidebook on this subject is as complete, so this is a first choice for those who follow the birds.

Kress, Stephen. **The Audubon Society Handbook for Birders.** New York: Scribner's, 1981. 322p. $17.95 (598.07)
Not a bird identification book, nor a book for the expert, this is a beginner's guide to the fine art of bird-watching. Kress touches on almost all topics likely to interest anyone involved with the subject, and his early chapters on equipment, record keeping, photography, and field trips are as precise and clear as they are well written. The second part of the book contains more directory information, with data on such things as state programs, bird trips, programs devoted to research, and ornithological societies. There is, too, an excellent annotated reading list and a list of supply sources.

Leahy, Christopher. **The Birdwatcher's Companion: An Encyclopedic Handbook of North American Birdlife.** New York: Hill & Wang, 1981. 902p. $29.50 (598.07)
Unquestionably, the most complete bird-watcher's guide is Terres, *Audubon Society Encyclopedia . . .* (q.v.), but if *The Birdwatcher's Companion* is no easier to carry, it is certainly less expensive. It is also an excellent work with good illustrations, accurate descriptions, and a wide enough scope to cover birds found in most areas of North America. Long essays on specific topics ranging from navigation to how birds bathe are followed by short entries under the common names of birds. There are about 25 pages of black-and-white drawings of some 45 bird families, as well as a limited number of color plates. The author needlessly adds material such as biographies of famous bird experts, but on the whole the book is well balanced and useful for both beginner and expert.

Peterson, Roger. **A Completely New Guide to All the Birds of Eastern and Central North America.** 4th ed. Boston: Houghton, 1980. 384p. $15; pap. $10.95 (598.2)
A Completely New Guide to All the Western Birds. 3rd ed. Boston: Houghton, 1972. 380p. $16.95; pap. $11.95 (598.2)
Over 3 million copies of the general field guide have sold since it was first published in the 1930s, and this is by far the most popular, most used of the

numerous guides available. Roger Peterson's name is synonymous with bird-watching. There are two separate volumes: (1) birds "found east of the Rockies," and (2) "a field guide to western birds." Both are equally basic in the identification of birds, and both are "bibles" for beginning and expert bird-watchers. Peterson gives field marks for each bird, i.e., he explains in great detail such things as its habits, how it flies, its songs, etc. There are numerous plates in color and black and white, and excellent line drawings. In the revised book on eastern birds the plates are opposite the descriptions. These compact little guides are known simply as "Peterson," and are a required item for anyone even remotely interested in accurately and easily identifying birds.

Simonds, Calvin. **Private Lives of Garden Birds.** Emmaus, PA: Rodale, 1984. 192p. $14.95 (598)

The author offers a chatty, yet informative, discussion about the typical birds that show up in most American backyards. Among the birds considered are swallows, jays, chickadees, sparrows, crows, and robins. Simonds manages to personalize the birds without being cute, and the data will interest anyone who is working around a garden. This is a bit too simple, though, for the seasoned bird-watcher.

Soper, Tony. **Birdwatch.** New York: Holt, 1982. 208p. $19.95 (598.29)

What does a bird-watcher watch? More precisely, how do you go about finding birds to watch and when you find them what do you look for? These and other basic questions for the beginner are answered in detail by an experienced British naturalist. Soper is more involved with explaining the joys of the art/sport than with specific identification, although there are photographs of British birds, many of which are found in North America. He explains the equipment needed and discusses the physiology, behavior, and habitat of birds. All of this is written with zest.

Terres, John. **The Audubon Society Encyclopedia of North American Birds.** New York: Knopf, 1980. 1,109p. $50 (598.297)

This book is extensive and expensive—which explains the use of the term "encyclopedia" in the title. The entries are arranged alphabetically and vary in length from a few lines to several pages. They include biographical data, the history of over 850 birds, definitions, and major discoveries on items of ornithological interest. According to the publisher, there are 1,675 illustrations (half in color) throughout the text. These are outstanding in terms of both reproduction and sympathetic treatment of the subject. Thanks to a massive number of cross-references, one may find anything needed. Without doubt, this is the most complete, most rewarding book about birds of North America, including Bermuda and Greenland. A first choice in any situation.

Terres, John. **Songbirds in Your Garden.** 3rd ed. New York: Hawthorn, 1980. 301p. pap. $5.95 (598.2)

How do you attract birds to your garden? The author, an expert in this field, gives you complete directions. He opens with feeding and attracting birds, moves on to birdhouses and birdbaths, and then offers specific suggestions on everything from plantings to trails that will encourage bird life. Terres has a marvelous style that is guaranteed to arouse interest in even the most neutral reader. The instructions have application almost everywhere, from the city to the country, and the book may be enjoyed by young people as well as adults.

U.S. Fish and Wildlife Service. **Home for Birds.** Washington, DC: GPO, 1980. 22p. $2.50 (I1.72:14/3)
An illustrated "do" and "don't" approach to the birdhouse, this pamphlet explains what types of birds like what types of birdhouses. Basic plans for simple houses are given, as well as information on the materials needed.

BIRDS (PETS)

Gerstenfeld, Sheldon. **The Bird Care Book.** Reading, MA: A & W, 1981. 224p. 11.95; pap. $6.95 (636.6)
Two major problems with home birds are diet and health. Both of these are of primary concern to the veterinarian-author, who gives useful advice applicable to almost any domesticated bird. There is also information on related subjects from breeding to selecting the bird itself. The section on wild birds is unsatisfactory, particularly as the author fails to point out the legal questions about ownership of these birds. Still, the chapters on health and care are strong enough to make the book worth considering.

Sutherland, Patricia. **The Pet Bird Handbook.** New York: Arco, 1981. 149p. $13.95 (636.6)
Here are detailed instructions on everything from buying a bird to housebreaking it, feeding it, and arranging for its supplementary diet. There is a brief section on health and breeding, but primarily the book is divided by type of birds and their care. The routines for training are particularly good; the illustrations adequate.

Teitler, Risa. **Starting Right with Budgerigars.** Neptune, NJ: TFH, 1983. 80p. $6.95 (636.6)
The ubiquitous budgie is a favorite pet bird. The author covers every conceivable interest of someone who has, or is considering purchasing, such a bird. There is a good section on the do's and don'ts of buying budgies. The feeding and care chapters are as thorough as they are helpful, and the author moves easily from general feeding patterns to methods of nail trimming. There are numerous illustrations throughout.

Vriends, Matthew. **Popular Parrots.** New York: Howell, 1983. 240p. $15.95 (638.8)
For some reason, parrots are back in style, and today few people know how to select and care for a parrot. That is where this book is useful. (The author is an ornithologist.) Full information is given, with numerous photographs, about the various types of birds. There is a particularly good chapter on the characteristics of different parrots, which will help in making a selection. Vriends explains how to feed and care for the bird once it is home, and what to do if it becomes ill. There are sections, too, on training and breeding.

BIRTHDAYS. *See* Entertaining & Parties

BLACKSMITHING

Bealer, Alex. **The Art of Blacksmithing.** Rev. ed. New York: Funk & Wagnalls, 1976. 448p. $19 (682)

Although dated, this remains the basic book on the subject for the beginner. After a historical overview, there is a precise description of the kinds of equipment used in blacksmithing. The various techniques for doing a number of tasks are explained and well illustrated and the coverage is such that almost any type of blacksmithing of interest to the nonprofessional is included, and this means horses to handicrafts.

McCraven, Charles. **Country Blacksmithing.** New York: Harper, 1981. 191p. $16.95; pap. $5.95 (682)

Directed to the individual who turns to blacksmithing as a way of making a living, not as a hobby, this is a down-to-earth, well-written manual. The author, who realizes the economic and technological pitfalls of the trade, is encouraging and a bit humorous. He leaves nothing to chance. Everything is covered here, from the type of training needed to the tools required and the kind of work that will more or less guarantee a living wage. There are projects (from tools and cabinet hardware to larger items used around a farm) that might be considered by the amateur, once the book is thoroughly understood. Precise directions are given for each of the items. Even the reader who may wish to learn no more about blacksmithing than basics can benefit from this excellent guide.

BLOCK PRINTING. *See* Graphic Arts

BLUEPRINTS. *See* Homes—Building & Construction

BOATS

See also Canoes & Kayaks; Navigation; Sailing

BUC New Boat Price Guide. Fort Lauderdale, FL: 1963– .   Annual. 1983 ed., 250p. $18 (623.8)

This is a reliable guide to basic retail prices of boats and engines (with separate entries for each). The information is from manufacturers, and includes such basics as the name or model, the type, and the specifications of interest to anyone doing comparative shopping. The same publisher issues a companion annual volume entitled *BUC Used Boat Price Guide* (1942–).

Mate, Ferenc. **Best Boats: To Build or Buy.** New York: Norton, 1982. 382p. $29.95 (623.8)

In his discussion of 27 basic types of pleasure boats, from skiffs to yachts, this knowledgeable author makes several points: (1) he explains how a basic hull may be turned into a variety of types, (2) he carefully points out the good and bad about each kind of boat, and (3) he tells the average reader what may or may not be done by way of how-to-do-it activities (although this is minimal). Mate does show how one may purchase the basics and by putting them together save considerable amounts of money. This may mean anything from a partially completed hull to different cabin features and various kinds of rigging. There are plenty of photographs and line drawings to make the points clear.

Nicolson, Ian. **Build Your Own Boat.** New York: Norton, 1982. 198p. $22.95 (623.8)

Specific instructions are given here on how to take a simple, bare, fiberglass hull, which the author assumes is the beginning point for the user, and outfit it for various kinds of use. The projects differ in difficulty and length of time to perform, depending on the ultimate use of the hull. The clear instructions are accompanied by numerous illustrations. The steps described are such that anyone who intends to buy a complete boat can use this as background reading on what to look for. *Note:* Originally published in England.

Roberts, John. **Fiberglass Boats: Construction, Repair, and Maintenance.** New York: Norton, 1984. 240p. $19.95 (623.8)

Anyone who either owns a fiberglass boat or is considering building a hull will profit from this detailed manual. Roberts claims that a good one-third of all pleasure boats are made of this material and he observes that in the not-too-distant future technological advances will extend the popularity of the form much further. The author opens with a step-by-step analysis of how the fiberglass boat is constructed. Here is a thorough discussion of the various materials and resins, as well as a detailed picture of how various parts of the superstructure are employed to reinforce and strengthen the hull. When he turns to repair and maintenance, Roberts considers the numerous sealants available, with their strong and weak points. There are other sections on how to discover potential and actual flaws in the hull.

Wood, Charles. **Building Your Dream Boat.** Centreville, MD: Cornell Maritime Pr., 1981. 508p. $26 (623.8)

Here "dream boat" means anything large enough to warrant docking. Whether it is a sail or power boat, Wood offers explicit plans on its construction. He points out that numerous books consider hull construction (see titles in this section), but few give detailed instructions on the more complex finishing of interiors. Wood considers every aspect from plumbing and upholstery to rigging the sails and/or installing the engine. The text is easy to follow and the instructions well illustrated; this is an excellent guide for anyone planning a project larger than a rowboat.

BOATS—MAINTENANCE & REPAIR

Barnes, Howard. **The Backyard Boatyard.** Camden, ME: International Marine, 1982. 127p. $10.95 (623.8)

The title is a trifle deceptive in that the author is not recommending that the boat owner turn the backyard into a major working area. There are laws against such activities, at least in most communities. He does give useful advice on how to use that space for minor repairs and maintenance of small boats. The unexpected sidelight is that Barnes is equally involved with the construction of such things as docks, hoists, cradles, and other elements of boating that are rarely considered in books. He gives specific, well-illustrated instructions for each project, and takes the reader step-by-step through the most economical approaches. The information is presented in such a way that even the novice should have no difficulty. A valuable and somewhat unusual book that will be of great use to almost any boat owner.

Harper, Max, and Dave Johnston. **The Repair & Restoration of Wooden Boats.** New York: Scribner's, 1980. 192p. $17.95 (623.8)

The title reveals the focus, but within this scope there is considerable material of value for anyone interested in building a wooden boat. Thanks to detailed plans and precise explanations of what is needed—from the type of wood to tools—much of the information is applicable to constructing a boat. Still, for those who simply want to make repairs and restorations, this is about as basic and reliable as one can get, particularly since both authors are established authorities. There are numerous illustrations that make the text even easier to follow.

BODYBUILDING

Darden, Ellington. **The Nautilus Bodybuilding Book.** Chicago: Contemporary, 1982. $15.50; pap. $8.95 (646.75)

The basic requirement for the reader is that he or she have access to Nautilus bodybuilding equipment, which is found in exercise studios throughout the country. (One can buy the complicated machines, but this is not usual, and certainly not required to use this book.) The author spends about half of the first part of his discussion explaining a somewhat complicated theory of exercise that depends, naturally, on the Nautilus unit. With that, he turns to specifics and shows how various routines, exercises, and methods may be employed using the machines. The book is not simply for building muscles, but can be used as a guide for anyone who wishes to keep in good health or to get relief, say, from a bad back.

Kennedy, Robert. **Natural Body Building for Everyone.** New York: Sterling, 1980. 192p. $10.95; pap. $5.95 (646.7)

Challenged by the photographs of many champions, the reader might want to go on to try for a similar physique. Addressed to both men and women, the manual explains the basics of what the author calls "natural body building." Weight training, diet, and good health are stressed. Each exercise is accompanied by photos and line drawings. The instructions are remarkably clear and easy to follow. With all that, there is no guarantee you will end up with a body beautiful, but you could be a trifle more healthy.

Manion, Jim, and Denie Walters. **Bodybuilding for Amateurs.** New York: Harper, 1984. 250p. $17.95; pap. $10.95 (796.4)

Written for the person who wants to become seriously involved in bodybuilding as a sport—not just as exercise—this is as basic as one can get. The authors point out the benefits of the art, emphasize how it helps to improve the mind as well as the muscles, and generally offer a noble set of reasons for participation in it. Both men and women are welcome. With that they turn to the illustrated exercises and explanations of equipment and approaches to the sport. There is a 24-week course, which is carefully explained. At the end, one should be able to enter competitions—and win. In addition, there is useful material on nutrition, general health, and related exercises. As of 1984, this is the best book of its type.

Marx, Gilda. **Body by Gilda.** New York: Putnam's, 1984. 230p. $18.95 (646.7)

What is different here is that there is no promise of an easy road to physical fitness. On the contrary, this experienced teacher offers only hard work and, in fact, insists the reader devote at least three hours a week to exercise. The diet menu, which is going to help remodel the body, is equally stringent, although it does permit a few luxurious binges. The exercises, from warm-ups to cooling-off periods, are clearly explained and illustrated in detail. None of them is unusual, and all follow standard patterns. An enthusiastic, well-written guide, this pulls no exercise or diet punches.

Schwarzenegger, Arnold, and Bill Dobbins. **Arnold's Bodybuilding for Men.** New York: Simon & Schuster, 1981. 240p. $17.50 (613.7)
The most famous of the bodybuilding experts explains how any man may develop into a movie star or a beach attraction. None of the suggestions is radical, and most are based on commonsense, well-tried isometric and stretching exercises. There are excellent photographs and the authors demonstrate a clear, sometimes even amusing approach. There is much reliance on standard equipment and there is also a section to show how one may train outside an exercise studio. With or without weights, with or without the sometimes strenuous exercises, this is a much-above-average book on the subject and one that offers good tips for anyone interested in good health, if not in developing a great body. See also the author's similar title, *Arnold's Bodyshaping for Women* (1979).

BOOK COLLECTING

Bradley, Van Allen. **The Book Collector's Handbook of Values.** New York: Putnam's, 1972– . 1983 ed., $29.95 (090)
How much is this book worth? If it is one of the 20,000 titles listed alphabetically here by author, the reader may discover its value immediately. There is a catch or two. All listings are worth at least $25, and the majority are American and English nineteenth- and twentieth-century classics. All are in mint condition. The result is that many titles of less worth, or in less than desirable condition, are not listed. For additional information on pricing see Bradley's excellent introduction and his bibliography. Those with titles not listed here might turn to the library for help; see, for example, *American Book Prices Current,* which is found in most large library reference sections.

Katz, Linda, and Bill Katz. **Writer's Choice: A Library of Rediscoveries.** Englewood Cliffs, NJ: Reston/Prentice-Hall, 1983. 255p. $15.95 (011)
This is compiled for the person who is seeking quality books that are not found on most reading lists. The titles cover all interests, and prove to be a great voyage of discovery for ardent readers. The "choice" consists of about 1,000 overlooked and neglected books. The "writers" are famous authors who nominated the books for this compendium. Each of the overlooked books is briefly described, and this is usually followed by a recommendation from one or more distinguished writers, usually explaining why they think the book should be read and reread. The contents are arranged in two parts: fiction, alphabetically by author, followed by nonfiction under broad subject headings. There is an author and title index as well as an index of the writers who recommended titles. Among those represented here with selections are W. H. Auden, Saul Bellow, Judy Chicago, James Dickey, William Kennedy, John Kenneth Galbraith, R. D. Laing, Carl Sagan, François Truffaut, Anne Tyler, and about 400 more, including a few musicians.

Peters, Jean, ed. **The Bookman's Glossary.** 6th ed. New York: Bowker, 1983. 223p. $21.95 (002)
Indispensable for any book collector, this guide gives clear explanations of about

2,000 terms used by collectors, book dealers, publishers, and those in related areas such as printing. The guide is of particular value for the current definitions of terms that are often just this side of slang, yet are essential to anyone working with books. There is even a good selection of terms associated with computers. Still and all, the basic use of the guide is for its definitions of common terms that anyone going through a dealer's catalog is bound to find.

Peters, Jean, ed. **Collectible Books: Some New Paths.** New York: Bowker, 1979. 294p. $19.95 (002.07)

A collection of essays by book collectors, librarians, and scholars, this book shows the reader how to start gathering books that are relatively inexpensive. The series of essays springs from the current economics of modern book collecting, which has put traditional rare books almost out of financial sight for the majority of collectors. There is advice, based on experience and love, on how to build a collection of everything from anthologies to paperbacks and even book catalogs. See also the related earlier work by the same author, *Book Collecting: A Modern Guide* (Bowker, 1977).

Tannen, Jack. **How to Identify and Collect American First Editions.** New York: Arco, 1976. 195p. $12.95; pap. $7.95 (020.75)

An experienced antiquarian bookseller (Biblo and Tannen) presents a wealth of specific information on American first editions. It is in two parts. The first section is a list of close to 300 American publishers with details on how to identify their first editions. There is clear data on difficult-to-decipher codes that determine first editions. The second section discusses good areas, such as detective fiction and private press books, for the beginner to build a collection. Although most of the price information is dated, the basic material is as applicable today as the day the book was published.

Wilson, Robert. **Modern Book Collecting.** New York: Knopf, 1980. 270p. $13.95 (002.07)

The owner of the well-known avant-garde Phoenix Book Shop in New York has written a clear, entertaining, and informative guide for the would-be book collector. Actually, much of the information will be of value even to experienced ones. Wilson moves from the basics of where to look for books to how to work with dealers and auction houses. There are numerous anecdotes (Wilson is a friend of many authors, and has known most of the illustrious ones). There is a useful section on first editions and a bibliography.

BOOKBINDING

Johnson, Arthur. **The Thames and Hudson Manual of Bookbinding.** New York: Norton, 1981. 224p. pap. $9.95 (686.3)

Thames and Hudson, of course, is a major British publisher, and this book reflects the British point of view. However, the result is not very different from an American approach (except for some terminology), and the manual turns out to be an excellent introduction to the art of hand bookbinding. The first section offers historical background, and then come the detailed instructions on the art. Explanations are clear, and the accompanying diagrams and illustrations are helpful.

U.S. Library of Congress. **Bookbinding and the Conservation of Books: A Dictionary of Descriptive Terminology.** Washington, DC: GPO, 1982. 297p. $27 (LC1.2:B64/3)

By "dictionary" the compilers really mean an encyclopedia of terms and terminology connected with bookbinding. Definitions may run a line or two, or be quite lengthy. The result is not only a handy place to turn for terms, but, if read carefully, a useful basic guide to the art.

U.S. Library of Congress. **Boxes for the Protection of Rare Books.** Washington, DC: GPO, 1982. 293p. $18 (LC1.2:B69)

Detailed instructions and step-by-step drawings show how to make eight types of book boxes for housing and protecting volumes that require special attention because of rarity, value, or condition. Loose-leaf, three-ring punch.

Young, Laura. **Bookbinding and Conservation by Hand: A Working Guide.** New York: Bowker, 1981. 273p. $35 (683.3)

Now the best, most complete guide to bookbinding in English, this offers the reader step-by-step instructions, usually illustrated. Each of the techniques has been tested by the author, an experienced bookbinder. Basic tools and materials are considered and explained. The numerous binding styles, finishing methods, and types of conservation work are discussed. There is a final section on conservation and its importance.

BOWLING

Pezzano, Chuck, and Herm Weiskopf. **Sports Illustrated Bowling.** New York: Harper, 1981. 130p. pap. $5.95 (794.6)

Anyone familiar with *Sports Illustrated* will realize that this manual offers two major things—excellent step-by-step illustrations of the primary bowling techniques, and a well-written text. There is an introduction on what is needed by way of equipment and skills, followed by the various methods of bowling, and finally tips on keeping score. Written by an experienced bowler, this is a fine beginner's guide.

Weber, Dick, and Roland Alexander. **Weber on Bowling.** Englewood Cliffs, NJ: Prentice-Hall, 1981. 144p. $12.95 (794.6)

Both for the beginner and those with some experience, this is a much-above-average guide to bowling. After fundamentals of the game are explained, the experienced authors get down to the finer points that separate amateurs from experts. Everything from reading the condition of a lane to the way pins fall is considered. Precise instructions, with illustrations, are given on different methods of delivering the ball.

BREAD

Jones, Judith, and Evan Jones. **The Book of Bread.** New York: Harper, 1982. 352p. $15.95 (641.8)

If anything about bread or any type of bread is left out of this guide, it probably deserves to be. Discussing both lesser-known and well-known types of bread and bread products (from bagels to English muffins), the authors clearly explain the ingredients and the techniques of making the breads at home. There are close to 250 recipes, and the illustrations nicely complement the text.

London, Mel. **Bread Winners Too.** Emmaus, PA: Rodale, 1984. 320p. $15.95 (641.8)

This is a direct, easy-to-follow guide to the baking of over 150 different types of bread. The recipes were submitted to the author by almost as many home cooks from various parts of the country. There is particular emphasis on nutrition, which is to say that almost all of the recipes are for whole grain flour. One may have a difficult time finding a white bread in the lot. There are various comments by the cooks, who become carried away from time to time with the spiritual nature of it all, but they do pause long enough to furnish the necessary details for a good bread. The book opens with a good background piece on the basics of the art. Illustrations are adequate. *Note:* This supplements and to a degree supersedes the author's earlier *Bread Winners* (1979).

Moore, Marilyn. **Baking Your Own: Recipes and Tips for Better Breads.** Hoopeston, IL: Prairie Craftsman, 1982. 96p. pap. $7.95 (641.8)

If you are looking for recipes and the perfect way to bake a wide variety of breads, this is useful. There are 11 sections, including "perfect white breads," "easy quick breads," and "taste-tempting pancakes and waffles." There is a short list of mail-order sources. Each section has a brief introduction and includes a dozen or more recipes that require a minimum of ingredients. The author has taught classes in bread baking, and has "spent a lifetime" creating bread recipes.

BRICKWORK. *See* Masonry & Brickwork

BRIDGE
   See also Games

Goren, Charles. **Play as You Learn Bridge.** New York: Doubleday, 1979. 116p. $5.95 (795.41)

This master tells the beginner how to play and win at one of the most popular games in the world—contract bridge. Working on the assumption that the reader can hardly tell a card from a checker piece, Goren literally spells out each step. His confident style, his attention to the slightest detail, and his obvious ability to explain things clearly make this one of the best, if not the best, beginner's books on the subject. Even practiced players may find it useful for the concise explanation of bidding practices.

Jacoby, Oswald, and James Jacoby. **Improve Your Bridge with Oswald Jacoby.** New York: McGraw-Hill, 1983. 140p. pap. $4.95 (795.41)

A collection of the famous master's bridge columns from newspapers, this is for the individual who already understands the game, not the beginner. The sections covering 125 bridge hands follow the basic pattern of illustrating the hands and then explaining how they are played. In a final part, the authors show hands played in particular games by famous players.

Reese, Terence, and Albert Dormer. **The Bridge Player's Alphabetical Handbook.** London: Faber, 1981. 223p. $19.95 (795.415)

Directed to the novice as well as the expert, this is a dictionary approach to definitions, problems, and arguments about almost every aspect of bridge. The two experts, who have written other works in this field, arrange the book in several sections. The subject is divided into such areas as bidding, card play, and tournament and rubber bridge rules and regulations. The definitions are filled with examples and are as clear as they are concise.

Stewart, Frank. **Better Bridge for the Advancing Player: An Introduction to Constructive Thinking at the Bridge Table.** Englewood Cliffs, NJ: Prentice-Hall, 1984. 234p. $15.95; pap. $6.95 (795.4)

This expert teacher presents about 90 representative hands, which move from intermediate to advanced status of skill and difficulty. The assumption is that the reader is now a good if not skilled player, and wishes more instruction. To that end, Stewart offers a hand and then asks the reader to decide on the appropriate bid. From there further questions are put. The correct answer, the correct final bid, and the proper opening lead are on the back of the pages. Well written and easy to follow, this is a fine guide.

Truscott, Alan. **Contract Bridge.** New York: Fell, 1983. 88p. $8.95 (795.41)

Truscott is a well-known bridge player and here he assumes the reader has little or no experience with the game. He begins with such basics as how to cut a deck and deal. Here, and at the end of each subsequent chapter, there is a quiz to test the reader. Beyond basics, he considers the art of bidding, evaluating a hand, keeping score, and other necessities. While this volume is brief, it is a fine beginning point for contract bridge players.

BUILDING & CONSTRUCTION. *See* Homes—Building & Construction

BURGLARY PROTECTION
See also Crime Protection

Cox, Wesley. **Crime Stoppers: Low Cost, No Cost Ways to Protect Yourself, Your Family, Your Home, and Your Car for Under $10.** New York: Crown, 1983. 150p. pap. $4.95 (643.16)

The author offers simple solutions to protecting property. Most of the ideas are inexpensive and easy to follow and the installation instructions are clear. Cox moves from how to reinforce the front door of a house or an apartment to the treatment of windows and other entry points for a burglar. Various locks and security devices are described, and there are instructions for building a simple alarm system. Following this, Cox discusses the car and explains ways of discouraging the theft of an auto or any of its parts. There is a less successful section on hiding valuables in the home.

Krotz, David. **How to Hide Almost Anything.** New York: Macmillan, 1978. 157p. pap. $3.95 (643)

Want to hide a diamond ring? The answer on how to protect yourself from burglars and other intruders is offered by an expert carpenter. Ample diagrams show how secret places may be constructed anywhere from between wall studs to drainpipes to electric plug plates. The suggestions are practical. The ultimate book for secretive readers. *Note:* An appendix, while less practical, does give tips on such things as how to hide nervousness and how to hide an affair.

MacLean, Jack. **Secrets of a Superthief.** New York: Berkley, 1983. 192p. pap. $5.95 (643.16)

While it is conceivable that this might be used by a would-be burglar as a manual or handbook, the actual value of the sometimes sensational confession is for the person trying to find protection against a thief. MacLean explains countless methods of "break and entry" with homey words of advice on how to fix a door or a window so it is tamperproof. The author draws on his own experience and that of other thieves, whom he interviewed in jail—where he was at time of publication. Despite the sometimes overdone prose and the overblown exploits, this is in the end sound advice from an expert.

Steed, F. A. **Locksmithing.** Blue Ridge Summit, PA: TAB, 1982. 170p. $14.95; pap. $6.95 (683)

For someone who wants to know the best type of lock around the home (or business), here is the place to turn. It is also a well-illustrated guide to the installation and repair of common locks. While most people will probably need the help of a professional locksmith for involved work, this is useful at least for simple projects.

U.S. Department of Justice. **How to Crimeproof Your Home.** Washington, DC: GPO, 1979. 20p. $2.50 (J26.2.C86/12)

Easy-to-follow, generally inexpensive ways to guard your home or apartment against crime are offered. Rudimentary steps are suggested to make the home safe when the owner is away. In no way dated.

CABINETMAKING. *See* Woodworking

CALLIGRAPHY

Baker, Arthur. **Foundational Calligraphy Manual.** New York: Scribner's, 1983. 90p. pap. $5.95 (745.6)

While this is more for the potential expert than for a beginner, with patience the latter should be able to master Baker's approach. Six steps are given for the formation of each letter, and the explanations and illustrations are exceptionally clear, with a single page devoted to a single letter. The precise method of holding the pen for the particular strokes is illustrated and specific instructions are given for all basic steps in mastering calligraphy. This is by far the best manual of its type available.

Lehman, Charles. **Italic Handwriting & Calligraphy for the Beginner: A Craft Manual.** New York: Taplinger, 1981. 146p. pap. $3.95 (745.6)

For years Lehman has been promoting the teaching of italic handwriting in schools, and here he demonstrates the type of guide to be used. It is for the beginner, and there are detailed instructions on all aspects of calligraphy from choosing pen, ink, and paper to various writing styles. There are scores of specimens illustrated, including the work of the author.

Wong, Frederick. **The Complete Calligrapher.** New York: Watson-Guptill, 1980. 185p. $19.95 (745.6)
This is a book for the intermediate student of calligraphy. If not "complete," it at least covers the primary concerns of a calligrapher. Wong opens with an adequate, if abbreviated, history of the art and then considers nine basic lettering forms and styles. These discussions are marked by a careful consideration of the importance of design. He then shifts to the technical aspects of calligraphy, and has a particularly good section on preparation of material for commercial use.

CAMERAS. *See* Photography

CAMPING
See also Hiking & Backpacking; Mountaineering; Survival Techniques (Wilderness)

Coleman, Harry. **Camping Out with Your Van or Minibus.** New York: Facts on File, 1983. 360p. $19.95 (796.7)
Old-timers hardly call camping out an occasion to draw up the van or minibus, but that is because they are old-timers. Today the use of vans is a favorite way of camping, and Coleman explains how to get the most out of this new turn. Primarily, he points out the best places to camp with a vehicle in every part of the world—not just in the United States. In fact, a good part of the book is concerned with planning the trip and tips on reading maps. Still, the largest part (some 220 pages) is a methodical approach to "facts about each nation and territory." Many countries are considered, and there is a fact sheet for each nation on everything from weather to dress codes. There is also valuable information on guidebooks, insurance, and equipment. Various tips on getting the most out of the vehicle in terms of sleeping, cooking, and general comfort are matched with sensible advice on maintenance and repair.

Ormond, Clyde. **Complete Book of Outdoor Lore and Woodcraft.** New York: Harper, 1981. 837p. $22 (796.5)
Whether the camper is going by water, foot, or horseback, this guide is one of the best available on what to expect and what to do in real wilderness areas. Experienced outdoors people may wish to consult detailed, specific guides; this is written for the beginner or for the amateur who wants a quick overview. The author imagines an individual who is alone against nature, much on the order of the early trappers or, for that matter, Native Americans. Being alone, what does one have to know? Ormond shows the camper the elements of catching or finding food and reading the skies for weather information, how to make various types of shelters, and how to stay healthy. Almost every conceivable situation is covered in this encyclopedic volume. The survival techniques alone make this an extremely valuable book for anyone who is contemplating more than a roadside stop. It is essential for those seriously involved with the out-of-doors.

Sparano, Vin. **The Outdoor Sportsman's Illustrated Dictionary.** New York: McKay, 1980. 179p. $12.95 (799.03)

While most sportspeople know the vocabulary of their favorite activity, whether fishing or mountain climbing, they may be lost in other areas. In order to make life easier for those who read books and magazines about the outdoors and discuss such matters with friends, Sparano has brought together the most common (and some downright uncommon) terms. Each is clearly defined, and there are numerous illustrations. Not everyone will agree with every definition, but on the whole it is one of the better specialized dictionaries of its type available.

CAMPING—GUIDES & DIRECTORIES

National Park Foundation. **The Complete Guide to American National Parks.** New York: Viking, 1981. 325p. pap. $7.95 (917.3)
  Listed by state, 357 national parks (including battlefields and historic sites) are described in this book. Information including the address, how to reach the park, its primary points of interest, and the various facilities is provided. Descriptions may vary in length from a few lines to many paragraphs, depending on the particular significance of the item. The official guide of the National Park Service, this is a basic resource for people who travel beyond the shopping center.

Rand McNally Campground and Trailer Park Guide. Skokie, IL: Rand McNally, 1971–   . Annual. 1982 ed., pap. $9.95 (796.54)
  A state-and-province guide to campgrounds, this is updated annually and, for that reason, it is reliable since it is always current. For each location the reader is given information on the basic facilities, costs (if any), size of site, and regulations. There are also notes on what to see. The state maps are in color and clearly show each of the sites. The primary coverage is of the United States and Canada, with some information on Mexico included.

Rhodes, William. **The Pocket Books Guide to National Parks.** New York: Pocket Bks., 1984. 384p. pap. $3.95 (917.3)
  This is more current than most guides of its type, and has the advantage of having more up-to-date information on such things as current lodgings in the parks. It is a paperback that is inexpensive and fits nicely into luggage. Beyond that, one finds the usual, e.g., a list of the 48 major national parks with day-to-day information on when they are open, their accommodation charges, if any, and other pragmatic facts. There is also material on the history of the park and what it has to offer in terms of wildlife and natural features.

Riviere, Bill. **The L. L. Bean Guide to the Outdoors.** New York: Random House, 1981. 299p. $15.50 (769.54)
  Produced by the nation's leading sporting goods and clothing store, this is a well-known, trusted, all-around guide to camping. The author considers major aspects of outdoor recreation, with the exception of hunting and fishing, which are covered in numerous other guides. Here the focus is on planning the trip, equipment, how to cook, how to camp in comfort, how to cope with anything that is likely to happen when the family or the individual shifts from the comforts of home to the hazards of outdoor living. The 11 chapters are divided not only by ways of enduring, but by special interests—from maps to canoes to backpacking. This is a superior book for the beginner, although a good deal of the information will be of

equal value to the veteran. *Note:* Despite the name, there is no mention of company products.

Satterfield, Archie, and Eddie Bauer. **The Eddie Bauer Guide to Family Camping.** Reading, MA: Addison-Wesley, 1983. 320p. $17.95; pap. $8.95 (796.5)

Almost as well known to campers as L. L. Bean, Bauer is a West Coast sporting goods store that dots periodicals with advertisements. Of course, you do not really need everything stamped by Bauer to profit from this camping advice. And the advice is credible, from what to do with young children while the family is camped by a lake to how much to budget for a two-week vacation. Most aspects of family camping are covered. The writing style and the information are much better than that often found in books of this type.

U.S. Department of the Interior. **Index of the National Park System and Related Areas.** Washington, DC: GPO, 1982. 94p. $4.75 (I29.I03:982)

Anyone seeking information on a national park will wish to turn here first. The guide, arranged state by state, not only includes basic information about the area's features, but gives a brief historical sketch of the park. In addition, the guide offers the locations and other information about related sites such as monuments, preserves, lakeshores, seashores, rivers and riverways, parkways, historic sites, military parks, and battlefields. The publication is updated every three or four years, so look for the latest edition.

U.S. National Park Service. **Camping in the National Park System.** Washington, DC: GPO. Annual. 1981 ed., 25p. $3.50 (I29.71:981)

Revised each year, this is an overview of camping in 103 national parks in every section of the country. Specific data are given on when the parks are open, facilities, costs, and safety rules. Usually the information for each park considers the availability of water, sanitation facilities, swimming, cooking facilities, boating, and the like.

A related publication by the same service, updated every two years, is *Visitor Accommodations, Facilities and Services Furnished by Concessioners in the National Park System* (115p., $5 [I29.2AC2]). This includes information on trailer parks, hotels, and other facilities in the parks. Specific information is given on costs and accommodations.

VanMeer, Mary. **Free Campgrounds, U.S.A.** Charlotte, NC: East Woods, 1982. 560p. pap. $9.95 (647.94)

State by state, in alphabetical order by name of town, park, or site, the author lists and briefly describes free campgrounds. The descriptions employ abbreviations for indications of such amenities as running water and activities. There are addresses to write to in each state for additional information. While it is true that "free" sometimes changes to "a small fee" from one year to the next, the information is likely to be accurate for the 1980s. Those in doubt may write state officials for updated facts, or consult the American Automobile Association or some such organization.

VanMeer, Mary, and Michael Pasquarelli. **Free Attractions, U.S.A.** Charlotte, NC: East Woods, 1982. 416p. pap. $8.95 (647.94)

Following the same state-by-state format as *Free Campgrounds, U.S.A.* (q.v.) this offers city-by-city, community-by-community attracctions that cost nothing. As one might suspect, the primary lists consist of parks, playgrounds, buildings, museums, zoos, and monuments. Often found, too, are companies that conduct special tours for visitors. A bit of background information is given for each attraction, as well as the hours it is open, the address, and sometimes the phone number. While much of this data is found in the standard travel guides, this book has the convenience of having it all in one place for all the states.

Woodall's Campground Directory. New York: Simon & Schuster, 1967–   . 2 vols. Annual. pap. $6.95 ea. (647.94)

A standard two-volume work, this is arranged alphabetically by state, then city. Under each heading one finds full information on private, state, and some federal camps, although many National Forest areas are not included. In addition to the usual information about each site, the publisher rates the various commercial areas. There are advertisements, but these do not seem to influence the selection or evaluation. Another handy feature is that at the head of each state there is a map clearly indicating the locations of the campgrounds. One volume covers the western United States and the other the eastern part of the country.

CANING. *See* Furniture

CANNING. *See* Food—Canning & Freezing

CANOES & KAYAKS

Bridge, Raymond. **The Complete Guide to Kayaking.** New York: Scribner's, 1978. 312p. $12.50; pap. $6.95 (797.1)

Among dozens of books on the joys of the kayak, Bridge's work remains one of the best. The reason is his thorough coverage of everything from how to select a kayak to how to use one in calm or turbulent waters. This compendium is good for the exciting information on racing and white-water touring. There are excellent sections, too, on the best places to use a kayak. The guide, except for the prices of the boats and the lack of some names new to the field since 1978, is in no way dated.

Davidson, James, and John Rugge. **The Complete Wilderness Paddler.** New York: Knopf, 1976. 188p. $10 (797.1)

Particularly useful for the basic information on canoe trips, this is in no way dated. In fact, it has the status of a minor classic among enthusiasts, and can be read as much for its sense of adventure as for its clear instructions. The authors begin with a white-water adventure in Canada. The month-long trip is described from beginning to end, from planning to the successful conclusion. Along the way are clear, well-illustrated instructions on handling a canoe, portaging, and what to do in case of capsizing. In fact, just about every conceivable problem or headache is described and explained, along with the delights and the successful solutions. The writers are lively, intelligent, and even downright poetic about the wilderness. The combination of superb prose and superb instruction is difficult to top.

Harrison, Dave. **Sports Illustrated Canoeing.** New York: Harper, 1981. 190p. $8.95; pap. $5.95 (797.1)

A basic approach to canoeing for the whole family, this is strong on instruction and technique. Written by an experienced paddler, the guide takes the beginner from the first moment of stepping into a canoe right through to confident day trips. The explanations are as clear as they are rudimentary. Not for the expert, but a first choice for anyone who wants to get started in the sport.

Huser, Verne. **River Camping: Touring by Canoe, Raft, Kayak, and Dory.** New York: Dial, 1981. 155p. pap. $12.95 (917.3)

Everything, and more than almost anyone would want to know, about how to enjoy—and survive—white-water boating is artfully explained in this excellent guide to the sport. As the subtitle indicates, the author discusses numerous crafts for speeding along the river. Each is explained in terms of benefits and drawbacks, and there is a particular focus on the importance of the right craft. Beyond that, Huser stresses the need to respect the environment, and his section on camping, which is first rate though brief, points up the advantages of destroying as little as possible. There is a short, yet good, section on safety, and the photographs nicely complement the text, which carries the reader down rivers of both the United States and Canada.

Sanders, William. **Kayak Touring.** Harrisburg, PA: Stackpole, 1984. 256p. $12.95 (797.12)

A basic guide to kayaks for the beginner, this is a love song to the versatility of the craft and its ease of handling. Sanders offers instructions on everything from the decision about what type and size of kayak to purchase (or make) to the steps needed for learning to operate it successfully. Various places are suggested for enjoyable touring. The tours are varied according to skill levels. Along the way, the author offers stories and anecdotes that will indicate to the reader the type of people involved in the sport. As an all-around guide, this is one of the best.

CARDS. *See* Bridge; Gambling & Betting; Games

CARPENTRY
See also Woodworking

Cassidy, Bruce. **The Carpenter's Bible: A Practical Step-by-Step Home-Repair Guide.** Garden City, NY: Doubleday, 1980. 147p. pap. $4.95 (643.7)

Written for the beginner, this is not so much a "bible" as a guide that stresses tools (about half the book), and concentrates on materials used in most homes from the floor to the ceiling. The writing style is just passable, but the information is generally accurate and the author's strong point is his definite recommendations on what to do and what not to do when considering home repairs. Used with other books in this area, it has its place.

Demske, Dick. **Carpentry & Woodworking.** Passaic, NJ: Creative Homeowner, 1984. 158p. $17.95; pap. $6.95 (684.08)

A good beginner's guide, this opens with simplified instructions and explanations of various types of materials and tools. Techniques for using both are carefully explained.

There are illustrated instructions, for example, on joining. The second half of the book is devoted to a group of 20 construction projects for the beginner. These range from the relatively simple, such as making a bench, to the more complex. For each project, there is a list of materials and tools needed, as well as diagrams and photographs. The step-by-step instructions are particularly easy to follow.

Feirer, John, and Gilbert Hutchings. **Guide to Residential Carpentry.** New York: Scribner's, 1983. 477p. pap. $14.95 (694)

As in other books by Feirer, the supposition is that the reader has some basic understanding of woodworking. Beyond that, it is assumed that the reader wishes to learn about basic tools, techniques, and approaches to carpentry that will be of use around the home. Here the two authors consider a broad range of activities, from simple repairs to adding a whole section to a house. The construction information is supported by numerous illustrations, many of which are in color. The text is clear and the coverage excellent.

Spence, William. **General Carpentry.** Englewood Cliffs, NJ: Prentice-Hall, 1983. 496p. $24.95 (694)

Essentially a textbook, this is still a useful manual for the amateur. The author, in a well-organized fashion, covers almost anything today's carpenter is required to know in home construction. (It is not a guide for cabinetmakers.) The book takes the reader from the beginning of home construction to the last nail. Along the way are definitions of terms, self-tests, and numerous illustrations.

Syvanen, Bob. **Interior Finish.** Charlotte, NC: East Woods, 1982. 126p. pap. $7.95 (694.6)

This is a beginner's book on various approaches to interior finish. While some knowledge of carpentry is assumed, directions are precise and clear enough so that a beginner should be able to follow all but the more complicated projects. Here are instructions on how to put up and finish sheetrock, fit baseboards, and lay hardwood floors. Every interior finish is considered, including shelving and cabinets. The text is nicely illustrated with helpful, well-placed line drawings.

U.S. Department of Defense. **Carpenter.** Washington, DC: GPO, 1979. 196p. $7 (D101.11:5-551)

This is an army technical and field manual that can be used as well by the layperson. The manual offers a basic course in carpentry for the individual who knows little or nothing about the subject. It is in no way dated and many of the tips and suggestions will save both time and effort.

CARPETS. See Rugs

CARS. See Automobiles

CARTOGRAPHY. See Maps & Map Reading

CARTOONS. See Graphic Arts

CATALOGS
  See also Indexes

Bachman, Ben, et al. **Shopping at Home for Camping and Outdoor Equipment.** New York: Facts on File, 1982. 172p. $15.95; pap. $9.95 (685.53)

This is for the person who hates to go to stores. The author offers a convenient compilation of about 150 firms from any one of which the shopper may order various types of camping and outdoor equipment. Complete information is given on how to obtain a catalog and what type of merchandise is offered. Each entry includes such information as the acceptance of credit cards, the firm's founding date, and the name of the company official to whom one can send complaints. The sample merchandise listed may or may not include a price. A product index allows rapid use.

Blackwell, Johnny. **Johnny Blackwell's Poor Man's Catalog.** New York: St. Martin's, 1981. 158p. $14.95; pap. $6.95 (680)

The catalog of a retail, home-building products dealer, Johnny Blackwell, this is actually a book of instructions about construction, gardening, photography, and several other categories. Before turning to the actual projects, the author gives background on both hand and power tools. After that there is offered a wide variety of plans for everything from a tool cabinet to a simple device to detect drafts in the home. Tips on window types of greenhouses and insulating a house vie for attention with simple approaches to fishing lures and equipping a darkroom. Most of this requires minimal skills, although some of the more involved projects assume some carpentry background.

Brand, Stewart, ed. **The Next Whole Earth Catalog: Access to Tools.** New York: Random House, 1981. 600p. pap. $16 (381)

Following the pattern of the well-known *Whole Earth Catalog* (1968), this is a descriptive list of close to 3,000 different items that may be of use in do-it-yourself projects or to someone in search of self-improvement or both. The arrangement is by broad subject headings (from energy to communications), and there is a useful index. The items vary from books to tools to audiovisual aids. Each is dutifully described and enough information is given so the reader may order it. Many of the described books and periodicals are available in libraries.

Conley, Marcia. **Free Stuff for Home and Garden.** Deephaven, MN: Meadowbrook, 1981. 123p. pap. $3.95 (011.03)

By "free," the compiler means anything that is literally free or costs less than $1. The result is a collection of primarily government, association, institution, and company pamphlets covering a wide variety of how-to-do-it subjects. Each subject is briefly described in terms of format and content.

De La Iglesia, Maria. **The International Catalogue of Catalogues.** New York: Harper, 1982. 245p. $21.95; pap. $10.95 (380.1)

If you want to buy English riding boots, French cookware, or an Italian pasta maker and you are not close to stores in large urban centers, this is a perfect guide. The author arranges by broad subject headings hundreds of items that can be purchased by mail from abroad. (Specific products are found through the index; the basic organization is by company and catalog.) For each entry, information is given on how to obtain the catalog, the number and type of items covered, and a price range. There is sensible information on what to avoid, what to check out, and how to process an order—as well as what to do when the order is not filled. Obviously, some specifics will change, but the author sought out, for the most part, reputable firms whose catalogs and products are likely to remain pretty much the same in the years ahead. *Note:* This is a much-expanded version of the author's *New Catalogue of Catalogues* (1975), which is useful but by now quite dated.

Druse, Kenneth. **Free Things for Gardeners.** New York: Putnam's, 1982. 127p. pap. $4.95 (635.9)

Most of the items here are government documents, company pamphlets, and other free or inexpensive materials (i.e., anything that costs less than $2). It is a valuable checklist, and is particularly useful for the extensive list of garden catalogs. Numerous how-to-do-it items are included.

Gottlieb, Richard, ed. **The Directory of Mail Order Catalogs.** Rev. ed. New York: Facts on File, 1981. 369p. $85 (659)

If you are looking for a given item or product and do not want to bother shopping in a local store, this may provide a solution. It is a list of mail-order catalogs put out by over 4,000 firms. Divided into 33 categories, from clothing to hobbies, this reference work offers immediate access to dealers who can fulfill your needs. In addition, there is an alphabetical product and company list. For each entry you will find the company name, address, and phone number, and sometimes the names of executives. There is a clear but brief description of the products, and some indication of the size, possible cost, and frequency of publication of the catalog. This is an expensive item and should be used in a library.

Hardigree, Peggy. **The Mail-Order Gourmet.** New York: St. Martin's, 1983. 272p. $15.95; pap. $8.95 (016.64)

Ordering specialized foods through the mails is by now fairly common. To make it easier, the author has compiled a list of offerings from about 150 different American concerns. Each product or service is explained, often with personal comments from the author. Sometimes her remarks seem a trifle overenthusiastic, but the book is a handy guide to places, prices, and products.

Hendrickson, Marilyn, and Robert Hendrickson. **2001 Free Things for the Garden.** New York: St. Martin's, 1983. 252p. $16.95; pap. $9.95 (635.9)

Name a type of plant, fruit, or vegetable and someone will give you a free catalog, pamphlet, or chart. The way to discover who is giving away what is to use this handy guide, which lists the freebies by type of plant. There are sections on gardening tools and related items. In addition to simple lists of groups, companies, and organizations, the authors give details on various aspects of gardening. *Note:* Some of the material does require a small payment—usually postage—but most is free.

Jorpeland, Elaine, and Ilsa Whittemore. **The Freebies Book: Hundreds of Things You Can Get Free (or Almost Free).** New York: Holt, 1981. 230p. pap. $4.95 (011.03)

There is a vast amount of material that is free, or almost free, from corporations, associations, and others anxious to advertise themselves. The freebies are listed here by general subject—from house to car to leisure-time activities. Under each subject are brochures, booklets, posters, films, and other items you need only ask for. Well, not quite. Some of the items do have a fee: $2 or less for printed materials, and no more than $25 for rental or purchase of film and related media. Each item has a short, descriptive annotation and there is a good index. Some of this dates rapidly, but most of the items will be available for years to come, and certainly through a good part of the 1980s.

LaRocco, Rich, ed. **Shopping at Home for Hunting and Fishing Equipment.** New York: Facts on File, 1982. 162p. $15.95; pap. $9.95 (688.7)

This follows the same format and approach as Bachman's *Shopping at Home for Camping and Outdoor Equipment* (q.v.). In fact, of the 150 companies listed, about 32 are duplicated in the Bachman catalog. Still, they nicely complement one another.

Lesko, Matthew. **Something for Nothing.** New York: Associated Pr., 1980. 71p. pap. $2.95 (011.03)

The emphasis is on where to find free or inexpensive information—not goods. For example, there is a section on how one may trace legislation through Congress, or find answers to questions concerning employment, business, social security, health, etc. The coverage is of both government and private agencies with a brief description (with phone number and address) of each source. There is a particularly helpful section devoted to what can be had by way of information—and free or inexpensive publications—from the various federal government departments. Much of this is dated, due to a change of administration in Washington, but the general outline remains the same and the guide is a useful source for locating sometimes difficult to find answers to pressing questions or needs.

McCullough, Prudence. **The New Wholesale by Mail Catalog.** New York: St. Martin's, 1982. 192p. $16.95; pap. $7.95 (381.2)

With a brief opening on how to order by mail, and what to avoid doing, this is a revised edition of a popular 1979 work. The author lists products that may be had for at least 30 percent below retail via the mails. Apparently some less-than-reliable firms listed in the first edition have been deleted, and the current work seems more accurate and trustworthy. Almost anything—from clothes to video—can be found in this handy catalog. By now, of course, the prices are dated, but the reader has at least a relative idea of costs and for that reason, as well as its listing some rather strange items, it is a valuable guide. *Note:* The first edition of this catalog was issued in 1979; it apparently is updated every three years.

See also a similar guide with considerable overlap, Sue Goldstein's *The Underground Shopper: A Guide to Discount Mail-Order Shopping* (Andrews & McMeel, 1983).

Sequoia, Anna. **The Complete Catalogue of Mail Order Kits.** New York: Atheneum, 1981. 255p. $14.95; pap. $9.95 (680.29)

Where can you find information on a build-it-yourself chair, boat, or toy, or a kit that supplies not only directions but all the vital materials? The answer is in this catalog, which covers over 1,000 mail-order kits, ranging from outdoor clothing and sporting goods to log houses and greenhouses. The sections are divided by subject and the author offers personal comments about each of the products. She finds most items good to excellent, and while one longs for a trifle more criticism, its lack is explained by the fact that she generally lists only items she believes worthwhile. While it is true that the actual kits become out-of-date, and prices tend to go up, the catalog is invaluable for ideas and for addresses of dealers where the individual may write for more detail and up-to-date prices.

Spitzer, Susan. **U.S. Mail Order Shopper's Guide: A Subject Guide Listing 3,667 Unique Mail Order Catalogs.** North Hollywood, CA: Wilshire, 1982. 217p. pap. $10 (659)

Under about 50 subject categories, the author covers the promised 3,000-plus catalogs, price lists, and related materials. The entry provides enough information to allow the reader to order the catalog. Lacking a proper index, it is more difficult to use than Gottlieb (q.v.), but it does include some items not found in that work.

U.S. Department of the Interior. **Maps for America: Cartographic Products of the United States Geological Survey and Others.** Washington, DC: GPO, 1981. $15 (I19.2:M32/12/981)

This is a guide to maps that are available from the U.S. government, particularly the Geological Survey, the Department of Defense, and the National Aeronautics and Space Administration. The handbook is nicely illustrated and in addition to the map listing, there is a well-written history and survey of map reading.

U.S. Government Printing Office. **Books.** Washington, DC: GPO, 1982– . Quarterly. (GP3.17/5)

This is a 50- to 60-page, illustrated guide to government publications, most of which are suitable for laypersons. Each issue contains about 1,000 publications, briefly described. These are arranged under various subject headings from agriculture to vacation and travel. Instructions on how to place an order are given in detail. There are no longer any free government publications listed in this bulletin, although some are reasonably priced. See also *The Consumer Information Catalog* (p. 76 in this book).

U.S. Library of Congress. **LC Science Tracer Bullet.** Washington, DC: GPO, 1977– . Irreg.

The Library of Congress publishes an ongoing series of how-to-do-it, self-help, eight- to ten-page pamphlets known as *LC Science Tracer Bullet.* Some are technical, but the majority are a helpful source of information for laypersons. Each pamphlet is free and is designed "to help a reader begin to locate published materials on a subject about which he or she has only a general knowledge." The material is listed by form, e.g., encyclopedias, handbooks, government documents, etc. Other information sources are added, such as the names of organizations. Available from the Science Reference Section, Science and Technology Division, Library of Congress, Washington, DC 20540. For additional information, see Ellen P. Conrad's article, "Who Was that Masked Librarian?" in *Reference Services Review* (Winter 1983, pp. 75–80). Conrad offers an alphabetical subject listing of the pamphlets, which range from "Aging and Airplanes" to "Windmills and Wood as Fuel."

Weiss, Jeffrey. **Free Things for Campers and Others Who Love the Outdoors.** New York: Putnam's, 1982. 125p. pap. $4.95 (011.03)

Most of the items here are government documents, pamphlets, and other free or inexpensive materials. Actually, "free" may include anything costing $2 or less. It is a valuable checklist and particularly useful for its extensive list of company catalogs. Numerous how-to-do-it items are included, and things such as free soap and matches.

Weiss, Jeffrey, and Susan Osborn. **The Information Age Sourcebook.** New York: Pantheon, 1982. 1,073p. pap. $12.95 (600)

There is no copyright on most government documents, and for this reason it is not unusual for a private publisher to reissue the documents in somewhat different forms. That is precisely what is done here, and the result is a collection of government pamphlets, brochures, and reports that are, for the most part, of the self-help/how-to-do-it variety. They cover everything from food and health plans to car purchase and repair. The information is reliable and quite current; includes an index.

CATS

Curtis, Patricia. **The Indoor Cat: How to Understand, Enjoy, and Care for House Cats.** Garden City, NY: Doubleday, 1981. 192p. $10.95 (636.8)

Drawing on experience, common sense, and the requisite love and understanding of cats, the author sets down rules and regulations for a happy home. The supposition is that the reader knows little or nothing about cats, and while the instructions are good, they are hardly for the veteran owner. Problems likely to face the cat owner are given in detail, including some rather gruesome reports on cat overpopulation and the need for neutering.

Frazier, Anita, with Norma Eckroate. **The Natural Cat: A Holistic Guide for Finicky Owners.** New York: Putnam's, 1981. 200p. $12.95; pap. $7.95 (636.8)

Every good cat book has one or two outstanding sections. Here, one is the authors' sound advice on grooming and handling. The cat is approached as a friend, not as something to be worked into an acceptable shape. The second outstanding feature is the focus on diet. Beyond that there are good-to-excellent tips on nutrition, training, health problems, etc.

Noyes, Patricia. **How to Talk to Your Cat.** New York: Holt, 1978. 118p. $6.95 (599)

The author is not kidding. She tells you how to talk to your cat, and, beyond that, how to interpret the animal's movements. For example, what is the difference between a contented mew and a cry of distress? Noyes explains it all. While based on her own experiences, the advice and the interpretation of the cat's moods seem fairly sound. Recommended by one cat lover, the book was read by two more. They both reported success, although they thought the author went a bit far at times in her appreciation of the cat's understanding of humans. All agree that the advice on everything from how to travel with a cat to getting a cat out of a tree makes this one of the best cat books about.

Pond, Grace, consultant. **Rand McNally Pictorial Encyclopedia of Cats.** Chicago: Rand McNally, 1980. 160p. $14.95 (636.8)

The outstanding feature of this book is the quantity and quality of photographs and other illustrations, many of them in color. Add the expertise of the internationally recognized author, and the book is a delight. The sum is a history, background, and running account of the cat. From the how-to-do-it point of view, there are brief yet accurate sections devoted to care, breeding, showing, and related matters. Major breeds are given the attention they deserve and described in enough detail to please any cat owner.

Richards, Dorothy. **How to Choose & Care for Your Cat.** Tucson, AZ: HP Books, 1982. 160p. pap. $7.95 (636.8)
This follows the format of the Palmer book on dogs (see p. 109 in this book). The first half lists and explains the various breeds, and each entry is usually accompanied by a photograph, often in color. The second section is concerned with the health, training, and grooming of the cat. It is a good book for the first-time cat owner, and should do much to ensure a happy relationship with the animal.

Sayer, Angela. **Cats: A Guide to Breeding and Showing.** New York: Arco, 1983. 143p. $16.95 (636.8)
A straightforward, easy-to-understand book on how to raise cats for show, this also has good advice on breeding. The experienced author indicates the types of cats likely to win, and what sets off a prize cat from a common one of the same breed. There are health and feeding tips that all cat owners will find useful. The rudimentary instructions are supported by black-and-white and color photographs.

Siegal, Mordecai. **The Good Cat Book: How to Live with and Take Loving Care of Your Cat.** New York: Simon & Schuster, 1981. 350p. $13.95 (636.8)
The expert on pets for *House Beautiful* explains precisely what the beginner should expect when a cat enters the house. The advice is practical, covering the basics from food to behavioral patterns. The writer's style is relaxed and easy to follow. The section on training is particularly good, but there is too much material on show breeds, at least for the beginner.

Siegal, Mordecai, ed. **Simon & Schuster's Guide to Cats.** New York: Simon & Schuster, 1983. 256p. $23.95; pap. $8.95 (636.8)
One of the more complete and current guides to the selection and care of cats, this is a basic approach to the subject. The authors write with vim and cover almost every aspect of owning a cat. In addition, there are superior illustrations, which sometimes go a bit too far in making the cat look almost human. At any rate, there is a good section on identifying the various breeds, and on their particular characteristics and needs. If the reader does not understand why a cat insists on going out-of-doors, or sleeping in a particular place, this book will make it clear. Countless aspects of the cat's personality are explored, and there is detailed advice on everything from feeding to health care.

Whitney, Leon, and George D. Whitney. **The Complete Book of Cat Care.** Rev. ed. Garden City, NY: Doubleday, 1980. 374p. $12.95 (636.8)
First published over 30 years ago, this is one of the most basic of the basic cat-care books. Here it is revised by the son of the author, himself a veterinarian with a deep love of cats. There are several outstanding aspects to this book. The first is the vast amount of material on the cat's anatomy and body func-

tions. (Some would say it is too much, but the author believes it essential for the true cat lover.) Next, diseases are listed in considerable detail, usually with suggested cures, even if that means a trip to the vet. There is, finally, an unusual section devoted to aging cats. In addition, the reader finds normal coverage of other aspects of care from nutrition to training. The book is well written, and there is an excellent index.

CAVING

Larson, Lane, and Peggy Larson. **Caving: The Sierra Club Guide to Spelunking.** San Francisco: Sierra Club Books, 1982. 311p. pap. $10.95 (796.5)

Over and over again, the Larsons make the point that caving can be a dangerous sport, so utmost precaution and reliance on experienced guides is strongly advised. With that, they give practical information on how to locate and get in and out of the cave. Sections and chapters are devoted to discussions of equipment, clothing, food requirements, and emergencies. There is material on the background of the sport, including a good explanation of the different types of caves and what to expect when going into each. Exploring techniques are given in considerable detail. This is the best book available on caving, and should be a first choice for anyone interested in spelunking.

CHAIRS. *See* Antiques; Furniture

CHECKERS

Wiswell, Tom, and Jules Leopold. **The Wonderful World of Checkers and Draughts.** San Diego: Barnes, 1980. 176p. $10 (794.2)

Although it is assumed that the reader knows the rules of checkers, if only in a rudimentary fashion, nothing else is assumed in this excellent introduction. The authors concentrate on problems, strategies, and actual games. In the more than 100 games discussed, there are numerous and startling twists, constructed in such a way as to puzzle and instruct. *Note:* Draughts is the name of the game in England.

CHEERLEADING
See also Baton Twirling

Neil, Randy. **The Official Cheerleader's Handbook.** New York: Simon & Schuster, 1979. 320p. $14.95; pap. $6.95 (371.8)

Cheerleading refers to many activities, but they all require certain basic skills, and these are explained by the author and the staff of the International Cheerleading Foundation. Written for the individual of almost any age, it is easy to follow and most of the movements are well illustrated. In fact, except for the necessary basic explanations of what cheerleading is about, each and every action is methodically handled by a series of carefully prepared photographs. The photos may not be that inspiring, but they cannot be faulted for lack of clarity. Equally good are the descriptive captions. There are sections on team activity and the necessary consideration of such things as fund raising, as well as the fundamentals of various sports where cheerleading is a major activity.

CHEESE. *See* Food

CHESS

Mednis, Edmar. **How to Beat Bobby Fischer.** New York: Quadrangle, 1974. 282p. $10 (794.1)

A reviewer for *Time* magazine called it "the most intriguing chess manual of the year." While written in 1974, this advanced approach to chess remains the best of its type. It is unusual on two counts. First, the writing style is superb; the author has as solid a command of the language as he does of the game. Second, the analysis of Bobby Fischer's 61 chess games is as clear as the accompanying diagrams. An added feature is that the author tries to explain the psychological triumphs of the chess champion. That this is aimed at advanced players should be stressed, because it is clearly not for the plodding beginner. Although written for the semi-expert, really intelligent beginners with more than a passing interest in the game will profit from a careful reading of this unique manual.

Pandolfini, Bruce. **Let's Play Chess: A Step-by-Step Guide for Beginners.** New York: Messner, 1980. 190p. $8 (794.1)

While specifically written for children and young people, this is an excellent beginner's guide for adults. The author, a U.S. National Chessmaster, leaves nothing to guesswork, defines all his terms, and provides directions that from first to last are exceptionally clear and easy to follow. Each lesson is graded in terms of difficulty, and is liberally illustrated. The complete game is covered, from setting up the pieces to special moves.

Russ, Colin. **Miniature Chess Problems from Many Countries: 400 Compositions with Solutions and Comments.** New York: St. Martin's, 1982. 262p. $11.95 (794.1)

A British chess expert offers both beginners and skilled chess players problems to be worked out with seven or fewer pieces. After an excellent introduction, which considers the essence of problem chess, the reader is led into the main content of the book. Here the problem is depicted on a large, clear diagram. The solution is on the opposite page. Solutions are in both descriptive notation and figurine algebraic. In addition, the author usually offers comments. A marvelous way to sharpen one's game, this is a superior book for anyone even remotely involved with chess.

Savage, Allan. **An Introduction to Chess.** Englewood Cliffs, NJ: Prentice-Hall, 1982. 196p. $12.95; pap. $5.95 (794.1)

Standard chess is taught here to the person who knows absolutely nothing about the game. Thanks to good illustrations, a clear explanation of chess notations, and a precise way of indicating moves, this is easy to follow. After the elements are described, the chess master discusses more complicated strategies and tactics, which include illustrated moves and games.

CHICKEN. *See* Cooking—Meats & Chicken

CHINA. *See* Antiques

CHRISTMAS. *See* Entertaining & Parties

CHRISTMAS DECORATIONS. *See* Handicrafts

CLEANING
See also Home Economics; Housecleaning

Moore, Alma. **How to Clean Everything.** 3rd ed. New York: Simon & Schuster, 1979. 240p. $9.95; pap. $2.95 (648)
Almost every conceivable method of cleaning such things as blankets and objects of art can be found in these pages. Cleaning agents are discussed, and specific steps are prescribed for getting rid of dirt. Various materials, from plastic to iron, are considered in terms of cleaning difficulty. The second part of the book is a useful guide to removing about 150 different kinds of stains and spots.

U.S. Department of Agriculture. **How to Prevent and Remove Mildew.** Rev. ed. Washington, DC: GPO, 1980. 15p. $2.50 (A1.77:68/8)
This pamphlet offers two considerations of mildew: how to remove it when it attacks clothing and other articles in the home, and what mildew is and how it can be kept in check. Hints on how to remove the odors from mildew are included.

CLIMATE. *See* Weather

CLOCKS & WATCHES

Fried, Henry. **The Watch Repairer's Manual.** Radnor, PA: Chilton, 1949–   . Irreg. 1983 ed., $17.95 (681.1)
First published in 1949, this is often updated and is a basic text for the would-be professional. It is also of value to the layperson who wishes to master the basics of watch repair. There are good illustrations augmenting the detailed instructions.

Whiten, A. J. **Repairing Old Clocks and Watches.** New York: Van Nostrand, 1981. 280p. $12.95 (681.1)
Written by a British expert, this is a basic guide that makes the assumption that the reader has some basic mechanical ability, particularly of the sort necessary to work with small parts. Given that skill and interest, the reader will discover how to take apart and repair almost any type of watch other than the digital variety. There are illustrations matching the detailed explanations. Separate chapters and sections are devoted to cleaning, adjusting the time setting, oiling, and case repair. With that, there is information on old clocks that includes advice on everything from pivots to hairsprings. There presently is no better general guide to the subject, and it is one the beginner should use to get a start. Most of the information will also be of interest and value to intermediate students of the art.

CLOTHING. *See* Handicrafts; Sewing

COCKROACHES

Frishman, Austin, and Arthur Schwartz. **The Cockroach Combat Manual.** New York: Morrow, 1980. 192p. $9.95; pap. $4.95 (648.7)
Anyone who has done battle with the cockroach knows that it is likely to be the winner, at least if given enough time. Still, there are methods of holding the bug in

place, and these two experts draw on most known battle plans. They range from the heavy artillery of professional pest control services to the sniper's specialized powders and formulas. In addition, the authors give a fascinating history of the cockroach, and zero in on four of the most common types. They answer the layperson's usual questions about the bugs, although they never guarantee that anything will absolutely and completely check the mighty cockroach.

U.S. Department of Agriculture. **Cockroaches: How to Control Them.** Washington, DC: GPO, 1980. 10p. $2.25 (A1.35:430/10)

There is probably no sure way of killing all cockroaches and ensuring they will not invade the home again. Still, this pamphlet at least offers practical suggestions. It is most useful for the instructions on how to use various insecticides effectively.

COCKTAILS. *See* Drinks

CODES

Kahn, David. **Kahn on Codes: Secrets of the New Cryptology.** New York: Macmillan, 1983. 343p. $19.95 (001.54)

Anyone (including teenagers) who is remotely interested in codes will find Kahn's exploration of the whole process a fascinating business. Actually, this is a collection of Kahn's various articles and other writings on cryptology over a number of years. They are grouped by subject, although sometimes the continuity and focus are a bit confusing. There is information on current ciphers and codes as well as historical data. While this is a far cry from the typical how-to-do-it book, it is required reading for anyone learning codes.

COINS

Bruce, Colin, II, ed. **Standard Catalog of World Coins.** Iola, WI: Krause, 1976– . Annual. 10th ed., 1983. 1,984p. pap. $32.50 (737.4)

Here the coin collector will find an accurate description of every coin minted in the world since about the beginning of the nineteenth century. Exhaustive information is given for each coin, as well as current prices. The illustrations are adequate. This is a basic guide for the serious collector and, as it is revised each year, the prices are relatively current and trustworthy. Related titles by the same publisher are *Standard Catalog of United States Paper Money* (1982), *Standard Catalog of World Gold Coins* (1983), and *Standard Catalog of World Paper Money* (2 vols., 1983). There are about half a dozen similar titles by the same publisher, most of which are revised either annually or every two or three years. They are particularly useful for information on current prices.

Coffin, Joseph. **The Complete Book of Coin Collecting.** New York: Coward, 1938– . Irreg. 1983 ed., $8.95; pap. $5.95 (737.4)

If not quite "complete," this does cover much the same ground as that found in Hobson and in Reinfeld and Hobson (q.v.). The difference is in the stress this places on ancient coins. True, modern coins are considered, and in some detail; but Coffin excels in his early history section. In addition, there is information on how to buy coins and where to buy them, as well as an excellent section on the problems of making the right selection.

A Complete Price Guide to Coins of the United States. Boston: H. E. Harris, 198l. 286p. pap. $3.95 (737.49)

Here the collector will find the market value of coins minted in the United States from 1793 to 1981. The listing is by denomination of coin, and then chronological. For each coin there is a physical description, the number minted, and prices based on various grades of the coin. A nine-point grading system from good to proof condition is used. Most coins are illustrated, and there is a brief history of American coins by Q. D. Bowers, a well-known expert. This is often updated; look for a later edition for years after 1981.

Doty, Richard. **The Macmillan Encyclopedic Dictionary of Numismatics.** New York: Macmillan, 1982. 355p. $34.95 (737.03)

Almost every aspect of money collection and coins is covered here, and most of the approximately 300 alphabetically arranged entries, which vary in length from a few lines to several pages, are well illustrated, with over 650 black-and-white pictures carefully keyed to the text. Another 25 pages of illustrations are in color. The scope includes all periods and all areas of the globe. The historical treatment is particularly worthwhile, and the author seems equally at home discussing ancient and modern methods of coin design, production, and distribution. In addition to the obvious attention to coins and paper money, the dictionary includes sections on other forms of currency. There is a good reading list.

Fell's International Coin Book. New York: Fell, 1953–   . Irreg. 1983 ed., $14.95; pap. $9.95 (737.4)

A beginner's guide. The strength of this volume lies in the brief history of coins and the detailed methods of identifying coins. A standard, updated list of the values of individual coins follows. Arrangement is alphabetical by country; most items are illustrated.

A companion volume also for beginners is *Fell's United States Coin Book* (1949–   , irreg). The tables give an accurate indication of the price of every coin minted in the United States, and it is nicely illustrated. More advanced collectors should consult *Fell's Guide to Coins and Money Tokens of the World* (1973–   , irreg).

A Guide Book of United States Coins. Racine, WI: Western Pub., 1946–   . Annual. 1983 ed, 256p. $5.95 (737.4)

This standard guide is considered a basic and essential part of every numismatic library and it ranks among the best-selling nonfiction books of all times. Prices for coins are based on the consensus of a board of experts. Prices are retail. (For wholesale prices, see the *Blue Book* by the same publisher.) While used primarily to check the cost of a coin, the guide is invaluable for its careful descriptions and history of regular issues and related areas such as commemorative coinages and territorial gold.

Hobson, Burton. **Coin Collecting as a Hobby.** Rev. ed. New York: Sterling, 1982. 192p. $7.95 (737.49)

The author starts his brief, yet well-written, discussion of the subject from the assumption that the reader knows little or nothing about coins. His narrative style is as conversational as it is informative, and opens with a justification for collection and closes with methods of identifying coins. There are good illustrations and most topics of interest to the amateur are covered in full.

Krause, Chester L., and Clifford Mishler. **Standard Catalog of World Coins.** Iola, WI: Krause, 1973–   . Annual. 1983 ed., 1,984p. $32.50 (737.4)

Generally called the "Krause Catalog" after its publisher, this is the basic guide to world coin prices. More than 1,300 coin-issuing countries, states, provinces, and cities are listed with coins minted from 1750 to the present. There are listings for more than 75,000 coins with more than half of them illustrated. The format can be a problem, particularly as thin paper is used and sometimes the print and illustrations bleed through from back to front. *Note:* This standard reference work is supplemented by the same author's and publisher's *Standard Catalog of 20th Century World Coins* (1981).

Lemke, Bob. **How to Get Started in Coin Collecting.** Blue Ridge Summit, PA: TAB, 1983. 214p. $19.95; pap. $12.95 (747.4)

A basic guide suitable for high school students and adults, this presupposes that the reader knows little about coins or collecting. All the required information is given from a history of coins to prices, investment possibilities, names of dealers, and the probable future of the hobby. In addition to coins, Lemke considers paper money, tokens, and medals; but except for one chapter, most of the focus in on U.S. money. There are adequate photographs. The writing style is relaxed and the information accurate.

Reinfeld, Fred, and Burton Hobson. **A Catalog of the World's Most Popular Coins.** New York: Sterling, 1956–   . Irreg. $19.95 (737.4)

One of the best of the numerous catalogs of coins, this offers complete coverage of both modern and ancient coins from the United States and the world. Many believe it is the most comprehensive of all the standard catalogs. It is carefully illustrated, and each of the coins is described in enough detail to make identification relatively simple. Current values are indicated for each entry.

Reinfeld, Fred, and Burton Hobson. **How to Build a Coin Collection.** Rev. ed. New York: Sterling, 1977. 160p. $10.99 (737.4)

Using a sample collection of basic coins, these world-renowned experts explain how to start, build, and maintain a personal collection. There is more to it than recognizing the difference between a French franc and an American quarter. In fact, so much is involved that the authors spend considerable time explaining what makes a coin valuable, or what makes one coin of the same type and year more worthwhile for a collection than another. They cover everything from mint marks to condition. A sample price list, a glossary of terms, and identification methods are included. The authors have several other titles, all of which are useful for either the beginner or the semi-expert.

U.S. Bureau of the Mint. **Domestic and Foreign Coins Manufactured by Mints in the United States, 1793–1980.** Washington, DC: GPO, 1981. 172p. $6.50 (T28:C66/2/793-982)

The most reliable guide to U.S. coins, this shows where the coin was minted, when, the number minted, and whether gold, silver, or other metals were used. Beginning in 1876, the U.S. Mint turned to foreign coins, and in the second half of the guide, data are given on this type of production, country by country.

Yeoman, R. S. **Modern World Coins: An Illustrated Catalog with Valuations.** Racine, WI: Whitman Coin Products/Western Pub., 1942– . Irreg. 1983 ed., 512p. $9.95 (737.4)

Periodically updated, this, along with the Krause catalog (q.v.), is considered basic. Arranged alphabetically by country, the catalog lists and illustrates the coins of each for the years 1850–1964. Sub-arrangement is by the type group, followed by precious metals such as silver and gold. Each section for a country opens with historic and geographic information. Yeoman has two other standard works, both distributed by Western: *Current Coins of the World* (1966– , irreg.) and *Handbook of United States Coins* (1941– , annual).

COLLECTIBLES. *See* Antiques

COMPUTERS

Beechold, Henry. **The Plain English Repair and Maintenance Guide for Home Computers.** New York: Simon & Schuster, 1984. 256p. $14.95 (621.38)

Sooner or later someone was going to come out with a manual of computer repair and maintenance suitable for the layperson. Beechold's makes the grade, although he is fighting an uphill battle in that no present-day computer is really simple enough for those other than trained electronics experts to repair. At the same time, there are basic maintenance routines that may be followed and simple repairs the skilled owner may attempt. Thanks to the clear writing style and the generous illustrations, there is enough information here to facilitate such things as repairing cable connections and lubricating and washing gears and heads. It is an easy-to-follow guide that will benefit anyone involved with or interested in computers.

Blotnick, Scully. **Computers Made Ridiculously Easy.** New York: BYTE/McGraw-Hill, 1984. 198p. $12.95 (621.3)

The title is not correct, in that nothing, but nothing, is going to make computers "ridiculously easy." Still, the author does come close, with an elementary explanation of everything from DOS to gates. Thanks to his splendid writing style, most terms and processes are at least easier to understand than they previously were. The text covers the basics of both software and hardware, and goes into more detail than is found in many beginning books of this type.

Buffington, Charlie. **Your First Personal Computer: How to Buy and Use It.** New York: McGraw-Hill, 1983. 326p. pap. $8.95 (001.64)

This is a solid, basic guide for the beginner. It is not for anyone already familiar with microcomputers and home computers. The author adequately describes what a personal computer is (and is not), and gives good advice on how to choose the right hardware for individual needs. While there is a reliance on current computers, many of the explanations are useful in a general way and can be guidelines for years to come. There are numerous sections on specific uses of the computer. This may be too general, too basic for some, but for most (and particularly those with little or no skills in this area) it is a good beginning, made even more so by the thorough and detailed coverage of various questions beginners are likely to ask about computers.

Crichton, Michael. **Electronic Life: How to Think about Computers.** New York: Knopf, 1983. 211p. $13.95 (001.64)

A popular writer (author of *The Andromeda Strain*) uses his skills to explain to laypersons what to expect in a computer and how to handle even the most complex problems of hardware and software. The first part of the book is devoted to reassurances that no one is going to be replaced by a computer, and that everyone can learn to be master of the machine. Then come practical notes on various types of software and hardware, including guidelines for evaluation and purchase. The book is particularly strong in the sections on word processing. There are numerous exercises and examples that involve the reader in the text. The unique contribution of this volume is the overall view offered by a truly literate and skilled writer. This is a good beginning for anyone who wants to enter into the world of computers.

D'Ignazio, Fred. **How to Get Intimate with Your Computer: A Ten Step Program for Relieving Computer Anxiety.** New York: McGraw-Hill, 1984. 155p. pap. $6.95 (001.64)

This is a book to help the person who is totally ignorant about computers. (It will be too simple for anyone remotely familiar with the subject.) Nothing is left to chance and everything is explained and defined. The arrangement is as logical as the overall presentation, which employs a ten-step procedure. The approach is something like teaching a person who has never driven before about an automobile. The various parts are indicated, but no effort is made to explain how or why they function. For example, programs are considered here, but no one has to worry about actual programming.

Dirksen, A. J. **Microcomputers: What They Are and How to Put Them in Productive Use.** Blue Ridge Summit, PA: TAB, 1982. 231p. $17.95; pap. $11.95 (001.64)

This is noteworthy for its clear explanations, its presentation, and the numerous flowcharts that help the beginner appreciate what is going on, particularly in terms of programs. Programming basics are featured, and there is a clear overview of the operation and potential of microcomputers in business and the home. *Note:* Translated from the Dutch and somewhat dated in terms of particular equipment.

Helms, Harry, ed. **The McGraw-Hill Computer Handbook.** New York: McGraw-Hill, 1983. 950p. $79.50 (001.64)

Anyone seeking basic background information on computers and programs can turn here for assistance. This compendium is divided into 30 chapters touching on all aspects of computer science from the history of computers to various types of time-sharing. The major program languages are discussed in separate chapters, and there are current materials on graphics, voice patterns, microcomputers, etc. Most of the material is well within the grasp of the layperson, and does not require a science background to understand. An unfortunate decision was to put the more technical terms in boldface. This is distracting, and of little real value as the glossary is incomplete. Still, a most useful work, and one that is sure to be updated—so look for the current edition.

Hillman, Howard. **Macmillan Complete Computer Buyer's Checklist.** New York: Macmillan, 1984. 120p. $7.95 (001.64)

This is a good introduction for the person who is in the market for a computer but knows little or nothing about them. By "complete" the author means all equipment, from the software to the printer, needed for a computer operation. There are general words of explanation for the beginner, followed by specific rules on what to look for and what to avoid when one has a particular mission in mind. The author realizes that people buy microcomputers for many purposes—from games to word processing. Given that, he offers evaluative checklists for each use. The guide has the advantage of being easy to understand and relatively up-to-date.

Hohenstein, C. Louis. **All about Hand-Held and Briefcase-Portable Computers: How to Use Them for Business and Personal Work.** New York: McGraw-Hill, 1984. 368p. pap. $9.95 (001.64)

Including both calculators and full-function computers, the author divides his book into three parts. The first is a consideration of basic units, memory, networking, and essential similarities and differences between various manufacturers of computers. The second part is a careful, detailed discussion of 20 basic models. Each computer is analyzed and there are numerous drawings and diagrams. Finally, there is a section on programs that may be used with the various hardware. The problem with any book of this type is that it dates quickly, and cannot include the latest innovations and models. At the same time, the guide is worthwhile for the overview it gives, for the specific advice on what to look for in computer models of this kind, and for the appreciation of differences in programs. It is a starting point for anyone who is trying to understand or shop for a microcomputer.

Ledgard, Henry, et al. **From Baker Street to Binary: An Introduction to Computers and Computer Programming with Sherlock Holmes.** New York: McGraw-Hill, 1983. 277p. pap. $10.95 (001.64)

Working with the premise that the computer should fit the user, not the user the computer, Ledgard and several contributors give a direct, easy-to-follow set of instructions leading to computer literacy. Nothing new, of course; but the difference is the clear writing style and the focus on fictional crimes to illustrate the points. Dr. Watson narrates the stories, in a nineteenth-century style, about Holmes trying to learn about the computer and its history. Holmes solves a mystery and then compares his method with that of the computer. There is a straightforward chapter on programs and what they are all about. Then comes a puzzle that has to be solved using material learned in the previous chapter or sections. This is all at the adult level (although it should also be of great interest to younger people).

McNitt, Jim. **The Art of Computer Management: How Small Firms Increase Productivity and Profits with Personal Computers.** New York: Simon & Schuster, 1984. 255p. $15.50 (658.02)

Written specifically for the person in small business, this guide points out what can and cannot be done with a computer to make that business more profitable. The author draws not on theory and advertising from computer firms, but from the experience of over 100 people in various types of small business operations. There is a consensus about several points. First, don't overspend; second, the program is considerably more important than the hardware; and third, the components must be flexible and should not be too complex. There are numerous other lessons scattered throughout the text, and summarized in the concluding section on how to select a computer. The primary value is the sometimes verbose explanations of the various types of functions, from spread sheeting to word processing, and how they are applicable in the average business situation.

McWilliams, Peter. **The Personal Computer Book.** 2nd ed. Los Angeles: Prelude Pr., 1983. 280p. pap. $9.95 (001.6)

This book is noteworthy for two reasons. As a basic guide to computers, it is a best-seller. Second, it achieved this status through its numerous illustrations and relaxed style. Some say there are too many puns and gags and that old-time engravings really do not fit, but this hardly detracts from the overall impression of an easy-to-understand, accurate, and demystifying approach to the personal computer. Advice is given on buying a microcomputer, and there is a name-brand guide (almost one-third of the book) that offers subjective opinions about the merits of the various products. Most of the focus is on basic background information and consumer advice, not on the actual operation of the computer. A major drawback: no index.

McWilliams is the author of several other books on computers, including *The Word Processing Book* (Prelude Pr., 1982), *Word Processing on the IBM* (Ballantine, 1983), and *The Personal Computer in Business Book* (Ballantine, 1983). All follow his skeptical yet informative style.

Meilach, Dona. **Before You Buy a Computer.** New York: Crown, 1983. 210p. $l5.95; pap. $8.95 (001.64)

The author offers a step-by-step system of deciding on which minicomputer or microcomputer is best for individual needs. There is complete information on the various types of hardware and software available, and the usual warning that it should be tried before purchase. The language respects the layperson and is free of technical terms and jargon. Computer language is translated freely. Unfortunately, product comparisons are not as detailed as many might wish.

Mick, Colin. **Working Smart: How to Use Microcomputers to Do Useful Work.** New York: Macmillan, 1984. 272p. $22.95 (001.64)

Written for the beginner, here is an easy-to-follow survey of hardware and software that can be of great help to anyone planning to use a microcomputer at home or in business. It has the advantage of being relatively current, and of covering the leading brands in both a critical and a descriptive way. A useful section shows how to trace basic problems in a system. There is an equally good part explaining why the user need not buy a whole package from one manufacturer, but can put together a less costly, more efficient system of terminals, printers, etc.

Osborne, Adam. **Introduction to Microcomputers,** Vol. 0: **The Beginner's Book.** 3rd ed. New York: McGraw-Hill, 1982. 240p. $12.50 (001.6)

This has the distinction of being the first popular computer book. (It was first published in 1975, and is a classic.) It is more detailed than any other guide for laypersons, and is particularly useful for its explanations of how the computer works, right down to the smallest part. This is not for the individual with no interest in technology, but for the type of person who wants to know as much about a computer as an amateur mechanic would want to know about the inner workings of an automobile. Parts of the book, however, may be read by even the least mechanically minded. The reason is that Osborne begins with a basic explanation of what a microcomputer is all about, including programming and software.

Other volumes, with self-explanatory titles, from the same publisher include: Vol. 1, *Basic Concepts;* Vol. 2, *Some Real Microprocessors;* Vol. 3, *Some Real Support Devices.*

Popenoe, Cris. **Book Bytes: The User's Guide to 1200 Microcomputer Books.** New York: Pantheon, 1984. 230p. pap. $9.95 (001.64)

It is rumored that there will be a great decrease in the number of computer books and periodicals. Still, they do continue to be published in vast numbers. Here is a guide to separate the best from the useless. Popenoe evaluates about 1,200 titles published from 1980 to early 1984. Some basic, older titles are included. There is complete bibliographic information for each of the titles and a short descriptive and evaluative annotation as well.

Ralston, Anthony, ed. **Encyclopedia of Computer Science and Engineering.** 2nd ed. New York: Van Nostrand, 1983. 1,665p. $87.50 (001.64)

Almost every aspect of computers and electronic data processing is considered in these review articles written for both laypersons and those who are nearly expert. Most of the material is well illustrated. Arrangement is alphabetical and the experts move from discussions of accounting to specific programs and hardware. The pieces run from brief, yet good, definitions to lengthy essays. Thanks to the 200 contributors and, one suspects, excellent editing, almost all of the material is well within the range of the nonexpert. The work is made easy to use by the addition of a detailed index. A first choice for anyone seeking basic information.

Rochester, Jack, and John Grantz. **The Naked Computer: A Layperson's Almanac of Computer Lore, Wizardry, Personalities, Memorabilia, World Records, Mind Blowers and Tomfoolery.** New York: Morrow, 1983. 335p. $15.95 (001.64)

Not a how-to-do-it book, but a general overview of the history of computers, and the odd facts and puzzles associated with their inventors and users. The result is a type of trivia collection that considers such things as the largest computer crimes in history, key moments in software history, and the IBM company song. Hardly essential, yet a nice change from the serious books on computers.

Rodwell, Peter. **The Personal Computer Handbook: A Complete Practical Guide to Choosing and Using Your Micro.** Woodbury, NY: Barron's, 1983. 208p. pap. $14.95 (001.64)

The editor of the popular *Personal Computer* magazine offers the layperson an easy-to-follow guide to the home computer. Avoiding technical jargon, Rodwell offers an overview in some 50 parts or modules, an arrangement that makes it possible to jump around at will. He covers hardware and what it does, software and what it does, and how to select a computer. There is also a good description of how a computer functions. Pleasant illustrations help to carry the text along. While the information on the 25 or so computers analyzed will date, the basic approach should be good for many years to come.

U.S. Department of Commerce. **Future Information Processing Technology.** Washington, DC: GPO, 1983. 251p. $6.50 (C13.10:500-103)

Anyone who is interested in the future of the computer, at least through 1997, will find this government study of value. It offers educated estimates on the development of the information processing industry—including technology. Topics covered include estimates of future system costs, impact of laws and regulations, shape of programs, etc.

U.S. Department of Commerce. **Microcomputers: A Review of Federal Agency Experiences.** Washington, DC: GPO, 1983. 146p. $5.50 (C13.10:500-102)

Probably no one has had more experience with micros than the federal government, and in this survey the pitfalls and the triumphs are listed. The information is gathered from interviews and research. Laypersons, particularly those selecting a microcomputer for the first time, will find the information invaluable.

Waxman, Robert. **Moonlighting with Your Personal Computer: An Insider's Advice on How You Can Earn Thousands of Extra Dollars.** New York: World Almanac, 1984. 160p. pap. $7.95 (001.64)

Have computer, will travel. Essentially, that is the message, and the author explains where to go and what to expect in the way of profits. Along the road to riches, he explains what is needed by way of hardware/software, who requires the services, what to charge, and how to market the business. The supposition is that the reader will be doing all of this part-time, although with a little ingenuity, luck, and good business sense, it is conceivable that the work might become a full-time profession. Waxman excels in two areas. First and foremost, he is good at showing the various opportunities available and what is required. Second, he is able to convince the reader that the real secret is self-confidence, and given such confidence nothing but success is ahead.

COMPUTERS—CHILDREN

Carlson, Edward. **Kids and the Apple.** Reston, VA: Reston, 1983. 218p. $19.95 (001.64)

Designed for children in about the seventh grade, this is an introduction to BASIC that an adult, with problems understanding such things, will appreciate too. Filled with associative memory guides, the manual traces the basic commands and what they mean and accomplish. There are 33 lessons, liberally punctuated with cartoons and drawings. While this may be too elementary for some, it is a day-by-day approach that guarantees an understanding of the computer language. *Note:* Modifications of the guide are available from the publisher for other computers.

Hammond, Ray. **Computers and Your Child.** New Haven, CT: Ticknor & Fields, 1984. 277p. $15.95; pap. $7.95 (001.64)

What role is the computer likely to play in the future of a child? What can the parent do to see that that role is useful and kept in perspective? What, by the way, *is* a computer and how does it function? Typical questions from typical concerned parents are addressed one by one and adequate answers are given. After supplying the standard background information on the computer, the author wisely divides the book into sections showing how various age groups use the computer. There is a good part, too, on computer use by disabled children. What sets the book apart from others is the author's concern with the fallout from technology. Some of it is good—e.g., it helps the child to reason and to speed up homework assignments, but some of it can be harmful. What is to be done with the student who becomes "hooked" on a computer? Is there any way to make room for a young girl in what is sometimes considered a male stronghold? The book ends with some information on microcomputers, but much of it will date quickly. Still, the overall impression of the book is that it is a good, basic guide for the involved parent.

U.S. Department of Education. **Computers in Education.** Washington, DC: GPO, 1983. 41p. $3.75 (ED1.2:C73/3/v1)
This is the result of a special conference on the subject of computers and computer literacy in the nation's schools. There is a particular focus on the need for additional research. The document reports the conclusions of the conference as reported by its chairman.

Williams, Frederick, and Victoria Williams. **Growing Up with Computers: A Parent's Survival Guide.** New York: Morrow, 1983. 288p. $15.95; pap. $7.95 (001.64)
What does a parent do when a child wants a video game or comes home with news about a computer in the classroom? The answers are all here. The Williamses, who have had wide experience working with children and computers, set out to explain the varieties of hardware and software, and what they do and do not do for the user. The ideas behind the child's programming are explained, as are the benefits of what may seem to be only games on video screens. Of course, particular attention is given to the type of technology likely to be used by the elementary to high school age child. There are some good sections on programs that may be used by both children and adults.

COMPUTERS—DIRECTORIES, DICTIONARIES & GUIDES

Baldwin, Ed, et al. **The First Family Computer Book: Your Family's First Home Computer System—What It Can Do, and How to Buy Wisely.** Radnor, PA: Chilton, 1984. 215p. pap. $12.95 (001.64)
One of the few computer guides written for the whole family, this claims that the proper choice of computer equipment can be used by everyone. The real bonus is the approach. The authors use everyday terms, avoid jargon, and underline points with clever drawings. The basics are considered, as are things to look for when buying a computer. Unfortunately, little attention is given to specific brands, and there might have been more emphasis on varieties of software. It is too elementary for some, but for those with absolutely no knowledge of the field. it is a fine beginning.

Bowker/Bantam 1984 Complete Sourcebook of Personal Computing. New York: Bowker/Bantam, 1983. 646p. $24.95; pap. $18.95 (001.64)
The "complete" in the title is accurate. In this useful reference work one finds a mass of directory-type information about computer hardware and software. The

guide opens with a basic discussion and overview of the subject. Whether this is needed is questionable, but it is at least useful. Following that is a directory of over 300 microcomputers and close to 3,500 programs. Each is briefly described, but not evaluated. There is also a list of various allied products from modems to disks. Then comes a bibliography of over 2,000 book titles—again simply listed without evaluative notes—as well as some 200 periodicals. There is other material as well, the most useful of which is the guide to 4,000 companies involved, in one way or another, with computers. Others may find the list of some 100 user groups and clubs throughout the United States of real benefit.

Rosenberg, Jerry. **Dictionary of Computers, Data Processing and Telecommunications.** New York: Wiley, 1983. 614p. $24.95; pap. $14.95 (001.6)

Here are some 10,000 entries that define and explain various aspects of computers. The three areas listed in the title are covered completely, although the definitions tend to be brief. The publisher plans to update this volume from time to time. Meanwhile, this is a first place to turn for easy-to-understand definitions of words connected with computers, data processing, and telecommunications.

Webster, Tony. **Microcomputer Buyer's Guide.** New York: McGraw-Hill, 1983. 351p. pap. $19.95 (001.64)

More than 180 different microcomputer manufacturers are considered and evaluated here. There are comparison charts that make it possible to see at a glance differences between various products. Grouped by manufacturer, the computers, along with peripherals (including software), are detailed in much the same fashion for each. The guide is invaluable as a source of evaluations and descriptions of particular parts or systems. *Note:* This is to be an annual publication, so look for the latest edition.

Willis, Jerry, and Merl Miller. **Computers for Everybody: 1984 Buyer's Guide.** Beaverton, OR: dilithium Press, 1984. 584p. pap. $19.95 (001.64)

A buyer's guide to close to 150 current microcomputers, divided by cost and type. For example, listings are under inexpensive ($600 or less); home and general purpose; business and professional; premium business; and portable. There is a general overview of the particular area, and then individual computers are described and evaluated. The evaluations are uniform, considering such things as ease of use, keyboard, video display, disk drive, etc. There is no comparison of the computers. One chapter considers the 12 most common computer lies told by salespeople. The half-truths and outright lies are explained so the buyer may be careful in reaching a decision. All of this is presented free of jargon, and where technical terms have to be used, they are carefully explained. In all, the authors ensure that the computer-buying task does not have to be a nightmare. It is basic to the beginner's bookshelf. *Note:* This is to be updated annually, so look for the latest edition.

COMPUTERS—PROGRAMMING & SOFTWARE

Bocchino, William. **Simplified Guide to Microcomputers: With Practical Programs and Applications.** Englewood Cliffs, NJ: Prentice-Hall, 1982. 256p. $34.95; pap. $15.95 (001.64)

This differs from many microcomputer guides in that in addition to information on how the computer works, the author adds ten programs. In BASIC, the programs are given in detail, i.e., written out line by line so that even the beginner may understand what is going on. The book includes a detailed glossary and scores of illustrations. *Note:* The binding is spiral bound, but sturdy.

Ditlea, Steve. **The Osborne/McGraw-Hill Home Computer Software Guide.** New York: McGraw-Hill, 1984. 202p. $11.95 (001.64)

Written for the typical family or individual with a home computer, not for the business or professional person, this is a use-by-use guide to software. The approach is to devote sections to specific types of requirements, from basic games and education for children to more sophisticated budget and word processing demands by adults. For each subject area, there is a good discussion of what can and cannot be expected from typical software, plus an evaluation. Specific software is considered for each of the tasks discussed by the author.

Glossbrenner, Alfred. **The Complete Handbook of Personal Computer Communications.** New York: St. Martin's, 1983. 325p. pap. $14.95 (384)

This differs from the majority of computer books in that the stress is not on the computer, but on data bases and other forms of information. The author not only considers the basic vendors, from Lockheed to BRS, but also discusses other more specialized services. Details are given on how to purchase these services, costs of services, types of equipment used, and even, in an extremely elementary way, how to search. (The problem is that searching is a highly skilled business, and Glossbrenner touches only on the difficulties.) The idea, though, is to open up for the layperson the wide, wide world of communication and information made possible by a computer and a telephone. In this he succeeds wonderfully well.

Glossbrenner, Alfred. **How to Buy Software.** New York: St. Martin's, 1983. 648p. $14.95 (001.64)

In this three-pronged attack on microcomputer software, the first section explains what software is and how it differs at various levels and types of use. Terms are clearly defined. The second part turns to the 30,000 to 40,000 different programs available for the personal computer and gives general methods of detecting what is good, bad, and indifferent. Here the author considers word processing, communication programs, electronic spreadsheets, and filing. The last part touches on, but really fails to review, specific software packages. This is a serious failing, and for other than some general programs the reader will have to go elsewhere for advice. Still, as a good introduction to the subject this is one of the best books now available.

Heckel, Paul. **The Elements of Friendly Software Design.** New York: Warner, 1984. 200p. pap. $8.95 (001.64)

Written for the would-be professional, not for the layperson, this is a manual for computer software writers. Heckel rightly points out that there is always a need for new software, or at least modifications, and he is concerned with the most efficient methods of preparation. He explains the basics that a programmer must master. Each of the steps is fully discussed and normally illustrated with examples. Thanks to an imaginative approach, and an appreciation of the need for clarity, this is a useful manual. It can be employed by the interested layperson as well as the professional.

Ledgard, Henry, and Andrew Singer. **Elementary BASIC as Chronicled by John H. Watson.** Chicago: Science Research Center, 1982. 264p. $20; pap. $12.95 (001.64)

The author of *From Baker Street to Binary* (see p. 65 in this book) employs the same approach to get the reader's attention. BASIC is taught by following the life and adventures of Sherlock Holmes. Problems and solutions are presented in a storylike fashion. The book is not only easy to follow but has the added advantage of teaching the reader a unique and fundamental approach to programming and computer-language concepts.

McGehee, Brad, ed. **Programmer's Manual.** 1982– . Annual. 1984 ed., 300p. $16.95 (001.6)

Following the plan of guides like *Writer's Market,* this is a list of places where free-lance computer programmers may sell their programs. Over 500 software publishers—including those of arcade games—are included, with information on what they need, what they pay, etc. In addition, there are articles on marketing, packaging, and copyright. There is even a section on how to prepare a user's manual for the program submitted. The book is divided into three main sections: type of computer, type of software, and alphabetical index.

Townsend, Carl. **How to Get Started with CP/M (Control Programs for Microcomputers).** Blue Ridge Summit, PA: TAB, 1982. 127p. $14.95 (001.64)

Many microcomputers have a CP/M system that allows the user to formulate and run software programs on floppy disks. As CP/M is a major element, the guide is of particular help to those with little or no knowledge of computers. The author, leaving nothing to chance, starts out with an analysis of microcomputers and other hardware, disks, word processing applications, etc. The guide is particularly useful where many are not, i.e., in step-by-step procedures that are clear and can be followed by the beginner.

COMPUTERS—WORD PROCESSING

Fluegelman, Andrew, and Jeremy Hewes. **Writing in the Computer Age: Word Processing Skills and Style for Every Writer.** New York: Doubleday, 1983. 254p. $19.95; pap. $12.95 (808.02)

Written specifically for the writer, although equally useful to students and others who compose papers, here is an exceptionally clear and methodical explanation of the word processor. The authors assume that the reader knows nothing, and so they begin with definitions and explanations of various kinds of software and hardware. They then move into a step-by-step analysis of how the typical word processing system operates. Specific applications are considered, and both the plus and minus aspects of the new way to write are discussed.

Foster, Timothy, and Alfred Glossbrenner. **Word Processing for Executives and Professionals.** New York: Van Nostrand, 1983. 173p. $17.50 (652)

This is an overview of the word processor and its use by people involved in business and professions. Because it stresses basics rather than individual word processing programs, it is likely to be of use for several years. The authors open with a history and background of the computer and the word processor. Using a step-by-step process, they illustrate, define, and explain basics from hardware and programs to a wide assortment of computer terms. Given the background information on the word processor, the reader is then invited to investigate various ways in which the processor can save time, frustration, and money. There are excellent examples of how it can be used in different situations. Less helpful, and likely to date, is a list of sources for software and hardware.

McWilliams, Peter. **The Word Processing Book: A Short Course in Computer Literacy.** Los Angeles: Prelude Pr., 1982. 240p. pap. $8.95 (651)
Employing the same approach of puns and old-time illustrations he uses in his successful *The Personal Computer Book* (see p. 66 in this book), the author offers a two-part approach to word processing. First, he explains what it is all about in terms acceptable to even the most technologically backward layperson. Second, he describes and evaluates the software for word processors and considers the pros and cons of popular types of hardware. Most people thoroughly enjoy his approach. Others are discouraged by the sometimes too elementary style, but for those there are more advanced books on word processors.

Naiman, Arthur. **Word Processing Buyer's Guide.** New York: BYTE/McGraw-Hill, 1983. 320p. pap. $15.95 (681.6)
There are scores of different approaches to word processing on the market. Which is best? The author, realizing that "best" is a relative term depending on the particular use of the word processor, sets out to give the answer(s). There is the expected opening section on the history and purpose of the word processor and how it operates. But Naiman is primarily concerned with software, not hardware, and here he turns to the 14 basic programs he thinks are the best. (Other word processor programs are discussed more briefly.) For each, he uses an evaluative procedure that allows the reader to determine the ease of use, speed, etc. The writing style is as clear as it is informative and this is one of the best books on word processing available. It is sure to be updated, so look for the latest edition.

Stern, Fred. **Word Processing and Beyond: The Introductory Computer Book.** New York: John Muir/Norton, 1983. 224p. pap. $9 (652)
Not just another book on word processing, this is a fresh look at a sometimes complex matter. The author has little reverence for technology but admits that the machine in the home or office saves time and donkey work. Just how it does so is explained, as he moves from the mechanics of the computer to the program and its basic operation. All of this is covered in different chapters, with adequate illustrations and the author's sometimes witty asides. Possibly the most useful sections are those on how to select the best word processing program for a particular need and the variety of printers. There are some reassuring parts on what to do when the computer or its allied components break down. The author has a fine writing style.

Zinsser, William. **Writing with a Word Processor.** New York: Harper, 1983. 117p. $12.95; pap. $5.95 (808.02)
"Maybe I'm not the last person in the world who would be expected to write with a word processor, but I'm one of the last." With this, the author of the best-selling *On Writing Well* sets out to explain in the first person how a middle-aged columnist acquired and learned to operate an IBM word processor. In 18

short chapters, he goes through the early stages of total frustration, through mild accomplishment, to success. (In fact, this book itself was composed on the word processor.) Along the way, he describes in everyday language what is involved in word processing and how the machine is operated. There is general information on disks, pagination, and so on, but no specific step-by-step guidelines for using the machine. It is more a general discussion about what to expect. The idea is: if *I* can do it, *you* can do it. Some basic discoveries will be applicable to other experiences, but primarily the charm and the unique quality of the book lie in telling everyone that a word processor can be, in fact should be, a replacement for the typewriter. The argument is as persuasive as it is intelligent. *Note:* There are no sections on what type of hardware to purchase.

CONJURING. *See* Magic

CONSTRUCTION. *See* Homes—Building & Construction

CONSUMER EDUCATION
See also Catalogs; Food—Purchase of; Indexes

Bartlett, Michael, ed. **The Book of Bests.** New York: Dodd, 1983. 433p. $15.95 (380.1)

When looking for the "best" products, most people turn to *Consumer Reports* or other consumer guides. Useful as these may be, they hardly touch on many of the items considered here. The compilers of *The Book of Bests* are interested in such luxury items as wine, food, vacation resorts, travel plans, music halls, etc. Their assumption is that the reader either has money to burn or, more likely, wishes to dream about spending time in the best penthouse in London. At any rate, information is given on where to find the best of these luxury items, how to order them through the mail or which people to contact to receive them, and, usually, how much they will cost. Prices are not always provided, but if you have to ask the cost, so the old saying goes, it is beyond your means anyway. Furthermore, one may take exception to the compilers' views of the "best," but these kinds of choices are always subjective. Besides, arguing with their judgments is half the fun!

Dorfman, John. **Consumer Tactics Manual: How to Get Action on Your Complaints.** New York: Atheneum, 1980. 239p. pap. $6.95 (640.73)

The first part lists alphabetically, with cross-references, common consumer complaints about everything from poor automobiles to poor appliances. Broader subjects from social security to the handicapped are also discussed. Usually quick advice is given on how to solve the difficulty, but in some cases there is reference to the second part, which gives detailed advice on how to fight for the consumer's rights. The author suggests sample letters, how to make phone calls, and even how and when to turn to a lawyer. There is a list of groups able to help–from the Federal Trade Commission to the local small claims courts, and a description of each organization and agency and how it may help in a particular battle. Also, valuable general advice is given on consumer rights.

Florman, Monte, ed. **Consumer Reports Guide to Electronics in the Home.** Boston: Little, 1984. 224p. pap. $10 (621.38)

The Consumer Union's ratings on products related to electronics are found in this handy compilation. Many of the studies are from *Consumer Reports* magazine, although they are sometimes updated and given in a somewhat different form. The product is named, the precise model number given, and then it is rated in a dozen or so ways. The top models are indicated, and there is necessary background information. For example, not only are home computers ranked, but there is good advice on what type is best for a specific need. Products range from telephones to computers and various high fidelity components. The editor takes the term "electronics" to mean almost anything plugged into a wall socket. Tests are on models produced through most of 1983.

Hatton, Hap, and Laura Torbet. **Helpful Hints for Hard Times: How to Live It Up While Cutting Down.** New York: Facts on File, 1983. 237p. $15.95; pap. $7.95 (640.73)

Anyone living on a restricted budget will find that this book measures up to the subtitle. The proof of the oxymoron is found in the ways suggested to budget for, select, and buy a house, car, and other necessities, as well as to handle maintenance and upkeep bills. Information is taken from government documents and from equally reliable books and pamphlets, many of which are cited. The advice is based on practical considerations, not dreams. The authors insist that the reader sit down and thoroughly analyze all aspects of income and outlay before moving in any direction. Just how to do such an analysis is built into each section. There are listed, as well, additional places to find information and fascinating tips on how to do things that save money, such as using toothpaste to clean almost anything in the house. The vital consideration is, of course, getting a cheap toothpaste.

Rinzler, Carol. **The Consumer's Brand Name Guide to Household Products.** New York: Lippincott, 1980. 240p. $9.95; pap. $5.95 (640.73)

The author does two basic things. First, she arranges common household products in alphabetical order by name of product. Second, she provides a detailed analysis of what each product does and does not do—but, most important, she adds such information as its safety factor, what it contains (including any harmful chemicals), and whether it is better, cheaper, or safer than its competitors. The information is augmented, fittingly enough, with a directory of poison control centers, a clear explanation of basic ingredients, and even a section on how to write a letter of complaint.

Stossel, John. **Shopping Smart: The Only Consumer Guide You'll Ever Need.** New York: Putnam's, 1980. 217p. $9.95 (640.73)

This goes a long way toward explaining what to look for when shopping. There is excellent advice on the basics of buying a car and other large-ticket items, as well as such things as the economics of a second house and the costs of vacations. All of this is laced with anecdotes and stories out of the CBS television show where Stossel is the consumer affairs editor.

Top Tips from Consumer Reports. Boston: Little, 1983. 319p. pap. $6.95 (640.73)

In the ongoing process of comparing various types of products, the researchers at *Consumer Reports* have learned scores of different things that will benefit the average person working in and around the home. For example, here one finds the best way to use everything from a wok and a pressure cooker to a spray gun and a booster cable for the car. What is the best way to wash dishes and the easiest way to grind coffee? How can one prepare a good soup and what are the various methods of using garbage bags? In a word, the editors more than meet the description of their subtitle, "how to do things better, faster, cheaper." One should stress the how-to aspect of this volume, because unlike many other *Consumer Reports* books this does not test specific products. It does show the reader how to use items in a most efficient way.

U.S. Office of Consumer Affairs. **The Consumer Information Catalog.** Pueblo, CO: Consumer Information Center, 1980–   . Quarterly. Free (Pr39.15-C)

This is a 16- to 20-page catalog listing and briefly describing U.S. government booklets of interest to consumers. Here you will find both free and inexpensive ($1.75 to $4.45) material "on how to fix your car; how to save money on food, health care, energy, and other household expenses; how to slim down and trim up; and many other interesting topics."

Weiss, Ellen. **Secondhand Super Shopper: Buying More, Spending Less, Living Better.** New York: Evans, 1981. 288p. $12.50; pap. $7.95 (640.73)

There are numerous good, even luxurious, buys in the secondhand shop. The trick is to tell what is really outstanding, what is really a bargain; and, of course, one must find the best places to do such shopping. Answers to these and related questions are offered by the author, who claims some 40 years of experience shopping in secondhand outlets. There are useful tips that should be of interest to everyone, even those who only occasionally look for something out of the ordinary in a secondhand store. Less useful is a section on starting a secondhand business. Most of the information is so basic as not to be dated.

The World Almanac Consumer Survival Kit. New York: World Almanac, 1983. 62p. pap. $1.50 (332.02)

This is a highly useful pamphlet that is primarily a compilation of government statistics on matters of interest to consumers, e.g., mortgage rates, social security regulations, life insurance, etc. Numerous charts and tables are included.

CONSUMER PROTECTION

Brobeck, Stephen, and Anne Averyt. **The Product Safety Book: The Ultimate Consumer Guide to Product Hazards.** New York: Dutton, 1983. 441p. pap. $9.95 (363.19)

Stop. Before you buy a product check to see if it is listed here. If it is included, do not buy it because, at least according to the authors, it may be hazardous. Exceptions: Some of the more than 1,500 products listed can be safe under certain circumstances, and these are carefully explained. Coverage includes everything from dangerous automobiles and cosmetics to common household products put on the market from about 1970 to early 1983.

Gilson, Christopher. **Consumer Revenge.** New York: Putnam's, 1981. 300p. $13.95 (381.33)

Don't just settle for an excuse—get your revenge. That is the strong message of a guide showing how average consumers may strike back at the garage that wrecks rather than repairs a car. This picture of the consumer as "the worm who turns" focuses on everything from bad products to nasty landlords. The problem: the actions require a considerable amount of iron will on the part of the consumer— and some are barely within the law. Still, it is good reading, particularly if the reader is downright angry.

Joseph, Joel. **How to Fight City Hall, the IRS, Banks, Corporations, Your Local Airport, and Other Nuisances.** Chicago: Contemporary, 1983. 200p. pap. $9.95 (343.73)

The ins and outs of getting justice for the consumer are explained here in detail. The vehicle for attaining justice is the law, so one needs some knowledge of how the law operates, although the author believes there is rarely a need for professional legal help. One needs to know only how to begin a lawsuit, not necessarily to follow through to the courts. Most of the time, the rudimentary steps are all that are needed, and each of these is given for a variety of problem situations from taxes to noise to a bad purchase. There are numerous legal forms to help the reader follow the pattern of attack. If all else fails, there are suggestions for when and how to bring formal legal action. A book with power, this is an important weapon for any aggrieved individual.

Newman, Stephen, and Nancy Kramer. **Getting What You Deserve: A Handbook for the Assertive Consumer.** New York: Doubleday, 1979. 328p. pap. $8.95 (381.3)

Two attorneys, both experts in consumer matters, tell how the average person can get the most out of consumer transactions. If goods or services are disappointing, complain. The authors give the laws governing such complaints, and there are lists of various places where one can go for help, such as federal consumer offices. Equally effective are the sections explaining how to avoid being a victim. Just about every aspect of the market is considered, from the door-to-door salesperson and the used car dealer to different vacation plans. Numerous charts and diagrams complement the text and explain what it means to look twice at any item or service. The basic advice is timeless.

Suthers, John, and Gary Shupp. **Fraud & Deceit: How to Stop Being Ripped Off.** New York: Arco, 1982. 144p. pap. $6.95 (362.8)

While no one thinks he or she is likely to be a victim of a con operation, there is always that outside chance. With that chance in mind, two district attorneys outline the major frauds and con schemes used to dupe the gullible, including some quite intelligent and sophisticated individuals. They offer a virtual catalog of swindles, and, if nothing else, it is a marvelous adventure in reading. It is also a guide in that the writers suggest ways to avoid such traps. The confidence tricks described range from the familiar stock and commodity frauds to the classic pigeon drop. Many are less esoteric and deal with familiar problems of home repair people, automobile mechanics, and phony cut-rate sales. The appendix includes a list of federal and state consumer agencies, as well as a glossary of terms used by the various con artists—and the police.

U.S. Department of Commerce. **How to Write a Wrong: Complain Effectively and Get Results.** Washington, DC: GPO, 1983. 16p (FT1.2:W93)

What is the best way to complain about a product or service? This publication shows the wronged individual precisely the right way to go about preparing a letter. Just what to include—and what to exclude—is clearly stated. *Note:* Sold only in packages of 100, $41.

U.S. Office of Consumer Affairs. **Consumer's Resource Handbook.** Pueblo, CO: Consumer Information Center, Dept. 601M, 1984. 116p. Free (Pr38.15:C-76)

Resolution of problems from aircraft noise to faulty computers is the promise of this free booklet, which is a directory of corporations and companies giving names, addresses, and telephone numbers of customer relations departments. Listings are in alphabetical order by company from Aamco Transmissions to Zenith Radio. Information is given on how to write letters of complaint, when and how to contact an attorney, and where to write for further information. There are extensive listings of Better Business Bureaus (state by state), county and city consumer protection offices, etc. There are also sections of information for handicapped people and the aged. *Note:* The handbook is frequently updated.

CONTESTS

Gadney, Alan. **How to Enter & Win Series.** New York: Facts on File, 1981–   . Approx. 200p. ea. $14.95; pap. $6.95

All titles in the series read *How to Enter & Win* [subject] *Contests.* As of mid-1984 they include *Black & White Photography, Color Photography, Fine Arts & Sculpture, Design and Commercial Art, Clay and Glass Crafts, Cooking, Fabric & Fiber, Fine Arts & Sculpture, Gardening, Jewelry & Metal Crafts, Fiction Writing, Film, Non-fiction & Journalism.*

All of these books have nearly identical introductions in which the author gives some background on the specific subject and then provides hints on how to succeed. The focus is primarily on listing contests or events one may enter, not on strategies for winning. As a directory of possible opportunities, it is hard to beat. Arrangement is by broad subject interests. Entries for the individual events are quite detailed, offering (1) the name of the event or contact person; (2) the purpose and scope of the event; (3) the address and any other vital information on rules; (4) complete data on entering fees (if any), royalties or payments (if any), contest rules (where applicable), and whatever is necessary to approach the situation intelligently. The books usually conclude with a full index by subject and category, as well as by event name, sponsor, and award. Individual titles are updated from time to time, and the reader should ask for the latest available.

Glasser, Selma. **The Complete Guide to Prize Contests, Sweepstakes and How to Win Them.** New York: Fell, 1980. 192p. $9.95 (790.1)

After years of experience in winning and advising others on how to win contests, Glasser reveals some of her innermost secrets. She moves easily from the best way to pen a limerick, name a product, or enter a sweepstakes. The grammar and style may be less than poetic, but almost every page is convincing proof that the author knows more about contests than almost anyone in the field. She is certain that anyone can make money by taking the time to study the psychological and practical twists of the games readers are asked to play. She may be right. At any rate, it is hard to find a better book on the subject.

Mincer, Richard, and Deanne Mincer. **The Talk Show Book: An Engaging Primer on How to Talk Your Way to Success.** New York: Facts on File, 1982. 256p. $14.95 (791.44)

Although directed to a limited audience, this is a unique guide that, when needed, is of considerable value. Its audience, as the title suggests, is the individual who is called on to appear on a television or radio talk show. How should one act? How should one promote oneself? Which subjects should be explored, and which avoided? What is the best type of clothing for a television appearance? This and countless other questions are answered by the authors, who have had years of experience on television, and know of what they write. In addition to basics, there is a good overview of the different types of shows, the technical side of broadcasting, and even a section on fees, agents, and bookings.

Sackett, Susan, and Cheryl Blythe. **You Can Be a Game Show Contestant—and Win.** New York: Dell, 1982. 130p. pap. $3.95 (791.44)

The first step is to become a contest participant. This is explained in detail, particularly in terms of what to do when your name is selected and it comes time for further investigation and interviews. Cleared for the show, what preparation is required, and how should one act when trying to win a prize? While general advice is given, the authors concentrate on the specifics of 15 popular quiz shows of 1981–1982 and what to do when you have been selected as a contestant. Less useful, and now dated, is the list of telephone numbers and names of people associated with these shows. More current data may be found in several television annual directories. An unusual kind of how-to-do-it guide, this seems reliable and sensible. Reading between the lines, the real question emerges: Does anyone want a prize that much?

COOKING
See also Bread; Desserts; Drinks; Food; Sandwiches; Wine

Ackart, Robert. **A Celebration of Soups.** New York: Doubleday, 1982. 260p. $19.95; pap. $10.95 (641.8)

Whether hot or cold, traditional or out of the ordinary, the soup of the day will be found in this guide. The directions are explicit, and the nature and kinds of ingredients are clear. There are some useful illustrations, and a section devoted to garnishes and other additions. The cookbook is suitable for both beginners and experts.

Anderson, Jean. **Jean Anderson Cooks: Her Kitchen Reference & Recipe Collection.** New York: Morrow, 1982. 560p. $19.95 (641.5)

Serialized in part in *Ladies' Home Journal,* this is a nice combination of practical cooking and gourmet delights. Anderson speaks to both the beginner and near expert and has something for almost every situation and occasion. The book opens with "kitchen reference," which is a guide to the selection and cooking of poultry, fish, meat, and vegetables. Most of the book consists of easy-to-follow recipes, all of which are explained in detail and usually with considerable, and justified, excitement. Thanks to the good writing style and the wide variety of menus and recipes, this is a basic book for most kitchens.

Anderson, Jean. **Jean Anderson's New Processor Cooking.** Rev. ed. New York: Morrow, 1983. 480p. $17.50 (641.58)

In her usual methodical syle, Jean Anderson suggests numerous recipes and approaches to the use of food processors and their numerous accessories. There is nothing unusual here except the great detail, for which the author is famous. Little is left to chance, and anyone who can read and has the necessary machine and the ingredients should create first-rate dishes.

Beard, James. **The New James Beard.** New York: Knopf, 1981. 625p. $16.95 (641.5)

A kind of summary of other Beard books, this marks a change from earlier works in that there is more emphasis on health and nutrition, as well as on fresher, lighter dishes. There are hundreds of recipes ranging from the simple to the difficult, but, as in all of his works, each is carefully explained and often nicely illustrated. The writing style is up to Beard's high standards, and the guide is by now another "classic" in the field. Among other titles by Beard worth considering, and published by Knopf, are *Beard on Food* (1974) and *James Beard's Theory and Practice of Good Cooking* (1977). Also, *The James Beard Cookbook* (Dutton, 1970) remains a basic cookbook.

Belsinger, Susan, and Carolyn Dille. **Cooking with Herbs.** New York: Van Nostrand, 1984. 261p. $20.50; pap. $15.50 (641.6)

What is nice about the herbs in this book is that most of them are readily available and none is an esoteric specimen found only in the wilds of Sussex. The authors hold the herbs under discussion to 20—from parsley to thyme—and devote a chapter to each. The reader follows the herb from a seed in a garden to a place on the table. Their history is detailed, as might be expected, and this is followed by gardening data. There are good line drawings of the individual herbs, and the recipes range from teas to desserts. An overall chapter considers storage of herbs and bits of advice the authors have found useful, including some lore on alchemy. Sources of supply in the United States and Canada are given. The recipes are as down to earth and appetizing as the style of this guide.

Claiborne, Craig, and Pierre Franey. **Cooking with Craig Claiborne and Pierre Franey.** New York: Times Books, 1983. 510p. $17.95 (641.8)

Unlike their equally popular *The New York Times Cookbook* (q.v.), this is devoted exclusively to recipes, some 600, which at one time or another appeared in the *New York Times*. The recipes are carefully detailed and explained, but the peculiar gift of the authors is their ability to describe every dish in such a way as to make it appear distinctive. While the emphasis is on American dishes, the authors include various recipes from European chefs. Some of these are a bit difficult, although they will be of great interest to dedicated cooks. Both men are aware of the health aspects of nutrition, and they make a special effort to include wholesome, fresh ingredients. There is, too, an interest in avoiding salt and substituting healthier spices and herbs. Even butter and cream are kept to a minimum.

Claiborne, Craig, and Pierre Franey. **The New York Times Cookbook.** New York: Times Books, 1979. 751p. $18.95 (641.5)

A combination of recipes, menus, and how-to-do-it, this is a basic cookbook for almost any kitchen. Based on 20 years of food columns for the *New York Times,* this is a revision of the original *New York Times Cookbook* (1961). With coauthor Pierre Franey, Claiborne offers specific directions on how to make everything from almond and dill stuffed eggs to somewhat more modest dishes. In addition to some 1,000 recipes there are chapters on cooking equipment, questions and answers about the art, and other related matters for both beginners and experts. There are numerous illustrations and the explanations are exceptionally clear and precise. Then, too, both men write with verve and style. The result is a first-rate cookbook.

Coulson, Zoe, ed. **The Good Housekeeping Illustrated Cookbook.** New York: Hearst, 1980. 512p. $11.95 (641.5)

First published in 1903, the basic Good Housekeeping cookbook is a classic often found in American kitchens along with Betty Crocker, Fannie Farmer, etc. It is of the same general type, in that the emphasis is on traditional recipes. There are some essential differences. Here the focus is on full-color illustrations, with each of the close to 1,000 dishes indexed and captioned in the first section of the book. The caption gives basic ingredients and preparation time and refers the reader to the text, where the individual recipe is given in detail, with numerous drawings demonstrating each step. Arrangement is by courses. It differs from the others too in that almost all of the emphasis is on the actual dishes, and there is not much material on the basics of cooking and food preparation. Another version of this same guide, arranged differently and without as many illustrations but with double the number of recipes, is *The Good Housekeeping Cookbook* (1973).

Crocker, Betty. **Betty Crocker's Cookbook.** Rev. ed. Racine, WI: Golden, 1978. 400p. $9.95; pap. $3.50 (641.5)

One of America's best-known cookbooks with over 1,500 basic recipes covering every situation, every type of meal. Directions are specific and easy to follow and rely primarily on ingredients that can be purchased in almost any store. There are sections devoted to taking the beginner through the basic steps of cooking and food preparation, accompanied by color photographs, charts, and diagrams.

Crocker, Betty. **Betty Crocker's Kitchen Secrets.** New York: Random House, 1983. 160p. $12.50 (641.59)

The famous kitchen expert does not offer recipes here, but does suggest countless ways to save time and effort by having a well-organized kitchen. In addition to tips on food preparation, she gives recommended methods of shopping for groceries and storing your purchases. The book is in two sections. The latter is involved with the basics of cooking (from various types of equipment to foods), while the former is concerned with various categories of foods—including hard-to-find advice and answers to questions likely to bother both beginners and experienced cooks. An easy-to-follow, handy book for most kitchens.

Damerell, Edna. **Twice Is Nice.** New York: Macmillan, 1984. 325p. $9.95 (641.5)
The title is a play on words and refers to leftovers. Here the author offers about 600 different methods of serving leftovers. Whether for an omelet or a stew, the directions are specific and easy to follow. Most of the recipes are fairly standard, although occasionally there is something to challenge the gourmet. As much a reminder as a guide, this is a useful approach for both beginners and intermediate cooks. Experienced hands may have their own ideas.

Farmer, Fannie. **The Fannie Farmer Cookbook.** 12th ed. New York: Knopf, 1979. 811p. $15.95 (641.5)
This is the standard American cookbook, which has been published since 1896 and continues to be revised every decade or so. The object is to show the beginner how to get the most out of cooking. At the same time there are recipes and hints here for even the expert. The focus is entirely on American eating habits, although not exclusively on American recipes and food. The book is divided into chapters and sections that, following the introduction on basics, discuss vegetables, fish, meats, and appetizers. The book is well illustrated and the recipes are easy to follow. Some may balk at this edition because it includes metric measurements, although standard American measurements are given too.

Franey, Pierre, and Richard Flaste. **Pierre Franey's Kitchen.** New York: Times Books, 1982. 262p. $14.95 (641.58)
While there is no guarantee that the reader who outfits a kitchen following the famed French cook's advice will become a good cook, this is at least a beginning. Here Franey carefully explains the equipment essential to producing a gourmet meal or a simple snack. He gives detailed information on 101 items from knives to pasta makers. In some cases he provides recipes in which he demonstrates how the item is best used. True, not everyone will need even a small portion of the equipment discussed here, particularly the more esoteric items. What it comes down to is a spirited, highly sensible discussion of cooking equipment that will be of benefit to almost anyone, even those who simply dream about the complete kitchen. *Note:* Much of this book is based on Franey's "Kitchen Equipment" column in the *New York Times.*

Garvan, Fran. **The Farmer's Market Cookbook.** Cambridge, MA: Harvard Common Press, 1982. 160p. $14.95; pap. $8.95 (641.5)
The weekly or even daily farmers' market is familiar to most urban Americans, so why a book on the subject? The answer is that Garvan offers a month-by-month, season-by-season description of what one is likely to find in these markets. (Unfortunately, the assumption seems to be that everyone lives in a temperate climate with markets open year round, but even for those in other climatic areas, the book is useful.) She discusses fruits, grains, meats, and vegetables and includes recipes. There is information, too, on how to shop—and even on how to operate a market.

Granseth, Sandra, et al., eds. **Better Homes and Gardens Kitchen Appliance Cookbook.** Des Moines, IA: Meredith, 1982. 240p. $14.95 (641.58)
What do you do with a microwave oven and a food processor? You turn to the first half of this guide, where you find complete instructions on how to use both for

better cooking. Beyond this, one finds illustrated sections and hints on the use of other basic aids from crêpe pans to woks to the fondue pot. The recipes are such that even those without the small appliances may want to purchase this book. All types of meals, all types of situations are considered, although the point of departure is always one of the appliances. While hardly an essential book, it is one that will remind the reader what to do with a gift appliance that is never used.

Huste, Annemarie. **Cooking with Annemarie.** New York: Perigee, 1984. 160p. $8.95 (641.5)

Teacher, caterer, chef, writer, Huste is as ebullient as she is witty about cooking. Here the stress is on enjoying the art. Her special skill is to present a gourmet dish in such a way that it will be a hit at the average family table. She stresses the importance of spending both time and money on the ingredients, and the book is an appeal for the good life in every home. Whether it is for a delectable fish dish or a dessert, the recipe is easy to follow and directions are meticulous. Huste is exhilarating to read.

Huxley, Judith. **Judith Huxley's Table for Eight: Recipes and Menus for Entertaining with the Seasons.** New York: Morrow, 1984. 506p. $19.95 (641.5)

Each weekend one might be entertaining a new group of guests. While one may use the same general recipes for a few weeks, there comes a time for a change. Gearing the turnover in guests to the seasons, this experienced author offers a month-by-month, 52-week series of menus that should delight visitors—and make life easier for the chef. Huxley begins each well-illustrated menu with useful information on what is, or is not, likely to be in season; the problems with shopping; the time involved and possible nightmares; and suggestions on how to bring it all off at the table. All the menus include advice on wines. There is wide variety in the monthly suggestions, and enough alternatives are given to make even the most fastidious cook happy. Thanks to the author's imagination, her concern with details, and her appreciation of the need for something new, something old, this book adds up to a superior work. Basic to almost every collection.

Ivens, Dorothy. **Main Course Soups & Stews.** New York: Harper, 1983. 320p. $13.95 (641.8)

By "main course" the author means a soup that will satisfy a ravishing hunger, and to this end she describes and gives recipes for a vast variety of dishes from those made with vegetables to others primarily of meat. She travels the world around for the suggestions and, if nothing else, there are some rare novelties. The book is not, and this is worth stressing, for the person looking for a simple, plain soup as an introduction to the main course. This is food for hearty appetites.

Klapthor, Margaret. **The First Ladies Cook Book: Favorite Recipes of All the Presidents of the United States.** Rev. ed. New York: Dutton, 1982. 238p. $20 (641.5)

Moving from Washington to Reagan, the author outlines the favorite foods of each president and gives menus and individual recipes. There is much about what goes on in the White House kitchen and dining room. While the recipes are hardly startling, and at times not even very appetizing, they are at least historically interesting. The book seems popular, too. It has gone through several editions and a new one is promised each time a new couple takes over the White House kitchen.

McCall's Editors. **The New Revised and Updated McCall's Cookbook.** New York: Random House, 1984. 510p. $17.50 (641.5)

Similar to many basic and popular cookbooks, this covers what every beginning and intermediate cook needs to know. There is the standard information on a well-equipped kitchen and on working methods, as well as about 1,000 recipes. Everything is carefully illustrated, nothing is left to chance, and even a total novice is able to follow the specific directions. If there is a problem about how to use a piece of equipment—from a blender to a microwave oven—here is the place to turn. If there is a question of how to prepare a meal for a party or for a couple, this is ideal. Most of the recipes are standard, but they are accurate and appropriate for the busy person. This is a new edition (the last being published in 1973), considerably updated, and should be found with other basic cookbooks in kitchens and libraries.

Meras, Phyllis, and Frances Tenenbaum. **Carry-out Cuisine.** New York: Houghton, 1982. 240p. $16.95; pap. $8.95 (641.5)

No, this is not a guide to food from McDonalds or other fast-food places. It is a guide to the actual recipes used in about 70 gourmet food shops around the United States, including almost 20 from New York City. The some 250 recipes are arranged by category. They have another advantage besides being tested taste treats. All are prepared in advance by the stores, so they may be made hours or days before they are served. The ingredients are scaled down so one does not make enough for a small army, and generally most of the items for the recipes may be purchased locally—at least in large urban centers with gourmet food stores. For the curious, there is a description of the shops that contributed to the volume.

Reader's Digest Farmhouse Cookery: Recipes from the Country Kitchen. New York: Norton, 1981. 400p. $24.95 (641.59)

This is a good cookbook, but the authors are staff members in the London office of the *Reader's Digest* and the focus is almost entirely on rural British foods, which may not appeal to all Americans. For example, the desserts are often extremely rich and the preponderance of meat dishes may run against current dietary habits in the United States. At the same time, the directions for basic English dishes, from fish to bread, are excellent and of wide appeal. Of particular interest is the emphasis on the historical development of various recipes from medieval to modern times— almost every recipe is introduced by a historical sketch.

Rombauer, Irma. **The Joy of Cooking.** Rev. ed. New York: Bobbs-Merrill, 1975. 930p. $15.95 (641.5)

Although first published in 1931, this is frequently updated and it is about as basic a cookbook as one can find for the average American family, and probably one of the best known. There are numerous reasons for its popularity and success, not the least of which is its wide scope. Here one finds not only the first lessons in how to cook, but related topics from mixing cocktails to checking foods for calories. There are well over 4,000 recipes ranging from the simple to the complex. Each is carefully explained and most cooks find them easy to understand and follow. Other sections of the work concern such diverse matters as pressure cooking, blenders, herbs, microwave ovens, canning, freezing, and other topics. Here is one book that really needs no introduction.

Roth, Sherrill. **The Country Gourmet Cookbook.** New York: Workman, 1981. 416p. $14.95; pap. $8.95 (641.5)

The "country" in the title is the particular focus of this cookbook, which stresses the use of farm-fresh ingredients and is arranged by month, with a specific project or technique to be mastered each month. In keeping with the organization, most of the projects are related to items introduced into the market at the same time of year. The real challenge is for the reader to grow or make the ingredients. This is of primary interest to those with a few feet of space for a garden or ready access to materials that allow the home production of such things as sausages and cottage cheese. The recipes, as down to earth as the authors, draw heavily on basic American eating habits.

Russo, Julee, and Sheila Lukins with Michael McLaughlin. **The Silver Palate Cookbook.** New York: Workman, 1982. 362p. $14.95; pap. $8.95 (641.5)

This is a cookbook for the person who wants to prepare truly elegant, different food, with a minimum of trouble. Directions are clear and the recipes do not require a tremendous amount of ability or training. The catch is that the title refers to a luxury shop that serves people with higher incomes in New York City. The result is that many of the suggestions are too expensive for the average reader. At the same time, there are just enough reasonably priced items to make it a grand book to turn to when trying to devise something that is out of the ordinary and in excellent taste—in both senses of the word. Most of the ingredients can be found in local shops, and the step-by-step instructions are carefully illustrated. An unusual, exciting, and challenging cookbook.

Sorosky, Marlene. **Marlene Sorosky's Year Round Holiday Cookbook.** New York: Harper, 1982. 320p. $18.95 (641.5)

Arranged by the calendar, with 23 specific holidays selected for consideration, this book offers ideas for festive meals. There are detailed menus and about 300 recipes. Approximately 100 photographs help the reader appreciate the intricacies of the given recipe or setting. The approach is practical, geared for a larger-than-average group of people at the table. There are even hints on what will or will not be suitable to freeze when there are leftovers.

Stobart, Tom. **The Cook's Encyclopedia: Ingredients and Processes.** New York: Harper, 1981. 547p. $22.95 (641.03)

Here is an alphabetically arrranged explanation of basic ingredients and processes employed in the kitchen. Occasionally, recipes are included to make a point or illustrate the use of a process, and recipes for preparing basic ingredients are duly given when the ingredient is not likely to be easily located. While this is written for the layperson, there is some fairly involved material, e.g., such things as types of food reactions and how they occur. At the same time, the author explains the difference between various types of olive oils, how to use nuts properly, the numerous approaches to alcoholic beverages, etc.

Sunset Cookbook of Favorite Recipes. Menlo Park, CA: Lane, 1982. 160p. pap. $5.95 (641.5)

A basic collection of about 400 recipes that may serve the novice in almost any situation. The illustrations, the clarity of the recipes, the constant encouragement, and the wide diversity of recipes add up to a useful book for almost any beginner.

Sunset Easy Basics for Good Cooking. Menlo Park, CA: Lane, 1982. 192p. pap. $9.95 (641.51)

An elementary guide containing about 350 recipes and good advice on the basics of cooking. Twelve chapters take the novice from the elements of the art through more sophisticated aspects. Along the way, there are definitions and illustrations of basic equipment and menu planning. The spiral binding allows the book to be used easily at the stove.

Sunset Ideas and Recipes for Breakfast and Brunch. Rev. ed. Menlo Park, CA: Lane, 1980. 96p. pap. $5.95 (641.52)

A standard work that has been revised twice offers ideas and easy-to-follow recipes. Few cookbooks have such imaginative menus for brunches, and everything is explained. The breakfasts, whether eggs or pancakes, are equally excellent. Nicely illustrated, often in color.

Time-Life Books. **The Good Cook Series.** New York: Time-Life, 1979– . 176p. $14.95

The series expands each year, but as of mid-1984 it included the following titles: *Poultry* (1979); *Beef and Veal* (1979); *Vegetables* (1979); *Fish* (1979); *Soups* (1979); *Classic Desserts* (1980); *Pork* (1980); *Salads* (1980); *Snacks and Sandwiches* (1980); *Egg & Cheese* (1980); *Pasta* (1980); *Pies & Pastries* (1981); *Breads* (1981); *Preserving* (1981); *Lamb* (1981); *Candy* (1981); *Cakes* (1982); *Dried Beans and Grains* (1982); *Terrines, Pâtés and Galantines* (1982); *Hors D'Oeuvre* (1982); *Shellfish* (1982); *Cookies and Crackers* (1982); *Variety Meats* (1983); *Outdoor Cooking* (1983); *Beverages* (1983); *Sauces* (1983); *Fruits* (1983); *Wine* (1983).

Using illustrations and step-by-step directions, the editors of this basic series indicate all of the procedures necessary to turn out a winning dish or meal. Many varieties of dishes are considered from the basic to the more advanced, and within the individual books one normally finds about 200 recipes. The easy-to-follow method should be of particular value to the relative beginner, albeit there are some rather difficult, exotic procedures along with more familiar types.

COOKING—AMERICAN

Beard, James. **James Beard's American Cookery.** Boston: Little, 1972. 877p. $12.95 (641.5)

Many consider this the definitive book on the subject of American cooking. It covers favorite and relatively unknown recipes and suggestions from the eighteenth to the twentieth century. In this respect, it is almost as much a history as a cookbook. (Also, Beard includes numerous foreign dishes that over the years have become American). As in all of the author's books, the directions are specific and each step is carefully and clearly explained. The various suggestions are for all levels of cooking skill and cover everything from simple soups to complex cakes and meat dishes. There are marvelous ideas for combining separate recipes into complete meals.

Better Homes and Gardens Classic American Recipes. Des Moines, IA: Meredith, 1982. 192p. $9.95 (641.57)

The "classic" recipes are gathered together by region alongside an "all American" section. There are close to 350 dishes which are familiar to most Americans—at least those living in the sections of the country where they are famous. Full details are given for each and there are numerous photographs, many in color. While most of the recipes are in other cookbooks, this has the advantage of placing them all in one work.

Crocker, Betty. **Betty Crocker's New American Cooking.** New York: Random House, 1983. 256p. $14.95 (641.59)

By "new," Betty Crocker means less emphasis on the American potatoes-and-meat diet and more on foods promising better health. This is one of several basic changes in the classic Crocker approach, an approach as familiar in American kitchens as the pans and the stove. In addition to the new emphasis on fresh vegetables and greater variety of foods, there is a distinct appreciation of fine cooking, with a nod to continental cuisine and ethnic choices. While this is the farthest removed from wild experimentation, it is solid enough to deserve the place it has in American cooking.

Foster, Pearl. **Classic American Cooking.** New York: Simon & Schuster, 1983. 512p. $16.50 (641.59)

The title's truth depends on one's interpretation. The author is an expert in the so-called New American Cuisine, and it is true that she cooks American style. The recipes, however, are both basic and esoteric, with the emphasis on the latter. The result is that typical Americans might feel they were eating foreign food when served dishes made from these recipes. Conversely, Americans with a taste for the unusual, who enjoy the New American Cuisine, will delight in the challenging approaches. For example, baked beans are laced with bourbon. Depending on point of view, this is a must or a total loss. Take your choice.

Mariani, John. **The Dictionary of American Food and Drink.** New Haven, CT: Ticknor & Fields, 1983. 477p. $19.95 (641.59)

The stress here is on American. One finds snappy, tasty, and sometimes highly imaginative approaches to the hamburger and hot dog. The focus is not on recipes, although there are numerous good ones scattered throughout the volume. The primary interest is on a sociological and historical study of American eating and drinking habits. There are detailed discussions of various aspects of behavior in kitchens, dining rooms, and public eating places. This special emphasis is matched only by discussions of words and their derivations. It is a marvelous book for browsing, and even for finding an unusual concoction of food and drink. It is not, however, your normal cookbook.

Prudhomme, Paul. **Chef Paul Prudhomme's Louisiana Kitchen.** New York: Morrow, 1984. 345p. $19.45 (641.59)

A best-seller, this is a collection of about 200 easy-to-follow recipes for Cajun and Creole cooking by a famous New Orleans chef. Despite the book's focus on Louisiana, almost all the ingredients are available in other parts of the country too. This is also true of the seasonings, which are the primary factors in the success or failure of the dishes. The chef shows the cook, who should have at least a basic command of the art, how to prepare such delights as gumbos, rabbit, and a great number of hot, spicy seafood and chicken delights. The illustrations are adequate, but do not measure up to the author's convincing enthusiasm.

COOKING—FISH & GAME & OUTDOOR

Better Homes and Gardens All-Time Favorite Fish & Seafood Recipes. Des Moines, IA: Meredith, 1980. 96p. (641.6)

A basic collection of about 200 seafood recipes that will have wide appeal for American families, this, like other guides by the same publisher, is easy to follow. It requires little previous knowledge of cooking, although some of the menus do assume some knowledge of the art. The division is by the method of cooking—fried, stewed, broiled, etc.—rather than by the kind of fish. The illustrations are numerous and helpful.

Bjornskov, Elizabeth. **The Complete Book of American Fish and Shellfish Cookery.** New York: Knopf, 1984. 498p. $18.95 (641.39)

Fish from both coasts are examined in such detail that the reader senses that the author knows more about the waters of America than almost anyone else. (There is more here on West coast varieties of fish than usually found in other cookbooks, albeit the emphasis is on the Northeast.) From the Pacific to the Atlantic, each major type of fish and shellfish is discussed. The author misses nothing, from how it should look when fresh, to how it should taste. The book opens with straightforward advice on basic preservation, cleaning, and cooking methods. Numerous recipes dot each chapter, along with suggested substitutes for fish that can't be found in the markets. Once the coast lines are explored, she moves into freshwater streams and lakes with the same thoroughness. One may quibble with some of the recipes, but on the whole they are well balanced and should meet the tastes of a wide variety of readers.

Cameron, Angus, and Judith Jones. **The L. L. Bean Game and Fish Cookbook.** New York: Random House, 1983. 640p. $19.95 (641.6)

From the people who bring you the catalog comes this first-rate book on what to do with the game and fish you caught while wearing those L. L. Bean clothes. The authors consider various types of game, and almost as many ways of cooking. Some of it may not have vast appeal—particularly the various squirrel recipes—but most is at least easy to understand and can be accomplished in the average, well-equipped kitchen. For those who like to rough it, there is a good section on cooking out-of-doors, although this makes it seem much simpler than it actually is in many situations. As almost every topic is covered, and always in a forthright fashion, this is an ideal book of its kind.

London, Sheryl, and Mel London. **The Fish-Lovers' Cookbook.** Emmaus, PA: Rodale, 1980. 427p. $16.95; pap. $11.95 (641.39)

Considered by some to be *the* best general cookbook for fish, this includes all the standard recipes plus a number of outstanding innovations. The authors offer more than 300 recipes for many varieties of fish, plus sage advice on how to purchase fish. There are excellent sections, too, on preparation before cooking and, where necessary, storage procedures. The division of the book is by type, i.e., by best-known and least-known fish, kinds of sauces, varieties of stews, etc. All of this is written with enthusiasm and a contagious appreciation for the joys of preparing and serving fish. It can be used by the beginner as well as by the nearly expert cook.

Marshall, Mel. **Complete Book of Outdoor Cookery.** New York: Van Nostrand, 1983. 384p. $26.50 (641.5)
This book has only one real problem—it is much too bulky to carry on a camping trip. That aside, it is one of the best available guides to all forms of outdoor cooking—here extended to mean not only on-the-trail foods, but backyard barbecues. The most valuable sections deal with how to prepare and cook fish and game you have caught yourself. Everything is explained, from building a fire to constructing a grill. The best way to clean fish and game is underlined with illustrations and there are numerous recipes that will increase the joys of the diner. In addition, there are tips on how to keep the out-of-doors clean and tidy and suitable for both people and animals. The writing style is chatty and informative.

Roden, Claudia. **Everything Tastes Better Outdoors.** New York: Knopf, 1984. 413p. $19.95 (641.5)
It is not just that everything tastes better when cooked outdoors, but that the way it is cooked there makes it seem especially delicious. This experienced author offers detailed, imaginative recipes that draw on the best in the world's kitchens. She does not limit herself to the United States, but travels from France to the Middle East to offer tasty, easy-to-prepare dishes. Along the way, she spices the text with anecdotes, history, and fables about cooking. There is a section on food that can be prepared indoors and then carried out onto the patio or backporch for eating. Barbecued and grilled recipes are also included. An extra touch is suggestions about where to eat when traveling, and the joys, for example, of eating freshly killed game.

Sleight, Jack. **Home Book of Smoke-Cooking Meat, Fish and Game.** Harrisburg, PA: Stackpole, 1971. 160p. $8.95 (641.4)
Writing for both the barbecue fan and the out-of-doors type, as well as the imaginative cook, Sleight offers easy-to-follow, specific directions on smoking a wide variety of meats. The instructions for curing leave nothing to chance, and the author offers plans to suit any budget—e.g., some of the smoking facilities are expensive, others extremely cheap. Each meat, fish, and game is considered in turn with step-by-step instructions. Many of the steps and plans are well illustrated. While this book is now over ten years old, little has changed except the prices. The directions are as good today as when the work was first published.

Sunset Picnics and Tailgate Parties. Menlo Park, CA: Lane, 1982. 96p. $5.95 (641.57)
A picnic need not be dull, or limited to sandwiches and cake. Using the back end of a station wagon offers a unique approach. Here are 142 recipes that can make the average picnic a delight. Most are for the beginner, and all are nicely illustrated, often in color. The book is organized by courses, i.e., by appetizers, soups, salads, and main dishes. And, yes, there are suggestions for sandwiches and desserts. There is even a section on how to organize the menu and the whole proceeding.

COOKING—INTERNATIONAL

Andoh, Elizabeth. **At Home with Japanese Cooking.** New York: Knopf, 1980. 254p. $15; pap. $9.95 (641.59)

A first choice for anyone interested in learning about Japanese cooking, this is recommended for its easy-to-follow recipes and for the excellent background material on techniques and equipment. The author is well qualified, as she has taught the fine art of Japanese cooking to Westerners who live in Japan. Recipes are carefully and completely explained, and are organized under broad methods of cooking and food preparation. The reader will have no problem following any of the directions or background material, but should be warned that Andoh takes this all seriously, and the guide is not one for the casual "let's try Japanese" tonight. It requires patience, if only to locate some of the ingredients. With that understood, it is basic in this area of cooking.

Casa, Penelope. **The Foods and Wines of Spain.** New York: Knopf, 1982. 458p. $17.95 (641.5)

With over 400 recipes and a separate chapter devoted exclusively to Spanish wines, this is by far the best overview of Spanish cooking available. The recipes range from the simple to the complex, and there is complete information on ingredients and detailed instructions. Of particular note are the sections on seafood, soups, and the meal-in-one-pot approach to dining.

Child, Julia. **The French Chef Cookbook.** New York: Knopf, 1968. 424p. $15.50 (641.5)

Probably the best-known cook in America, if only for her television program, Julia Child offers a classic book on French cooking. Actually, it developed out of the television series, and includes all of the basics of the art from sauces to pastries. Instructions, often illustrated, are exceptionally clear and easy to follow, even though many of the recipes are quite complex. This is certainly one of the better guides to French cooking and a good starting point—at least for those with some experience in basics.

Child has written numerous other cookbooks, also published by Knopf and, to a lesser or greater extent, based on her long-running television series. All are recommended. Among the better known are *Julia Child & More Company* (1979), *Julia Child & Company* (1978), *From Julia Child's Kitchen* (1975).

David, Elizabeth. **French Provincial Cooking.** Harmondsworth, England: Penguin, 1969. 584p. $1.45 (641.59)

While not a recent publication, this remains a classic and is highly recommended by Julia Child, who states: "Mrs. David is one of the most distinguished writers on gastronomy in the English language. She is deeply knowledgeable and her works are always fully researched; she is a wonderful stylist, and this happens to be one of the very best books on French provincial cooking. I think one reason it hasn't been widely used in this country is that for one thing, the book was not translated from British English into American English, which often puts people off, and two, that neither Mrs. David's publishers nor Mrs. David herself have made any effort to be known in this country. It is a very fine book and one that should be in the library of anyone who is serious about cooking and especially French cooking" (*Writer's Choice*, Reston, 1983, p. 230).

Granseth, Sandra, et al., eds. **Better Homes and Gardens Classic International Recipes.** Des Moines, IA: Meredith, 1982. 192p. $9.95 (641.4)

This is a beginner's guide to the eating habits and traditional recipes of 15 areas of the world, from our neighbors Mexico and Canada to distant Thailand. Each section has a brief introduction to the particular diets of the area discussed. Recipes are usually accompanied by explanatory notes on their historical background. This combination travel, cook, and history book is in the usual striking *Better Homes and Gardens* format with abundant full-color photographs and illustrations.

Grigson, Jane. **Jane Grigson's Book of European Cookery.** New York: Atheneum, 1983. 256p. $24.95 (641.5)

One of England's best-known and most famous food writers, Grigson is enthusiastic about good cuisine while maintaining a commonsense attitude toward its pretensions. Her views are expressed in this lavishly illustrated and highly readable overview of the cooking of ten European countries. Presentation is by country with recipes and a prefatory discussion of what constitutes the basics of that nation's cooking style, e.g., Portugal uses mayonnaise in ways quite different from those of most other countries. There are some 300 recipes and each one is carefully formulated so it can be followed step-by-step. At the same time, the author does leave something up to the cook, since she makes the assumption that her audience is literate and imaginative. Grigson has a fine appreciation for the differences between home cooking, which is pretty much what is represented here, and the restaurant variety. A first place for beginners to turn, but not for experts. The book was originally published in England and some terms are not explained in American vocabulary.

Hom, Ken, and Harvey Steiman. **Chinese Technique: An Illustrated Guide to the Fundamental Techniques of Chinese Cooking.** New York: Simon & Schuster, 1981. 345p. $17.95 (641.5)

Some claim there are almost as many Chinese cookbooks as Chinese, but this is one of the best and can be considered a first choice. A generous use of pictures (there are over 1,000) that complement an orderly text result in easy-to-follow directions for simple to complex dishes. Each step in the recipe is illustrated, and there are close to 30 steps in difficult recipes. The sections on vegetables, noodles, meats, seafood, etc., are as comprehensive as they are well written, and there are thorough instructions on the use of various cooking devices such as the ubiquitous wok.

Jaffrey, Madhur. **Madhur Jaffrey's Indian Cookery.** Woodbury, NY: Barron's, 1983. 200p. pap. $7.95 (641.5954)

One of the best general books on Indian cooking, with 120 superb recipes, this is by a woman well known to English television viewers who have followed her series there on the subject. She is also the author of *Invitation to Indian Cooking* (1975). Here she uses pretty much the same introduction as in the 1975 guide, but everything else is updated. For anyone familiar with Indian cooking, the directions—for both recipes and the setting up of an Indian approach to cooking—are clear enough. The beginner will want to spend time with the introduction in order to become familiar with the sometimes unusual spices and methods of preparation.

Lee, Karen, and Alaxandra Branyon. **Chinese Cooking Secrets.** New York: Doubleday, 1984. 368p. $22.50 (641.59)

Carefully illustrated, and with each recipe meticulously detailed, here is a Chinese cookbook that should be of constant value to both the intermediate-level and
the expert cook. Lee places considerable emphasis on complicated dishes, and
while there are clear enough preparatory explanations of what is to be done, some
readers might get lost. Still, the real value of the book, and one that sets it apart
from numerous titles in this area, is its attention to detail. Lee spends much of her
time explaining the so-called secrets of preparation, the need for careful planning,
and adaptation of basic cooking techniques to new approaches. There are particularly good instructions concerning less well known ingredients.

Marshall, Lydie. **Cooking with Lydie Marshall.** New York: Knopf, 1982. 510p.
$17.95 (641.59)

An expert teacher and French cook, the author offers the reader some basic hints
on good cooking as well as involved techniques requiring expert skill and tremendous patience. All of this is done with specific, clear directions and in a witty,
confident style. There are some 22 basic lessons that begin with relatively easy
dishes and conclude with more complex recipes. While not for the beginner or
even the average experienced cook, this is ideal for the individual who wants a
challenge and seeks to create truly superb meals.

Pepin, Jacques. **Everyday Cooking with Jacques Pepin.** New York: Harper, 1982.
194p. $15; pap. $8.95 (641.59)

How does the average French chef cook at home? This book, based on a television series, does not give all the answers, but it indicates a probable direction, and
in an enthusiastic, winning style. The text and the illustrations are geared to the
average cook, not the expert. The foods are basic to France, as they may well be
basic to American tables once the fear of French cooking is overcome. Emphasis is
on ease of preparation and most of the ingredients can be found without difficulty
in U.S. stores. If nothing else, Pepin demonstrates that plain recipes can be turned
into marvels with a little imagination and care. Among French cookbooks this is
one of the best, at least for the beginner or for the person who wants to get a tasty
dish on the table with speed and not too much trouble.

Roden, Claudia. **A Book of Middle Eastern Food.** Rev. ed. New York: Knopf, 1974.
453p. $10 (641.59)

This remains the best, if not always the easiest to follow, cookbook on Middle
Eastern food. By "Middle Eastern" the author means countries where the Arabic
language is dominant and the religion is Muslim. The author writes with flair and is
as involved with cooking and foods as are the masters of the art. Depending as they
do on vegetables, few meats, and relatively easy-to-find spices, the recipes and
meals suggested here now have wider appeal than when the book was first published. The recipes cover every aspect of the menu from hors d'oeuvres to desserts,
and there are some clever drawings.

Tropp, Barbara. **The Modern Art of Chinese Cooking.** New York: Morrow, 1982.
623p. $24.50 (641.59)

There are scores, possibly hundreds, of books on Chinese cooking, but this is one of the best. It deserves this accolade for at least three reasons. First, the author, an American cook, writes with clarity and wit. She imbues her menus with an appreciation for the modern and the historical, and at all times understands that the average reader is cooking not for the emperor, but usually for a small group. Second, the basics are presented in an easy-to-understand fashion. The description of the method of cooking is matched with a clear explanation of the type of equipment and ingredients necessary, as well as the specialized techniques required. Third, the recipes themselves are straightforward, and while sometimes complicated, can be followed from beginning to end without a sense of impending disaster. Finally, where a dinner is involved, the author not only considers individual dishes, but advises on other items from desserts to wines. She hardly begins to cover all the possibilities of Chinese cooking, but this is by far the best overall introduction.

Volokh, Anne, and Mavis Manus. **The Art of Russian Cuisine.** New York: Macmillan, 1983. 448p. $19.95 (641.59)

The Russians are not coming. They have arrived, at least in the kitchen. The secrets of Russian cooking are revealed here—and in such a way, and with such precision, as to win over any cook. Recipes range from the traditional, even well-known dishes to unusual desserts. While some of the ingredients may be a trifle hard to get at the local store (or too expensive), there is a useful guide to mail-order houses that will supply what is otherwise unobtainable. Descriptions of Russian methods of doing almost everything in a kitchen are interwoven with recipes and menus. The result is a marvelous insight into an area of the world too little understood in the United States. The various sections of the book are introduced by quotations from literature and history, as well as anecdotes. This may or may not add to the value of the book, but it certainly livens it up. With this work there is no need for any other Russian cookbook, at least for the modest kitchen. For those with expansive tastes or an inordinate love of Russian cooking, other titles might be in order, but only as supplements.

Von Welanetz, Diana, and Paul Von Welanetz. **The Von Welanetz Guide to Ethnic Ingredients.** New York: Houghton, 1982. 731p. $20.95 (641.59)

Here the adventuresome cook is offered explanations of about 1,000 ingredients used in various ethnic recipes and kitchens. Arrangement is geographic—from Africa to various regions of the United States—and within each section ingredients are presented in alphabetical order. The product is clearly defined and there is an explanation of how it is used. There are about 150 recipes that serve to demonstrate the practical application of the ingredients. A useful list of ethnic cookbooks is included.

COOKING—MEATS & CHICKEN

Dyer, Ceil. **Chicken Cookery.** Tucson, AZ: HP Books, 1983. 160p. pap. $7.95 (641.6)

Everything you ever wanted to know about chicken, from selecting to frying, is found in this inexpensive cookbook. Thanks to the relatively low price of chicken, it is a favorite food. Dyer shows how it may be served in about 200 different ways.

Most of the suggestions are simple, the recipes basic. There are some recipes for turkey and duck and hints on stuffing.

Grigson, Jane. **The Art of Making Sausages, Pâtés, and Other Charcuterie.** New York: Knopf, 1980. 349p. pap. $6.95 (641.66)

Originally published as *The Art of Charcuterie* (1976), this is a classic, and is highly recommended by Julia Child. With a flair for the practical, both in her approach to cooking and in her witty, down-to-earth style, the author explains the thousand and one variations on making the most out of that unprepossessing animal, the pig. While the focus is on French techniques, the author is aware of the peculiar needs of American and English cooks, and she manages to explain French terms, equipment, and methods in such a way that the instructions can be followed easily. There are topical chapters, each with background details, on everything from pâtés and galantines to using the extremities and the fat.

House & Garden Editors. **The Art of Carving.** New York: Simon & Schuster, 1978. 79p. pap. $3.95 (642)

While almost all basic, general cookbooks include a series on carving, this is a guide devoted exclusively to the subject. The result is a much more detailed approach, and one that will be of help to both beginners and experts. The steps involved in carving everything from a roast to wild fowl are given in detail, usually accompanied by specific photographs of each action. There is a good section, too, on the various types of knives to employ, as well as a discussion of how to fillet fish.

Lobel, Stanley, and Evan Lobel. **How to Be Your Own Butcher.** New York: Perigee, 1983. 127p. pap. $7.95 (664.90)

Numerous cookbooks have sections or chapters on how to cut up and carve meat, but no book is as detailed as this excellent, well-illustrated manual. Here the title means just what it says: how to butcher, not simply to prepare one or two cuts of meat. The authors maintain a prestigious meat market in New York and they realize the importance of proper boning and cutting. In fact, their display cases are works of art, expensive art. The book is organized by various types of meats (from chicken to game birds, from pork to lamb). In each, the authors consider what is to be cut and how it can be prepared for cooking. There are excellent sections, too, on equipment, from knives and butcher blocks to freezers. The text is fairly easy to follow, although it is evident that some dexterity is required to be a real master (as are the authors) rather than just an everyday butcher.

Nickerson, Doyne, and Dorothy Nickerson. **The New 365 Ways to Cook Hamburger and Other Ground Meat.** Rev. ed. New York: Doubleday, 1983. 240p. $12.95 (641.6)

There are ways to eat hamburger other than out of a paper carton from a fast-food dispenser. Just how many ways there are, and how one may save money by using them, is demonstrated in this revised edition of the ultimate hamburger book. Here are recipes for meatballs, meatloaves, the traditional hamburger in the bun, and scores of other combinations, including soups and pies. While little of this will meet a gourmet's rigorous taste, it certainly will please the average American family. There are good sections on other forms of ground meat, but none compares with the major focus on hamburger.

COOKING—NATURAL FOODS

Baggett, Nancy, et al. **Don't Tell 'em It's Good for 'em.** New York: Times Books, 1984. 288p. $15.50 (641.5)

The idea is simple enough. The average family will enjoy natural foods and a good diet when meals are prepared in such a way that the members do not realize "it's good for 'em." There are close to 275 recipes, most of which are easy to follow and require minimum effort. Possibly more important, most of the recipes are for standard dishes from roasts to pies. The difference is that fat, salt, and sugar are virtually eliminated—this in keeping with National Cancer Institute recommendations. Instructions are clear, and the particular dish is accompanied by a nutritional score. There is good background information on how to use substitutes for fats and sugars and the benefits of a healthy diet. Well written, with a dash of humor and much common sense, this is a basic book for most kitchens.

Gerras, Charles, ed. **Rodale's Basic Natural Foods Cookbook.** Emmaus, PA: Rodale, 1984. 899p. $21.95 (641.56)

The basic book on natural foods cooking, this is as useful as it is massive, as precise as it is imaginative. Pulling together over 1,500 recipes is only one of the book's missions. There is also a good introduction to cooking, which could be applicable to any situation, as well as commonsense advice on everything from the well-equipped kitchen to how to purchase and store foods. Specific sections are devoted to cooking that relies on vegetables and other natural ingredients. White flour, sugar, and salt are not included in the recipes, but there are numerous substitute products from the sea and the fields. This can be used both for daily cooking and for special diets. It is as well organized, illustrated, and written as any cookbook now on the market.

Herman, Barry, and Bill Lawren. **The Long Life Gourmet Cookbook.** New York: Simon & Schuster, 1984. 352p. $15.95 (641.5)

Craig Claiborne and several other well-known cooks now advise people on how to eat like a gourmet without salt, sugar, or fatty ingredients. Here is another member of the growing ranks of experienced cooks with similar advice. Herman, a former chef at the Pritikin Longevity Center, offers different approaches, different recipes that may be used at various times of the year and on various occasions. The author succeeds in making the bland brave and the nutritious nice. He relies on everything from herbs to fruits to lend flavor to the some 350 recipes. While there is no breakdown of the dietary elements, the various recipes certainly appear to be healthful and promise to be tasty.

Hewitt, Jean. **The New York Times New Natural Foods Cookbook.** Rev. ed. New York: Times Books, 1982. 480p. $16.95 (641.5)

First published in 1971 and updated in 1982, this is a basic guide to recipes that will appeal to those interested in cooking with natural foods. There are specific instructions, including notes on ingredients and on vegetable dishes, poultry, pasta, and related items. The book is well written, and the recipes imaginative and tasty. A first choice for cooks with an interest in the subject. *Note:* This edition includes 250 more recipes than the 1971 presentation, and here the author has deleted the candy and red meat sections.

Johnson, Roberta, ed. **Whole Foods for the Whole Family.** New York: New Amer. Lib., 1984. 320p. $10.95 (641.5)

The La Leche League, an advocate of breast-feeding, has gathered recipes from many of its members. The focus is on health and what the editor calls "whole foods," which may include anything that is natural or homemade. The real value of the guide is not so much the individual recipes as the emphasis on family cooking, with ideas for all three meals of the day. Here and there are excellent suggestions for truly American dishes. An added bonus: a short section (about 39 pages) of recipes that children may use. Originally published in 1981.

Low Cost Natural Foods. Emmaus, PA: Rodale, 1982. 96p. pap. $5.95 (641.5)

Most natural foods are unnaturally expensive, and it costs a lot to stay healthy. Recognizing this, Rodale Press offers suggestions for about 75 dishes where the main ingredients are healthful, inexpensive, natural foods. Long on grains and beans, short on delicacies, the book may have limited appeal to anyone who can afford more expensive ingredients. Still, the recipes are reasonably priced and are good enough that it warrants a place on shelves of cooks dedicated to natural foods. *Note:* It is not only for vegetarians, and there are a few suggestions that include nonvegetarian ingredients.

Proulx, E. Annie, and Lew Nichols. **The Complete Dairy Foods Cookbook.** Emmaus, PA: Rodale, 1982. 296p. $15.95 (641.6)

How to Make Everything from Cheese to Custard in Your Own Kitchen is the claim of the subtitle, and the claim is fulfilled. The guide is a combination cookbook, history of dairy products, and explanation of the characteristics of basic dairy foods. While some of the information (how to pasteurize) is a trifle esoteric—at least for the urban reader—most of it is quite practical and suitable for the average kitchen. There are specific instructions for every activity from making butter and ice cream to preparing yogurt. There are numerous recipes, some of which may strike the reader as austere. Photographs of dairy equipment and black-and-white drawings complement the text.

Wason, Betty. **Soup-to-Dessert High Fiber Cookbook.** New York: Rawson, 1976. 248p. $9.95 (641.5)

High-fiber recipes are now found in scores of cookbooks. Nevertheless, this 1976 book remains one of the best because it is more complete than the others and has masses of information of interest to anyone involved with high-fiber foods. Wason offers numerous recipes that cut back on sugar and fats and draw heavily on whole-grain cereals, nuts, vegetables, fruits, and similar ingredients. The recipes cover the whole spectrum from breakfast to dinner, from first courses to desserts, and all of them are as tasty as they are easy to follow. Some of the information on ingredient availability is dated, but almost all of the work can be consulted today with confidence.

COOKING—PASTA

Beard, James. **Beard on Pasta.** New York: Knopf, 1983. 236p. $14.95 (641.8)

The author's name alone ensures that this is an exceptional book, and one that will find its way to the top of scores of books on the same subject. Almost anything by Beard can be considered reliable, and this is no exception. Here the master considers such things as how to make pasta and how to combine it with other dishes. Recipes, while not dominant, are used to accentuate each of the chapters. Needless to add: many of the recipes are unusual, yet practical so as to gain praise for both the amateur and the expert. No kitchen can afford to be without this guide, at least if pasta is on the menu more than once a year.

London, Sheryl, and Mel London. **Sheryl & Mel London's Creative Cooking with Grains & Pasta.** Emmaus, PA: Rodale, 1982. 308p. $16.95 (641.6)

Depending entirely on grains and pasta for tasty dishes, the Londons offer hundreds of ideas and recipes to make these readily available ingredients a major part of a diet. Arrangement is alphabetical by grain, from barley and bulgur to wild rice. For each, full details are given on what it is and how it may be employed in the kitchen. One section is devoted to pastas made from grains. There are good illustrations and the recipes are quite easy to master.

Sunset Pasta and Cook Book. Menlo Park, CA: Lane, 1980. 96p. $5.95 (641.82)

Arranged by various pasta shapes, such as squares and tubes, this is an elementary guide to making and cooking pasta. The 250 recipes and directions are illustrated with color photographs and are easy to follow. There are suggestions not only from Italy, but from Greece and even Japan. The pasta includes both side and main dishes.

COOKING, QUICK

Better Homes and Gardens Complete Quick and Easy Cookbook. Des Moines, IA: Meredith, 1983. 348p. $24.95 (641.5)

This work is not for the gourmet cook. It is a book for the person who is not reluctant to use convenience foods, short cuts, and just about any other device in order to come up with a quick meal. Quick does not necessarily mean offensive to the palate and to the eye, for most of the recipes and menus are good to excellent. The best sections deal with culinary techniques and equipment and helpful hints on saving time. The contributors, experts all, offer a wide range of choices that should appeal to every member of a fast-moving family. The illustrations are numerous and good.

Burros, Marian. **You've Got It Made.** New York: Morrow, 1984. 250p. $13.50 (641.5)

The food editor of the *New York Times* offers menus for about 50 quick, easy-to-prepare meals. They are primarily for serving two to four people, though they can be cut back or slightly expanded. In fact, the book concludes with some 15 menus that are ideal for a dinner party of 10 to 15 people. The emphasis on nutritional foods and fresh ingredients, as well as an analysis of such things as the calories and sodium content per serving distinguish this work from others of its kind. Also, the author has an excellent writing style and her imaginative approach to food is unusual.

Crocker, Betty. **Betty Crocker's Working Woman's Cookbook.** New York: Random House, 1982. 160p. $10.95 (641.5)

In the best tradition of the usual Betty Crocker cookbooks, here are uninspired yet useful methods by which the working woman can save time in the kitchen. There are slightly over 300 recipes covering almost every conceivable menu, occasion, or time of year. There are even symbols to indicate which dishes may be prepared in advance of the meal. The format, as one might expect, is handsome, and there are numerous colored illustrations.

Dannenbaum, Julie. **More Fast & Fresh.** New York: Harper, 1982. 240p. $14.95 (641.5)

The recipes are fast (usually no more than minutes are required), and the ingredients fresh (the author insists on readily accessible fresh products), but the person who follows the plan is likely to gain weight. Which is to say that these imaginative food approaches may be used, but should not be relied on too frequently because there is often a heavy dependence on such things as cream and butter. That aside, this is a fine book of ideas, particularly for the person who wants a break from the often complex menus suggested by other books.

Franey, Pierre. **The New York Times More 60-Minute Gourmet.** New York: Times Books, 1981. 296p. $12.95 (641.5)

The 60 minutes in the title represents, according to the author, the approximate time necessary to prepare and cook a complete gourmet meal. The assumption is that the reader is a fairly experienced cook, but given that, the goal may be reached without undue difficulty. The basic section includes recipes for the dinner menu (with a main dish and a salad or vegetable). There are then chapters on desserts and appetizers that may be fitted into the 60 minutes, or take only a little more time to complete. There are good illustrations. *Note:* This is the companion volume to the author's earlier *The New York Times 60-Minute Gourmet* (1979).

Smith, Cathy, et al. **Food.** Seattle, WA: Pacific Search, 1982. 154p. pap. $7.95 (641.5)

This is written specifically for the beginning cook and for the individual who may be forced to prepare a meal on a single burner. All of the recipes are simple, yet tasty; all require a minimum of equipment; all need only a short time to prepare. The introduction is for the person who begins without any idea of the difference between boiling water and stirring a sauce. Basics are clearly explained and there are about 125 different recipes. For seasoned cooks, most of this will be nightmarish because the choice is so limited; but for others, and particularly those cooking only for themselves, it is a lifeline.

Sunset Casserole and Cook Book. Menlo Park, CA: Lane, 1980. 96p. pap. $5.95 (641.82)

The one-pot dish is a favorite for many cooks, and here the different methods for casseroles are carefully explained with many illustrations, usually in color. Coverage is international, although many of the recipes are American. A useful feature: noting the cooking time required and the time it takes to reheat leftovers.

COOKING—VEGETABLES

Ballantyne, Janet. **Garden Way's Joy of Gardening Cookbook.** Pownal, VT: Garden Way Pub., 1984. 336p. $22.50; pap. $14.95 (641.6)

Once the garden vegetables are picked, how should they be cooked? Working on the assumption that the reader has a garden (or is near a good greengrocer), the author explains numerous approaches. She has a wide variety of suggestions and cooking methods. The 420 recipes include the proper cooking time and are in enough detail for both beginners and experienced cooks. Color photographs.

Burpee, Lois. **Lois Burpee's Gardener's Companion and Cookbook.** New York: Harper, 1983. 248p. $14.95 (641.6)

This is written by a partner of the famous seed company that is known to almost every gardener. Here the author combines information on cooking and gardening with a discussion of how to plant the vegetables that will later grace the table. Close to 50 vegetables are considered, and there is advice on everything from the proper gardening and kitchen tools to growing and cooking tips. The mixture may be too much for those who are simply gardeners or cooks, but those who combine both efforts will thoroughly enjoy this well-written, nicely illustrated work.

Candler, Teresa. **Vegetables the Italian Way.** New York: McGraw-Hill, 1980. 236p. $12.95 (641.6)

Drawing on family recipes, common sense, and the types of vegetables readily available during specific seasons of the year, this experienced author offers an amazing variety of recipes. Like any good Italian, she depends on bringing out flavors with numerous herbs and sauces. Most of the 250 recipes require from 5 to 30 minutes' preparation, and while a few are fairly complex, the majority are easy to follow. There are desserts based on vegetables, such as carrot cake and zucchini cake, and items such as dips. While a vegetarian may use this book to advantage, it does feature numerous preparations that require meat or poultry.

Halsey, Johanna, and Patricia Halsey. **The Green Thumb Harvest.** New York: Random House, 1984. 270p. pap. $8.95 (641.6)

A low-priced, easy-to-follow book on how to cook vegetables in a way to ensure that all around the table will clean off their plates. Many of the 250 recipes are outstanding for their ease of preparation and for use of in-season vegetables, fruits, and herbs. Recipes are from the authors' Green Thumb farmstead and from some of its customers. Here and there, the directions are not quite clear, the authors assuming that the reader knows as much as they do about, for example, measurement of ingredients. The majority of ideas, though, are within reach of the average cook, and not so exotic as to be impossible to prepare.

Morash, Marian. **The Victory Garden Cookbook.** New York: Knopf, 1982. 374p. $25; pap. $14.95 (641.6)

A vegetable cookbook that developed out of the television show "Crockett's Victory Garden," this offers a truly different approach. The author stresses not only the recipe, the dish, and the meal, but the actual planting, growing, and harvesting of the ingredients. The nongardener is shown how to shop for the best vegetables, and there is sound advice on how to store and can them. There are about 800 tested recipes for some 40 easy-to-grow vegetables. Arrangement is by vegetable, beginning with asparagus. All of this is accompanied by beautiful photographs of vegetables growing or about to be eaten. There is a nice, personal, relaxed touch to the book, which offers commonsense approaches to gardening and cooking.

Nyerges, Christopher. **Wild Greens and Salads.** Harrisburg, PA: Stackpole, 1982. 204p. $10.95 (641.6)

For those who like to live, if only in part, off the land, this is your book. The author describes some 40 plants and wild greens, most of which can be readily found in backyards or the countryside, which you can collect and mix in a salad or use as a separate, delightful dish. Many of the greens, from asparagus to chickweed, are familiar, but Nyerges does include a few more exotic types. And to be on the safe side, each is not only described but shown in a clear line drawing. Best times for harvesting are stressed and the recipes are both imaginative and easy to follow.

Scaravelli, Paola, and Jon Cohen. **Cooking from an Italian Garden: Over 300 Classic Meatless Recipes from Antipasti to Dessert.** New York: Holt, 1984. 354p. $18.45 (641.5)

Not just another Italian cookbook, but one that is extremely well written, easy to follow, and has the added bonus of drawing on the best European meatless dishes. Most of the ingredients are to be found in American markets, albeit few of them are going to be as fresh as the two authors wish. The recipes range from breads and appetizers to main courses, including marvelous soups and fondues. The main dishes draw heavily on pasta and vegetables. Desserts are the least expansive part of the book, yet quite adequate. While all of this may be followed by a beginner, it is really a better cookbook for someone with a little experience. Given that, the guide demonstrates how delicious vegetarian dishes can be when prepared properly.

Sherman, Kay. **The Findhorn Family Cook Book: A Vegetarian Cookbook Which Celebrates the Wellness of Life.** Boulder, CO: Shambhala, 1982. 152p. pap. $7.95 (641.5)

Here is the place to find out how to prepare a vegetarian dish or banquet that will have wide appeal and will not be a strain for either the cook or the person who sits down to the meal. The recipes suggest delicious treats, and all have been adequately tested. True, the Findhorn spiritual community does sometimes get carried away by ideology, but for the most part this is a minor (and, for many, agreeable) part of the cookbook. The northeast Scotland community is by now famous for its natural food approach, and even a cursory glance through this book will explain why the fame is well deserved. The recipes are clear and range from soups and salads to breads and desserts. It is a joy to read and to use.

Shulman, Martha. **The Vegetarian Feast.** New York: Harper, 1979. 319p. $12.95 (641.56)

Among the scores of vegetarian cookbooks, this is about as basic and good as one can hope to find. It is by now a classic in the field and is particularly valued as a source of delicious recipes and intriguing suggestions. The author believes the vegetarian need not suffer to claim that title, and in page after page demonstrates the glory of imaginative cooking. Most of the ingredients are readily available, although some are found only in health food stores and outlets. The directions are precise, the explanations clear, and the result is an excellent cookbook not only for the vegetarian, but for any individual who cares for refined tastes and meals that look as good as they taste. See also her *Fast Vegetarian Feasts* (New York: Dial,

1982, pap., $11.95), which has more of the same excellent ideas, but includes the time it takes to prepare each dish—usually 10 to 25 minutes.

Sunset Menus & Recipes for Vegetarian Cooking. Menlo Park, CA: Lane, 1981. 96p. pap. $5.95 (641.8)

Best for its numerous and imaginative recipes, this follows the pattern of other Sunset guides. There are illustrations, many in color, and useful diagrams and charts showing how to measure foods for amounts of protein, calories, etc. The recipes are easy to follow and are for both beginners and intermediate-level cooks. Experts will probably wish to skip this.

COSTUME. *See* Entertaining & Parties; Sewing; Theater

CRAFTS. *See* Handicrafts

CRIME PROTECTION
  See also Burglary Protection; Self-Defense

Castleman, Michael. **Crime Free.** New York: Simon & Schuster, 1984. 288p. $16.95 (364.40)

A journalist has scanned the literature and come up with a compilation of ideas on how to deter crime in and near the home. This guide differs from others in that the primary focus is on community prevention of crime, an area with which the author is particularly familiar. There is a section, too, on what to look for in a con game or a swindle. Other chapters consider how to get over being a victim, or helping someone else in that psychological state of mind, and how to ward off a criminal assault.

Dobson, Terry, and Judith Shepherd-Chow. **Safe and Alive: How to Protect Yourself and Your Family, and Your Property against Violence.** Boston: Houghton, 1981. 152p. pap. $4.95 (362.8)

The primary safeguard against violence is to be calm and prepared. The two authors, both experts on security measures, block out various areas of possible danger—from the home to the street—and show what the individual should do when confronted by a robber, a burglar, or someone committing a gratuitous crime. The advice is conservative, and does not rely on carrying a weapon or expertise in combat. There seems to be almost as much on how to prevent crime as on what to do when confronted with immediate danger. A reliable, commonsense guide that will be of help to anyone.

Fike, Richard. **How to Keep from Being Robbed, Raped & Ripped Off: Personal Crime Prevention Manual for You and Your Loved Ones.** Washington, DC: Acropolis, 1983. 239p. $14.95; pap. $8.95 (362.8)

Specifics are given here on various self-defense tactics and exercises. The how-to-do-it sections are indicative of what can be done, and thorough enough to be of use to the average layperson. In addition, Fike covers such things as burglar alarms, safe locks, hiding places, etc. Still, the primary emphasis is on how to move about with a sense of security through the use of careful precautions, all of which are listed and explained. The focus is on the home and business. There is a special section devoted to advice for children.

Lipman, Ira. **How to Protect Yourself from Crime: Everything You Need to Know to Guard Yourself, Your Family, Your Home, Your Possessions, and Your Business.** Rev. ed. New York: Avon, 1981. 248p. pap. $2.95 (364.4)

This offers basic information for use by the layperson. It does not require technical skill to implement, and most of the suggested aids can be purchased at a local store. There are excellent sections on what to do in an emergency situation. *Note:* This was first published in a slightly different form by the U.S. Law Enforcement Assistance Administration (1980).

McNamara, Joseph. **Safe & Sane: The Sensible Way to Protect Yourself, Your Loved Ones, Your Property and Possessions.** New York: Perigee, 1984. 224p. $8.95 (362.88)

A police chief shows how one may safeguard the home and neighborhood against crime. This guide differs from others of its kind in two ways. First, the author has an excellent section on steps older people can take to safeguard themselves and their property. This is rarely considered in such depth. Second, he has a better understanding of the criminal mind than most, and offers commonsense approaches to crime that are not always found in these guides. In addition, the book urges the reader to follow sensible, not daring, methods of protection.

Schwarz, Ted. **Protect Your Home and Family: A Commonsense Guide to Personal Safety.** New York: Arco, 1983. 256p. pap. $8.95 (362.8)

Here is good advice on how to protect the home against thieves, where and where not to hide valuables, and how to establish alarm systems that function properly. There is a particularly useful section on the protection of children. Actually, the author goes beyond the home and offers practical tips on safeguarding boats, cars, bikes, and even planes. With advice as practical as it is easy to understand, this is one of the better approaches to home safety now available.

U.S. Department of Justice. **How to Crimeproof Your Business.** Washington, DC: GPO, 1979. 28p. (J26.2:c86/12)

This pamphlet pinpoints ways you can protect your business from robbery, shoplifting, employee dishonesty, and more.

U.S. Department of Justice. **You, Yours and Crime Resistance.** Washington, DC: GPO, 1979. 61p. $2.10 (J1.14/2:C86)

This offers general, yet practical, tips on various aspects of crime prevention. The suggestions range from what to do when attacked or robbed to how to keep an inventory of possessions in your house. The advice is not likely to date quickly.

CROQUET

Osborn, Jack, and Jesse Kornbluth. **Winning Croquet: From Backyard to Greensward—the Skills, Strategies and Rules of America's Most Sophisticated Outdoor Sport.** New York: Simon & Schuster, 1983. 224p. $17.95; pap. $9.95 (996.35)

No *Alice In Wonderland* game this. Here the authors are out for blood, and they demonstrate methods of winning and winning again. If you think of this game as a leisurely way to pass a few minutes, this is not your book. If you take up the wooden mallet to win, there is information on how to accomplish your goal— specifically, on drills and on how to hold the mallet and hit. There are some rather uninteresting illustrations, but the prose is fine.

CROSSWORD PUZZLES

Baus, Herbert. **Master Crossword Puzzle Dictionary.** Garden City, NY: Double-day, 1981. 1,693p. $19.95 (793.7)
   For crossword puzzle fans who do not eschew the use of a dictionary, this is one of the best available. Arrangement is by the word used as a clue in the puzzle. There are about 200,000 such words, followed by what the publisher claims are over 1 million answer words. Sometimes there are 75 answer words for a single clue word, in which case they are subdivided by the number of letters in each word. Variations on spelling are noted, although not all the time. This is about as exhaustive a dictionary as is now published, although it will not appeal to the proudly independent puzzle fan.

Donner, Michael, and Norton Bramesco. **The Illustrated Encyclopedia of Cross-word Words.** New York: Workman, 1982. 384p. $15.95; pap. $8.95 (793.73)
   Unlike numerous other crossword dictionaries, this has several unique and valu-able educational features. First, there are more than 1,000 illustrations. Second, there is a section of categories that helps the reader locate elusive subjects. Third, there are clear definitions of those ubiquitous two-to-six letter words that dot every crossword puzzle. Finally, there are over 3,000 often-used terms. Pronunciations of the words are included.

Kurzban, Stan, and Mel Rosen. **The Complete Cruciverbalist: Or How to Solve and Compose Crossword Puzzles for Fun and Profit.** New York: Van Nostrand, 1981. 167p. $9.95 (793.73)
   A three-pronged attack on the crossword puzzle, this is not for the individual who takes pride in solving puzzles without any outside aids. It is for someone who wants to know how to make up a crossword puzzle. The third section gives precise explanations of this feat for five different types of puzzles. There is also a short section on how to sell a puzzle. Still, the real benefit of this book for the nonpurist is in its second part, where the authors give strategies and ideas for solving five basic types of puzzles, i.e., the kinds most likely to be found in newspapers and magazines. Less useful is the first part, which discusses the history of puzzles.

Pulliam, Tom, and Claire Grundman. **The New York Times Crossword Puzzle Dictionary.** New York: New York Times Books, 1977. 727p. $7.95 (793.73)
   The standard crossword puzzle dictionary, this follows the pattern of listing basic clue words with numerous synonyms that might fit into a crossword.

CRYPTOLOGY. See Codes

CUSTOMS. See Entertaining & Parties

CYCLING. See Bicycling

DANCE

Clarke, Mary, and Clement Crisp. **The Ballet Goer's Guide.** New York: Knopf, 1981. 367p. $19.95 (792.8)

For the beginning ballet fan who is trying to understand what is going on, this is ideal. Numerous illustrations augment the direct, uncomplicated explanations of about 100 commonly performed ballets. Various interpretations of a particular ballet are noted, and the majority of dances are closely related to a particular company or dancer. There is background material on the principles of dance, basic positions and movements, primary dancers, and related matters.

Frich, Elisabeth. **The Matt Mattox Book of Jazz Dance.** New York: Sterling, 1983. 128p. pap. $12.95 (793.3)

Teaching someone to dance by numbers is not easy. An instructor is certainly preferred. Still, the intermediate to skilled dancer can learn much from a book. Here the author wisely relies as much on photographs of each movement as she does on text. The learning process is based on that of Matt Mattox, a well-known teacher. Frich opens with the traditional warming-up exercises and then moves into the various dance steps, which range from the relatively basic to the complex. Each step is illustrated. One can presumably glide across the dance floor with the book in hand and, at the end of several sessions, be more than a passable jazz dancer.

Livingston, Peter. **The Complete Book of Country Swing & Western Dance, and a Bit about Cowboys.** New York: Doubleday, 1981. 236p. pap. $10.95 (793.3)

Western dance is interpreted here to mean almost anything this side of the formal dance floor. The result is a comprehensive guide with numerous illustrations for each and every step described. The instructions are easy to follow and, given a bit of practice, the average person should have no difficulty mastering the dances. Most of the material is quite basic. Less useful: sections on the life and times of the cowboy.

Loren, Teri. **Dancer's Companion.** New York: Dial, 1978. 275p. $7.95; pap. $3.95 (793.3)

Written for the aspiring young dancer, this is one of the best guides available. It is in no way dated, and the 14 chapters cover every aspect of the art likely to interest the dance student. There are sections on selecting a teacher, nutrition, practice, etc. The book will be of value to both parents and young dancers.

Marx, Trina. **Tap Dance: A Beginner's Guide.** Englewood Cliffs, NJ: Prentice-Hall, 1983. 165p. $18.59; pap. $8.95 (793.3)

Anyone can tap dance. That is the claim of the author, who makes her point with step-by-step directions that are carefully illustrated. Take the book in hand and follow the instructions. Of course, anyone who is serious about it will need a teacher, but for someone who is simply curious or for a child who wants to learn basics, this is a solid point of departure. The various types of dances are described and there is additional information on tap dancers who became great personalities and on the history of the form.

Sawyer, Phyllis, and Pat Thornton. **Aerobic Dancing a Step at a Time.** Chicago: Contemporary, 1981. 99p. pap. $5.95 (613.7)

A brief yet well-illustrated guide to the basics of aerobic dancing, this includes not only precise instructions on the dances but good background information on health as well. The dances vary in difficulty and in type, but all are considered step by step, usually with illustrations. There are sections on stretching, methods of warming up and cooling down, and general exercise. For a somewhat more detailed approach see Jacki Sorensen's *Aerobic Dancing* (New York: Rawson, 1979).

DATA BASES. *See* Computers

DECORATING. *See* Interior Decoration

DESSERTS

Anderson, Jean. **Unforbidden Sweets: More Than 100 Classic Desserts You Can Now Enjoy without Counting Calories.** New York: Arbor, 1982. 203p. $15 (641.86)
Directed to dieters, this offers classic desserts that can be enjoyed without counting calories. The secret of this popular cookbook writer is to prepare the desserts without high-fat ingredients by substituting such things as egg whites, skim milk, yogurt, and low-calorie sweeteners. Recipes include pies and cakes, cookies and sauces, and the author guarantees all may be eaten in moderation without putting on weight.

Crocker, Betty. **Betty Crocker's Cookie Book.** Racine, WI: Golden, 1980. 96p. pap. $3.95 (641.5)
The recipes are traditional, although the compiler does include basic cookie recipes from many Western European countries. The directions are as easy to follow as the ingredients are specific, and there are numerous illustrations. Aside from the straightforward recipes, there are sometimes less useful hints on how to gift wrap cookies and make constructions out of the basic cookie design. Still and all, one of the best all-around approaches to the subject and sure to be a solid favorite among children and adults alike.

Cutler, Carol. **The Woman's Day Low-Calorie Dessert Cookbook.** Boston: Houghton, 1980. 213p. $9.95 (641.8)
The distinct and compelling reason for selecting this "watch the waist but eat desserts" cookbook over scores of others in the same field is that the author relies completely on natural sweeteners and avoids packaged mixes and shortcuts. Nothing chemical or dangerous is used here, just downright good ingredients combined in good-to-excellent recipes. The various desserts include a vast array of appetizing cakes, cookies, and pies. The author dutifully notes the number of calories in each serving (most are under 100). The recipes require limited culinary ability and almost all the ingredients are found in local markets. Thanks to the solid advice, the wit of the author, and her skill in finding low-calorie desserts, this should be a required item in any kitchen where the waistline is a concern.

Heatter, Maida. **Maida Heatter's Book of Great Chocolate Desserts.** New York: Knopf, 1980. 428p. $15 (641.63)
When it comes to recipes for "disastrous-to-the-waistline marvelous-to-the-

palate" desserts, there is nothing comparable to Maida Heatter's by now classic presentation. She has two distinctive qualities at work here. First and foremost is her knowledge of the meaning of the phrase "chocolate desserts." It is almost mystical, certainly appreciated only by those who would gladly swap almost anything for a great chocolate treat. Second, she deals with specifics and it is perfectly possible to make all of the delights she describes. Directions are complete and easy to follow, and the results are rarely disappointing.

Heatter, Maida. **Maida Heatter's New Book of Great Desserts.** New York: Knopf, 1982. 477p. $17.50 (641.8)

There may be better cooks who instruct the reader on how to make desserts, but it is unlikely. This is a follow-up to the author's original *Book of Great Desserts* (1974) and it is just as marvelous, just as elegant. It offers a new, imaginative collection of easy-to-follow, although sometimes quite involved, recipes. Here one finds recipes for pies, cakes, cookies, muffins. Each opens with an explanation of the ingredients and equipment needed. Heatter favors baked goods, but she does include tempting recipes for other products from ice cream to custards. The directions are precise, and the style is informal. The basic problem: Weight gain is a guaranteed by-product of these delightful after-dinner suggestions.

Warrington, Janet. **Sweet & Natural: Desserts without Sugar, Honey, Molasses, or Artificial Sweeteners.** Trumansburg, NY: Crossing Pr., 1982. 145p. $15.95; pap. $7.95 (641.8)

This should work. The recipes for people who cannot eat sweets sound inviting enough. They are easy to understand, and most of the ingredients are readily at hand. The sweet tooth is nurtured by the natural delights of fruits and some spices, such as cinnamon. A sampling, though, shows that anyone addicted to sugar is not going to be satisfied. This is no fault of the author, who has done her best, and one may argue that the various dishes are better than nothing. At any rate, it certainly is worth a try—and in many cases the book may be an absolutely necessary part of a kitchen.

DINOSAURS. *See* Fossils

DOGS

American Kennel Club. **The Complete Dog Book.** New York: Howell, 1929–   . Irreg. 16th ed., 1979. 768p. $12.95 (636.7)

The most complete all-around encyclopedia about dogs, this is a standard reference guide. Each breed is clearly identified and described with its history and development. There is a black-and-white photograph for every dog, as well as several group color photographs. Various sections are devoted to breeding, dog shows, health, nutrition, etc. Limited to AKC breeds, this does not include some rather popular animals found in various parts of the country, not to mention the rest of the world. Readers should watch for the newest edition, particularly as the 1979 edition does not take into account the AKC's own change in the division of breeds.

Barnes, Duncan, ed., and the Staff of the American Kennel Club. **The AKC's World of the Pure-Bred Dog.** New York: Howell, 1983. 344p. $29.95 (636.7)

Sponsored by the American Kennel Club, this is a general overview of the pure-bred dog. In some five sections, it moves from the various types of breeds to a piece on the dog in literature and art. Little of this is original, but the essays devoted to the dog in art, and the illustrations, many in color, make this a useful title for the lover of dogs.

Burnham, Patricia. **Playtraining Your Dog.** New York: St. Martin's, 1980. 273p. $12.95 (636.7)

Among dog-obedience books, this is a favored guide. Here the author takes a debatable approach. She strongly believes in working obedience training into games that will be fun for both the animal and the trainer. Beyond this, she gives all the usual, necessary background data as well as sensible advice on improving the dog's disposition and performance. Burnham has another important thing in her favor: She writes extremely well, and the book is a joy to read. The illustrations are good and well placed.

Caras, Roger. **A Celebration of Dogs.** New York: Times Books, 1982. 253p. $12.95; pap. $6.96 (636.7)

Familiar to millions of radio listeners and television fans, Caras is an entertaining and informative authority on animals, and, more particularly, dogs. He also writes a column in *Ladies' Home Journal* and in several newspapers. With that kind of background he is well suited to write a popular book on the history of dogs and the relationship between these animals and humans. This loosely organized volume relies on anecdotal material about certain breeds, but it is always accurate and eminently readable. There are excellent although brief descriptions of more common breeds. There is not much direct how-to-do-it material here, but anyone who owns and loves a dog will want to read the book for the indirect information it gives about the pet—and the reader.

Caras, Roger. **The Roger Caras Dog Book.** New York: Holt, 1980. 292p. $16.95 (636.7)

The well-known pet expert turns his attention to dogs, and the result is a chatty, accurate guide to help someone select a dog, care for it, and generally enjoy having the animal around the house. Basic questions are answered and problems are discussed, and there is useful data on each breed—including how much exercise may be needed to keep the dog healthy. Caras seems particularly good at identifying the problems that a dog is likely to cause around the home, and offering practical solutions to them. Another strong attribute is his obvious appreciation of the differences in types of dogs and owners, and he stresses that the two should be matched.

Carlson, Delbert, and James Giffin. **Dog Owner's Home Veterinary Handbook.** New York: Howell, 1980. 365p. $15.95 (636.7)

What can the dog owner do when a pet becomes ill? If it is ill enough, of course, a trip to the veterinarian is essential, but for simple diseases, this manual will answer most questions. The two veterinarian authors approach the subject by looking at the dog in sections—literally and figuratively. Each part of the dog's body is illustrated and descriptive text explains likely diseases and what to do when illness strikes. There is also a useful summary on the inside front cover, i.e, "Index of Signs and Symptoms." The well-written text covers various other matters from emergency treatment to drugs and pregnancies. One of the best and certainly one of the easiest books of this type to read.

Clarke, Anna. **Canine Clinic: The Veterinarian's Handbook to the Diagnosis and Treatment of Your Dog's Health Problems.** New York: Macmillan, 1984. 298p. $17.95 (636.7)

Symptoms of diseases and canine upsets are clearly described here by an experienced veterinarian. Each symptom is followed by methods of prevention and treatment, often accompanied by illustrations. The result is a much-above-average handbook for the dog owner who may want to avoid a visit to the vet, or at least understand what is going on when the dog is taken to the pet hospital. Much of the information may be used daily, since Clarke offers ways of preventing disease and troubles. Nutrition is another important element in the dog's health, so the author provides some advice on what types of commercial foods to use. The down-to-earth, practical information is easy to follow. When a vet is needed, she specifically so advises. In fact, there is a section on how to select a vet, when to call one, and what to expect. Illustrated throughout, this is carefully and clearly written.

Glover, Harry, ed. **A Standard Guide to Purebred Dogs.** Rev. ed. New York: Macmillan, 1982. 472p. $24.95 (636.7)

While this overlaps somewhat with the AKC *The Complete Dog Book* (q.v.), it has the advantage of including breeds not found in that standard reference work. Each dog is described in full with a black-and-white photograph. (There are separate sections of colored photographs.) Extinct breeds are described in the final part.

Kalstone, Shirlee. **Dogs: Breeds, Care and Training.** New York: Dell, 1982. 560p. pap. $4.95 (636.7)

Basics from how to choose a dog to what to look for in order to avoid a high-strung animal are clearly explained. There is much room for choice in that each AKC breed is discussed in detail and illustrated by a line drawing. There is sufficient material to help the owner discover what may be wrong with a dog's diet or how to prepare the animal for a show, and good sections on training. *Note:* Kalstone is the author of the now out-of-print *The New Dog Encyclopedia* (Harrisburg, PA: Stackpole, 1970), which rivals in coverage the standard AKC *The Complete Dog Book* (q.v.).

Loeb, Jo. **Supertraining Your Dog.** Englewood Cliffs, NJ: Prentice-Hall, 1980. 240p. $9.95 (636.7)

Here the author is more concerned with real problem dogs than with basic training. True, the first third or so of the book is devoted to the conventional rules of training, but following this, the author discusses specific problems. For example, Loeb covers conventional housebreaking methods, but goes beyond these to consider why a dog does not fit into the normal training pattern. The same approach is employed for aggression, health difficulties, wandering, etc. While not the best overall training book available, it is tops for someone with a dog who simply refuses to follow the usual training patterns.

Messent, Peter. **Understanding Your Dog.** New York: Stein & Day, 1983. 159p. $12.95 (636.7)

This English specialist in animal behavior takes a long look at dogs as pets and concludes that there are two basic ways to train, or, if you will, understand a dog. First, one uses the Pavlovian approach, which calls for the animal to do a certain thing on a given signal. Second, the reward-and-punishment syndrome is a support for the Pavlovian method. He advises using this system because he believes strongly in the intelligence of dogs and their ability to communicate with humans, if only indirectly. There are additional well-defined explanations about other aspects of the dog, from its history and background to how it reacts with other animals. The laudatory foreword by Konrad Lorenz is deserved, for this is one of the better books for anyone with a dog.

Milani, Myrna. **The Weekend Dog.** New York: Rawson/Scribner, 1984. 256p. $14.95 (636.7)

What is the best dog for the person who works and cannot be home to watch the animal? According to this veterinarian-author, it depends on the particular personality and life-style of the owner. Still, the real focus is on the characteristics of individual dogs. There are detailed explanations of what sizes and types make the best part-time pets—and, equally, the kind that make the worst. The author provides instructions on how to care for the animal, what to do when it gets sick, and how to handle a dog that insists on leaving calling cards about the house. She is particularly good at suggesting basic training methods. Throughout, she illustrates her major points with case histories. The author writes with authority, knowledge, and a sprightly original style that makes sometimes old advice sound new. A useful book, actually, for anyone, not just the weekend walker.

Palmer, Joan. **How to Choose & Care for Your Dog.** Tucson, AZ: HP Books, 1982. 160p. pap. $9.95 (636.7)

For the person who cannot decide what type of dog to buy, the first half of this guide outlines the different breeds and explains the pros and cons of each. Complete information is given on everything from degree of friendliness to how much the dog is likely to eat. Each, too, is identified with a photo, some in color. The second half tells the reader what to do with the dog when it is taken home—and there is the familiar advice on training, exercise, grooming, health, etc. The assumption is that the reader knows little or nothing about dogs, but by the time the book is closed that same reader will be on the way to becoming an expert.

Palmer, Joan. **An Illustrated Guide to Dogs.** New York: Arco, 1982. 240p. $9.95 (636.7)

A simple, direct guide to close to 200 breeds of dogs, this illustrates each family and gives a brief description of them. Their suitability as pets may be gauged by the precise information on how much the animals eat, how difficult they are to care for, their exercise requirements, etc. Arrangement is by size of dog.

Pitcairn, Richard, and Susan Pitcairn. **Dr. Pitcairn's Complete Guide to Natural Health for Dogs and Cats.** Emmaus, PA: Rodale, 1982. 280p. pap. $10.95 (636.70)

It is important to stress "natural" in the title. The authors are strong believers in the holistic approach to ensure the health of the dog or cat. And to that end, they explain the various basic diets and health treatments for raising animals. Much is made of feeding the dog natural foods, and avoiding canned or dried products. The arguments for this are persuasive and reasonable. When the animal becomes ill, specific remedies are given as well as treatments ranging from acupuncture to homeopathy. There is an excellent section on specific diseases and substitutes for the usual pills and chemicals. The appendixes include names of sympathetic veterinarians in various parts of the country and a list of sources for supplies. Among dog and cat care books, this is one of the very best.

Tortora, Daniel. **The Right Dog for You.** New York: Simon & Schuster, 1980. 381p. $12.95 (636.7)

How do you select the right dog? According to the author, you match the dog's temperament with your own. In order to ensure a good match, he carefully describes the characteristics of each breed under 16 points. He then goes on to describe self-administered tests that will help the prospective dog owner match a life-style with that of the dog. Sometimes, to be sure, there is no match. The author's conclusion: Forget a dog. This is all done with scientific objectivity, at least as far as the dog's traits are concerned. One may argue a bit with the human side of it all, but the idea seems sound enough and the result is a useful, even delightful guide.

Volhard, Joachim, and Gail Fisher. **Training Your Dog.** New York: Howell, 1983. 239p. $12.95 (636.7)

Both authors are experienced trainers, and well known to dog lovers. Both have a sure touch with animals (and people), and here they demonstrate why they are leaders in their field. Beginning with the first steps in dog-obedience training, the authors take the reader and the dog through a series of lessons. The easy-to-understand lessons are based on numerous approaches, even numerous schools of training, and represent what the authors believe to be the best overall general plan. The direct instructions, coupled with excellent photographs and line drawings, make this an exceptionally good training book for beginners and experts alike.

Woodhouse, Barbara. **No Bad Dogs: The Woodhouse Way.** New York: Summit, 1982. 127p. $13.50 (636.7)

There probably is no better-known, or for that matter better-qualified, dog trainer than Barbara Woodhouse. Her authoritative speaking voice and expert handling of dogs are familiar to television viewers. Here she reiterates the techniques that make her able to handle any type of dog. Most of the training is really of the owner rather than of the dog, and Woodhouse explains in detail what types of approach the owner must take—including necessary equipment and techniques. She has words of advice for those with difficult dogs and gives sensible tips on how to solve common problems such as the dog jumping on guests. An excellent title, not only for the person who wants to train a dog, but for the dog lover who already has a well-behaved animal.

DOLLS
See also Antiques; Handicrafts

Dodge, Venus, and Martin Dodge. **Making Collector's Dolls.** New York: Sterling, 1984. 167p. $18.85; pap. $9.95 (745.5)

The two authors combine their skills to offer instructions for making 30 different types of dolls. These range from the relatively simple (rag) to the extremely complex (clay), but almost all assume that the reader has some knowledge of crafts. Less-experienced people should turn to more basic works. Martin Dodge meticulously illustrates the specific instructions of Venus Dodge, and the patterns are outstanding for their clarity. There is an excellent section on clothing and other additions, again with full-sized patterns. Coverage is historical, in that the ladies are drawn from medieval to twentieth-century models.

Guild, Vera. **Dollmakers' Workshop.** New York: Hearst, 1981. 160p. $19.95 (745.59)

Here the doll is primarily of rag construction, and the emphasis is on simple designs that do not require abundant sewing skills. Thanks to the author's artistic sense, the patterns are quite superior. Illustrations are clear and the step-by-step instructions include what materials to use.

Holz, Loretta. **Developing Your Doll Collection.** New York: Crown, 1982. 243p. $16.95 (688.7)

The best feature of this guide is its clear explanation of what constitutes a collectible doll and where it may be found and purchased. The explanations, both here and throughout, are augmented by numerous clear photographs. Other aspects of the book include sections on restoration, storage, and display. There are even tips on how to sell dolls. The appendix includes a valuable list of doll museums and organizations devoted to such matters.

King, Constance. **The Collector's History of Doll's Houses, Doll's House Dolls and Miniatures.** New York: St. Martin's, 1983. 608p. $40 (745.59)

The operative word here is "history," although there are some useful sections on collecting and the restoration of old dollhouses, miniatures, etc. The author works on the correct assumption that anyone interested in the hobby must know its origin in Europe and America, and to that end she provides encyclopedic descriptive matter for the doll's house art from the seventeenth century to the 1960s. There are numerous color and black-and-white illustrations throughout, and while most of the focus is on the houses, the author does consider the individual dolls and the furnishings. Well written and carefully executed, this is a massive volume, but worth the study.

Lavitt, Wendy. **Dolls.** Collectors' Guides to American Antiques. New York: Knopf, 1983. 478p. pap. $13.45 (745.59)

Thanks to numerous color illustrations, this is a full, excellent guide to collecting dolls. It follows the pattern of others in the series (for details, see the discussion of the Ketchum book on chests, p. 8 in this book). The individual dolls are described in detail and there is a good introduction to the problems and joys of collecting.

McCall's Big Book of Dollhouses & Miniatures. Radnor, PA: Chilton, 1984. 286p. pap. $12.95 (745.5)

Following the usual pattern of McCall's, here are step-by-step instructions, usually accompanied by illustrations, on making various kinds of dollhouses. These range in size and difficulty, but the majority are well within the capacity of the intermediate-level craftsperson. In addition, there are instructions for making miniature furniture, as well as rugs and even bedspreads. As much an idea book as one for instruction, it is a joy to look through.

McCracken, Joann. **Dollhouse Dolls.** Radnor, PA: Chilton, 1980. 167p. $14.95; pap. $8.95 (745.59)

Just about anything the doll maker may need in order to construct a doll is included in this brief yet helpful guide. After generalities about fashioning a doll, the author gives step-by-step instructions. These, accompanied by numerous black-and-white photographs, cover every aspect of the process from shaping heads and bodies to face painting and hair. There is a good list of suppliers appended.

McElroy, Joan. **Dolls' House Furniture Book.** New York: Knopf, 1977. 222p. $15 (745.59)

Although published in 1977, this is in no way dated and is, in fact, a basic book for dollhouse furniture. Complete illustrated instructions are given on the construction of numerous miniature pieces. The step-by-step instructions are easy to follow, although it is assumed that the reader has the same keen eyes, the same degree of patience, as the author, who made all of the furniture illustrated here. McElroy has a good sense of balance and design, and the furniture she recommends is extremely attractive.

Marsten, Barbara, and Christine Makowski. **Step-by-Step Dollmaking.** New York: Van Nostrand, 1981. 144p. $16.95 (745.59)

One of the best books on the subject, this is, as the title indicates, a basic approach for the individual who is interested in making different types of dolls. The patterns and projects move from the relatively simple to the more complex. There are particularly good illustrations—many in color—leading the reader through the various steps. The full-size pattern pieces may help the reader considerably. In addition, one finds information on basic doll-making processes, sewing suggestions, and time-saving hints. Most of the patterns follow traditional lines, and all are in good taste.

Merrill, Virginia, and Susan Richardson. **Reproducing Period Furniture and Accessories in Miniature.** New York: Crown, 1981. 309p. $25 (749.1)

For anyone concerned with the construction or purchase of miniature furniture, this is a basic guide by the leading experts on the subject. About one-third of the book describes the characteristics of seven different period styles. There follow some 35 patterns, as well as 42 designs for needlework. Then, too, there are examples of furnished rooms, carefully explained, and an excellent reference chart that points out characteristics of each period. It all ends with a glossary and a list of sources of supplies, which are sometimes difficult to locate.

Seeley, Mildred, and Colleen Seeley. **Doll Collecting for Fun & Profit.** Tucson, AZ: HP Books, 1983. 144p. $14.95 (688.72)

The ins and outs of doll collecting for the beginner—not the experienced—is the focus of this well-illustrated book. Working on the premise that the reader knows little or nothing about how to locate dolls, determine their value, or recognize the various types, the authors explain all. There is even a section on repair and cleaning. While the writing style is a bit too simple for some, it has the benefit of being easy to understand. Also, the book is quite thorough within its stated scope.

Smith, Harry. **The Art of Making Furniture in Miniature.** New York: Dutton, 1982. 288p. $32.50; pap. $21.95 (745.59)

A sumptuous, well-illustrated volume, this is by an expert who can explain as much about furniture in general as about how to build miniature furniture. Given this double expertise, the author offers specific directions on how to construct a wide variety of small furniture from chests and cradles to beds and chairs. Various periods are considered. Every step is explored, including the type of tools needed and the various desirable woods and finishes. Work with limited kinds of metals is discussed, too. The book is written for both the amateur and the expert.

Westfall, Mary. **The Handbook of Doll Repair and Restoration.** New York: Crown, 1980. 282p. $15.95 (688.7)

The title adequately explains the scope, but a hidden benefit of this fine manual is that careful reading will make it possible for even the beginner to detect replicas. Replicas are a major headache for the collector because the doll market increasingly is seeing rising prices. Beyond the detection element, and aided by good illustrations, is the main purpose of the book, which is to show how to restore and repair dolls. Complicated procedures are explained in detail, as are the specialized tools needed. The best of its type.

Worrell, Estelle. **The Dollhouse Book.** New York: Van Nostrand, 1964. 125p. $9.95; pap. $5.95 (745.59)

While more than 20 years old, this remains one of the best guides to dollhouses. After a brief history of the form, the author considers various types of dollhouses and furniture. She moves from the earliest seventeenth-century examples, through the French provincial, to colonial, nineteenth-century, and modern examples. With that come detailed patterns and instructions for actually making the houses and various types of furniture and accessories. Most of this requires considerable skill, and it is not for the fledgling amateur. The plans are carefully thought out, though, and the experienced should have no difficulty in constructing the various dollhouses.

DRAMA. *See* Theater

DRAWING. *See* Graphic Arts; Painting (Art)

DRINKS
  See also Wine

Cotton, Leo. **Old Mr. Boston Deluxe Official Bartender's Guide.** Rev. ed. New York: Warner, 1982. 224p. pap. $5.95 (641.8)

This is a basic guide to just what goes into a specific type of drink. All of the ingredients are given, as well as the proportions, and even the amateur mixologist will have no difficulty following the directions. The steps in preparing a drink are carefully spelled out in such a way that it would be difficult not to get the final concoction correct. This distiller is also responsible for two related guides that are equally useful: *Mr. Boston Cordial Cooking Guide* (1982) and *Mr. Boston Spirited Dessert Guide* (1982), both distributed by Warner.

Duffy, Patrick, and Robert Misch. **The Official Mixer's Manual.** Rev. ed. New York: Doubleday, 1983. 190p. $10.95 (641.8)
Here are specific directions on how to serve, mix, and prepare close to 1,500 different drinks. All types of beverages are included, from wine and beer to liqueurs. The directions are specific and the book is particularly useful in relating a given drink or drinks to particular meals or types of food. The usual added features include material on glasses, measurements, wine vintages, etc.

Grossman, Harold, and Harriet Lembeck. **Grossman's Guide to Wines, Beers and Spirits.** 7th rev. ed. New York: Scribner's, 1983. 638p. $29.95 (641.2)
Primarily for the person who sells wine, beer, and spirits, not necessarily the consumer, this is a standard reference work that has gone through seven editions. It owes its popularity to several things, not the least of which is its comprehensiveness and a highly readable style. Anything to do with drink is included, e.g., how beer is made, distributed, and sold. While a commercial guide, its wide coverage makes it a valuable work of interest to anyone deeply involved in the subject.

Mares, William. **Making Beer.** New York: Knopf, 1984. 170p. pap. $7.95 (641.8)
Unlike the step-by-step manual offered by Reese (q.v), this is more of an overview of the small-business aspects of an industry with romantic overtones. Mares hopes to start his own brewery, but soon finds it is out of his reach. With most of the focus on the small brewery, there is little real space for how-to-do-it material. True, there are recipes and instructions, but they are not detailed enough, and in no way are they as adequate as those found in Reese. Still, Mares's book is an extremely well-written guide that will be of interest to any home brewer.

Mario, Thomas. **Playboy's New Bar Guide.** New York: Playboy, 1982. 400p. pap. $3.95
An inexpensive yet good guide to drinks, this is based on the author's 1954 manual, which is found in many libraries and homes. Mario has the ability to explain simply quite complicated drinks, but the real triumph is the book's organization and presentation of basic information. Here even the novice will quickly learn the difference between a rum- or brandy-based drink, and come to understand the variations possible in a punch bowl. Wines are treated in somewhat less depth.

Morris, Stephen. **The Great Beer Trek: A Guide to the Highlights and Lowlights of American Beer Drinking.** Brattleboro, VT: Greene Pr., 1984. 130p. $10.95 (641.2)
Most American commercial beer tastes like little more than flavored water, at least to hearty beer drinkers familiar with European drafts. Still, there are some exceptions, and in a tour of the United States the author discovers some substitutes for the bland drink. These are listed at the end of each chapter with the names and addresses not only of local breweries (both big and small), but individuals known

in the region for their home brew. The author even includes beer-can collectors. At the same time, this is a travel book in which Morris is as much enthralled by the company in a Texas bar as he is with the commercial beer. The result is a guide that will entice anyone remotely interested in the brew, or in American travel. An unbeatable combination.

Reese, M. R. **Better Beer and How to Brew It.** Pownal, VT: Garden Way Pub., 1981. 128p. pap. $6.95 (641.8)

The ideal book for the person who wants to make home brew, this explains every step in detail and has illustrations to underline the major points. There is a full description of the specific equipment needed, as well as the type and amount of ingredients. The language is simple and there is no jargon or technical terminology. Aside from the straightforward procedures for making beer, the author offers about 20 other approaches with increasing degrees of difficulty and sophistication.

DRIVING. *See* Automobiles

EARTH (UNDERGROUND) SHELTERED HOMES. *See* Homes—Building & Construction

EDIBLE WILD PLANTS. *See* Food; Mushrooms

ELECTRONICS
See also Radio; Telephone; Television

Iannini, Robert. **Build Your Own Laser, Phaser, Ion Ray Gun & Other Working Space-Age Projects.** Blue Ridge Summit, PA: TAB, 1984. 390p. $21.95; pap. $13.95 (621.3)

The title is to be believed. The author actually does show the reader how to construct this mass of space war weaponry. There are three catches. First, the materials needed are sometimes expensive and esoteric. Second, while the dangers of some of the projects are indicated, too much trust is placed in the judgment of young people. (It can be assumed that adults can take care of themselves, although even this may be optimistic.) Third, it presupposes a knowledge of basic electronics, which some readers will not have. Given those three reservations, one can accept this as a reliable, current guide to a subject of interest to many people. The directions are specific, and the accompanying illustrations clarify difficult concepts. Operating and testing instructions are noted, too. Not all of the projects are complicated. There are some, such as telephone-tapping devices and other voice technological works, that are relatively easy for the electronics fan.

Veley, Victor, and John Dulin. **Modern Electronics: A First Course.** Englewood Cliffs, NJ: Prentice-Hall, 1983. 670p. $21.95 (621.38)

This is an encyclopedic textbook of electronics, and while written for students, it is of equal benefit to amateurs and others who wish to have a handy guide on the subject close at hand. Various aspects of electronics are considered, and there are summaries and problems in each chapter. As it is fairly basic, the textbook would be a useful work to employ with more advanced or more specialized guides.

EMBROIDERY. *See* Needlecrafts

ENERGY CONSERVATION. *See* Homes—Energy Conservation

ENGINES. *See* Automobiles; Boats

ENLARGING. *See* Photography

ENTERTAINING & PARTIES

Bride's Magazine. **Bride's Lifetime Guide to Good Food & Entertainment.** New York: Congdon & Weed, 1984. 300p. $25 (642.4)

This is for the young bride, and has little to convey to the experienced hostess. The purpose is to offer entertainment hints and recipes that are as American as the magazine, and as simple to follow as most of the prose in *Bride's*. Whether the subject is tips on buying food or preparing for a small party, the instructions are rudimentary, and notably lacking in imagination and difficulty. This, of course, is as planned, and as a guide for the audience the magazine has in mind, it works well enough. One would hope, though, that the reader would soon grow out of the title's "lifetime" into more adventuresome stages.

Chambers, Wicke, and Spring Asher. **The Celebration Book of Great American Traditions.** New York: Harper, 1983. 192p. $15.50 (394.2)

What do you do to celebrate a special holiday? That is to say, what is the appropriate kind of party, gift, or particular approach to the day? The answers, arranged by the name of the holiday, are given here. There are both the usual (July 4, Christmas, birthdays) and the unusual (starting traditions where none exist, funerals). The approach is practical, often humorous, and carefully considered. The book is well designed and includes many useful illustrations.

Chase's Annual Events: Special Days, Weeks and Months in 1984. Chicago: Contemporary, 1957– . 1983 ed., 192p. pap. $12.95 (394.26)

Arranged by day, here are over 4,000 celebrations and sometimes downright mad occasions. Coverage is from state to state and country to country, and "event" is translated to mean anything from a holy day to an astronomical phenomenon. Anyone looking for an excuse to develop a theme for a program will discover 5 to 11 entries for each day of the year. There is a handy, although not entirely accurate, index by the name of the event.

Kraus, Charles, and Linda Kraus. **Charles the Clown's Guide to Children's Parties.** Rolling Hills Estates, CA: Jalmar, 1983. 320p. pap. $9.95 (793.2)

A professional who has spent a good part of his time making children's parties successful, Charles Kraus passes on what he has learned to harried parents. The advice is good because it is based on a real understanding of what children enjoy and on an appreciation of the parent with a limited amount of time and/or income. The golden mean is stressed in all things connected with a party. There are the usual tips on what the youngsters want to eat (junk food for the most part, but it can be improved) and what the parent might do to get everything going. The best section concerns party activities, and here the authors are sometimes ingenious.

Marzollo, Jean. **Birthday Parties for Children: How to Give Them, How to Survive Them.** New York: Harper, 1983. 176p. $11.95; pap. $4.95 (793.2)

Getting right to the heart of the matter, the author asks how busy, intelligent parents can give a birthday party for a child (1 to 10 years old) and still retain their sanity and some money in the bank. The answer is a good-natured, practical, and quite imaginative approach to different types of parties. In general, keep them short and keep the number of guests down. The book is divided into two sections—ages 1 through 3 and 4 through 10. For every party the author gives a round of useful information from menus to decorations to games. Everything is carefully explained, even down to the rules for games in a birthday contest. Well written, this will be a blessing to the parent who does not want to spend hours or days preparing for the event. Numerous line drawings help things along.

Post, Elizabeth, and Anthony Staffieri. **The Complete Book of Entertaining.** New York: Harper, 1981. 384p. $14.95 (642.4)

Good information on drink, food, etiquette, table settings, flowers, etc., makes this useful for the person entertaining two to three people or a brigade. The guide will have a particular appeal to those who want rules and regulations. There are no "ifs" or "buts" here—everything is spelled out as being correct or incorrect. There is a special focus on larger parties and the need for rented equipment, catering services, etc. Still, whether for entertaining those few people or for the few times in one's life when such large parties are required, this is *the* book to have for help. There are detailed explanations of various other types of gatherings, including a good section on children's parties. The first part deals with party preparations and offers practical information on everything from guest lists to flower arrangements. The second part is concerned with specific types of parties, and for each suggested menus and recipes are included.

Reed, Marjorie, and Kalia Lulow. **Entertaining All Year Round.** New York: Ballantine, 1983. 211p. pap. $12.95 (395.3)

A celebrity who loves parties, Marjorie Reed offers more than 30 plans for successful entertaining. These range from relatively simple ones for a few guests to complicated ones for many. The directions are complete and cover such topics as what to have for dinner, when and how to send out invitations, what to do a few days or a few hours before the party, etc. The author introduces her detailed program with some general advice on what constitutes a good party. There are recipes as well as innovative types of menus.

Reed, Marjorie, and Kalia Lulow. **Marjorie Reed's Party Book: Entertaining with More Style Than Money.** New York: Ballantine, 1981. 161p. pap. $6.95 (642.4)

Personality and planning seem more important than money in throwing a superb party (although cost is a factor the wise planner can't overlook). Given this premise, these two experts show how to do just about everything from developing a theme, to sending out invitations, to deciding what foods should be served. The authors claim that anyone can give a great party by using a detailed checklist. The book is particularly valuable for its overall view as well as for hints on how to save money.

Shannon-Thornberry, Milo. **The Alternate Celebration Catalogue.** New York: Seabury, 1982. 192p. pap. $8.95 (394.2)

Here "alternate" means a fresh way to celebrate holidays throughout the year, whether at formal parties or informal family gatherings. This catalog of ideas is an effort to divorce holidays from commercial sales pitches—to show that there is more to Easter, for example, than purchasing expensive Easter eggs and clothing. This is accomplished by informing the reader about inexpensive projects, suggesting books and other reading matter, and listing organizations that are particularly in tune with specialized holidays. The information is conveyed in short articles or essays, often with good drawings. Sometimes the mission overrides the ideas, and from time to time one wishes the author were not quite so dedicated to the noncommercial way of life. But this is a subjective response, possibly not shared by others. The point remains that this is a useful, imaginative approach to the observation of holidays and celebrations. Even those who still want to keep their credit cards will find much of value and interest in these pages.

Stewart, Martha, and Elizabeth Hawes. **Entertaining.** New York: Potter, 1982. 310p. $35 (642)

Whether the party is for a couple or for 300 guests, the reader will find just the right menu here to ensure success. Other books are better for the finer points of entertaining, for here the focus is on food. The chapters are divided into types of parties, with large weddings at one extreme and intimate gatherings at the other. There are also divisions by type of food from cocktails to omelets to massive dinners. The recipes are detailed, exact, and easy to follow. There are good tips, too, on the presentation of the meal, including table settings and flower arrangements. All of this is served up in a handsome format that includes numerous colored illustrations.

Williams, Milton. **The Party Book: Everything You Need to Know for Imaginative Never Fail Entertaining at Home.** Garden City, NY: Doubleday, 1981. 224p. $16.95 (642)

The supposition here is twofold. First, the vast experience of the author in giving parties should be of value and interest. This is true, since he carefully explains what goes into his entertaining and how it can be duplicated. Second, there is a focus on parties given for certain holidays and for specific ethnic groups, which the author assumes will be useful. It is, at least for most readers. The ethnic parties may have a more limited appeal, yet they too suggest a wealth of ideas. Good illustrations, clear writing, and a sense of humor make this a good book for almost anyone. There is a catch. For the more elaborate parties, and there are many of these, the party giver must have considerable sums of money to support the effort. Still, even here, one might cut corners, and, again, the ideas are important.

EXHIBITIONS

Witteborg, Lothar. **Good Show! A Practical Guide for Temporary Exhibitions.** Washington, DC: Smithsonian Institution Pr., 1981. 172p. $17.50 (069.5)

What steps does one have to take to mount a small or medium-sized exhibition of art, crafts, or any other subject? Detailed answers are given by an expert in such matters. The author begins with the basic planning required to hold a show, and then moves on to such topics as space requirements, individual booths, construction of walls, booths, flooring, etc. There is even a section on making it easy for the handicapped to view the exhibition. Sources of equipment and a further-reading list are given, and the whole is supported by good line drawings, tables, charts, and diagrams. Written specifically for the person who knows little or nothing about such matters, this is the guide to make the staging of a show a success.

FALCONRY

Ford, Emma. **Birds of Prey.** Newton Centre, MA: Branford, 1983. 64p. pap. $8.95 (799.23)
   Admittedly this is an esoteric subject, but for those who are interested in falconry (the "birds of prey" in the title), it is a good guide. There is an overview of the different breeds of birds and then general instructions on training them. The text is supported by over 40 beautiful color photographs and even for the person who is not interested in the actual care and training of the bird, it is a fascinating book to read.

FARMING

Bartlett, J. V. **Handy Farm and Home Devices and How to Make Them.** Cambridge, MA: MIT Pr., 1981. 304p. pap. $7.95 (600)
   An oddity, this appeared in Australia over 30 years ago. It is a reprint, and at first view would seem to be of little value to modern readers. Look again. Thanks to the precise directions, the universal value of the devices and tools, and the truly ingenious labor-saving ideas, the book is one of the best of its kind. It may be used by auto buffs, farmers, homeowners, campers, and the just plain curious. Here are projects, tools, and directions on how to save time and effort in daily living. Some instructions are a trifle hard to follow, but this is the exception. Most of the projects are simple, requiring a minimum of skill and tools. The illustrations are good.

Bultitude, John. **Apples: A Guide to the Identification of International Varieties.** Seattle: University of Washington Pr., 1984. 323p. $50 (634)
   While not the usual identification guide, this is certainly different enough to warrant consideration by the reader who has ever puzzled over selecting the best apple. An expert in such matters, the author describes over 250 different national and international varieties. There is detail (too much for most readers) on everything from the shape and size of the apple to its ideal color and the season for its best development. Along the way are hints concerning flavor. Although this is essentially a scholarly guide, it may be of value to involved laypersons.

Burch, Monte. **Building Small Barns, Sheds and Shelters.** Pownal, VT: Garden Way, 1982. 224p. pap. $10.95 (690.89)
   The title, while literally a description of scope, really fails to point up the value of the book for the average homeowner. Thanks to extremely detailed instructions, charts, and illustrations and an exceptionally clear presentation, most of the advice on construction of small buildings will be useful for anyone, not just the farmer or homesteader. True, livestock buildings are the major focus, but in showing the

reader how to build a small shed or barn the author indirectly demonstrates how the same building might be used, with slight modifications, for storing tools or as a workshop.

Deming, Dick. **Back at the Farm.** New York: Van Nostrand, 1982. 288p. $17.95; pap. $10.95 (636.19)

For anyone who wants to give up urban life and try living "back at the farm," this is a fine introduction. It is not, however, for the experienced. The author assumes the reader is completely green to the delights of farming, and spells out each and every step necessary to establishing a farm. Particular attention is given to raising animals—including bees and fish. There are informative sections, too, on vegetables and fruit. In fact, those who may never make it back to the farm will enjoy reading about life outside the city.

U.S. Department of Agriculture. **Farm Lighting.** Washington, DC: GPO, 1981. 13p. (A1.9:2243/2)

Despite the title, this is a useful guide for anyone planning even a minimum of outdoor lighting, e.g., around a recreation area, backyard, swimming pool, etc. There is also a section on indoor lighting. Both parts consider types of fixtures, placement, and so on.

U.S. Department of Agriculture. **Handbook of Water Harvesting.** Washington, DC: GPO, 1983. 45p. $4 (A1.76:600)

Water harvesting is a way of collecting and conserving water. Various methods of storing rain and excess water supplies are given in detail. The guide shows how to design, build, and maintain different kinds of systems that can be used to provide water for animals or domestic use.

U.S. Department of Agriculture. **Living on a Few Acres.** Washington, DC: GPO, 1978. 432p. $13 (A1.10:978)

This is the 1978 *Yearbook of Agriculture,* and like all works in this series, it is devoted to a single subject. (The 1981 yearbook, for example, focuses on the importance of U.S. agriculture in helping to feed the world.) Here experts consider the pros and cons of someone starting up a small farm, i.e., 10 to 50 acres. Details are given as to types of farms to consider, equipment, financing, and most important, the types of crops likely to bring profit.

U.S. Department of Agriculture. **Report and Recommendations on Organic Farming.** Washington, DC: GPO, 1980. 94p. $5.50 (A1.2:Or3/3)

Here government experts present an easy-to-understand, basic approach to organic farming—for both the beginner and the established farmer. There is a section on the history and background of organic farming as well as chapters on research, methods of beginning, and its likely future in this country. More emphasis is given here to an overview rather than to specific instructions. A related document is the *Organic Farming Act of 1982* (Y3.Ag 8/1-97SSS).

Weisburd, Claudia. **Raising Your Own Livestock.** Englewood Cliffs, NJ: Prentice-Hall, 1980. 314p. $15.95; pap. $7.95 (636.2)

Once back on the farm, then what? In this well-written guide, an experienced farmer suggests raising livestock, not only for personal use, but for sale. The author covers the purchase and care of such animals as goats, cattle, swine, chickens, and even horses and dairy cows. After an introduction on basics, Weisburd moves into specific instructions for each type of livestock. There are numerous illustrations to enhance points about health, care, feeding, and breeding of animals.

FENCES & WALLS

Chamberlin, Susan. **Fences, Gates & Walls: How to Design and Build.** Tucson, AZ: HP Books, 1983. 160p. pap. $9.95 (643.55)
    What kind of fence, gate, or wall do you want or need? The author suggests an answer by beginning this guide with photographs of various designs of these objects in use throughout the United States. Specific instructions are given on how to select materials for and build a fence or wall. The book is particularly helpful for its suggestions on a wide range of materials that might be employed, and for the variety of situations in which a protective surrounding is needed. The drawback is that the author tries to cover almost too much. Where one would want a more complex fence or wall, it would be better to turn to a book dedicated specifically to that type of project.

Proulx, Annie. **Plan and Make Your Own Fences and Gates, Walkways, Walls and Drives.** Emmaus, PA: Rodale, 1983. 225p. $16.95; pap. $11.95 (643.55)
    This differs from many how-to-do-it books about beautifying the area around the house in that the author draws on a historical background and other books (to which she makes general reference) to show how one can learn to make outstanding replicas from the past, and puts particular emphasis on the use of materials such as stone and wood that may already be about the house and grounds. The result is an idea book for everything from post and rail fences to patios and flagstone walks. The step-by-step instructions are clear, and are usually accompanied by illustrations.

Ramsey, Dan. **The Complete Book of Fences.** Blue Ridge Summit, PA: TAB, 1983. 242p. $19.95; pap. $12.95 (631.2)
    By "complete" Ramsey means he treats basic types of fences in separate chapters. For example, there is a section on the traditional picket fence and still another on wire fences. In each chapter or section there are illustrations and details on materials and construction. Other suggestions for protection range from landscaping devices to walls. In terms of design this is not a good guide. Chamberlin (q.v.) offers a much better approach. But in terms of how-to-do-it, with complete coverage of the subject, Ramsey is about as basic as one can get.

FENCING

Shaff, Jo. **Fencing.** New York: Atheneum, 1982. 125p. $9.95 (796.8)
    A university fencing coach explains how the sport is played, marking each position and thrust with good photographs. In addition to the author's concern with various aspects of the fencer in action, she discusses as well various types of equipment, the basic weapons employed, exercise, coaching, and even fencing in drama. All of this is done briefly, yet with style. It is a fine introduction to the art.

FIELD GUIDES. *See* Animals—Field Guides

FIRE PREVENTION

Blair, William. **Fire: Survival & Prevention.** New York: Barnes & Noble, 1983. 176p. pap. $3.95 (628.9)

Relatively easy, inexpensive steps may be taken to protect oneself from fire in the home. Here, a Chicago fire commissioner explains what to do to guarantee a high degree of safety, and what action to take if a fire should nonetheless develop (an escape plan should be worked out and rehearsed). For example, as a precautionary measure, he urges the use of smoke detectors and fire extinguishers. The author also offers suggestions for reacting to fires in cars, hotels, and mobile homes, among other places.

National Fire Protection Association. **Fire Protection Handbook.** New York: The Association, 1904– . Irreg. 1983 ed., $43.50 (363.3)

While this is written for professionals, much of the information will be of value to anyone contemplating fire protection for a home, a business, or another type of building. Specific data are given on the types of construction that guarantee maximum protection, and there are sections on various kinds of fire-fighting aids.

Smith, Dennis. **Dennis Smith's Fire Safety Book: Everything You Need to Know to Save Your Life.** New York: Bantam, 1983. 141p. pap. $2.95 (628.92)

A veteran New York fire fighter explains how to prevent a fire, and, if one breaks out, what to do to save life and property. The advice covers a wide range of situations from home and business to travel locations. The focus is on the typical reaction to fire (panic) and the need for training, education, and common sense to ensure calm, measured steps to fight the fire. Possibly even more important are the suggestions on how to prevent fires—from careful attention to the heating sources in a home to the best type of smoke detector. Most of this is supported with useful illustrations.

FIREARMS. *See* Fishing & Hunting

FIREPLACES & STOVES

Bortz, Paul. **Getting More Heat from Your Fireplace.** Pownal, VT: Garden Way, 1981. 156p. pap. $5.95 (697.1)

If there is a fireplace in the home, this book will explain how to get more effective heat from that source. The author is concerned with how to improve the efficiency of the fireplace, that is, how one can enjoy a fire without losing a vast amount of heat up the chimney. Sections cover basic instructions on chimney and fireplace maintenance and techniques for adding various inserts and accessories. There is a good glossary and a list of manufacturers.

Harrington, Geri. **Fireplace Stoves, Hearths & Inserts: A Coal & Wood Burner's Guide & Catalog.** New York: Harper, 1980. 178p. $20; pap. $8.95 (683.8)

When you have a fireplace and a chimney and want to install a wood-burning stove, what do you do, and where do you turn for equipment? The answers are here, as well as suggestions for the use of coal-burning stoves. The method is to detail and list specifications for a wide variety of possibilities. There are illustrations and a list of manufacturers. The advice is such that the book will not rapidly go out of date, and the basic information on such things as pollution, types of wood to purchase, and basics on equipment will always be useful.

Harrington, Geri. **The Wood Burning Stove Book.** Rev. ed. New York: Collier, 1979. 234p. pap. $7.95 (697)

What is the best wood stove for your particular needs? The reliable answer is here, along with complete coverage of some 70 models. There is even a glossary, and the book is frequently updated. The related title, with more information about growing and gathering wood and safety tips about wood burning, is *Heating with Wood* (Butterick, 1978).

Morrison, James. **The Homeowner's Guide to Coalburning Stoves and Furnaces.** New York: Arco, 1981. 172p. $11.95; pap. $6.95 (697)

While Americans fought to get away from coal-burning stoves and furnaces after World War II, the high cost of energy now makes them desirable—at least for some. For them, the author gives the advantages of the coal-burning stove, and there is a good discussion of the various choices of stoves and furnaces available. There is a section, too, on boilers and safety and standards. The part devoted to the possible difficulties and problems with coal is objective, although understandably not overstressed. There is a good list of sources of equipment and information aids.

Traister, John. **All about Chimneys.** Blue Ridge Summit, PA: TAB, 1982. 232p. $13.95; pap. $8.95 (697.8)

The subtitle is "building, using, maintaining and repairing" chimneys, and Traister is more or less true to his promise. More, in that he considers related matters from the proper firewoods and stoves to methods of building a good blaze. Less, in that there are only general instructions, usually with adequate illustrations, for the construction of chimneys. He is concerned not only with fireplaces and chimneys in the home, but with outdoor units as well. While all of this serves as a good introduction to the subject, and may be quite enough for masons and bricklayers, others should turn to more specific manuals for actual chimney construction.

U.S. Department of Energy. **What about Fireplaces.** Washington, DC: GPO, 1980. 18p. $2.25 (E1.28:DOE/TIC-11)

This is a brief explanation of the benefits and drawbacks of using an existing fireplace to heat, or partially heat, a home. There are computations on the relative costs of fireplaces for heating.

FISH AS FOOD. *See* Cooking—Fish & Game & Outdoor

FISH (PETS)

Axelrod, Herbert, and L. P. Schultz. **Handbook of Tropical Aquarium Fishes.** Rev. ed. Neptune City, NJ: TFH, 1983. 718p. pap. $8.95 (639.84)

Axelrod is a well-known authority on tropical fish, and has written numerous works on the subject. This is a standard guide in the field, and is now in its third revision. The book begins with basic information on aquariums and the plants one may use to make the structures more appealing and healthy for the fish. There is also somewhat dated information on tropical fish diseases. The point of turning to the book, however, is for accurate descriptions of the basic types of tropical fish. There are more than 400 entries, fully illustrated, with not only complete descriptions of the individual fish, but useful data on such things as the food they eat and their temperature requirements.

Note: For an encyclopedic approach to the same subject, see the author's *Exotic Tropical Fishes* (rev. ed., 1983). The 1,300-plus pages come in loose-leaf form and literally cover every type of tropical fish. Much too detailed for the person with an ordinary hobby, it is a useful guide for unusual problems.

Braemer, Helga, and Ines Scheurmann. **Tropical Fish: Everything about Freshwater Aquariums and the Selection and Care of Fish.** Woodbury, NY: Barron's, 1983. 80p. pap. $3.95 (639.3)

Everything the beginner needs to know about tropical fish, and a bit more, is found here. This short, concise guide may be of limited use to the expert, who will want a more comprehensive approach, but for others it is ideal because it is uncomplicated and straightforward. There are numerous color photographs to support the brief descriptions, as well as some good drawings. In addition to identifying the best types of tropical fish for the home, the authors answer questions such as what type of aquarium is necessary and how often and what one should feed the fish. There is even a section on diseases and decorations, the latter being somewhat more garish than many readers will find acceptable. This book is a good starting place.

Paysen, Klaus. **The Larousse Guide to Aquarium Fishes.** New York: Larousse, 1981. 230p. pap. $10.95 (639.3)

First published in 1970, this is a translation of a German work that will be of great help to both beginners and people who already have tropical fish as their hobby. There are over 600 color photographs of fishes in their natural habitat. These are cross-referenced to descriptive material, which has additional line drawings and suggestions on the best conditions and care for raising and maintaining the particular type of fish. The book is well indexed, and will be of great help to anyone trying to identify a fish, or, more likely, attempting to determine whether the fish should be included in the home aquarium.

Sterba, Gunther, ed. **The Aquarium Encyclopedia.** Cambridge, MA: MIT Pr., 1983. 605p. $35 (639.3)

From tank to fish, from plants to filter systems—it is all here, and in considerable detail for both the amateur and the expert. This is *the* basic reference work for anyone involved with aquariums, whether one tank or a building filled with fish. There are some 1,000 illustrations, in black and white and in color, that augment the text. Explanations, definitions, and discussions of both major and minor matters are given in full. There is basic information on the various families of fish, as well as invertebrates and plants often found in aquariums. There are excellent discussions, too, of fish physiology and behavior, as well as diseases, water problems, filters, etc. As in most encyclopedias, the longer articles tend to deal with general topics such as diseases, while the shorter pieces cover specific, sometimes quite small, items of interest. Although originally published in Europe, the work is suitable for Americans, and the translation is good.

Vevers, Gwynne. **The Pocket Guide to Aquarium Fishes.** New York: Simon & Schuster, 1980. 180p. pap. $6.95 (639.34)

The difference between a guppy and a goldfish is evident even to the casual viewer, but when it comes to finding differences between related families of fish and being able to identify one from the other, this guide will prove useful. Thanks to striking illustrations, most in full color, and meticulous descriptions, even an amateur may be able to detect and name the elusive fish that finds its way into an aquarium. Beyond that, the author gives directions on how to select, care for, and breed various types of tank fish. There is even advice on diseases and on differences between freshwater and saltwater fish. Carefully organized and well written, this is one of the better books in this field.

FISHING & HUNTING

Bay, Kenneth. **How to Tie Freshwater Flies.** New York: Winchester, 1974. 151p. $10 (688.7)

A combination of first-rate photographs, some in color, and the excellent explanation of fly-tying techniques guarantees first place for this book in its category. The author has a pleasant writing style and he is able to combine the joys of fishing with the routines of tying flies. He gives specific instructions for each type of fly, and shows the kinds of tools and materials necessary. Even the most awkward beginner, not to mention the near expert, will profit from the close-up photographic illustrations that are an integral part of the explanation of basic patterns for wet and dry flies.

Fisher, Jeffrey. **The Fish Book.** Verplanck, NY: Emerson, 1981. 128p. $8.95 (799.1)

The obvious empathy between the author and the subject need not be labored, but if anyone is interested in learning the basics of fishing, turn to Fisher. Beginning at the beginning, Fisher explains the different approaches to catching fish and what type of gear is needed. There is even an explanation of how to bait a hook and how to scale a fish for cooking. The style is brisk and even humorous, but the advice is solid enough, right down to various fish recipes. There is also a section on canning, pickling, or otherwise preserving the day's catch.

Lee, David. **Fly Fishing: A Beginner's Guide.** Englewood Cliffs, NJ: Prentice-Hall, 1982. 190p. $16.95 (799.1)

Nicely illustrated, easy to read, and much fun to look through, this is by far one of the best guides of its type. The author has wide experience in the sport, and covers every aspect of it, from equipment to landing the fish itself. The writing style is as enthusiastic as it is informative. The guide is not just for beginners, but for anyone short of an expert.

McClane, A. J. **McClane's New Standard Fishing Encyclopedia and International Angling Guide.** 2nd ed. New York: Holt, 1974. 1,156p. o.p. (799.1)

Almost anything anyone ever wanted to know about angling is in this massive encyclopedia. The subject matter is arranged alphabetically, and there are illustrations on nearly every page. Each article is the work of an expert, and the information is quite reliable. Of particular value to fishing enthusiasts are the complete descriptions of individual species of fish. In addition to the basics about fishing, there is considerable related material, ranging from aquatic biology to discussions of algae and fish diseases. This is the basic encyclopedia in the field, and it is updated about every ten years.

O'Connor, Jack, et al. **Complete Book of Shooting: Rifles, Shotguns, Handguns.** Rev. ed. Harrisburg, PA: Stackpole, 1982. 376p. $24.95 (683.4)

A basic book on firearms, this is divided into the fundamentals of rifle shooting, hunting with the rifle, target shooting; fundamentals of shotgun shooting, hunting with the shotgun; trap and skeet shooting; safety and care; and handgun shooting. Various authors describe the weapons, show how they are to be used and fired, and then consider rules of the shooting game. The illustrations are adequate, but in no way match the quality of the text, with its enthusiastic writers who are dedicated to a safe, sane use of firearms.

Ovington, Ray. **Basic Bait Fishing.** Harrisburg, PA: Stackpole, 1984. 160p. pap. $9.95 (799.12)

How does one land a fish with a worm or a grasshopper? Actually, few amateur or experienced lake or stream enthusiasts need much instruction—or at least they think they don't. True, one should consult books for the more socially acceptable fly fishing, but why have a manual on bait fishing? The answer is given by an expert who goes considerably beyond bait to explore other aspects of the sport. Parenthetically, there is more to bait than a worm, as the author patiently explains. He is as concerned with the proper type of rod and line for freshwater and saltwater fishing as he is about what is on the hook. There are some startling methods of fishing detailed in this book that should be welcome to beginners and experts alike.

Ovington, Ray. **Tactics on Bass.** New York: Scribner's, 1983. 278p. $19.95 (799.1)

Ovington is a major figure in the world of fishing, and his delightful tract on trout (*Tactics on Trout*) is a classic. In this book he turns to bass, and with a combination of how-to-do-it and philosophical ruminations so familiar to readers of his other work, he develops still another book for any fishing enthusiast. Which is to say that one does not have to have an abiding love of bass to appreciate this book, although bass are about as plentiful as water and a favored fish almost all across the country. There is much general fishing lore and many solid ideas on the art of fishing. There are details on everything from types of lures to tricks of catching bass that give this work a very specific tone. The author's marvelous writing style, his sure grasp of the subject, and his abiding love of the sport make this required reading.

Pfeiffer, C. Boyd, and Irv Swope. **The Practical Fisherman.** Piscataway, NJ: New Century, 1982. 224p. pap. $12.95 (799.1)

With the emphasis on "practical," the authors introduce the layperson to the joys of fishing. The assumption is that the reader knows nothing about the sport but wishes to fish.. These two outdoor writers manage to cover about every possible situation from freshwater to saltwater fishing, from various types of gear and boats to insect repellents. They believe in covering lakes, streams, and oceans with equal care. The result is a fine introduction, which dedicated fishing fans might follow up with more detailed guides to specific aspects of the sport.

Rosenthal, Mike. **North America's Freshwater Fishing Book.** New York: Scribner's, 1982. 272p. $15.95 (799.1)

What is the best kind of tackle for landing freshwater fish? The author explains this and the finer points of fly fishing, baitcasting, and spinning to novice anglers. Specific directions are given in the second part of the book, where the methods of catching 22 different species are considered. The author is a practical fisherman who loves the sport. The book is well illustrated and organized.

Sparano, V. T. **Complete Outdoors Encyclopedia.** 2nd ed. New York: Harper, 1980. 610p. $16.95 (799)

Extremely well illustrated, this differs from many general outdoors guides in that the emphasis is on fishing and hunting. These areas are covered in some depth, and include such things as selecting cartridges and guns and tackle and fishing rods. Identification and handling of various types of fishing and hunting equipment are considered in detail. Related matters, from camping and boating to trail blazing, are considered with equal skill. There is a now somewhat dated list of agencies that the hunter or fishing enthusiast will find of value.

U.S. Coast Guard. **Anglers Guide to the United States Atlantic Coast.** Washington, DC: GPO, 1974–1977. 8 vols. 16–25p. ea. $9–$9.50 ea. (C55:308An4)

These eight books are filled with charts showing where various types of game fish are usually found, and identifying fishing and boating facilities on the Atlantic Coast. There are illustrations of species of game fish likely to be found around a given area of the coast, as well as discussions of local fishing conditions and characteristics. All volumes are printed in large (16" x 14") format.

The eight volumes include Passamaquoddy Bay, Maine to Cape Cod; Nantucket Shoals to Long Island Sound; Block Island to Cape May, New Jersey; Delaware Bay to False Cape, Virginia; Chesapeake Bay; False Cape, Virginia to Altamaha Sound, Georgia; Altamaha Sound, Georgia, to Fort Pierce Inlet, Florida; and St. Lucie Inlet, Florida, to the Dry Tortugas.

U.S. Coast Guard. **Anglers Guide to the United States Pacific Coast.** Washington, DC: GPO, 1977. 139p. $8.50 (C55.308:An4/2)

This includes a series of section-by-section maps showing the more frequently fished areas, the species of fish commonly taken, and the facilities available on the Pacific Coast. Included too is an illustrated roster of over 200 game fish.

Wisner, Bill. **The Fishermen's Sourcebook.** New York: Macmillan, 1983. 320p. $23.99 (799)

Here is an encyclopedic approach to fishing by a well-known author and *Newsday* fishing writer. Wisner covers almost every conceivable topic of interest to the fishing enthusiast, from identification of game fish to an extensive analysis and review of equipment. Various approaches to catching fish—from flies to worms—are considered, as are the leading places to engage in the sport. All is organized in an easy-to-follow fashion, and the writing is professional, quite up to the best of his previous books and columns.

FLEA MARKETS. *See* Secondhand Trade

FLOWERS. *See* Gardening; Nature Study

FLOWERS, DRIED

Wiita, Betty. **Dried Flowers for All Seasons.** New York: Van Nostrand, 1982. 138p. $18.95 (745.92)

If the reader thinks the only way to dry flowers is in the pages of a book, consider the microwave oven. More conventional methods, of course, are carefully described as well, and this is the first place to turn for detailed information on the art. In addition to explaining the different approaches to drying flowers, the author offers many suggestions on their use in decoration. A useful feature is the arrangement of projects by the types of flowers available at certain periods of the year. There are good illustrations, including some color photographs.

FLYING. *See* Airplanes, Military; Airplanes—Piloting; Balloons; Gliding

FOLK ART. *See* Antiques; Handicrafts

FOOD

See also Cooking; Drinks; Mushrooms; Wine

Coyle, Patrick. **The World Encyclopedia of Food.** New York: Facts on File, 1982. 780p. $40 (641.03)

Everything, and then some, that the average reader wants to know about the history and background of food can be found in this alphabetically arranged encyclopedia. There are about 4,000 entries, which concentrate on little-known facts and distant lore. The illustrations are numerous—well over 300 black-and-white photographs and drawings and some 50 color plates. It should be emphasized that the book is not directed to someone who is looking for specific recipes or meal plans, nor to the scholar. It is a popular treatise for the individual who never gets enough information about food.

Elias, Thomas, and Peter Dykeman. **Field Guide to North American Edible Wild Plants.** New York: Van Nostrand, 1983. 286p. $22.95 (581.63)

According to these expert botanists, there are some 200 fairly common edible wild plants in North America—plants that can be used to make tasty dishes. While the authors provide only a few recipes, they do offer illustrations, usually color photographs, of each of the plants; detailed descriptions of each; various methods of cutting while at the same time preserving the growing plant; and maps and other keys indicating likely hunting grounds. They include information about how each plant may be used—in a drink or as a spice, for example—and in what season it flourishes. There is also a useful guide to poisonous plants that closely resemble their benign cousins. As authoritative as it is useful, this is a basic guide.

Ensrud, Barbara. **The Pocket Guide to Cheese.** New York: Perigee, 1981. 138p. pap. $4.95 (641.373)

A handy paperback, this should serve anyone who wanders into a delicatessen or cheese emporium and is lost trying to make decisions over which cheese to buy. The author, who writes as well as she explores the world of cheese, divides her book into sections by country. Under each she gives the standard cheeses with outline information on such things as taste, appearance, etc. Numerous illustrations, including maps, help matters along. Particularly useful: sections on matching cheeses with wines, suggestions for selection and serving, and an index that lists each cheese by name.

Hillman, Howard. **The Art of Dining Out.** New York: Pocket Bks., 1984. 89p. pap. $5.95 (380.14)

An expert on food, wine, and the good life offers a conversational approach to the fine art of getting the best meal for the money when eating out. The first and most important step is selecting the proper restaurant, and here Hillman suggests how one goes about making the choice. Once seated, how does one order wine, determine the best dish, handle the waiter, overcome accidents, and in general have a good time? All of these and scores of other questions are answered from a practical, not a theoretical, point of view. The confidence the author shows is contagious, particularly when supported by various suggestions and even a glossary of translated items from the typical Italian or French menu. One might wish to slip this into a pocket or purse and consult it when the waiter indicates a tip is in order. *Note:* The suggestions are primarily for an individual or a couple, but there is some advice on dealing with larger groups.

Redenbacher, Orville. **Orville Redenbacher's Popcorn Book.** New York: St. Martin's, 1984. 97p. pap. $4.95 (641.6)

An odd mixture of anecdotes, autobiography, history, recipes, and unabashed public relations, this is the kind of book one accepts or rejects quickly. In the latter category will be those who object to the fact that the author is so well known. Redenbacher claims to be the source of the best popcorn about (Redenbacher's Gourmet Popping Corn). He is somewhat obsessive about the subject, and his charm becomes slightly trying. On the other hand, where else can one find close to 60 recipes for popcorn, each and every one of them different?

Root, Waverley. **Food.** New York: Simon & Schuster, 1980. 602p. $24.95 (641.03)

Almost anything you want to know about food will be found in this "authoritative and visual history and dictionary of the foods of the world," as the subtitle puts it. The author, a leading historian of food, is as witty as he is authoritative. He arranges the entries in dictionary order and moves with ease from the aardvark to the Zulu nut. Root combines directions on how to cook with folklore, history, and short essays on everything from the development of certain types of vegetables to varieties of meat. The illustrations, some in color, are excellent, and the coverage is truly wide. Although not the first place the reader is likely to turn for a recipe, it is an unsurpassed source of ideas and background information to enliven the kitchen and the table. The author also has written *The Food of France* (1973) and *The Food of Italy* (1977).

U.S. Department of Agriculture. **Cheese Varieties and Descriptions.** Washington, DC: GPO, 1978. 151p. $2.75 (A1.76-54/978)

This basic guide includes considerable details on cheese and cheese production.

The writing style is not all it should be, but the data are accurate and the information is more complete than that found in some commercial books.

U.S. Department of Agriculture. **Meat and Poultry Products: A Consumer Guide to Content and Labeling Requirements.** Washington, DC: GPO, 1981. 23p. (A1.77:236)
   How can you tell the grade of meat or poultry and its consequent taste? This government bulletin gives details on what those product labels mean.

U.S. Department of Agriculture. **Storing Vegetables and Fruits in Basements, Cellars, Outbuildings and Pits.** Washington, DC: GPO, 1980. 18p. $2.25 (A1.77:119/4)
   While written for a farm family, much of the advice here will be of value to anyone who buys and stores more than a day's supply of vegetables and fruits. There are clear instructions on types of facilities needed, how to prepare existing storage places, and temperature and humidity considerations.

FOOD—CANNING & FREEZING

Hood, Joan, and Vivian Donald. **Will It Freeze?** New York: Scribner's, 1982. 192p. $12.95 (641.4)
   Can you, should you, freeze bread, duck, or string beans? To find the answer the reader looks up the food in this alphabetically arranged guide. After each item the authors give the yes or no signal (a missing product indicates a no), and then suggests the best time to freeze, containers needed if any, and defrosting instructions. There are handy tips on how to pack a freezer, what to do when it switches off, and how to handle refreezing. Written by British experts, this book is one of the easiest of its kind to use, and is reliable.

Sunset Canning, Freezing & Drying. Menlo Park, CA: Lane, 1981. 128p. $4.95 (641.4)
   This nicely illustrated guide covers the basic types of food preservation. The book is divided into the three major sections of the title, and each opens with a general explanation of the process as well as its advantages and disadvantages. There are step-by-step directions for each process, as well as information on various types of equipment that may be needed. The guide concludes with recipes that draw on the knowledge imparted in each section. One of the best introductions to the subject, this is recommended for beginners of almost any age.

U.S. Department of Agriculture. **Home Canning of Fruits and Vegetables.** Washington, DC: GPO, 1983. 31p. $3.25 (A1.77:8/12)
   Basics of canning are offered here in this illustrated guide. The procedures are those guaranteed to save both money and time. The photographs, tables, and other illustrations make this extremely easy to follow.

U.S. Department of Agriculture. **Home Freezing of Fruits and Vegetables.** Rev. ed. Washington, DC: GPO, 1982. 48p. pap. $3.50 (A1.77:10/8)
   This is a two-part pamphlet. The first section sets down general rules for the purchase, preparation, and freezing of fruits and vegetables. The second section

considers specific types of products and gives equally specific instructions on freezing.

Walker, Charlotte. **Freezing & Drying.** San Francisco: Ortho, 1984. 96p. $5.95 (641.6)

How to freeze or dry almost any food product is described and carefully illustrated here. Following the usual pattern of Ortho guides, the book is clearly written and there are detailed diagrams and illustrations, many in color. The freezing section covers everything from meat and fish to vegetables and baked goods. Smoking and oven drying are featured in the part devoted to drying foods. Suitable for beginner and intermediate-level cooks.

FOOD—PURCHASE OF

Hodgson, Moira. **The New York Times Gourmet Shopper: A Guide to the Best Foods.** New York: Times Books, 1983. 368p. $15.50 (641)

Practical tips on how to recognize the best, the freshest, fish or one of 187 types of mustard are only a few of the hundreds of pieces of advice liberally scattered throughout this illustrated guide. The focus is on how to shop with skill and bring home not only the bacon, but the best and most interesting bacon. The sections on fresh food are particularly good. Here the author explains how vegetables are grown, what to check for when shopping, and how to store produce. Sections end with recipes. The guide is useful for any part of North America, and, for that matter, the world. It is a joy simply to dip into and read.

Powledge, Fred. **Fat of the Land: What's Behind Your Shrinking Food Dollar—and What You Can Do about It.** New York: Simon & Schuster, 1984. 287p. $15.95 (338.4)

Anyone who shops in a supermarket will profit from reading this guide. A *New Yorker* writer offers a rare view of the actual marketing of food. He shows how a particular crop moves from farm to home, and explains the built-in costs and profits that boost the price of that product. In fact, those in the middle seem to make most of the money—up to 70 percent of the $300 billion or more Americans spend on food. Powledge offers basic hints for shoppers, including careful checking of prices, shopping from a list, and avoiding impulse buying. He believes the ultimate solution to high costs may be a simple one: Americans should simply stop buying the overpriced items.

Salsbury, Barbara, and Cheri Loveless. **Cut Your Grocery Bills in Half: Supermarket Survival.** Washington, DC: Acropolis, 1983. 133p. $14.95 (640)

This gets off to a not-all-together encouraging start when Salsbury explains how she stockpiled an eight months' supply of groceries before her wedding. However, she is good to her promise of revealing methods of halving grocery bills. She looks at dozens of different ways of saving money—from using coupons and following advertisements to making lists—and suggests the good and bad points of each. All this takes a considerable amount of time and effort, although if the reader is as dedicated as the author, half as much in love as she is with shopping, it should be a joy to follow. Others will find just enough good material to justify a cursory glance.

U.S. Department of Agriculture. **Buy Economically: A Food Buyer's Guide.** Washington, DC: GPO, 1981. 29p. (A1.77:235)

This is a simple, direct plan of attack for the individual who wants to know the best way to save money in the supermarket. Tips are given on what to look for in meat and produce, and there are even instructions on carving a chicken. This guide is often updated.

FOOTBALL

Barrett, Frank. **How to Watch a Football Game.** New York: Holt, 1980. 240p. pap. $7.95 (796.33)

Written for both young people and adults, this offers a virtually complete survey of football and suggests what to watch for in the game. The history of the game is given, as are major plays and players. There is a clear explanation of fundamental techniques, as well as a detailed discussion of various strategies. A highlight of the book is the interviews and discussions about the game with players and coaches, as well as some officials.

DeLuca, Sam. **Football Made Easy.** Middle Village, NY: Jonathan David, 1983. 193p. pap. $6.95 (796.332)

Written primarily for the fan, although of great interest to the active player, this guide takes each position and demonstrates what is involved in playing it. The role of the position within the team, the attributes needed by a player, and the basic as well as the wilder possibilities of the game are explored in considerable detail. Although the whole book is dedicated to giving the fan a better idea of what is going on down on the field, there is a final chapter that is simply called "How to Watch a Football Game." Actually, it is a summary and conclusion. *Note:* This is a somewhat different version of the author's earlier *Football Handbook* (1975).

FOSSILS

Glut, Donald. **The New Dinosaur Dictionary.** Secaucus, NJ: Citadel, 1982. $19.95 288p. (567.9)

This will be of great value to the individual who wants to identify various dinosaurs found in museums. (Needless to add, it will be of particular joy to many youngsters. Even those who cannot read will delight in the excellent illustrations.) For each genus there is a brief entry with basic characteristics noted. Particularly useful is the identification of the type of fossil that gives evidence of a genus. The large, handsome format suits the subject.

Lambert, David. **A Field Guide to Dinosaurs: The First Complete Guide to Every Dinosaur Now Known.** New York: Avon, 1983. 256p. pap. $8.95 (567.91)

True, no one needs a guide to identify a dinosaur. It is usually nicely done by museums. Still, given the dinosaur's great popularity, it seems only fitting to have at least one entry on identification. This book provides a lively, well-written discussion of the class, as well as sections devoted to each type. There is enough information here on the size, eating habits, and probable behavioral patterns to satisfy the majority of lay readers. In addition, one finds maps, illustrations, and diagrams to help isolate the peculiar features of one's favorite dinosaur. It is an exaggeration to claim the book is "complete," but it comes close and certainly will meet the needs of the average dinosaur fan between 5 years of age and 100.

Thompson, Ida. **The Audubon Society Field Guide to North American Fossils.** New York: Knopf, 1982. 846p. pap. $12.50 (560.97)

A basic guide for the collector of fossils, this has over 400 color photographs to help identify findings. There are also maps, but these are of indifferent quality. A precise description is provided for each item, including possible age. Arrangement is by shapes of typical specimens, and both marine and freshwater plants, insects, vertebrates, and invertebrates are covered. In addition, there is other useful information ranging from how to collect fossils to a list of good locations in which to hunt for them.

FRAMES, PICTURE. *See* Picture Frames

FREEZING. *See* Food—Canning & Freezing

FRISBEE

Roddick, Dan. **Frisbee Disc Basics.** Englewood Cliffs, NJ: Prentice-Hall, 1980. 48p. $8.95 (796.2)

An award-winning frisbee expert tells young people how to get into the winner's circle. There are explicit warming-up exercises, followed by the basic positions one must assume to control the frisbee. Drawings and numerous photographs show the reader how to throw, catch, and manipulate the disk. There is also a section on purchasing frisbees. While written for those in grades four to eight, it is a suitable manual for any age group.

FRUIT. *See* Food; Vegetable & Fruit Gardening

FURNITURE
See also Antiques; Interior Decoration; Woodworking

Alth, Max, and Charlotte Alth. **The Furniture Buyer's Handbook: How to Buy, Arrange, Maintain, and Repair Furniture.** New York: Walker, 1980. 240p. $14.95; pap. $9.95 (645)

The kinds of things to look for in furniture, besides appearance, are not often considered in basic manuals. Here is an exception, and the Alths point out how to discover whether a piece of furniture is properly joined (or just nailed or glued) and what are the best finishes, among other checkpoints. The rules are applicable to both new and antique furniture, and there are sections on both, including a good discussion of two extremes—rattan and high-tech furnishing. There are less-useful sections on maintenance and cleaning, as well as some hints on purchasing rugs and carpets. Adequately illustrated.

Alth, Max, and Charlotte Alth. **Making Plastic Pipe Furniture.** New York: Everest House, 1981. 154p. $13.95; pap. $8.95 (684.1)

How to make high-tech furniture with a minimum of expense and effort is the promise of this introductory book. It fulfills the promise with easy-to-follow directions, photographs, and diagrams for building 11 pieces for indoor and outdoor use. There is an introductory section on techniques and necessary tools, and an explanation of the materials to be employed. In this case it is white polyvinyl chloride pipe that you can purchase from a hardware or plumbing supply house.

Ball, R., and P. Campbell. **Masterpieces.** New York: Hearst, 1983. 144p. $22.45 (684.10)

Too many do-it-yourself furniture books give excellent instructions, yet fail to offer patterns suitable for homes where aesthetic taste is as important as durability. Trying to put things right, the authors suggest furniture patterns that have special artistic merit since they were the creations of famous artists. These range from the Matisse chair to a Picasso sideboard. The original is reproduced in detail and with step-by-step directions. True, not all pieces are comfortable; yet all are marvels of aesthetic imagination. There are enough good ideas here to make this an invaluable guide, particularly when used in conjunction with one of the more specific how-to-do-it furniture books featured in this section.

Ball, R., and P. Cox. **Low Tech: Fast Furniture for Next to Nothing.** New York: Dial Pr., 1984. 219p. $14.95 (645)

By "low tech" the authors mean the ability to convert other people's discards into furniture. This means the imaginative use of everything from pieces of board and pipe to dismantled or somewhat less than new cabinets. The found objects may be converted into a wide variety of items from tables and seating to delights for the bathroom. Each conversion is explained and there are illustrations and line drawings to show how the change is effected. The specific instructions are supported by methods of construction in the appendix. The nice thing about the guide is its emphasis on good design and the ease with which most of the projects can be carried out.

Bavardo, Joseph, and Thomas Mossman. **The Furniture of Gustav Stickley: History, Techniques and Projects.** New York: Van Nostrand, 1982. 175p. $18.95 (684.1)

The so-called mission style in American furniture is the product of the work and genius of Gustav Stickley. Near the beginning of this century he lent dignity to oak furniture, and foresaw the growing awareness of the simple line as opposed to the baroque line of the Victorian era. His history, as well as a detailed study of his furniture, is given in this excellent guide, which will be of considerable value to anyone interested in antiques. An added bonus: The authors give plans and precise directions on how to build nine pieces of Stickley-designed furniture. The directions are often those set down by the designer himself.

Brann, Donald. **How to Build Colonial Furniture.** 3rd ed. Briarcliff Manor, NY: Easi Bild Directions, 1982. 258p. pap. $6.95 (684.1)

Here are detailed plans for 12 different types of colonial furniture. The plans and text are truly definitive in that absolutely nothing is left to chance, and if the reader is careful the product will be precisely like those pictured. Plans vary from simple tables to chairs and cabinets. They are suitable for young people, as well as adults.

Davis, Kenneth, et al. **Restoring and Reupholstering Furniture.** Emmaus, PA: Rodale, 1982. 177p. $21.95 (684.1)

This is probably the best book on furniture restoration for the amateur, and while it has an English bias, almost all the information is applicable to the American reader. Instructions are supported by illustrations (many in color) on almost every page. The first section gives information on restoration of furniture in general. This is followed by specific projects, which range from chairs to tables. The second half is dedicated to reupholstering and it includes several projects, e.g., redoing a sofa. Thanks to the clear writing style, the illustrations, and the format, this is the ideal starter book for anyone interested in the subject.

Dudgeon, Piers, ed. **The Art of Making Furniture.** New York: Sterling, 1981. 192p. $21.95 (684.08)

What sets this apart from dozens of books on making furniture is the fact that it is a compilation of plans for 30 pieces of furniture by 11 expert designers. Most of the pieces are excellent and fulfill two purposes—they are a handsome addition to the home, and they are relatively easy to construct. Good photographs help the user follow the specific directions. There are also notes on woodworking and certain tools. An added feature is the list of sources of wood to be found state by state.

Feirer, John. **Furniture & Cabinet Making.** New York: Scribner's, 1983. 512p. $17.95 (684.10)

This book, explaining the basic techniques of the art, is written specifically for the person who wishes to improve his or her home, not for the would-be specialist. Except for a few sample projects, there are no specific plans for furniture or cabinets. The focus is on the general skills one needs to master, as well as the tools and materials involved. The book is divided into several broad subject areas from furniture styles to finishing. The text is clear and relatively easy to follow—although the author expects the reader to be an enthusiast, and not someone simply looking for a tip or two on a given type of work. The illustrations are good, and there are some outstanding line drawings of projects.

Graham-Barber, Lynda. **The Furniture Book.** New York: Pantheon, 1982. 159p. pap. $9.95 (684.10)

The point of this book is to demonstrate how easy it is today to buy knockdown, kit furniture. The author is not interested in showing how to build furniture, but how to assemble it. She first discusses the various options open to the reader who may wish to order kit furniture. She explains what is available, relative costs, difficulty of assembly, etc. And while specific directions are not given for assembling all of the furniture, she does have a general introduction to the topic, nicely illustrated with step-by-step details for three basic kits. There is a representative list of suppliers and a bibliography. The primary benefit of this guide is to indicate still another approach to relatively inexpensive, imaginative furniture.

Kinney, Ralph. **The Complete Book of Furniture Repair and Refinishing.** New York: Scribner's, 1981. 276p. $17.95 (684.1)

The word "complete" is not out of place in this title. From establishing a workshop to various types and materials needed for furniture repair and refinishing, the author covers every conceivable situation and type of furniture. The step-by-step instructions are carefully illustrated, and there are numerous photographs, diagrams, and charts. Whether the author is explaining how to cane a chair or refinish a scratched surface, it is all done with exceptional clarity. There is even a section on cleaning furniture.

McGiffin, Robert. **Furniture Care and Conservation.** Nashville, TN: American Association for State and Local History, 1983. 233p. $17.95 (749.1)

In this work, the author, a museum curator, emphasizes the conservation of furniture, particularly antiques. Despite the professional involvement of the author and the publisher, most of the information is of interest to laypersons. Many out-of-the-way facts and considerations found here are not often included in more popular works. For example, there is information on such things as temperature control, storage, moving, and touching up scratches and deeper wounds. Particular emphasis is placed on care that will not damage the original finish. There is some material on repair, but it tends to be too general for most situations. Good black-and-white illustrations are provided.

Miller, Bruce, and Jim Widess. **The Caner's Handbook.** New York: Van Nostrand, 1983. 143p. $25.50 (684.1)

A highly specialized guide, this is the best of its kind. By caning the authors mean wicker, rush, rawhide, splint, Danish cord, etc. The prose style is as enthusiastic as the information is practical, and the instructions are precise. Each step is profusely illustrated with line drawings and photographs. The book ends with a good reading list and a list of suppliers.

Nelson, John A. **Antique Furniture Reproduction.** New York: Van Nostrand, 1982. 126p. $13.95 (749.1)

How to accurately reproduce 15 different pieces of Early American furniture is carefully explained. Included are such pieces as a Shaker drying rack, a Chippendale mirror frame, a Dutch child's bench, and a blanket chest. Each project is fully described and illustrated with enough detail so that any competent woodworker will be able to carry it through to completion. After a drawing and photograph of the finished piece, the author offers step-by-step directions for each item. There are precise dimensions given, as well as recommendations as to types of wood, finishing, and so on.

Nesovich, Peter. **Reupholstering at Home: A Do-It-Yourself Manual for Turning Old Furniture into New Showpieces.** New York: Crown, 1979. 164p. $12.95; pap. $7.95 (684.1)

This is a detailed, beautifully illustrated guide for both beginners and those already familiar with upholstery fundamentals. The author begins with 20 basic steps everyone should follow when they contemplate a project of upholstering. There is information on what types of materials and tools are needed, where to begin, and what should or should not be done in the initial stages of planning. Then specific types of furniture are illustrated and explained in considerable detail, right down to how much material will be needed. One of the best books available on the subject.

Rodd, John. **Repairing and Restoring Antique Furniture.** New York: Van Nostrand, 1982. 240p. pap. $9.95 (684.1)

How does a professional cabinetmaker restore a valuable antique? The secrets are spelled out here, in projects from totally dismantling a piece of furniture to repairing loose joints and renewing leather. The instructions are precise—for everything from chairs and drawers to cabinets—and there are numerous drawings and black-and-white photographs. The assumption is that the reader has an antique worthy of the effort and the skill and patience for such restoration.

Small, Hydee. **The Complete Bed Building Book.** Blue Ridge Summit, PA: TAB, 1979. 432p. $12.95; pap. $7.95 (684.1)

This explains methods of constructing various types of beds and accessories to the amateur. Each of the projects is clearly described and there are numerous illustrations and diagrams to help the reader. The author is as authoritative in explaining the construction of cradles as he is in discussing the merits and drawbacks of waterbeds.

Sunset Editors. **Furniture Upholstery.** Menlo Park, CA: Lane, 1980. 112p. pap. $4.95 (684.1)

Here are step-by-step instructions on basic upholstering. Each of the steps is carefully explained and usually illustrated. There are sections on the tools and equipment needed as well as the various types of materials. Quite basic, this guide is for the beginner.

Watson, Aldren. **Country Furniture.** New York: New Amer. Lib., 1976. 274p. pap. $4.95 (684.1)

Useful for both the how-to-do-it fan and the historian, this is a well-illustrated overview of American colonial furniture. The author, whose excellent line drawings dominate the book, traces the beginnings of woodworking in the United States and then shows precisely how basic pieces were constructed. He stresses not only techniques, but tools and woods used. There is a fine glossary of woodworking terms, and even excerpts from the inventories and records of early furniture makers.

Watts, Simon. **Building a Houseful of Furniture.** Newtown, CT: Taunton, 1983. 211p. $18.95 (684.10)

Here are "43 plans with comments on design and construction" that the average home craftsperson can build without too much difficulty. In order to ensure ease of construction and a minimum of frustration, the author gives specific directions for every step of fabricating the basic types of furniture, from tables to beds and desks. Furthermore, each step is illustrated with photographs and drawings, so there can be no misunderstanding. The styles are subject to some variation since a cabinet-maker may change a piece from traditional to modern by eliminating or adding a small feature. (Not everyone will be pleased with the aesthetics of the plans, particularly the chairs, but this is a matter of taste and has nothing to do with the skills of the author.) The assumption of the book is that the reader knows the basics, although Watts does give necessary information on various finishes, woods, etc.

GAMBLING & BETTING

Ainslie, Tom. **Ainslie's Complete Guide to Thoroughbred Racing.** New York: Simon & Schuster, 1979. 470p. $16.95 (798)

By the author of the equally excellent *How to Gamble in a Casino* (q.v.), this is a basic guide to horse races, written for the beginner who wants to know the ins and outs of the sport. There are thorough discussions of riders and trainers and how these affect the probability of winning. Ainslie covers various methods of betting, from the legal to not so legal, and considers ways of laying a bet. There is a good section on bloodlines, numerous statistics, and information on previous winnings, records, etc. This is one of the first places to turn before going to the track. True, some of the specific information may date, but the general rules and approaches will not.

Ainslie, Tom. **How to Gamble in a Casino: The Most Fun at the Least Risk.** New York: Morrow, 1979. 224p. $10.95 (795)

Explanations of basic casino gambling games are described here. The author, an experienced gambler, also considers such things as the probable odds of winning, and what to do when faced with a difficult gambling decision. Directed to the novice who enjoys gambling but does not make it a habit, the book assumes little or no knowledge of each of the games described. The directions are easy to follow and the author has a winning writing style. It is fine for beginners and amateurs, but of limited value to would-be experts.

Alvarez, A. **The Biggest Game in Town.** Boston: Houghton, 1983. 185p. $13.95 (795.41)

While a far cry from the typical "how-to-do-it" gambling treatise, this is a superb analysis of what it takes to be a gambler. The British author examines the lives and careers of several major Nevada gamblers, and in his careful scrutiny of their backgrounds, methods, and reactions to winning and losing, he establishes the world of professional gamblers as totally apart from the one the rest of us live in. The focus is on the Las Vegas 1981 "World Series of Poker" and the various gamblers who participate in it. Through both interviews and observation, Alvarez offers a complete, reasonably objective guide to the gambling personality. It is fascinating and repellent. Alvarez is a highly literate, lively writer who captures the essence of gambling for anyone even remotely interested in the subject.

Ankeny, Nesmith. **Poker Strategy: Winning with Game Theory.** New York: Basic Books, 1981. 189p. $11.95 (795.41)

Using mathematics and probability, the author demonstrates how a careful player may win in draw poker. Much is made of game and probability theory, but this is always explained in terms of the hands and the game. Thanks to Ankeny's clear writing, this is a guide that is as easy to follow as it is comprehensive. Among numerous titles of its type, this is a basic and superior overview of the subject.

Berger, A. J., and Nancy Bruning. **Lady Luck's Companion.** New York: Harper, 1979. 288p. $13.95 (795)

Not limited to cards and dice, this guide covers all forms of gambling likely to be available to Americans. From the racing track to the stock market, the authors are quite at home. Their basic advice is simple: Be cautious. There is hardly any new material here, or even anything of help to the dedicated gambler. It does excel, though, in its quick, generally reliable overview. For detailed accounts, the gambler should turn to more specific books.

Beyer, Andrew. **The Winning Horseplayer: A Revolutionary Approach to Thoroughbred Handicapping and Betting.** Boston: Houghton, 1983. 192p. $12.95 (798.4)

The secret is in first watching the horse actually race. Beyer, a sportswriter who has written several books on how to beat the horses, here comes up with a traditional scheme of evaluating a horse, point by point, as it is in motion. After that, one is able to decide (using Beyer's numerical system) whether to put money on the horse. Trip handicapping is a method that may or may not work, depending on how observant the bettor happens to be on that day. Beyer is a marvelous writer who is deeply involved with the sport and enlivens every page with a good story. Even nonbetting types should enjoy this book.

Biracree, Tom, and Wendy Insinger. **The Complete Book of Thoroughbred Horse Racing.** New York: Doubleday, 1982. 364p. $14.95 (798.4)

The book lives up to its title and covers almost everything a dedicated follower of the horses wants to know. Using lists and anecdotes, the authors discuss famous horses, races, jockeys, and personalities. While this is not a book for someone who wants to discover a specific method for betting, the information given is of the type required for evolving a betting scheme. There are good illustrations, a detailed index, and both current and historical facts about the subject. Perhaps of less interest is the narrative about two race horses from their first steps to the winner's circle.

Brunson, Doyle. **Super/System: A Course in Power Poker.** Las Vegas, NV: B & G Pub. Co., 1979. 605p. $15 (795.4)

One of the all-time great poker players, Brunson writes a guide that is about as trustworthy as any the reader is likely to find. Writing about it, the author A. Alvarez comments: "Like the title, the prose will not win any prizes—except for the unwavering determination to split every infinitive. But as a postgraduate guide to the intricacies of high level, high stakes poker the work has no equal. . . . Brunson takes . . . basic knowledge for granted. . . . The strategies that interest him are those by which the experts outmaneuver each other when they are playing the fine edges" (*The New Yorker,* March 14, 1983, p. 66).

Ortiz, Darwin. **Gambling Scams: How They Work, How to Detect Them, How to Protect Yourself.** New York: Dodd, 1984. 310p. $15.95 (795)

Anyone who gambles should sit down and read this book carefully. Ortiz points out what every professional gambler knows—it's a jungle out there, with numerous people cheating, lying, and trying anything else to balance the odds in their favor. Precisely what the cheating procedures are in different gambling situations are explained from a to z. Ortiz considers common games from cards to con operations. In addition, he gives solid advice on how to avoid being a victim.

Scarne, John. **Scarne's Guide to Casino Gambling.** New York: Simon & Schuster, 1978. 352p. $9.95 (795.01)

This is one of the best all-around guides to gambling. The casino games are considered in a uniform fashion. Each is explained, with a brief historical background, and then there is statistical data on the chances of winning or breaking even. One of the best sections is devoted to debunking sure-to-win systems. Scarne laces his statistics, warnings, and explanations with numerous anecdotes, and the whole is a joy to read. Although some of the data on casinos are a bit dated, the basic information is solid.

Silberstang, Edwin. **Playboy's Guide to Sports Betting.** New York: Harper, 1982. 336p. $14.50 (796)

Although some people think that most sports betting is a game of chance, others, particularly those attracted to this guide, believe it is one of skill. That is the opinion of the author, who methodically explains how to place a bet on basic sports, in almost any acceptable situation. His particular interests are football, boxing, hockey, basketball, and baseball. Each of the pro teams is carefully considered and charted as one would the performance of a race horse. The author indicates how to keep abreast of this type of calculation, so the book will not go out of date soon. Silberstang covers almost every variable, and if his figures are correct he deserves the boast in his subtitle, namely that a reader can "win big" with his guide. Even for nonbettors, the lore of sports is so well handled here that it makes for entertaining reading.

Silberstang, Edwin. **The Winner's Guide to Casino Gambling.** New York: Holt, 1980. 272p. $12.95 (795)

The secret to beating the casino, or at least breaking more or less even, is careful play. Just how careful one has to be and what moves to make or avoid are discussed here by a literate, experienced gambler. There is no easy approach, Silberstang points out, but common sense and precise attention to detail result in a sure way to win. He is strong on mathematical formulas, and keeping track of what cards are played. The discussion of craps and blackjack, for example, is as much a lesson in probability and mathematics as in gambling. Various types of games are explained to show the mathematical odds and the best type of play to ensure success. The explanations are clear and meticulous, although they generally require of the reader a good memory and an ability for mental computation.

Yardley, Herbert. **The Education of a Poker Player.** New York: Pocket Books, 1961. 167p. (795.42)

Yardley's guide is one of the classics in the field of gambling. The assumption is that the reader knows little or nothing about the game of poker, and the author takes it from there to a successful win. His advice is accurate and conservative so the book is ideal for the beginner. With practice, one then might pass on to Brunson (q.v.).

Zolotow, Maurice. **Confessions of a Racetrack Fiend.** New York: St. Martin's, 1983. 144p. $10.95 (798.4)

The subtitle explains the scope and audience: "how to pick the 6, and my other secrets for the weekend horseplayer." The author, an experienced writer who just happens to be involved with horses, is a cautious man. His advice, unlike that found in scores of books of this type, can be trusted and followed. The reason is that he blows the whistle when the reader is too far over his or her financial head. In fact, he spends as much time with warning signals as with winning. The idea is to have fun, not to go bankrupt or try for millions. Convinced the track is relaxation, Zolotow shows how to improve relaxation with the fun of gambling. He has some first-rate tips on handicapping, and basic background advice on how to read a racing form. An enlightened and entertaining guide.

GAME (WILD). *See* Cooking—Fish & Game & Outdoor

GAMES
    See also Billiards; Bridge; Checkers; Chess; Croquet; Frisbee; Gambling & Betting; Puzzles; Sports; Word Games

Brandreth, Gyles. **The World's Best Indoor Games.** New York: Random House, 1981. 304p. $15.50; pap. $6.95 (793)
    From cards to dice to paper, the author explains the fundamentals of over 300 games that can be played in the home. These are grouped under broad subject headings. Stars are used to designate their complexity and provide a key to the age group for which the game is best suited. Clear instructions, usually with illustrations, accompany each game. The materials needed to play are duly noted. This is an excellent survey of basics from chess to tiddledywinks.

Charlton, James. **Charades: The Complete Guide to America's Favorite Party Game.** New York: Harper, 1983. 151p. $11.95; pap. $6.68 (793.24)
    The dictionary defines charades as "a guessing game in which each syllable of a word to be found is represented by a tableau or by dramatic action." Charades may be one of the oldest parlor games in the world, and here the author offers a brief history. With that, he launches into a description of various categories of hidden terms and how they should be handled by the players. The last part of the book is less helpful because here Charlton offers easy-to-difficult names from such things as plays and landmarks. That detracts from some of the fun because it cuts down on the exercise of imagination. Still, the instructions on how to win and how to baffle opponents are particularly good, and even the photographs of anxious players move things along.

Holmes, John. **Fantasy Role Playing Games.** New York: Hippocrene, 1981. 224p. $14.95 (794)
    Both a how-to guide and a basic explanation of fantasy games such as Dungeons and Dragons, this is for amateurs and experts alike. The author gives brief, often fascinating histories of the games, as well as a rationale for the apparent violence found in many of the more involved ones. Holmes edits the basic rules for Dungeons and Dragons, so he knows of what he speaks. After the history, there are basic rules on how to play the games. The book concludes with addresses of game distributors, manufacturers, and related magazines. There is a useful section on the computer's role in these entertainments. The illustrations are passable, but hardly up to the quality of the discussion and the reference value of the guide.

Newman, Frederick. **Mouthsounds: How to Whistle, Pop, Click and Honk Your Way to Social Success.** New York: Workman, 1980. 127p. pap. $5.95 (790.1)
    Some people never learn to whistle. Still, the vast majority can learn, particularly

when aided by an expert such as Frederick Newman. Here explicit, easy-to-follow instructions, complete with diagrams, drawings, and photographs, ensure success. Beyond the whistle, the author offers close to 65 other sounds that are guaranteed to bring attention to oneself. Among the delights are honks, various rude noises, and a great number of animal calls. Worthwhile for anyone who has ever longed to whistle for a cab or give out a loud raspberry.

Orlick, Terry. **The Second Cooperative Sports & Games Book.** New York: Pantheon, 1982. 226p. $18.50; pap. $8.95 (796.1)

Something on the order of Weinstein's *Playfair* (q.v.), this is more expansive in that it includes rules and regulations for about 200 games and sporting events—as contrasted with about 60 in *Playfair.* The books are much alike, though, in their plea for cooperation rather than competition, in showing methods whereby groups can work together in fun and sports. Here the arrangement is by different age groups, and the activities are for everyone from young children to adults.

Provenzo, Asterie, and Eugene Provenzo. **Play It Again: Historical Board Games You Can Make and Play.** Englewood Cliffs, NJ: Prentice-Hall, 1981. 243p. $16.95; pap. $7.95 (794.2)

The board games are limited to 17 from various times and countries. Complete instructions are given on how to make the boards and the pieces. There are detailed rules, often from historic sources. Most of the material is simple enough for a youngster to make and to play, although just as much of it should be of equal interest to adults.

Rovin, Jeff. **The Complete Guide to Conquering Video Games: How to Win Every Game in the Galaxy.** New York: Macmillan, 1982. 407p. pap. $5.95 (794)

Over 150 video games are explained in varying detail, but the real value of this exhaustive guide is the ratings. Just how challenging is a particular game? Rovin scores the play on its overall value and in terms of such things as graphics and response to commands. He gives useful tips on how to improve player strategy and then, through a series of cross-references, takes the reader to equally difficult (or less difficult) games in other categories. Home games are emphasized, but there is some attention paid to arcade games as well. *Note:* A second volume is planned, and the publisher says the basic guide(s) will be periodically updated, so look for the latest edition.

Sessoms, Bob. **The New Fun Encyclopedia.** Vol. 1. Nashville, TN: Abingdon, 1983. 240p. pap. $9.95 (793)

Games, games, and more games are suggested here for various home and outdoor situations. The author explains more than 500 simple games that require a minimal expenditure of money and effort. The rules are simple and most games demand little equipment. Arrangement is by specific type of activity (from campfire to birthday party) and for various sized groups. The entertainments are for children and teenagers with a few suitable for adults. Sessoms opens with sections on leadership skills and methods, which most readers will probably want to skip. *Note:* The "new" in the title suggests the original work by E. O. Harbin, *The Fun Encyclopedia* (1940). While this is an update, much of Harbin is still useful.

Weinstein, Matt, and Joel Goodman. **Playfair: Everybody's Guide to Noncompetitive Play.** St. Luis Obispo, CA: Impact, 1980. 250p. pap. $8.95 (793)

If competition is not the point of a game, then this is the perfect guide. The authors explain how to play over 60 different types of games (for almost as many different age groups and types of people) that stress cooperation. There is a fascinating introduction in which the authors define their concept of play—one held, incidentally, by many groups outside the Western world. The emphasis is on sharing and cooperation, whether a close-knit organization, or in a family, or with strangers. Illustrated instructions for each of the activities follow. There is even a part devoted to methods of making up games, and people to contact for additional information.

GAMES—CHILDREN

Athey, Margaret, and Gwen Hotchkiss. **Complete Handbook of Music Games and Activities for Early Childhood.** Englewood Cliffs, NJ: Prentice-Hall, 1982. 218p. $15.50 (372.8)

A game book with a difference—this is built around some 300 different musical diversions for juvenile entertainment and education. The idea is to instruct children while they are enjoying themselves. This is accomplished by teaching fundamentals of music, such as rhythm and singing, around specific types of games. There is some material of interest only to teachers, but most of the book, including a fine chapter on how to point up the joys of classical music to youngsters, will be of value to parents of preschool children and those in first through seventh grades.

Bell, Sally, and Dolly Langdon. **Romper Room's Miss Sally Presents 200 Fun Things to Do with Little Kids.** New York: Doubleday, 1983. 161p. $7.95 (790.1)

When kids are driving their parents mad, when it is raining outside and everything, including television, fails to interest them, then the time has come to turn to this book. Two experts on projects and games, as well as the needs of young children, have gathered together 200 "fun" things to keep youngsters occupied and happy. The book is arranged by the length of the activity, the type of activity, projects for given situations, etc. There is a list of projects for a complete day (starting at 7:00 A.M. and running through 8:00 P.M.) as well as for sick days, rainy days, and parties. All of them are suitable for preschool children, although many will also appeal to older youngsters. All, too, have been tested on the "Romper Room" program, and found effective in holding the participants' attention.

Gregson, Bob. **The Incredible Indoor Games Book.** Belmont, CA: Pitman Learning, 1982. 187p. pap. $10.95 (794)

Here are "160 group projects, games and activities" that can help children (aged 6 to 16) pass the time when the weather keeps them inside. Instructions are specific and easy to follow, and most of the games and activities are illustrated with line drawings. Each game follows a specific format in that the reader is told the number of players, how long it takes to play, etc. Materials needed for the projects, which tend to be simple and easy to find around the home, are listed.

Harwood, Michael. **Games to Play in the Car.** New York: St. Martin's, 1983. 96p. pap. $6.95 (794)

Originally published in 1967, this has only a few revisions, yet it remains helpful in alleviating boredom for children traveling by car. The games and projects are such as to interest not only the youngster but the parent as well. The numerous ideas range from the well known to the unexpected, and are accompanied by delightful illustrations. There is some space given to safety, and tips on easing the driver's tension.

Jacobson, Willard, and Abby Bergman. **Science Activities for Children.** Englewood Cliffs, NJ: Prentice-Hall, 1983. 198p. $16.95 (507.8)

How can a parent interest a five- to ten-year-old child in science? The authors provide the answer with about 100 different projects, activities, games, and related ideas. The approach is familiar enough. There are easy-to-carry-out experiments showing, for example, how plants develop from seeds or why it is possible to move certain objects with ease. Full instructions are given, both for the parent and the child. A helpful list of needed materials accompanies each project. There are numerous illustrations to enliven the text.

Shank, Carolyn. **A Child's Way to Water Play.** New York: Scribner's, 1983. 112p. pap. $7.95 (790)

Striking a balance among safety, education, and fun, the author offers a sensible guide for parents who wish to introduce their children to water and, eventually, swimming. This physical education teacher, who starts out with a baby in a tub, discusses how to make the infant feel at home in water and how to overcome any of its fears. She introduces various types of play for all age levels, with numerous suggestions on how even nonswimming parents can become engaged in the activity. There are sections on how to handle the child in a pool, a lake, or even at the ocean. There are good line drawings and photographs.

Sobel, Jeffrey. **Everybody Wins.** New York: Walker, 1982. 116p. $12.95 (793.01)

Here are some 360 games for children aged three to ten, and they differ from most games in that, as the title says, everyone wins. The focus is on the noncompetitive, and whether it is musical chairs or a version of tag, the winner is anyone who plays. Even where victory is built in, the author offers suggestions to reverse the process, i.e., he advocates a type of scoring that allows even the slowest to emerge at one time or another as a member of the winning side. The emphasis on team play rather than on individual merit will also appeal to many. Instructions are complete and there are numerous illustrations.

GARAGE SALES. *See* Secondhand Trade

GARDENING.
See also Greenhouses; Herbs; Insects, Garden; Landscape Gardening; Organic Gardening; Plants; Pruning; Trees & Shrubs; Vegetable & Fruit Gardening

Better Homes and Gardens Complete Guide to Gardening. Des Moines, IA: Meredith, 1979. 551p. $19.95 (635)

Here is almost everything from how to grow peas or petunias, how to cope with insects and poor soil, and even sections on indoor planting. Instructions are easy to follow, quite specific, and it is always clear what part of the country is being referred to, i.e., particular attention is given to climatic conditions. Illustrations, which primarily include colored drawings and photographs, are excellent and always closely related to the text. The writing style is good, and follows the approach found in the magazine *Better Homes and Gardens*. *Note:* Some of the material is from the publisher's You Can Grow Series (*Annuals You Can Grow, Vegetables You Can Grow,* etc.) published earlier.

Brookes, John. **The Garden Book.** New York: Crown, 1984. 287p. $22.50 (712.6)
   A truly sumptuous gardening book, this features more than 1,000 illustrations, almost half in full color, and various plans for garden layouts. The real strength of the book is in its garden plans. The author suggests 25 different types of various size and complexity. The materials needed are explained, as well as the different kinds of planting.

Bush-Brown, James. **America's Garden Book.** Rev. ed. New York: Scribner's, 1980. 819p. $22.50 (635.9)
   A standard work from the New York Botanical Garden, this is an accurate, illustrated overview of gardening. (There are numerous black-and-white illustrations, but none in color.) Each chapter considers a different aspect of gardening or type of plant. For example, the section on perennials is as detailed as anyone is likely to find in a general gardening book. Each basic plant is described, along with what it requires for maximum growth and beauty. Obviously some plants grow in one place, some in another, and it is the wide choice this book offers that makes it so useful. Other sections deal with fertilization, weeding, pruning, plant diseases, herbs, patios, and just about anything else of concern to the average gardener.

Church, Thomas, et al. **Gardens Are for People.** 2nd ed. New York: McGraw-Hill, 1983. 256p. $37.50 (712.6)
   Among dedicated gardeners, Church is about as well known as anyone. A prominent landscape architect, he died in 1978, just as he was in the middle of revising this book. It was successfully completed by colleagues, right down to many new illustrations. In fact, the photographs, most in black and white, dominate the text. It is more a book for browsing than a how-to-do-it title, but there are enough ideas in a few pages to more than warrant its inclusion here. The ideas range from the placement of trees to overall landscape plans, often for Californian homes of less than modest proportions. Despite the obvious interest in expensive design, the bits of advice Church offers on almost every page are generally adaptable for the gardener with only a ten-foot plot. It is a joy to read and to contemplate.

Graham, Sharon. **1001 Tips for Successful Gardening.** New York: Dutton, 1983. 145p. pap. $6.95 (635)
   Its convenience is the best reason for turning to this guide. The author arranges odd bits of helpful information under specific garden subjects—from broad family plant names and types of herbs to lawns and houseplants. One quickly locates the topic of interest and there finds brief hints on basics, as well as out-of-the-way items such as novel ways to control insects or to transplant. Everything is easy to understand, and well within the budget and skills of the average gardener.

Hall, Walter. **Barnacle Parp's Guide to Garden & Yard Power Tools.** Emmaus, PA: Rodale, 1983. 254p. $18.95; pap. $11.95 (681.7)

Hall is Parp and Parp is Hall, and, unfortunately, the two are sometimes so cute as to stand in the way of otherwise good advice. Style aside, here is a useful, basic guide to help someone select and maintain garden tools. Basics, of course, may be found in issues of *Consumer Reports*, but Hall goes much further. Aside from specific recommendations, he tells how to maintain the various tools, which ones are best for specific situations, and how to make simple repairs and tune-ups. There is a most useful troubleshooting guide, as well. One of the best sections is on the typical small motor that powers most of the tools. It is explained, and useful instructions are given on how to keep it running properly. While some information on particular tools will date, the basics on maintenance and repair will be good for years to come. Numerous illustrations support the text.

Huxley, Anthony. **Huxley's Encyclopedia of Gardening for Great Britain and America.** New York: Universe Books, 1982. 373p. $17.50 (635.9)

A dictionary approach to gardening, with over 2,000 entries, this not only defines terms, but in most cases provides specific instructions on planting and care. Thanks to the handy arrangement, and the replacement of British terms with those familiar to Americans, this is a most useful and handy reference guide for almost any gardener. The writing style is as clear as the numerous illustrations—including color plates and line drawings—are helpful.

Kramer, Jack. **The Everest House Complete Book of Gardening.** New York: Everest House, 1982. 382p. $29.95 (635)

What sets this apart from other large, general gardening books is Kramer's ability to deal with quite basic gardening problems while not avoiding complexities. The format is outstanding, with frequent charts and tables, as well as profuse illustrations (some in color) to underline every important point. The content follows the usual pattern, e.g., opening sections on tools, followed by a full array of garden plants from bulbs to trees. The book is well planned and organized, although here and there the instructions are a bit vague. Advanced gardeners will find the information too elementary, but it is a wonderful place for the novice to start.

Kramer, Jack. **Your Garden in the City: How to Plant It, Build It, and Grow It.** New York: Crown, 1982. 278p. $19.95 (635.9)

Taking into consideration the unpredictable amount of sunlight, the usual small plot, and the problems with pollution, Kramer offers hope for the urban gardener. He gives specific advice on how to design a garden that will be best for the city dweller. The gardens are illustrated, and are of various sizes and types, including small patches on balconies and roofs. Once the basic pattern is established, he launches into a discussion of constructing everything from fences to walks and containers. Beyond this point, the material begins to repeat what is found in other books, including Kramer's own (q.v.), e.g., the usual advice on flowers, plants, trees, vegetables, herbs, etc. The real strength is not so much in the basic growing advice as in the planning and the hope the author holds out for the gardener who must be satisfied with a small gardening area. Kramer ends with 11 plans that may be modified for city gardens.

Lacy, Allen. **Home Ground: A Gardener's Miscellany.** New York: Farrar, 1984. 270p. $14.95 (635.9)

The garden columnist for the *Wall Street Journal* is a highly literate, amusing, and cultivated gentleman. He writes with style and verve about how he became a gardener and why it is such a satisfying way to spend time. The rambling history of his introduction to the garden is a far cry from the usual how-to-do-it guide, but it builds from that point to where he explains the ins and outs of his own gardening efforts. One may learn much from his ten-year experience, including sources of information and facts about special plant species. In fact, the dedicated gardener will be grateful for the numerous and unusual listings of various organizations, as well as Lacy's favored books and his other individual touches. This is a book to make anyone want to rush out and start digging. It may be a bit short on specific information, but it more than makes up for it in enthusiasm, history, and garden lore.

Lloyd, Christopher. **The Adventurous Gardener.** New York: Random House, 1984. 231p. $17.95 (635.9)

An English horticulturist offers instructions on how to plant and what to plant, and along the way provides sensible advice on many aspects of gardening. The book is for the experienced gardener, particularly as Lloyd assumes that the reader understands gardening terminology and is familiar with most of the plants mentioned. Everything here is much above average in terms of style and wit. The major drawback is the assumption that the gardener is functioning in an English climate. This definitely gives one pause when considering a selection of certain types of shrubs, plants, and trees.

Loewer, H. Peter. **Peter Loewer's Month by Month Garden Almanac for Indoor & Outdoor Gardening.** New York: Putnam's, 1983. 175p. pap. $8.95 (635.9)

A conversational, cheerfully illustrated guide, this has a particular strength in the step-by-step instructions for carrying out less-than-common projects. For example, there is a good section on herbs that can be grown in and out of doors, and another on cooking unusual garden plants. Each of the hints is accompanied by a drawing, and there is a list of outstanding garden magazines and books, as well as places to buy seeds and supplies. The author lives in upstate New York, so the book is particularly suited to the Northeast, but most of the material is applicable elsewhere.

Logsdon, Gene. **Wildlife in Your Garden.** Emmaus, PA: Rodale, 1983. 268p. $14.95 (635.04)

What do you do when a raccoon shows up in your suburban backyard? How can you attract birds and small wildlife to enliven your family half-acre? These questions have become more and more common as people become conscious of animals who seem to thrive in and around urban communities. The answers to these questions are provided in a tiresome style (the author insists on using such characters as the "Dumb Farmer" or the "Widow Lady" to tell his stories). Still, despite the archness, the advice is sound. The author is particularly good at advising the reader on types of fences and other barriers that will keep animals out. He is equally wise in the ways of attracting the wildlife via such things as bird baths and feeders. Then, too, there is much accurate lore on animal identification and even on cooking raccoons or squirrels. The author may not know style, but he does know animals.

Mitchell, Henry. **The Essential Earthman: Henry Mitchell on Gardening.** Bloomington, IN: Indiana University Pr., 1981. 244p. $12.95 (635.9)

Written for the compulsive, impulsive urban gardener, this guide differs from most in that the author, an enthusiastic garden columnist for the *Washington Post*, is more concerned with the joys of gardening than with formal results. Try this or that, he says, as long as it makes you happy. At the same time, Mitchell offers sound advice, good rules of thumb for both amateur and experienced growers. He has favorite plants, landscape designs, and trees, and he is quick to point these out. His style is both flamboyant and relaxed, his approach both calm and excited. He is, in a word, the perfect gardener in love with his work.

Naimark, Susan, ed. **A Handbook of Community Gardening.** New York: Scribner's, 1983. 180p. $14.95; pap. $7.95 (635)

A gardening subject of growing interest is covered by the Boston Urban Gardeners. They consider the steps necessary to establish and maintain a flourishing, trouble-free garden for the whole community. In addition to expected sections on what to raise, and how to do it, there are the unique chapters on such things as organizing a group, tips on sales, and the best types of sites. Problems that may arise when several people are involved are examined and solutions suggested.

Ortho Library Series. San Francisco: Ortho, 1977– . 96–112p. ea. $5.95 ea.

The series expands each year, but as of mid-1984 included the following titles: *All about Annuals* (1982); *All about Bulbs* (1981); *All about Perennials* (1981); *All about Fertilizers, Soils and Water* (1980); *All about Ground Covers* (1982); *All about Growing Fruits and Berries* (1982); *All about Houseplants* (1982); *All about Landscaping* (1981); *All about Lawns* (1981), available in three regional editions; *All about Pruning* (1979); *All about Roses* (1977); *All about Tomatoes* (1981); *All about Trees* (1982).

The Ortho series is well thought of among gardeners and professional horticulturists. These standard gardening guides are useful in almost any situation. They are noteworthy for their scope, excellent coverage, and relatively low price. In addition, there is a strong emphasis on color photography, brief yet practical information for the average gardener, and a useful arrangement and index that allow for easy consultation. The books rely on tables and charts to summarize much of the data. All climatic zones are considered, and dutifully noted for the various types of annuals or perennials. There are good, although sometimes dated, lists of suppliers. Several of the books offer brief glimpses of special or historical gardens where the subject of the guide is featured. These underline the attention given to plans and diagrams to help the gardener in landscaping.

The Ortho Problem Solver. San Francisco: Ortho, 1983. 1,022p. $149.95 (635)

Possibly the most massive (8 pounds) and most expensive of the gardening books, this is the problem solver for gardeners. Approximately 2,000 major problems are analyzed. These are primarily diseases caused by, or augmented by, such things as bad soil, insects, poor light, unsuitable climate, etc. For each analysis, the guide offers photographs and illustrations to drive home the points. All aspects of the garden are considered from flowers and trees to lawns and even house plants. While it is true that many solutions include use of the publisher's garden products, there is no reason not to use other controls. The book is exhaustively indexed, extremely well organized, and updated with pages that are sent the buyer. This is the ultimate reference tool in this area, and if you cannot afford a copy of your own, turn to the library and/or a gardening store that handles Ortho products.

Ortho's Complete Guide to Successful Gardening. San Francisco: Ortho, 1983. 504p. $24.95 (635)

Filled with luxurious photographs of equally rich gardens, this is more a book to dream over than one that is likely to explain how to design a garden for a typical home. Beyond this, though, the work can be useful day by day. There is basic information on types of flowers and plants, when and how to grow them, and what to watch for by way of disease and other problems. There is good information on vegetable gardening and trees, less on houseplants. Numerous illustrations, charts, and diagrams make everything clear. While this may not be entirely necessary, it is a useful book to supplement other general gardening volumes.

Page, Russell. **The Education of a Gardener.** Rev. ed. New York: Random House, 1982. 382p. $19.95 (712.2)

In a lengthy, perceptive review of what has come to be a minor gardening/literary classic, a critic observed that while this is an overview of expensive gardens, planned by the author and "hopelessly out of the average gardener's reach," it is of invaluable help to any enthusiast. Actually, Page has much to do with "those of us struggling to make sense of a city backyard or three quarters of a disheveled country acre. Page is a class act, but there is something for everybody." Primarily, the lessons are ones of aesthetics and design, which are as natural to the author as painting was to Picasso, and just as impressive. The average gardener will learn more here about what a garden is really about than in scores of how-to-do-it works. This should be obvious to anyone who examines the numerous gardens Page has planned. Incidentally, the reviewer believes Page has designed more gardens since his career began in 1928 than any other individual in history. The prose style is as imaginative and challenging as the message. And while the photographs do not always adequately illustrate his words, they are at least indicative of genius. Page "is a gardener, first and last, and to those who share his passion that says it all." (Quotations from review by Eleanor Perenyi, *New York Review of Books,* April 14, 1983.)

Reader's Digest Illustrated Guide to Gardening. Pleasantville, NY: Reader's Digest Association, 1978. 672p. $22.50 (635)

Three thousand line drawings and photographs (some in color) augment the easy-to-follow text in this basic book, which will answer most questions about the home garden. The sections are arranged in such a way that the reader begins with a selection of shrubs, trees, plants, and seed and is shown, step-by-step, how to make a success with each. There are discussions, too, of some indoor plants, herbs, and vegetables.

Sunset Editors. **Gardening & Landscaping.** Menlo Park, CA: Lane. Various dates. 80–96p. ea. pap. $3.95–$5.95 ea.

Among titles in the series in print as of 1984 are *African Violets: How to Grow* (1977); *Azaleas, Rhododendrons, Camellias* (1982); *Basic Gardening: Introduction* to (1981); *Cactus and Succulents* (1978); *Decorating with Plants* (1980); *Desert Gardening* (1967); *Garden Color/Annuals & Perennials* (1981); *House Plants: How to Grow* (1976); *Landscaping & Garden Remodeling* (1978); *Lawns and Ground Covers* (1979); *Orchids: How to Grow* (1977); *Roses: How to Grow* (1980); *Vegetables & Berries: How to Grow* (1982); *Western Garden Book* (1979).

All of the guides follow a format combining color photographs, line drawings, and explicit directions. The books are divided into three or four main sections that cover the basics of the topic. They are noteworthy for their illustrations, which are carefully linked to the text, and the step-by-step analysis of each situation. Although published in California, the majority of the titles are of use in any part of North America. Among gardening series, they are highly recommended.

Sunset Introduction to Basic Gardening. 3rd ed. Menlo Park, CA: Lane, 1981. 160p. pap. $5.95 (655.9)

Specific, readily understood instructions are given on everything from preparing the garden to picking the flowers. In between are discussions of fertilizers, weeding, pests, tools, and numerous other subjects. Illustrations—color plates, line drawings, diagrams, charts—accompany almost every paragraph. The book ends with a useful glossary and an index. The guide is revised every five or six years.

10,000 Garden Questions Answered by 20 Experts. 4th ed. New York: Doubleday, 1982. 1,507p. $16.95 (635)

A standard guide used by many gardeners, amateurs, and semi-professionals, this is ideal because of its easy-to-use arrangement. Various types of gardens, plants, and problems are handled in specific sections. Each section is written by an expert in that subject and they cover topics like soils, fertilizers, lawns, vegetables, plants, etc. Each part has numerous illustrations, charts, and diagrams. State-by-state coverage is offered for planting and basic problems, and there are numerous useful lists added. First published in 1944, this is a classic in the field, and is encyclopedic in scope.

Time-Life Encyclopedia of Gardening Series. New York: Time-Life, 1971– . Approx. 160p. ea. $11.95

The series apparently ended in 1979. It includes *Annuals* (1971); *Roses* (1971); *Landscape Gardening* (1971); *Lawn and Ground Covers* (1971); *Flowering House Plants* (1971); *Bulbs* (1971); *Evergreens* (1971); *Perennials* (1972); *Flowering Shrubs* (1972); *Trees* (1972); *Foliage House Plants* (1972); *Vegetables & Fruits* (1972); *Herbs* (1977); *Wildflower Gardening* (1977); *Greenhouse Gardening* (1977); *Ferns* (1977); *Pests and Disease* (1977); *Gardening under Lights* (1978); *Decorating with Plants* (1978); *Garden Construction* (1978); *Cacti and Succulents* (1978); *Orchids* (1978); *Pruning and Grafting* (1978); *Easy Gardens* (1979); *Miniatures and Bonsai* (1979); *Vines* (1979); *Shade Gardens* (1979); *Rock and Water Gardens* (1979); *Japanese Gardens* (1979); *Winter Gardens* (1979).

Although by now somewhat dated, this remains one of the better Time-Life Book Series, and most of the information will be useful to both beginners and intermediate-level gardeners. Following the normal pattern of these series, each volume is filled with color illustrations and step-by-step instructions. The arrangement varies, but essentially consists of background information on the subject, easy identification of common plants and varieties (with good pictures), and an alphabetically arranged section where one may turn for advice on everything from disease to fertilization and watering. Little is left to chance, and every step is carefully explained. Most of the books are as applicable in one part of the country as in another. The problem may be that some subjects are covered too briefly.

Wallace, Dan, ed. **The Natural Formula Book for the Home and Yard.** Emmaus, PA: Rodale, 1982. 336p. $17.95 (648)

What ingredients can you put together to make a suitable, safe fertilizer, insect spray, or cleaner? The formulas for these and scores of other household products are given with clear directions both as to the proportions and substances to use. In the appendixes there are useful lists of chemical substances and sources of ingredients, as well as lists of mail-order suppliers and manufacturers. The practical suggestions include not only formulas, but safe, quick ways of doing such things as cleaning the house and fixing the yard.

GARDENING—INDOORS
   See also Greenhouses; Plants

Dressler, Robert. **Orchids: Natural History and Classification.** Cambridge, MA: Harvard University Pr., 1981. 352p. $27.50 (584.15)

While not a how-to-do-it book in itself, this is a basic guide for anyone interested in growing orchids, even on a modest scale. What it does do is identify and detail the more than 20,000 known species of orchids. Written for both laypersons and scholars, this guide is the definitive work on the subject. It is illustrated with marvelous and numerous plates.

The Essentials of Bonsai. Beaverton, OR: Timber Pr., 1982. 108p. $9.95 (635.97)

Here is a clear, well-illustrated guide to growing a miniature tree or plant. The author opens with methods of propagation, moves on to problems of maintenance (and they are many), and has a lengthy section on training the bonsai into various forms. This is a difficult art, at least if carried beyond the rudimentary first few months, and the author considers all of the problems while giving due attention to the questions of beginners. It is a fine guide for the novice, although of limited help to anyone more experienced with bonsai.

The Gardener's Catalog People. **The Gardener's Catalog 2: A Complete Compendium for Indoor, Outdoor, Hydroponic and Greenhouse Gardeners.** Rev. ed. New York: Morrow, 1983. 320p. $12.95 (635.9)

The first edition of this appeared in 1974, and was considered a triumph of design, being superb for reference use. It remains so in the latest edition, with necessary updates in the various sections and more illustrations. The pictures are often from old woodcuts and give the book the appearance of reliability firmly based on age and experience. However, the real point is that the coverage is complete, compact, and well organized. The immediate facts (from how much light a plant needs to how much fertilizer a rose requires) are easily accessible. There even is a list of mail-order houses, periodicals, and organizations involved with gardening.

Halpin, Anne, ed. **Rodale's Encyclopedia of Indoor Gardening.** Emmaus, PA: Rodale, 1983. 902p. $29.95 (635.9)

Divided into broad categories based on houseplant varieties, here is an easy-to-read book for both dedicated and beginning home gardeners. Each section—ferns, herbs, succulents, orchids, bromeliads, etc.—includes well-placed line drawings and color photographs. The plants are carefully described, and there is information on how to keep them out of harm's way. The details on care are particularly useful. There are chapters on related matters such as bonsai and terrariums.

Hitchcock, Susan. **Wildflowers on the Windowsill: A Guide to Growing Wild Plants Indoors.** New York: Crown, 1983. 192p. $12.95 (635.96)

Wildflower seeds, nicely packed in cans, are now available to scatter over a backyard. People who enjoy such things will be delighted with a book on growing wildflowers at home. It is not easy, although Hitchcock seems to have mastered the art for the simpler, more hearty varieties. She explains where to secure seeds and/or plants, and what to do with them in terms of light, temperature, food, and so on. She has a special section on terrariums, which are particularly suitable for the types of plants one finds growing in forests. Some may question the desire to grow wild weeds on the windowsill, but for those who wish to do so, this guide is as useful as it is unusual and well illustrated.

Kramer, Jack. **An Illustrated Guide to Flowering Houseplants.** New York: Smith, 1981. 160p. $6.95 (635.9)

Assuming that the reader knows little or nothing about houseplants, this expert author carefully describes each one and then candidly discusses the chances of the plant's surviving and blossoming. Some make it through a season, but do not flower; others flower and rapidly die. Many, of course, are completely successful, and it is with these that Kramer is primarily concerned. Still, he suggests that the reader make choices based on home conditions and personal preferences. The book is pocket-size and easy to carry about when looking for just the right plant.

Kramer, Jack. **1,000 Beautiful House Plants and How to Grow Them.** Rev. ed. New York: Abrams, 1982. $24.95 (635.96)

The primary arrangement here is alphabetical, by name of the specific house plant. Each is briefly described, and there is basic information on where it grows best, types of lighting required, water needs, etc. Most are illustrated, often with color photographs. In addition, there are sections on basic planting requirements, using a greenhouse, pest control, and problems that may plague the average indoor gardener. There is a good glossary and the usual bibliography and list of suppliers. The book differs from others because of its easy-to-follow arrangement, numerous illustrations, and good writing style.

The New York Times Book of House Plants. New York: Quadrangle/New York Times, 1983. 288p. pap. $9.95 (635.9)

A detailed guide to popular house plants, this is particularly useful for the good illustrations provided and the practical hints on what to do to keep plants healthy. There is a fine section on the 100 most popular plants one is likely to find in garden shops. Arrangement is alphabetical by name of plant, with sections on various aspects of the art such as growing plants under lights and varieties suitable for children. There is a list of suppliers and societies in the appendix.

Ortho Books Editors. **All about Houseplants.** San Francisco: Ortho, 1982. 96p. pap. $5.95 (635.96)

This is a no-nonsense approach to houseplants that are likely to thrive in the average home. Exotic varieties, which may prove difficult, are excluded. The book is divided by type of plant. Specific instructions are given on such things as food, amount of light required, potential problems, and preferred soil. Most of the plants are illustrated in color, and there is a good index.

Stewart, Christine. **Bonsai.** Salem, NH: Merrimack, 1983. 112p. $16.95 (635.97)

As an introduction to bonsai, this is useful because of the clear instructions and the author's examples, which are well within the capabilities of the average person. Specific information is given on how to select a plant and how to train it over the years. Illustrations, usually in color, show the plants and the step-by-step procedures necessary for outdoor or indoor training. While originally published in England, this is equally useful in the United States.

Sunset House Plants. Menlo Park, CA: Lane, 1983. 112p. pap. $5.95 (635.96)

One of the more popular books in the massive series of Sunset Books, this is a revised edition of an earlier work. The revision includes new color photographs showing how to use houseplants to liven up any room. There are specific instructions on the selection and placing of plants, their daily care, repotting, and problems with disease, pruning, propagation, and feeding. The most common varieties for all parts of the country are listed here in alphabetical order by name of plant. There is a standard description, including what is needed for maximum success, and each plant is illustrated with a color photograph. This is a handsome, basic book for any plant grower.

GEMS. *See* Precious Stones

GEOGRAPHY. *See* Travel

GIFTS. *See* Handicrafts

GLASS
   See also Antiques

Graham, Boyd. **Engraving Glass: A Beginner's Guide.** New York: Van Nostrand, 1982. 127p. $18.95 (748.6)

The choice of books is pretty much limited when you are interested in basic lessons in engraving glass. (An earlier guide, which is out-of-print, but still useful, is Barbara Norman, *Engraving and Decorating Glass,* McGraw-Hill, 1972.) Employing numerous photographs and illustrations, the author uses a step-by-step approach. It is possible for the beginner to use the book without the aid of an instructor. The focus is on the use of the diamond burr. There is a good list of suppliers and even a section on how to display your work.

Isenberg, Anita. **How to Work in Stained Glass.** Radnor, PA: Chilton, 1972. 237p. $13.95; pap. $8.95 (748.5)

The instructions for the beginner who is interested in making stained glass are authoritative and clear. Most steps are illustrated, and the authors discuss windows, shades, sculpture, jewelry, and other forms of stained glass. There is a good section on tools and materials. Unfortunately, there is no glossary nor are there good examples of classic pieces of stained glass. Aside from that, it is a basic text in the field.

Isenberg, Anita, and Seymour Isenberg. **How to Work in Beveled Glass.** Radnor, PA: Chilton, 1982. 225p. $19.95; pap. $14.95 (748.2)

Beveled glass is a style of working with glass that consists primarily of knowing how to taper and polish it. This may sound simple enough, but it can be quite intricate, and requires considerable skill and patience. The authors cover all aspects of the art, and most of the steps are illustrated with good black-and-white photographs. The authors write as well as they form, design, and fabricate glass, and the book is a basic one in this field.

Mount Tom Stained Glass Artisans. **Starting Out in Stained Glass.** New York: Arco, 1983. 148p. $14.95; pap. $8.95 (748.502)

Working with stained glass really requires a first-rate teacher, although individuals with a minimal art background and some ability and experience with glass should be able to learn on their own. The present guide is an excellent beginning. Thanks to step-by-step instructions accompanied by carefully matched photographs, the reader is able to follow the various processes. There is an explanation of the type of equipment and materials needed, and suggestions for patterns within the novice's capabilities.

GLIDING

Gannon, Robert. **Half Mile Up without an Engine.** Englewood Cliffs, NJ: Prentice-Hall, 1982. 198p. $18.95; pap. $9.95 (629.13)

Sailplaning is the game, and nerve and skill the name of that game. Gannon does not give detailed instructions on how to build, buy, or fly, but does offer enough historical and technical information to help the beginner appreciate what is involved with sailplaning and soaring. There is a good section on the legal requirements, where they exist, to become a pilot. The author shows the steps a student might go through to become proficient, but, again, these are not detailed. There are some good-to-excellent black-and-white photographs, which give the reader some idea as to the shape of the sport. Actually, the best part of the guide is the author's enthusiastic explanation of what it is like to be "a half mile up without an engine."

Wills, Maralys. **Man Birds: Hang Gliders and Hang Gliding.** Englewood Cliffs, NJ: Prentice-Hall, 1981. 242p. $17.95 (797.55)

Here is a combination how-to-do-it and historical information on a dangerous yet popular sport. Wills explores the background of hang gliders from early times and in the process points out that people have been, and can be, killed while soaring through the air. There are definite skills required, besides bravery, and these are dutifully explained. The author next turns to the heart of the matter—how the gliders operate and the processes necessary to fly them under various conditions.

Obviously, it takes more than a book to teach one how to fly, but this is a good introduction and preparation for actual instruction. The text concludes with a list of various hang gliding sites throughout the United States, as well as some records set as of early 1980.

GOLF

Harvey, John. **The Golfer's Repair and Maintenance Book.** Chicago: Contemporary, 1984. 95p. pap. $5.80 (796.35)

An easy-to-follow paperback, this explains the basics of keeping a set of golf clubs in shape. The author shows how to do everything from repairing a club's shaft to improving a grip. Tools necessary for maintenance are discussed. The illustrations are adequate.

Hobbs, Michael, ed. **In Celebration of Golf.** New York: Scribner's, 1982. 212p. $19.50 (796.35)

Celebrating the celebrities of the golf game, various sports writers contribute chapters and sections to a book that is more about the great players than about the rules of the game. It is assumed that the reader has a high interest in golf, knows how to play, and hopes to learn a bit more by reading about the experts of both early and later days. So while not a how-to-do-it book, this collection of approaches and attitudes of the memorable players, along with their advice and explanations, will serve any golfer well.

Kaskie, Shirli. **A Woman's Golf Game.** Chicago: Contemporary, 1982. 198p. $13.95 (796.35)

According to the author, the average woman does not have the strength to play golf the way men do, so she introduces compensatory approaches to the game. The key is improved coordination and a good eye. Drawing on the experience and advice of women golfers, Kaskie turns her attention to stance, the golf swing, various clubs to use or to avoid, problem shots, etc. There is a good section on equipment for women. What is less appealing, at least for the individual trying to master the game, is the chatty biographies of leading women golfers. These are written well enough, but do not seem to belong in the book. There are good illustrations.

Kennington, Donald, ed. **The Sourcebook of Golf.** Phoenix, AZ: Oryx, 1981. 255p. $39.95 (016.79)

The history of golf, stories of the great golfers, and much more will be found in what was originally a British look at the game. Essentially, the book is a collection of short essays and a list of reference books, periodicals, and primary groups in golfing. Only about 70 pages is devoted to material on playing. A useful guide for future reading and a good although by now somewhat dated directory, this will appeal primarily to the golf expert.

GRAPHIC ARTS

See also Antiques; Painting (Art); Printing

Ballinger, Raymond. **Design with Paper in Art and Graphic Design.** New York: Van Nostrand, 1982. 144p. $29.95 (702.8)

Here is a catalog, not a how-to-do-it presentation per se, of the history of paperwork. The ideas alone more than justify its publication. Anyone looking for something different in a valentine, a cutout or an extremely complex crafted paper should turn here first. Ballinger covers the topic with illustrated examples and just enough text (often no more than a caption) to explain the particular novelty. The book is a springboard to creativity, and a joy to browse through.

Bridgewater, Alan. **Printing with Wood Blocks, Stencils & Engravings.** New York: Arco, 1983. 159p. $19.95 (761)

Combining historical facts about woodblock printing with details on techniques and projects one can undertake, this manual provides basic information on the process of relief printing. It is directed to the beginner, and it presupposes little or no knowledge of printing. Each process, as noted in the title, is described with dutiful attention to its development over the years. With that, there is a project, with the necessary instructions for gathering materials and using tools. The directions are well illustrated. While hardly inspirational or imaginative, this is a good place to start for anyone interested in the subject.

Campbell, Alastair. **The Graphic Designer's Handbook.** Philadelphia: Running Pr., 1983. 192p. $12.95 (686.2)

Information for beginners, intermediates and, to a lesser extent, experts in the graphic arts is not easy to find in one source. Thanks to a compact style and an appreciation of what is important, the author has achieved that goal. Almost everything needed to understand and work in the graphic arts is included. There are numerous graphs, charts, and illustrations to summarize and support the text. Campbell considers various aspects of graphic arts from the methods of reproduction of photographs and line drawings to typefaces, and the opportunities now open to matching type with the overall design. Of more interest to the person in the field is the data on business matters, from what and how to charge to estimate analysis.

Thoma, Marta. **Graphic Illustration: Tools and Techniques for Beginning Illustrators.** Englewood Cliffs, NJ: Prentice-Hall, 1982. 175p. $29.95; pap. $12.95 (741.6)

The subtitle states precisely what the book is and thanks to the clear presentations and the numerous illustrations it is one of the best guides to illustration available. Basic techniques are considered and then specific methods from line drawing to ink washes are examined. Ideas for subjects and methods of making the material truly graphic are discussed. The book concludes with information on how to become a professional illustrator. The guide is as useful to the amateur who only wants to illustrate as a hobby as it is to the potential expert.

GREENHOUSES

See also Gardening—Indoors

Pierce, John. **Home Solar Gardening.** New York: Van Nostrand, 1982. 164p. $14.95 (635.04)

An expert on greenhouses covers numerous varieties, from free-standing models, to those attached to the home, to substitutes built into windows or roofs. Chapters are devoted to the selection of the proper type of greenhouse, what to grow, how to get the project started, problems that may arise, costs, and just about everything else of interest to either the beginner or the near expert who may be looking to expand a space. The text is illustrated and there is a good reading list.

Steinbrunner, Marion. **Greenhouses: From Design to Harvest.** Blue Ridge Summit, PA: TAB, 1982. $17.95; pap. $11.95 (631.58)

Most of the emphasis here is not on building a greenhouse, but on determining whether one is feasible, and, if so, its placement and maintenance. Much of the book is devoted to planning and utilization, but the author is fully aware of the fact that "greenhouse" may mean anything from a simple addition in a window to a massive structure. All types are considered, with benefits and drawbacks noted. There is a good section on the importance of site, and specific advice is given on heating and cooling. Once the greenhouse is in place, the author shifts to information on what to plant, how to care for the plants, and odds and ends about the joys of the art. There is a list of greenhouse suppliers, as well as eight do-it-yourself plans approved by the U.S. Department of Agriculture. The latter should not be undertaken unless the reader is quite good with tools. There are illustrations throughout.

Walls, Ian. **The Complete Book of Greenhouse Gardening.** New York: Quadrangle, 1975. 447p. $14.95; pap. $8.95 (635.9)

There is no more complete book on greenhouse gardening. While it has a British focus, and is not a current publication, all of the information is still applicable. A candid, clear discussion of what type of greenhouse is best in specific situations of climate (and budget) is a highlight. Vegetables, fruits, and flowers are given equal attention, and numerous illustrations help to identify the varieties. An extensive section on pests, with methods of cutting their lives short, is followed by an excellent index.

Wolf, Ray. **Gardener's Solar Greenhouse: How to Build and Use a Solar Greenhouse for Year 'Round Gardening.** Emmaus, PA: Rodale, 1984. 160p. pap. $14.95 (690.89)

Wolf tells the reader precisely what type of freestanding greenhouse is best, and then proceeds to give all the details (illustrated) necessary to build the structure. The only option one has is whether to have the greenhouse above or in the ground. The no-ifs-and-buts approach will be appealing to people who cannot make up their own minds, and who long for the ultimate guide. Wolf claims his building is based on years of research, and the 190-square-foot greenhouse is the ideal one for most laypersons. He figures costs (as of late 1983) to be between $4,000 and $5,000, but without labor included. There are complete instructions on how to select and prepare a site, as well as the necessary data for heating equipment, air cooling, etc. Nothing is left to chance, and in many ways (if one agrees with the author's conclusion), this is the best greenhouse book for the home builder now available.

GUITAR
See also Music

Ferguson, Jim, ed. **The Guitar Player Book.** Rev. ed. New York: Grove, 1983. pap. $11.95 (787.6)

Guitar Player magazine is the basic how-to-do-it title in the field. Each issue contains articles on folk and popular music, as well as step-by-step instructions on playing the guitar—popular, not classical. Drawing from those columns and articles, the editors offer what is essentially an anthology of material from the magazine. The text is divided in several ways. There are interviews with living musicians and historical pieces on the greats of the past. The heart of the book is advice on how to buy, care for, and play a guitar. The instructions are basic, and yet can be of benefit to an intermediate-level player as well as a beginner. The latest edition has a section devoted to newer aspects of the instrument, including the guitar synthesizer and some additional modifications that have influenced playing over the past few years. Considered a handbook and a manual by players, this is an excellent overview and starting point for almost anyone. *Note:* Often updated, so look for the latest edition.

GUNS. *See* Fishing & Hunting

GYMNASTICS

Sands, Bill, and Mike Conklin. **Everybody's Gymnastic Book.** New York: Scribner's, 1984. 255p. $19.95 (764.4)
 A coach (Sands) and a sportswriter offer a detailed overview of both men's and women's gymnastic trials and events. There are sections on the history and evolution of the sport, training, competition, and related matters. There is a list of gymnastic programs, as well as the best clubs, and excellent and numerous photographs. While short on precise instructions, the book does offer the best summary of the sport and it is required for any collection in this area.

Smith, Morgan. **An Introduction to Sports Acrobatics.** New York: Beaufort, 1983. 89p. pap. $8.95 (796.47)
 A guide for beginning gymnasts of high school and university age, this is concerned with basic maneuvers and exercises. Each is carefully explained, most are illustrated with photographs, and possible problems are analyzed in detail.

Thomas, Kurt, and Kent Hannon. **Kurt Thomas on Gymnastics.** New York: Simon & Schuster, 1980. 225p. pap. $8.95 (796.4)
 A leading gymnast explains what the sport is all about in a combination how-to-do-it, history, and downright inspirational book. There are illustrated sections on training and related matters, although a good part of the book is autobiographical. Thomas works his personal revelations into the development of gymnastic art so they complement each other. Viewers will profit from an excellent chapter on how to watch the various events.

HANDICRAFTS
 See also Carpentry; Woodworking

Better Homes and Gardens Easy Bazaar Crafts. Des Moines, IA: Meredith, 1981. 96p. $4.95 (745.5)
 Here are 88 different objects one can make with a minimum of expense and trouble. The idea, of course, is to provide material for the local bazaar. The items

range from dolls and toys to baked goods, and most have been thoroughly tested. In fact, almost all at one time or another appeared in *Better Homes and Gardens*. Each project is thoroughly illustrated, usually in color, with complete details on each step. The expectation is that the user is at least able to sew, cook, or use a hammer; aside from that, the instructions are basic and easy to follow.

Better Homes and Gardens Handcrafted Gifts & Toys. Des Moines, IA: Meredith, 1984. 225p. $16.95 (745.5)

Following its usual pattern, the publisher offers an extensively illustrated, step-by-step guide to about 150 projects that can be made by almost anyone. The patterns, if not wildly imaginative, are practical and easy enough to follow. They are for everything from simple toys to somewhat more complex needlework, and in the appendix there is advice on simple sewing techniques. What is not especially helpful is a section about people who are experts at crafts.

Better Homes and Gardens Treasury of Christmas Crafts & Foods. Des Moines, IA: Meredith, 1980. 384p. $18.95 (745.59)

Ranging from recipes to gifts to handicrafts, this is a basic approach to what can be done at home during the Christmas season. Its unique feature is that many of the ideas come from countries around the world. The guide assumes the existence of a vigorously active host who desires to know what is suitable in needlework for the holidays or what might be a quaint ornament for the tree. Directions are specific and easy to follow, and most are accompanied by illustrations in color.

Houston, Julie, ed. **Woman's Day Bazaar Best Sellers.** New York: Van Nostrand, 1983. 168p. $18.50 (745.5)

Woman's Day offers uncomplicated, easy-to-make handicrafts, and about 175 of their better suggestions are compiled here. These range from clothes and toys to Christmas decorations. Every project is generously illustrated, usually with color photographs, and the explanations are brief and remarkably clear. While the focus is on material that may be sold at a bazaar, almost all the suggestions could be used for gifts or as additions to the average home.

Katz, Ruth. **Wrap It Up! Creative Gift Wrapping for All Occasions.** New York: Doubleday, 1983. 202p. $11.95 (745.54)

This is a guide for both the beginner and the experienced wrapper. The author opens with fundamentals of wrapping and then provides instructions for making specific parts, from bows to boxes. She stresses time and time again that once the basics are mastered, the readers should depart into their own imaginative territories. There are few ready-made projects; the emphasis is on individual expression. There are good colored illustrations to emphasize her points.

Linsley, Leslie. **The Great Bazaar.** New York: Delacorte, 1981. 176p. $15.95 (745.5)

Here is a writer who knows almost everything there is to know about organizing fund-raising bazaars. She explains her techniques and findings in a conversational yet sensible fashion. Whether a sale features small, inexpensive things or is on a grand scale, the author has useful suggestions. The heart of the book is how to make things to sell. She examines various ideas and products that can be turned into profit, and offers hints on displays.

Linsley, Leslie. **Million Dollar Projects from the 5 & 10¢ Store.** New York: St. Martin's, 1982. 160p. $18.95 (745.5)

Send an experienced interior decorator or artist into the traditional five-and-ten-cent store and he or she will come out with material to decorate any room in high style. How is that possible? It primarily requires a good eye, an even better imagination, and an ability to transform "kitsch" into beauty. That is what this book is about. The author shows the reader how to transform about 100 inexpensive products (from T-shirts to towels to lamps) into good-looking items. Specific directions are given, and the materials and tools needed are itemized. There are photographs and some patterns. Generally the transformation is amazing, and well within the abilities of most people.

Nast, Regina. **Baby Things to Make.** Tucson, AZ: HP Books, 1983. 160p. pap. $7.95 (745.5)

Here are some 70 different items of varying difficulty to make that are guaranteed to delight the parent and, one supposes, the baby. Instructions are clear, precise, and supported by black-and-white illustrations, as well as some color photographs. The guide is for both the beginner and intermediate-level craftsperson, although a few projects (such as a detailed quilt) require more experienced hands.

Oliver, Libby, et al. **Colonial Williamsburg Decorates for Christmas.** New York: Holt, 1981. 80p. $9.95; pap. $5.95 (745.92)

A slim volume, yet thanks to the imaginative energy of the author and her coauthors, this is one of the best titles for ideas on Christmas decorations. As the title suggests, the approximately 40 different ideas are based on Colonial Williamsburg designs, and they range from wreaths to notions for the tree. Each project is carefully explained and accompanied by step-by-step illustrations.

Pettit, Florence. **How to Make Whirligigs and Whimmy Diddles and Other American Folk Craft Objects.** New York: Crowell, 1972. 349p. $6.95 (745.5)

Detailed instructions are found here on how to make more than 20 folklore items. Beyond that, and of equal interest to many readers, is the historical background offered for most of the objects. There are good illustrations of art originally crafted by pioneers, Native Americans, and Eskimos. While written for adults, the book will be of some value for young people who have the necessary skill in using tools.

Reader's Digest Crafts & Hobbies. Pleasantville, NY: Reader's Digest, 1979. 456p. $20.50 (745.5)

This book excels in its number of detailed illustrations and its comprehensive coverage. There are close to 40 different crafts considered, and these range from the usual (ceramics and printmaking) to the unusual (collage and string art). Each of the crafts is explained in terms of materials, tools, skills, and time involved, and several basic projects are suggested. The book can be used by both beginners and intermediate-level craftspersons, and it is one of the best overviews available. Little of the material is dated.

Reader's Digest 101 Do-It-Yourself Projects. New York: Reader's Digest/Random, 1984. 384p. $25 (684)

Following the usual pattern of *Reader's Digest* manuals, this has an abundant number of illustrations (6 to 12 per page) of the step-by-step procedures and the finished product. The result is predictable in that almost anyone can build these 101 items, which may be used in almost every part of the home. The editors presuppose that the reader is familiar with basics and tools. Wisely, they list the projects by the level of skill and experience required. Within that system, one finds the dollhouses, cabinets, chairs, or toys divided by household areas, from the bedroom to the kitchen. The index makes it possible to attack the projects from the point of view of various techniques from metalwork to woodworking.

Roth, Sandra, and Beverly Bieker. **Creative Gift Wrapping.** Charlotte, NC: East Woods, 1982. 110p. pap. $6.95 (745.54)

Using line drawings, black-and-white photographs, and a clear style of explanation, the two authors show how to wrap just about any type or size of package so it appears festive—and in good taste. There are over 100 different methods explained, not simply those involving paper and ribbon. Other materials, from cardboard to just plain paint, are considered. Wrappings are clearly labeled for the appropriate event or occasion.

Sterbenz, Carol, et al. **The Decorated Tree: Recreating Traditional Christmas Ornaments.** New York: Abrams, 1982. 160p. $22.50 (745.59)

Following the normal format of Abrams art books, this is a handsomely illustrated guide to about 55 traditional Christmas tree ornaments. Everything from a pattern to required materials is given and even a novice should be able to make the less complex items. Actually, the authors rate the decorations in terms of their difficulty of construction. There are both general and particular directions for making such objects, as well as a glossary of common terms.

Stoneback, Jean. **333 Easy-to-Build Fun Projects for Your Home.** Blue Ridge Summit, PA: TAB, 1981. 294p. $15.95; pap. $8.95 (745.5)

These are 333 projects ranging from items for pets to simple gifts. Although the coverage is too broad, this book does offer guidance for the person who wants ideas for home-built projects. Almost all can be made in a short time using a minimum of materials. The explanations are clear, instructions are illustrated with line drawings, and there is a chapter on materials.

U.S. Department of Defense. **Craft Techniques in Occupational Therapy.** Washington, DC: GPO, 1981. 511p. $10 (D101.11:8–290)

Although intended for the occupational therapist, this illustrated book may be used by anyone interested in crafts since it provides a basic set of instructions and background for all the major arts and crafts. It includes the common tools that are used for each craft.

Vermeer, Jackie. **The Bazaar Handbook.** New York: Van Nostrand, 1980. 145p. $15.95 (745.5)

The beauty of this guide to items that can be made for a bazaar is its attention to detail and its specific instructions. Given the simplicity of most of the projects, this is an ideal source of inspiration when time and money are short. The step-by-step patterns are illustrated, often with photographs in color. Less useful is the information on the organization of a bazaar.

HANDWRITING. *See* Calligraphy.

HANG GLIDING. *See* Gliding

HEATING. *See* Homes—Energy Conservation; Solar & Wind Power

HERBS

Flannery, Harriet, and Robert Mower. **Gardening with Herbs.** Ithaca, NY: Cornell University Pr., 1980. 39p. $1 (635)
  This 40-page bulletin represents the work done in the extensive herb garden at Cornell. Of particular value are the various methods suggested by the authors to identify 50 common, basic herbs. They offer an identification key that can be used by even the uninformed layperson. There is also a useful reading list.

Foster, Gertrude, and Rosemary Louden. **Park's Success with Herbs.** Greenwood, SC: Park Seed Co., 1980. 192p. $9.95 (635.72)
  Written by a mother-and-daughter team, both experts on herbs, this is an extensive account of herbs. There is a separate page for each herb, describing the plant, noting how it is to be used, and often including several recipes in which the herb is an important ingredient.

Stobart, Tom. **Herbs, Spices and Flavorings.** New York: Viking, 1982. 320p. $15.95 (641.6)
  The author of the much-used *The Cook's Encyclopedia* (see p. 85 in this book) employs his urbane style and meticulous attention to detail in this fine overview. The arrangement of the 400 items is alphabetical. The history and origin of the particular herb, spice, or flavoring are discussed, and suggestions are given for its use. (Flavorings are defined in terms of wines, mushrooms, liqueurs, etc.) While the terminology is British, and here and there a bit confusing, the coverage is international and it is hard to imagine any item not covered in this volume. There are some good illustrations, as well, and a list of plants by families.

Swanson, Faith, and Virginia Rady. **Herb Garden Design.** Hanover, NH: University Press of New England, 1984. 192p. $30; pap. $15.95 (635.7)
  Anyone planning a herb garden should begin with this book. Here are 51 well-thought-out and considered plans for gardens of various sizes and types. Nothing is left to chance. Both the numerous illustrations—which include diagrams and drawings—and the text cover all aspects of the garden plan from how it should be structured to necessary fences, and even trees and other plants. The book opens with a small, average herb garden for the beginner and then moves on to larger, sometimes extremely ambitious efforts. There is detailed information on both common and rare herbs, and nothing is left out. In addition, the authors include illustrated sections on famous herb gardens of the world.

HIGH FIDELITY. *See* Radio

HIKING & BACKPACKING
  See also Camping; Mountaineering; Survival Techniques (Wilderness)

Bridge, Raymond. **America's Backpacking Book.** New York: Scribner's, 1981. 390p. $17.95 (796.5)

Beginning at the beginning, the author explains how to plan a camping and/or hiking trip and what equipment is essential. He moves from the relatively simple—a family outing—to the much more complex. In the latter category are some fine chapters on mountaineering and crossing difficult terrain, such as deserts. The author is most helpful in the down-to-earth suggestions about types of equipment and materials needed, as well as advice on how to camp in comfort.

Elman, Robert, and Clair Rees. **The Hiker's Bible.** Rev. ed. New York: Doubleday, 1982. 148p. pap. $4.95 (796.51)

Thanks to its enthusiasm and fine writing style, this is much above average and particularly well suited to the beginning hiker. Every step is clearly explained—from clothing to methods of walking. There is a good section on major equipment, and a state-by-state listing of trails, their conditions and lengths. The appendixes include a vast amount of reference material from addresses of hiking groups, to bike-hiking data, to campsites and outfitting sources. There is no index, but there is a massive table of contents. Suitable for all ages.

Fletcher, Colin. **The Complete Walker III: The Joys and Techniques of Hiking and Backpacking.** Rev. ed. New York: Knopf, 1984. 645p. $19.50; pap. $11.95 (796.5)

A classic and about as basic as one can get, this was first published in 1969 and has been twice updated. The work's reputation is due to the author's excellent writing style, his enthusiastic advice, and, above all, the detailed and explicit instructions. There are numerous helpful illustrations and lists of various types of equipment, suppliers, organizations, and related matters. There is not a topic that Fletcher does not cover. He even explains the best type of flashlights, not to mention clothing and sleeping equipment, to buy. The book is for the beginner, the intermediate, and even the expert. The latter particularly will share the author's intelligent approach to nature and his constant plea for never tempting nature too far. A definitive guide, this is the first place to turn whether the reader is planning a day's walking trip or a month or more of backpacking.

Hart, John. **Walking Softly in the Wilderness: The Sierra Club Guide to Backpacking.** Rev. ed. New York: Random House, 1984. 510p. pap. $8.95 (796.5)

Like other Sierra Club publications, this places considerable emphasis on ecology and the need to maintain the wilderness. In fact, almost every bit of advice is laced with this concern and, for that reason, it is particularly good for younger people who may just be breaking into backpacking and camping. At any rate, all bases are covered in an informative fashion. Hart moves from what is needed by way of equipment to how to prepare for the trail. Once the hike begins, he has specific instructions on both the joys and the problems likely to arise. While there is really little new here, it is refreshingly written and the solid organization of the guide makes it easy to find specific bits of information. It is also an inspiration and a plea to maintain the environment.

Maughan, Jackie, and Ann Puddicombe. **Hiking the Backcountry: A Do-It-Yourself Guide for the Adventurous Woman.** Harrisburg, PA: Stackpole, 1981. 237p. pap. $9.95 (796.5)

No matter where one hikes, no matter what the conditions, the authors seem to be ahead of the reader in that they cover the situation and offer constructive suggestions on how to make the most of the experience. Thanks to this nearly complete coverage, the book is as suitable for men as for women. This is particularly true in sections devoted to basics. Beyond that, the authors explain the physiological differences between men and women that are likely to affect the hiker. In each case they draw on documented studies and their own experiences to show what the differences may mean when hiking. The writing style is lively and the authors obviously love the adventure of the outdoors.

Sandi, Michael. **Sports Illustrated Backpacking.** New York: Lippincott, 1980. 224p. $9.95; pap. $5.95 (796.5)
The strength of this guide is its wide coverage. The author assumes that the reader knows little or nothing about backpacking and camping, and the discussion opens with a clear explanation of what is involved. The advice is applicable to any part of the country, or, for that matter, the world. Sandi then moves to specifics, from simple hiking with children to more advanced camping. As in other *Sports Illustrated* manuals, this is noteworthy for the abundance of excellent photographs and illustrations.

U.S. Department of Agriculture. **Backpacking.** Washington, DC: GPO, 1981. 52p. $3.50 (A1.68:1239)
The Forest Service puts great stress on safety and precaution in this illustrated brochure, yet the information is well presented and almost as lively as that found in commercial works. There are some excellent tips on how to make backpacking considerably easier than it first may appear. Specific information is given on various types of equipment, campsites, and even bear-proofing.

HOBBIES. *See* Name of specific hobby, e.g., Book Collecting; Coins; Stamps; etc.

HOCKEY. *See* Skating

HOLIDAYS. *See* Entertaining & Parties

HOME ECONOMICS
See also Housecleaning

Bacharach, Bert. **How to Do Almost Everything.** New York: Simon & Schuster, 1970. 340p. $9.95 (640)
How to paint a house faster, how to keep cut flowers longer, and how to remove stains from your clothes are only three of hundreds of practical bits of advice collected by this popular columnist. Usually direct, simple methods are stressed—methods that have worked for the author and others. The first section is general and covers everything from clothes to pets and hobbies. The second part is devoted to cooking hints. There is a good general index and a separate food index. True, much of this can be found in specific reference works, but the charm here is the "almanac" approach, with a little bit of something for almost everyone.

Ballard, B. Gay, and Tracy Craig. **Home Care & Upkeep.** San Francisco: Ortho, 1983. 96p. pap. $5.95 (648)

Primarily a guide to cutting the work of housekeeping short, this moves from room to room, from problem area to problem area about the home. Helpful suggestions will be found on how to clean and care for everything from carpets to doors and windows. There is a section, too, on removing stains from furniture and rugs, and one devoted to the control of bugs and insects. The information is presented carefully, and the directions (nicely illustrated) are easy to follow.

Consumer Guide Editors. **The Ultimate Householder's Book.** New York: A & W, 1982. 672p. $17.95 (640)

While this is a hodgepodge of 4,000 suggestions, tips, and ideas on how to do almost anything—in or out of the home—it has the distinct advantage of being comprehensive. In fact, such a wide range of subjects is covered, from the usual treatment of stains and cooking to the unusual method of basement planning, that the book is virtually an encyclopedia. Unfortunately, it tends to wander, and tips on diet and health care somehow do not quite seem to fit, although they are balanced by imaginative ideas about decoration and entertaining. There are numerous illustrations and the text is easy enough to follow. The lack of any real focus makes it a secondary item in this area, but one that serves as a good fallback when all else fails.

Cruse, Heloise. **Hints from Heloise.** New York: Dutton, 1980. 530p. $12.95; pap. $6.95 (640)

How to do almost anything around the home—that is the promise of the author the *New Yorker* calls "the premier household-hints columnist of all times." Here she has taken, and sometimes modified, suggestions found in her syndicated newspaper column "Hints from Heloise." The brief cures, formulas, hints, suggestions, etc., cover hundreds of individual problems from how to get rid of odors in a refrigerator to a sure cure for exterminating the elusive roach. There are shortcuts here for removing stains, fixing squeaky floors, cooking, cleaning, and even forming human relationships. A good index and numerous cross-references make most of this material easy enough to find. The prose style is relaxed, too much so for some people, but it is easy to follow. The hints themselves are good, and according to the publisher there have been few, if any, complaints.

Douglas, Erika, ed. **The Family Circle Hints Book.** New York: Times Books, 1982. 284p. $12.95 (640.2)

One of the more popular parts of the *Family Circle* magazine is "The Reader's Idea Exchange," where hints are given on how to make life easier and more orderly around the home. Numerous suggestions from that column are collected here and organized in an easy-to-follow fashion. The editor claims all of the ideas have been tested and proved suitable for safety and good living. The "hints" range from travel ideas to decorating and kitchen aids.

Hirsch, Gretchen. **Womanhours: A 21-Day Time-Management Plan That Works.** New York: St. Martin's, 1983. 144p. $10.50; pap. $4.95 (640.43)

Actually, the average reader may not want to stick to the 21-day program offered here, but that does not matter. Even a cursory reading of the book will help. The author begins each day with a lecture on how to select out of the 24 hours those activities that are most necessary, rewarding, and helpful. Once this is decided (at least where there is room for decision), Hirsch explains various approaches to making efficient use of each hour. The problem with all of this is the assumption that the reader needs so much guidance, but if one accepts that, the book is close to ideal. The author offers many insights as well as practical tips on how to make the most out of time. A few of these should prove of value to even the most skeptical.

Jabs, Carolyn. **Re/Uses: 2133 Ways to Recycle and Reuse the Things You Ordinarily Throw Away.** New York: Crown, 1982. 182p. $18.95; pap. $8.95 (640)

The title tells it all, but the author offers a surprise on almost every page. Arranged in alphabetical order by item, the hints and suggestions range from what to do with wastepaper, old newspapers, and milk cartons to various types of tin cans and bottles. For many of the entries there are good line drawings, and often there is directory-type information that leads the reader to organizations that can help in the recycling process. Most ideas are conventional enough, but here and there are some real mind-bogglers such as using old chewing gum to clean typewriter keys, or saving pull tabs from beverage cans for various types of clothing adornment. While much of this will serve only an individual who is determined to save things at almost any cost—and sometimes considerable energy—it also offers less strenuous ideas for young people and adults who are simply looking for imaginative new . craft ideas.

McCullough, Bonnie R. **Bonnie's Household Organizer.** New York: St. Martin's, 1980. 184p. pap. $4.95 (640)

A basic guide to the organization of housework, this is the best of its kind, and fully lives up to the promise of the subtitle, "the essential guide for getting control of your home." Most of the suggestions, hints, and organizational patterns are based on common sense rather than fashion—hence, the book is not likely to date. The author moves from methods of making the most out of limited space to wise suggestions on shopping. The formulas and ideas are useful for singles or for large families. The writing style, illustrations, and charts and diagrams work nicely together. A must for anyone seriously interested in learning how to overcome organizational problems in the home.

Mitchell, Harris. **1200 Household Hints You Wanted to Know.** New York: Everest House, 1982. 252p. pap. $9.95 (640)

What is the easiest way to remove wax? How can one take out spots on clothing? What can be done when the fireplace smokes? What are the basics of wiring in the home? Answers to such questions are found among these 1,200 hints, arranged by broad subjects. One turns directly to the topic or consults the index. Answers are brief yet accurate, and cover everything from common cleaning and maintenance procedures to repairs and improvements about the house. This is an extremely handy guide for almost any common (and not so common) household problem.

Schofield, Denise. **Confessions of an Organized Housewife.** Cincinnati: Writer's Digest, 1982. 192p. pap. $6.95 (640)

Here is a management approach to organizing a house, and while the title narrows the audience, the book would actually be of equal help to a man who took any interest in the home. What the author has done is not to offer simple tips, but to apply management techniques to the running and command of every part of the mansion from kitchen and children's room to basement. Needless to say, the book is well organized. It not only demonstrates how to make the most out of the least amount of space and time, but goes into some detail on how to fit in outside activities with the housework.

HOME INSPECTION

Becker, Norman. **The Complete Book of Home Inspection.** New York: McGraw-Hill, 1980. 172p. pap. $8.95 (643)

A professional home inspector tells the reader what to look for in making a decision on whether to buy a house. He moves from basement to attic and, in an easy-to-follow, step-by-step approach, lists what the buyer should check. There are checklists, forms, and charts. For each item, whether studs or siding, Becker explains what should be correct and what can be wrong. Numerous illustrations and photographs aid the reader's understanding of potential problems. Even after a home is purchased, this guide would be useful in making corrections before problems become catastrophes.

HOMES. *See* Apartments; Appliances; Bathrooms; Carpentry; Fences & Walls; Fireplaces & Stoves; Homes—Additions; Homes—Building & Construction; Homes—Energy Conservation; Homes—Maintenance & Repair; Homes—Remodeling; Interior Decoration; Kitchens; Masonry & Brickwork; Painting & Wallpapering; Plumbing; Solar & Wind Power; Tools; Woodworking

HOMES—ADDITIONS

Browne, Dan. **Multiply Your Living Space: How to Put an Addition on Your Home at a Cost You Can Afford.** New York: McGraw-Hill, 1979. 120p. $12.95 (690.8)

Instead of serving up the usual techniques and procedures for remodeling, Browne offers time-saving methods. Charts show how much time each of these unconventional approaches takes, and whether it is worth it to the reader. Equal emphasis is placed on unusual materials—often at a considerably lower cost than conventional brick and cement. There are tips on cutting costs by buying directly from suppliers. While this is not for the beginner, it is for the amateur on his or her way to becoming an expert. It is an excellent companion to the Daniels title (in the Homes—Remodeling section), which stresses conventional, easy-to-follow methods.

Consumer Guide Editors. **Add-a-Room.** New York: Simon & Schuster, 1980. 192p. pap. $8.95 (643.7)

What makes this a different kind of guide for an old problem is the easy-to-follow directions and the large number of illustrations. It is conceivable that a complete novice might become an experienced builder simply by following the directions and pictures. At the same time, there is practical advice at the preliminary stage. Should, for example, a room actually be added to the house, or would it be better to remodel an existing space—say an attic, garage, or basement? There is excellent advice on when and how to contact a professional architect, carpenter, plumber, etc. Each step in construction is noted, from major (walls and foundations) to minor (patching walls). Cost figures—by now somewhat dated—are given and the methods of estimating costs are explained carefully.

Landis, Michael, and Ray Moholt. **Patios & Decks: How to Plan, Build & Enjoy.** Tucson, AZ: HP Books, 1983. 160p. pap. $9.95 (690.89)

This is more an idea book than a detailed how-to-do-it approach. Thanks to excellent illustrations and an extremely clear style of presentation, almost anyone should be able to design a patio or deck by using this guide. The various projects are described in terms of design and type of construction. The authors make much of the possibility of solving problems through proper planning, and for each situation there are numerous illustrations. The solutions are the work of imaginative architects, not just Saturday-afternoon builders. In fact, there are numerous conversations between architects and landscape designers that do much to explain the need for careful planning. Less detail is given on actual construction, but there is excellent advice on tools and materials.

McConnell, Charles. **Building an Addition to Your Home.** Englewood Cliffs, NJ: Prentice-Hall, 1982. 261p. $19.95; pap. $10.95 (643.7)

For the individual who has the courage to actually put up a major home addition, this is the ideal book. The author gives specific directions, and begins where all construction begins, at the foundation. With that he supplies data on everything from walls and floors to plumbing—all in logical order. He then moves into the area of maintenance and repair, which will have a wider audience than the more ambitious first section. A noteworthy part is the detailed section on how to save and use energy. He provides plans for such things as a new lease on life for the water heater and the construction of a solar water heating system. The illustrations are good, and the instructions precise.

Wolverton, Ruth, and Mike Wolverton. **How to Convert Ordinary Garages into Exciting Family Rooms.** Blue Ridge Summit, PA: TAB, 1981. 406p. $18.95; pap. $10.95 (643.55)

When more living space is required, any guide that shows how to turn underutilized room into living room is bound to be welcome. That is precisely what the Wolvertons do, offering a dozen specific types of conversions. There is a useful background section on the whole question of conversion with realistic methods to estimate costs, materials, labor, etc. It is assumed that the reader has some understanding of carpentry. The authors do offer basic information on tools required and various building techniques, but these are minor, and for that type of help one should turn to a more general guide. Even for those who are not going to do the conversion themselves, this book is useful to indicate the steps and costs involved.

HOMES—BUILDING & CONSTRUCTION

Brann, Donald. **How to Build a Low Cost House Above or Below Ground.** Rev. ed. Briarcliff Manor, NY: Easi Bild Directions, 1982. 226p. pap. $6.95 (690.83)

The author and the publisher are responsible for several how-to-build-it books, and this one is typical. Here the emphasis is on detailed plans—detailed to a point where absolutely nothing is missing, right down to the last nail. Basics are considered from a to z, although it is assumed the reader does have some knowledge of construction. The house may not be everyone's dream, but it is truly "low cost" and a clever builder should have no difficulty making modifications.

Carter, David. **Build It Underground: A Guide for the Self-Builder and Building Professional.** New York: Sterling, 1982. 208p. $14.95; pap. $7.95 (690)

With the recognition that energy is saved in underground construction and reliance on the earth to conserve heat and provide natural cooling, this guide is particularly helpful. There are instructions for building underground homes, most of which are accompanied by illustrations. The text is written primarily as an overview, and will be of benefit, as the title suggests, to both beginners and experts. If nothing else, it indicates possibilities, although anyone going ahead with actual construction will need more detailed planning. Related areas discussed include landscaping, building permits, property purchase, etc. There is a minimum of data on commercial structures.

Clifford, Martin. **Basic Drafting.** Blue Ridge Summit, PA: TAB, 1980. 270p. $12.95; pap. $7.95 (604.2)

Carefully and completely illustrated, this is a basic approach to drafting and mechanical drawing for the interested layperson. The explanations are particularly clear, and the author assumes that the reader knows nothing about the subject. There is an opening discussion of tools and materials, followed by a detailed section on basic techniques. Simple projects are considered. The book may be of less benefit when, toward the conclusion, it becomes more complicated. *Note:* Those with an advanced interest in the subject can consult Frederick Giesecke's basic textbook, often revised, entitled *Technical Drawing* (New York: Macmillan, 1936–   ).

Edelhart, Mike. **The Handbook of Earth Shelter Design.** New York: Dolphin/Doubleday, 1982. 235p. $11.95 (728)

Here the home is literally buried in earth to protect it from the elements and to ensure much better heating and cooling in all seasons. What makes the text different from others is its drawing on experiences of those who have owned, or currently own, such homes, and builders with experience in the field. This is primarily a decision type of book in that it will help the potential buyer decide whether the earth shelter is best for individual needs. There are good illustrations and clear explanations.

Hibshman, Dan. **Your Affordable Solar Home.** New York: Random House, 1983. 124p. pap. $7.95 (690.86)

By "affordable" the author means $20,000 or less for a passive solar heating system for a home. Specific plans and instructions are provided for variations of cost, difficulty, type of home, and location. The primary focus is on the smaller home—in fact, the contents of the book are the result of a California contest in which designers were asked to bring in plans for under $20,000. Even with this relatively low cost, the author admits it is too much for some, and offers alternative suggestions.

Hoffman, Eric. **Renegade Houses.** Philadelphia: Running Pr., 1983. 153p. $19.80; pap. $7.95 (690.83)

Builders offer many different approaches to the construction of a home for the person who wants either an inexpensive dwelling or one that is truly different from all others about. Some of it is a bit extreme—e.g., there are plans for tree houses. At the same time, most of the advice is applicable to many construction schemes. For example, most of the homes are designed to save energy, and one might incorporate these ideas into a more conventional structure. While complete details on individual homes are not given, specific features are provided. The text is accompanied by good diagrams, line drawings, and photographs.

Mackie, Allan. **Building with Logs.** 7th ed. New York: Scribner's, 1981. 91p. pap. $11.95 (694.2)

Originally published in Canada, this is a superior and thoughtful guide. Superior, because it is the work of a man who has had a great deal of experience in the construction of log homes. Thoughtful, because Mackie believes there is more to a house than building it, and he points up the necessary aesthetic components of the successful log home. In addition to the usual step-by-step instructions, the author gives a history of log cabins and indicates the best trees for use in this type of construction. A companion work (with plans for houses from little more than one room to over 3,000 square feet) is the author's *Log House Plans* (1981, $12.95) from the same publisher.

Merritt, Frederick, ed. **Building Design Construction Handbook.** 4th ed. New York: McGraw-Hill, 1982. 1,408p. $75 (690)

Intended for the builder, this standard handbook can be used by the interested amateur for guidance. It is divided into over 20 sections, each of which focuses on a particular topic. The first, for example, is concerned with building systems, which include basic materials, techniques, construction methods, etc. In other sections, one finds information on lighting, types of construction, design, and even a section on the effects of natural catastrophes on a building. Each part is written by an expert and is illustrated. Particular attention is given to design specifications. A new edition is planned for the late 1980s.

Ramsey, Dan. **Building a Log Home from Scratch or Kit.** Blue Ridge Summit, PA: TAB, 1983. 250p. $17.95; pap. $11.95 (690.1)

Whether for romantic reasons, finance, or pure aesthetics, Americans have a love affair with log cabins. Here the author, an expert builder, explains the nitty-gritty of what is involved in putting up a home—and this in itself may give many pause. For those who wish to go on, the illustrated instructions are close to ideal. Every aspect of construction is covered, and it is conceivable that an amateur would be able to proceed by using this book. It is equally apparent that carpentry skills are needed. For those who want to contract the work out there is material on site selection and choosing a builder (and a kit).

Sievert, Manny. **The Art of Log Building.** Blue Ridge Summit, PA: TAB, 1982. 303p. $17.95; pap. $9.95 (694.2)

An expert himself, Sievert understands both the difficulties and the benefits of building a log house. He assumes that the reader has some natural talent for carpentry, but from that point he gives detailed instructions on such topics as how to select and cut the right logs and put on the finishing touches. There are adequate photographs and line drawings, but the instructions for plumbing, lighting, etc., are too quickly passed over, and here one is likely to need another source. Still, this is by far the best book on log houses available and can be used profitably by anyone interested in the subject.

Sterling, Raymond, et al. **Earth Sheltered Residential Design Manual.** New York: Van Nostrand, 1982. 251p. $24.95; pap. $16.95 (690.8)
 A technical manual, this is for anyone with some experience in building who wishes to consider a home virtually surrounded by earth as a method of saving on energy and some building costs. The assumption that the reader has at least a basic understanding of engineering and/or building sets this off from others of its type, as does the sponsor: the U.S. Department of Housing and Urban Development. It is extremely useful for those with the necessary background.

Traister, John. **Basic Blueprint Reading for Practical Applications.** Blue Ridge Summit, PA: TAB, 1983. 295p. $18.95; pap. $12.95 (604.2)
 What does a blueprint tell the trained observer? That is precisely what the author sets out to explain for the average layperson who may have to consult blueprints for work around the home or in a hobby. Each line, each term, each variation, is carefully defined. Obviously there are differences in varying types of work, and Traister considers these, from mechanical drawings to architectural renderings. Everything is nicely illustrated. In addition, there is a fascinating discussion on how the blueprint is drawn and reproduced. Here, too, the author tells what equipment is required. It is conceivable that once the book is finished the reader will be capable of making blueprints, but the primary focus is on reading them.

Underground Space Center, University of Minnesota. **Earth Sheltered Homes.** New York: Van Nostrand, 1981. 125p. $16.95; pap. $9.95 (728)
 Here are good descriptions, usually accompanied by both black-and-white colored photographs, plans, and drawings, of 23 outstanding earth-sheltered homes in the United States and Europe. Each home represents a different approach in size and cost as well as in technological design. The information is such that the careful reader can employ it for design ideas. It is not so specific that one could work only from this book to build a home, but it does give essential details that might assist one in drawing up plans. There is a list of builders and designers who specialize in such work.

U.S. Department of Housing and Urban Development. **Designing Affordable Houses.** Washington, DC: GPO, 1983. 21p. pap. $1.75 (HH1.2:D46/3)
 This is a brief yet useful guide for someone contemplating designing and building a one-family home. The primary benefit is that there are numerous, well-thought-out floor plans for different houses of various size.

U.S. Department of Housing and Urban Development. **Guide for Earthquake Design.** Washington, DC: GPO, 1980. 60p. $3.75 (HH1 6/3:H75)
 While few people may need this type of guidance, for those who do and are contemplating building a home, it is invaluable. It clearly shows what design

features must be built into the home and where the house should or should not be located for maximum safety.

Wade, Herb. **Building Underground: The Design and Construction Handbook for Earth-Sheltered Houses.** Emmaus, PA: Rodale, 1983. 289p. $19.95; pap. $14.95 (690.8)

This handbook offers the reader a home that is literally buried. The only visible sections are the front door and select space for windows or access to light. As unlikely as this may sound, the plans for at least eight such houses are considered. In addition, the author gives instructions on basics from selection of a place for the home to roof construction and how to cope with solar designs. Using eight different situations and plans, he offers specific case histories that illustrate the problems involved. There are illustrations throughout, and the text is easy to follow. It is an excellent introduction to the subject, but it should be stressed that it is not a step-by-step how-to-do-it book. It is an overview that allows readers to decide whether this type of construction is for them.

HOMES—ENERGY CONSERVATION
See also Solar & Wind Power

Coffee, Frank. **The Self-Sufficient House.** New York: Holt, 1981. 213p. $17.95 (696)

Taking the reader through the house and outside it, the author shows how its systems may be made more livable and certainly more economical to operate. There are good discussions of insulation, solar energy, sewage draining systems, heating plants, etc. For most of these ideas, the author offers detailed descriptions of specific houses where the suggestions have been applied. There is a list of product sources and a good bibliography. The primary benefit of this guide: the overview it gives, and the possibilities it suggests for energy saving.

Dawson, Joe. **Seeking Shelter.** New York: Morrow, 1983. 190p. $17.95; pap. $9.95 (643.12)

Here the shelter is a home that is energy efficient, and the seeker is looking for help on how to select such a house. Most people, of course, have a wider vision, but this is useful as subsidiary reading. All aspects of heating and cooling are considered, and within its narrow range the book is quite helpful.

Duncan, S. Blackwell. **The Home Insulation Bible.** Blue Ridge Summit, PA: TAB, 1982. 366p. $16.95; pap. $9.95 (693.8)

What is the best type of insulation for a particular home? How much will it cut down on heating and cooling costs? What will it cost to install? Are there dangers in using insulation? These and numerous other questions are answered directly and indirectly—i.e., calculations, charts, diagrams, and text help the individual discover the actual figures for his or her situation. However, this is primarily a reference work. It is *not* a how-to-do-it for the individual engaged in a home-insulation project.

Fossel, Peter. **Keeping Cool: A Sensible Guide to Beating the Heat.** New York: Putnam's, 1984. 145p. pap. $7.95 (640)

The obvious way to stay cool in a home is to buy an air conditioner. While this is considered in one section, the author is more involved with alternatives he says are ultimately more satisfactory, and less expensive. The solutions vary, but they depend primarily on good insulation, ventilation, and proper landscaping. Each of these is explained in depth, as is the use of solar energy to maintain an even temperature. Nontechnical, practical, and well written, this is an excellent guide for the person planning either to build a home, or to extensively remodel a dwelling.

Fossel, Peter. **Keeping Warm: A Sensible Guide to Heat Conservation.** New York: Perigee, 1983. 204p. pap. $6.95 (697)

Keeping warm is a matter of knowing how to heat a house and how to keep out the cold. While the secrets may translate into highly expensive renovations and new equipment, they do not have to. The author examines both approaches with good, easy-to-follow discussions of various alternative heating methods. He is particularly helpful in the consideration of stoves and fireplaces. The solar heating section, reminiscent of many found elsewhere, is not really complete enough. There is, though, an interesting examination of other ways to keep warm, including the use of proper bedding. Heat loss, and what can be done to check it, is examined. All of this is conveyed in an easy-to-follow writing style, with the aid of numerous auditing devices and charts. It is primarily useful as a good summary of current thinking on heating. *Note:* This is one of the few books to include a discussion of apartments as well as houses.

Hotton, Peter. **So You Want to Build an Energy-Efficient Addition.** Boston: Little, 1983. 242p. pap. $14.95 (643.7)

When it comes to adding an extra room to the house, or remodeling the garage into a living space, how can one make them energy efficient? A detailed answer is given by the author, a well-known expert in the how-to-do-it field. He offers some fairly basic approaches such as wall insulation and using various products to create necessary seals against the weather. There are good sections on related matters from plumbing to painting and wiring. All of this is explained in detail, with sufficient illustrations to make the text clear. There is nothing really new here, except the much better than average writing style of the author, and a useful glossary of terms associated with energy-efficient homes. It is a book suitable for both beginners and experienced amateurs.

Jones, Peter. **Weekend Home Energy-Saving Projects.** Van Nostrand, 1984. 120p. $18.50; pap. $10.95 (644)

The projects described here are for the average homeowner who is handy with tools. They are guaranteed to save energy, and most are well enough known. The claim is that one may carry them out in steps that require only a small amount of time. Here are explanations, diagrams, illustrations, and hints on everything from insulating the attic to caulking windows. There is a treatment of the proper installation and use of wood-burning stoves. In addition, there are sections devoted to explaining how one can save electricity and heat through a judicious use of appliances. More ambitious projects consist of constructing basic solar heating units—projects one suspects were added and do not really fit the typical "weekend" project category.

McClintock, Michael. **Homeowner's Energy Investment Handbook.** Andover, MA: Brick House, 1982. 116p. pap. $8.95 (693.8)

Can one really save money by cutting energy costs? What are the necessary steps in successfully insulating a house? And what other things can you do to cut back on heating expenses in your home? The author explains what is and is not to be done. What makes this guide particularly useful, and different, is its clear method of figuring costs and savings by using such things as solar heat, wood-burning stoves, greenhouses, wind generators, underground construction, etc. McClintock considers each option and how the investment compares with what might be saved were the money simply put into a savings account. Besides the basic economics, he offers direct advice on how to find the worst energy leaks in your home and how to plug them with or without the aid of professionals.

Morris, David. **Be Your Own Power Company.** Emmaus, PA: Rodale, 1983. 326p. $15.95; pap. $9.95 (621.31)

This solution is hardly feasible for many people, but for those who are able, the formation of one's own electric power company solves numerous energy problems. What is needed to set up such an operation—from the technological to the financial and legal concerns—is covered here in considerable detail. Various types of power sources are discussed, ranging from the more familiar wind power to the less well known photovoltaic sources. The book is based on government regulations, which are now written to encourage such enterprises.

Norback, Peter, and Craig Norback. **The Consumer's Energy Handbook.** New York: Van Nostrand, 1981. 362p. $19.95; pap. $14.95 (333.7)

What sources are available for supplying energy in the home? This book begins with a thorough discussion of this question, and moves from the traditional sources (wood, oil, and coal) to recent applications of solar energy. There is a useful description of the ideally energy-efficient home. The second section is concerned with practical ways of conserving heat, and the last section is a somewhat dated directory of various energy organizations and government groups listed state by state. The book is now out of date in its particulars, but the general discussion is excellent and a good place for the beginner to start.

Powell, Evan, and Ernest Heyn. **Popular Science Book of Home Heating—and Cooling.** Reston, VA: Reston, 1983. 371p. $16.50 (697)

Using the style of *Popular Mechanics,* including the same approach to combining various forms of illustrations, two experienced editors offer an overview of modern home heating principles and possibilities. They cover the general theory of heating and cooling and particular products, often right down to installation instructions. Probably because there is now so much written on wood-burning stoves and solar heating, these two areas are not discussed in much depth. The primary focus is on traditional forms of heating and less conventional approaches such as heat pumps. As a general examination of possibilities, this is an exceptional book. Once a method has been chosen, books offering specific heating and cooling projects will be more helpful.

Ross, Fred. **Fuel Alcohol: How to Make It, How to Use It.** 2nd ed. New York: St. Martin's, 1981. 176p. $9.95; pap. $4.95 (662.66)

As the title states, this is a manual for learning how to make and use fuel alcohol. Precise information is given regarding the necessary ingredients—which vary, the basics of fermentation, and what equipment is needed for distillation. There are necessary licenses to obtain, too, and these are noted. Once it is made, the alcohol may be used in different ways, and these are carefully explained. There is a section on gasohol, which at one time was considered a good substitute for gas. Other uses, from home heating to driving various types of machinery, are discussed. There are lists of places where materials may be purchased, and sources of information.

Rothchild, John. **Stop Burning Your Money: The Intelligent Homeowner's Guide to Household Energy Savings.** New York: Random House, 1981. 258p. $15.50; pap. $5.95 (696)

The author, who has had both theoretical and practical experience with energy-saving methods, offers the reader some highly useful methods of saving money. He discusses furnaces, insulation, appliances, water heaters, and just about anything else that is involved with energy-related bills. For each, he shows ways of improving efficiency, or, in some cases, gives advice on totally new approaches or equipment. The book is particularly useful for its numerous charts and diagrams, which are often used to compare various methods in terms of cost and ease of use. Rothchild, for example, generally takes a dim view of most solar heaters, fireplaces, and wood- or coal-burning stoves. The book ends with a list of suppliers and manufacturers.

Shelton, Jay. **Jay Shelton's Solid Fuels Encyclopedia.** Pownal, VT: Garden Way, 1983. 268p. pap. $12.95 (697)

By "solid fuels," Shelton means primarily wood and coal. By "encyclopedia" he means a detailed discussion of the fuels and the various places they are burned—from stoves and fireplaces to furnaces. He is concerned not only with the best types of fuel, but with methods of installing heating plants. All of this is carried out in a thorough, detailed fashion—so much so that the book is a good reference work for someone trying to decide on a given type of heating system or for the person who needs help with buying such a system. There are illustrations and definitions of terms.

Sherman, Steve. **Home Heating with Coal: Energy for the Eighties.** Harrisburg, PA: Stackpole, 1980. 208p. pap. $8.95 (697.04)

The author calls for a return to coal, at least in those areas where coal remains plentiful and cheap. He shows the advantages of using this fuel, and goes into considerable detail to explain the best types of stoves and other heating devices to use, and the different varieties of coal available. Much of the focus is on the stove. Not only are the various types explained, but there is information on how to install and maintain them. A handy list of major manufacturing firms of stoves is included.

U.S. Community Services Administration. **No More Heat? A Self-Help Booklet.** Washington, DC: GPO, 1981. 30p. $2 (CSA1.9:6143)

An emergency self-help government pamphlet, this gives the reader full instructions on how to handle a no-heat situation. Sections cover such things as sudden failure of the furnace due to lack of fuel or mechanical ills and how to keep warm without a furnace. Also, there are suggestions on the prevention of frozen pipes when you leave home, and a checklist of things that can be done to prevent heat-related emergencies.

U.S. Department of Agriculture. **Cutting Energy Costs: The 1980 Yearbook of Agriculture.** Washington, DC: GPO, 1980. 397p. $9.50 (A1.10:980)
Each year *Yearbook of Agriculture* focuses on a single topic. The 1980 annual is concerned with just about anything anyone would want to know about how to conserve energy and how to get the most for the heating dollar. There are scores of suggestions and hints, including illustrations of various how-to-do-it projects for home energy saving. Considering the price and the wide scope, this is a best buy in the energy field.

U.S. Department of Commerce. **Energy Conservation in Buildings: An Economic Guidebook for Investment Decisions.** Washington, DC: GPO, 1980. 150p. $5 (C13.11:132)
Although this is technical and requires an understanding of mathematics and a minimal appreciation of accounting, for those with the requisite skills it is an excellent guide to figuring out just how much can be saved by various energy-conservation methods. There are illustrations and case studies that support the explanations. Still, it is for the individual willing to spend some time and effort in computation, not for the casual beginner.

U.S. Department of Energy. **Find and Fix the Leaks.** Washington, DC: GPO, 1981. 29p. $2.50 (E1.89:0006)
Subtitled "a guide to air infiltration reduction and indoor air quality control," this pamphlet explains how to save energy by plugging up holes. Since up to one-half of the energy used to heat or cool a home may literally go out the window, there is money to be saved by stopping the leaks. The procedures, many of which are inexpensive, are clearly explained. Most can be carried out by the homeowner without outside help.

U.S. Department of Energy. **Tips for Energy Savers.** Washington, DC: GPO, 1981. 30p. $2 (E1.25:0037/1)
The title tells all. Here are a number of practical and quite inexpensive suggestions for saving energy. There is a valuable map showing the type and kind of insulation best suited for homes in various sections of the country.

Vaughn, Lewis. **Chilton's Guide to Home Energy Savings.** Radnor, PA: Chilton, 1982. 225p. $15.95; pap. $10.95 (643.7)
Where does all the heat from a home go? Much of it is wasted, and Vaughn opens this useful manual by describing the various escape patterns that make home energy costs so high. This is followed by a discussion of the various methods and techniques that will hold heat in the house and cut costs. There is no one method of saving for every house, but the basic approaches are considered in some detail. After a discussion of everything from weather stripping to insulation, the author considers various types of heating plants and fuels. Vaughn offers enough information for those who are going to do the work themselves, or for others who will hire it out and want some notion of what is going to be involved in the labor. The text is

well illustrated and there are numerous charts and graphs that the reader can use to figure specific heating solutions.

Wahlfeldt, Bette G. **The Energy Efficient Home—101 Money Saving Ideas.** Blue Ridge Summit, PA: TAB, 1982. 277p. $19.95; pap. $12.95 (644.2)

While there is nothing new here, the organization and the writing style are such that this serves as a fine guide for the beginner trying to save heating costs in a home. The advice is practical, with numerous explicit drawings and photographs. Basically it is arranged under "101 money saving ideas," which include insulation, heating and cooling, problems of condensation, maintenance of the fireplace, etc.

Wing, Charlie. **House Warming with Charlie Wing.** Boston: Little, 1983. 204p. $24.95; pap. $16.95 (697)

Here the primary focus is on how to conserve heat, how to keep it from going out the cracks in the house. Concerned with both old and new homes, Wing offers suggestions useful to anyone remodeling, building, or, for that matter, trying to cut back on fuel bills while living in an established home. There are various sections on types of insulation and their applicability to given situations. In addition, the author goes through each part of the home and points out what can be done to cut condensation, air flow, heat loss, etc. The book is carefully written and the text is supported by useful illustrations.

HOMES—MAINTENANCE & REPAIR

Alth, Max. **Do-It-Yourself Roofing and Siding.** New York: Hawthorn, 1979. 210p. pap. $4.95 (643)

The roofing instructions are clear and easy to follow, but pretty much limited to basics, i.e., asphalt shingles or rolls. As in Alth's other manuals, each step is clearly explained and usually illustrated. The book excels in detail. For example, there are specific directions and photographs showing just how a shingle should fit around a chimney. Instructions for siding follow the same procedures. There is good advice on what materials to purchase, how to buy them, the types of tools needed, etc. Costs are indicated. While the beginner might want to try this book, it really is aimed at someone who is familiar with the basics of home repair and maintenance.

Alth, Max. **The Handbook of Do-It-Yourself Materials.** New York: Crown, 1982. 344p. $17.95 (643.7)

By "materials" the author means building materials ranging from concrete and brick to lumber and plastic. Alth has a systematic approach for each. He groups the materials by class and then considers which is best for a given type of project or situation. Costs are considered and he discusses the good and bad points about working with the specific items—including such things as how they are cut and shaped. There are illustrations on every page and the drawings and photographs do much to clarify various points. This guide will be of great use to both the amateur and the expert.

Better Homes and Gardens Complete Guide to Home Repair, Maintenance & Improvement. Des Moines, IA: Meredith, 1980. 552p. $19.95 (643.7)

Among the best of the numerous home-repair books, this can claim its distinction for several reasons. First, it boasts close to 3,000 line drawings that support the text in all areas—plumbing, wiring, or fixing appliances. It is equal to and in some cases better than the basic *Reader's Digest Complete Do-It-Yourself Manual* (q.v.). Second, there is a fine illustrated section on the types of tools needed. Finally, in the "improvement" chapters one finds solid advice on the installation of everything from new fences to skylights. Throughout, the explanations are brief yet clear; the language is free of jargon and technical terms; and coverage is complete.

Better Homes and Gardens Step-by-Step Household Repairs. Des Moines, IA: Meredith, 1982. 96p. pap. $5.95 (643.7)

The leaky faucet, the stopped-up drain, the door that will not close—all these and hundreds of other problems are addressed here. Following the publisher's usual format, the book depends as much on good illustrations, diagrams, and drawings as it does on text. The result is a general guide for the inexperienced layperson who wants simple, easy-to-follow directions for returning life to normal. There are guides more detailed than this one, but here is a good beginning, and it cannot be topped for illustrations.

Better Homes and Gardens Your Windows and Doors. Des Moines, IA: Meredith, 1983. 160p. $9.95 (690.18)

Here is one of the All about Your House Series with the rich illustrations, usually in color, and step-by-step instructions. Various types of new, replacement, and reconstructed windows and doors are considered. There is a good section on heating loss through these openings, and what can be done to prevent it. Beyond the obvious, the editors cover such things as locks and even alarms. Every aspect of the subject is covered with the thoroughness associated with this fine series.

Bragdon, Allen, ed. **The Homeowner's Complete Manual of Repair & Improvement: A Do-It-Yourself Bible.** New York: Arco, 1983. 576p. $19.95; pap. $14.95 (643.7)

A fundamental one-volume guide for almost any homeowner. Here one finds easy-to-follow, sensible advice on everything from painting a single room to a house, from repairing a dripping tap to installing plumbing. Step-by-step instructions, usually with illustrations, carry even the amateur through to success. A nice feature is that for each job the author lists the tools to be used and the probable length of time needed to complete it. A brief index helps the reader find what is wanted in one of six sections. The descriptions are clear, and the coverage is as complete as that found in any work of this type. It would be a first choice for all but the most expert. *Note:* This replaces *Petersen's Home Repair & Maintenance Guide*—the name under which it was first published.

Consumer Guide Editors. **Do It Yourself and Save Money.** New York: Harper, 1980. 708p. $14.95 (640)

A systematic plan is established for the accomplishment of approximately 500 do-it-yourself projects around the home, from replacing a sash cord to building shelves to home canning. In a few short paragraphs, liberally illustrated, the guide establishes what tools and materials are needed and precisely how difficult the task is likely to be for the beginner. For projects for which more detailed information is required, such as the alteration of clothes and the installing of insulation, the reader may prefer specialized books. This is ideal as an overview and for items not usually treated in how-to-do-it books.

Family Handyman Magazine Staff. **America's Handyman Book.** Rev. ed. New York: Scribner's, 1980. 405p. $16.95 (643)

This is a standard, rather well-known general guide to repairs and maintenance around the home. First published in 1961, it is found in many houses and workshops. There are numerous sections, which take the reader through each part of the home from basement to attic and clearly explain repair and maintenance procedures as well as basic improvements. The illustrations are numerous and good. The text is written for the beginner, and almost all of the instructions are easy to follow and require no real prior knowledge. Among general books of this type, this is one of the best, although the emphasis should be on "general." For particular situations, one would be better off with specific guides.

Jensen, Tom. **Skylights: The Definitive Guide to Planning, Installing, and Maintaining Skylights and Natural Light Systems.** Philadelphia, PA: Running Pr., 1983. 112p. $19.80; pap. $8.95 (690.15)

This may not be definitive, but it comes close to answering most questions on the subject. The author shows how to decide whether a skylight is practical, where it should and should not be installed, what type to select, how to put it into place, and how to maintain it. There is a list of manufacturers of skylights and related equipment. The illustrations are numerous, fair to good in quality, and generally add to an understanding of the written instructions.

Jones, Peter. **Outdoor Home Repairs Made Easy.** New York: Butterick, 1980. 158p. pap. $4.95 (643.7)

This is a different type of home-repair book in that the whole text concentrates on the exterior of the house. Jones is concerned with simple, easy-to-follow instructions for both major and minor repairs and remodeling. He gives specific directions, usually with equally specific line drawings, on such things as repairing a leaky roof, replacing a piece of siding, or working on a fence. A good deal of the manual is concerned with roofing and siding, including exterior painting.

McClintock, Mike. **Getting Your Money's Worth from Home Contractors.** New York: Harmony, 1982. 179p. $11.95; pap. $5.95 (643.7)

When one sets out to find a contractor for a job around the home, what are the rules? This former contractor explains them in detail—what to look for in carpenters, roofers, etc., and what to avoid. Once several rules are identified, the author explains how to ask for estimates and bids and how these may be properly evaluated. It is not just the lowest price, but the qualifications of the people bidding one should be interested in. There are sections on supervision, problems that may arise, and final settlements. McClintock also has excellent advice on how to deal with a contractor when the job is not satisfactory.

McClintock, Mike. **The Home How-to Source Book.** New York: Scribner's, 1984. 368p. $24.95; pap. $14.95 (643)

Under ten broad subject headings from home building to design, McClintock, the author of several how-to-do-it books, lists the names, addresses, and phone numbers of the various government and public organizations, businesses, associations, and societies that can be of help in how-to-do-it projects. Each of the 1,500 sources has a brief, descriptive annotation. The author is careful to point out that he is not evaluating the sources listed. The guide is thorough; the information supplied includes precisely what an organization or individual firm has to offer and at what price. Most of the country is covered, and there is no particular place favored, although urban centers do have the greatest number of listings. Probably of most help is the index, where one can find information on such things as where to get help in replacing a stained glass window or a difficult-to-find special tool.

McClintock, Mike. **The Homeowner's Handbook.** New York: Scribner's, 1980. 238p. $12.95; pap. $5.95 (643)

A broad, effective look at almost anything of interest to the would-be or actual home owner, this is noteworthy for its close examination of potential problems. The author, a former *Popular Mechanics* editor, is concerned with what can go wrong in a house. He is like a doctor who is strong on diagnosis but leaves the actual cure to others. Here he examines the home from basement to roof, shows what to look for to detect termites or a leak. Hardly an area is outside his scrutiny, and the text is matched by detailed photographs and drawings. Beyond the trouble-shooting, the author gives advice on finding and dealing with contractors and repair persons. There are also good sections on preventive maintenance and energy-efficiency tips.

Manners, David. **Planning and Building Your Home Workshop.** New York: Harper, 1980. 220p. pap. $4.95 (684)

A *Popular Science* publication, this is written for the beginner and explains the fundamentals of a well-conceived home workshop. It accommodates most budgets, although by now some of the materials suggested are quite expensive. Of most use are the plans and planning sections that show the reader how to build a workshop. There are numerous illustrations, diagrams, and charts. *Note:* The author discusses not only the typical home shop, with its tools, lighting, and power sources, but also specialized workshops such as an electronics repair shop and one in which plumbing is of central importance.

Nunn, Richard. **Popular Mechanics Guide to Do-It-Yourself Materials.** New York: Hearst, 1982. 151p. pap. $8.95 (691)

Written for the person who frequents self-service lumber yards and hardware sources, this guide quickly explains what material to use for a given project or repair. The book is organized by various work projects from electrical to plumbing and construction. Under each is a brief yet clear discussion of the primary materials and products available, and how they differ from one another. There are numerous tables and illustrations. Information on repair problems is included.

Popular Science. **Do-It-Yourself Yearbook.** New York: Van Nostrand, 1981–   . Annual. Various paging. $17.50 (643.7)

A variety of experts supply current information that will be of value to how-to-do-it enthusiasts. There are sections on new tools; various techniques for repair, construction, and remodeling; and a number of simple to fairly complex plans and projects for the home. These range from the ubiquitous magazine rack to the computer corner. All are illustrated with photographs and line drawings, and the style of writing is familiar to those who read *Popular Science*. The problem with this annual is twofold: (1) it tends to cover too many and too varied types of projects, and (2) the information may or may not be adequate, depending on who wrote or edited the contribution. Given these reservations, it is a useful idea book. *Note:* This is the first in a projected series of annual volumes that will follow the same basic pattern.

The Reader's Digest Complete Do-It-Yourself Manual. Pleasantville, NY: Reader's Digest, 1973. 600p. $15.95 (643)

Many declare this to be the best of the home and repair books, because the text and the numerous illustrations (over 2,000) so nicely complement each other. The directions are succinct but understandable, and almost anything that can go wrong in a house is considered—including an excellent section on furniture repair and another on financing. There are useful discussions of concrete work, painting, plumbing, and electricity and, of course, the necessary tools for each type of work. In addition, the compilers offer 50 different projects for making such things as toys and cabinets. The one drawback, at least for some, is that the text is sometimes too brief, particularly for the beginner.

Reader's Digest Home Improvement Manual. New York: Random House, 1983. 384p. $21.50 (643.7)

The focus of this manual, as the subtitle suggests, is "renovating, modernizing, and adding space to your home." It is for the individual who is prepared for major work, including such things as adding closets or a greenhouse or finishing an attic. By "remodeling" the guide means everything involved, and most sections consider not only design, but related matters such as electrical and plumbing work as well as structural problems. Following the pattern of other *Reader's Digest* how-to-do-it books, this has numerous illustrations and a clear, precise text. The 2,000-plus diagrams, drawings, cutaways, etc., are tied directly to the instructions so that one may look as one reads. There are sections, too, on what must be learned about building codes, reading plans, and other factors of major construction. Hardly for the novice, this is for the experienced worker, or someone with an urge to gain experience. Within the scope of its purpose and audience it is one of the best books available.

Sunset Books Editors. **Building, Remodeling & Home Improvement.** Menlo Park, CA: Lane. Various dates and paging. pap. $3.95–$5.95 ea.

Among titles in the series in print as of 1984 are *Basic Plumbing Illustrated* (1983); *Bathrooms* (1980); *Bedroom & Bath Storage* (1982); *Bedrooms* (1980); *Children's Rooms & Play Yards* (1980); *Energy-Saving Projects* (1981); *Family Rooms, Dens, Studios* (1979); *Fireplaces* (1980); *Flooring* (1982); *Garage, Attic, Basement Storage* (1982); *Home Lighting* (1982); *Kitchen Storage* (1981); *Solar Remodeling* (1982); *Wall Coverings* (1982); *Wall Systems & Shelving* (1981); *Windows & Skylights* (1982). Additional related titles are in the Outdoor Building Series and include *Basic Masonry Illustrated* (1981); *Decks: How to Plan & Build* (1980); *Fences & Gates* (1981); *Garden & Patio Building Book* (1983); *Hot Tubs, Spas, Home Saunas* (1979); *Patios & Decks* (1979); *Roofing & Siding* (1981); *Swimming Pools* (1981).

Note: Complete Home Storage (1984, $9.95) incorporates *Kitchen Storage; Bed-*

room & Bath Storage; and *Garage, Attic, Basement Storage* (with slight revision) in one volume.

All of the guides follow a basic format that combines color photographs, line drawings, and explicit directions. The books are divided into three or four main sections. They are noteworthy for the illustrations, carefully linked to the text, and the step-by-step analysis of each situation. Although published in California, the majority are of use in any part of North America. Among home-improvement series, they are highly recommended.

Swezey, Kenneth, and Robert Scharff. **Formulas, Methods, Tips and Data for Home and Workshop.** Rev. ed. New York: Harper, 1979. 670p. $17.50 (602)

Arranged by broad subjects, this offers an approach to almost any home-workshop or about-the-house problem. The solution usually is a full discussion of how to use a product, from paint to cleaners. What sets this book apart, however, are the formulas and sometimes unique methods of doing difficult jobs. For example, the authors offer approaches to paint removing that actually work. See, too, their section on cleaners that not only save money but are more effective than many commercial products. When it comes to showing the reader how to accomplish a difficult job—whether cutting glass or preparing chemicals for an attack on garden pests—this is hard to beat. Fully indexed and with many tables, charts, and illustrations, this is by far one of the best general manuals of its type.

Time-Life Books. **Home Repair and Improvement Series.** New York: Time-Life, 1976– . 128p. ea. $11.95 ea.

The series expands each year, but as of mid-1984 included the following titles: *Space and Storage* (1976); *Paint and Wallpaper* (1976); *Basic Wiring* (1976); *Masonry* (1976); *Plumbing* (1976); *Weatherproofing* (1977); *New Living Spaces* (1977); *Heating and Cooling* (1977); *Kitchens and Bathrooms* (1977); *Roofs and Siding* (1977); *Floors and Stairways* (1978); *Advanced Wiring* (1978); *Outdoor Structures* (1978); *Doors and Windows* (1978); *Cabins and Cottages* (1978); *Home Security* (1979); *Adding-On* (1979); *Working with Wood* (1979); *Built-Ins* (1979); *The Old House* (1979); *Outdoor Recreational Areas* (1980); *Walls and Ceilings* (1980); *The Home Workshop* (1980); *Repairing Furniture* (1980); *Special Purpose Rooms* (1981); *Porches & Patios* (1981); *Advanced Woodworking* (1981); *Fireplaces & Wood Stoves* (1981); *Repairing Appliances* (1981); *Working with Metal* (1982); *Working with Plastics* (1982); *Advanced Masonry* (1982); *Cleaning* (1982); *Energy Alternatives* (1982); *Small Engines* (1983); *Landscaping* (1983).

As in all of the Time-Life Books series, the emphasis here is on illustrations and step-by-step instructions. The books presuppose little or no knowledge of any of the areas, although experience indicates that steps are sometimes omitted because the editors believe the reader understands a basic that is not explained. The result is that on occasion one must refer to other books. Still, for those who have had at least a limited amount of experience in home repair and construction, the guides are ideal. In addition to the extremely clear instructions, fully supported by illustrations, there are color-coded diagrams that help to explain the basic operations. Where appropriate, the guides show a before, during, and after sequence so one can check one's success in executing the various steps. One might quibble with the fact that the models are all clean, smiling, and looking totally relaxed, but this is to be expected. All in all, one of the publisher's better series and certainly worth considering.

U.S. Department of Agriculture. **Painting Inside and Out.** Washington, DC: GPO 1978. 26p. $1.50 (A1.77:222)

Basics on surface preparation and how to select the right paint for the interior or the exterior are offered in this brief yet carefully written guide. It is an ideal place to begin, and none of the advice is dated. Particularly useful is the explanation of how to paint and what basic equipment is needed.

HOMES—REMODELING

Abrams, Lawrence, and Kathleen Abrams. **Salvaging Old Barns & Houses: Tear It Down and Save the Pieces.** New York: Sterling, 1983. 128p. pap. $7.95 (691.26)

Most if not all books about houses tell you how to build or repair them. This one is concerned with the fine art of how to "tear it down and save the pieces." While not many people are going to be involved with such procedures, for those who are this is the complete guide. There are instructions on everything from determining the value of a structure, to dismantling it piece by piece, to selling or otherwise disposing of the parts. Despite the title, most of the emphasis is on homes—there is a chapter on barns. A bonus for everyone is the illustrations showing how parts from other structures may be used in a home.

Ching, Francis, and Dale Miller. **Home Renovation.** New York: Van Nostrand, 1983. 338p. $22.95; pap. $15.95 (643.7)

Why this instead of another book on home renovation? The answer is threefold. First, the information is current, and this is important when dealing with new materials. Second, the authors have a logical plan of attack that focuses on conversions, additions, and improving available space. Third, they offer numerous details not found in other books of this type and are particularly good at the step-by-step instructions, which include analyses of what is or is not to be done. Beyond this, one finds the usual attention to various parts of the home, from the attic to the basement, delivered in a clear and crisp writing style with helpful illustrations.

Daniels, M. E. **How to Remodel and Enlarge Your Home.** Indianapolis, IN: Bobbs-Merrill, 1978. 208p. pap. $8.95 (643.7)

One of the most practical and easy to follow of the remodeling books, this is basic and should be one of the first choices for a beginner. Its excellence is due to several things. The writing style is clear, the directions precise, and the illustrations augment the text nicely. The construction methods are simple and effective and require neither particular tools nor specialized skills. The author from time to time does suggest when a professional should be consulted, and often recommends close consultation with suppliers about materials. There is an emphasis on the need to use particular techniques—no generalizations here. Finally, almost all areas for remodeling are considered from the foundation to the roof.

Grow, Lawrence. **The Third Old House Catalogue.** New York: Macmillan, 1982. 220p. pap. $9.95 (728.3)

No longer completely current, yet extremely useful, this is a listing and brief description of about 3,000 services, products, materials, guides, etc., that the individual is likely to use at one time or another in remodeling an old house. The annotations consider both content and use, and the guide covers American homes from the earliest up to the 1930s. There is a particular emphasis on nineteenth-century houses, although even here most of the suggestions would be applicable to other types of restoration. The alphabetical list of suppliers and dealers is somewhat dated, but still sound. *Note:* This is an update of the author's *Old House Catalogue* (1976) and *The New Old House Catalogue* (1980). Any of these is useful, although of course the most recent has more current information on suppliers, products, and services. Look for further updates.

Hutchins, Nigel. **Restoring Houses of Brick and Stone.** New York: Van Nostrand, 1982. 192p. $29.95 (643.7)

Most restoration guides are concerned with wooden homes. As the title suggests, this book fills a necessary gap. Here the author turns to eighteenth- and nineteenth-century homes to show the problems and solutions involved with brick and stone. The book is winning because the author is as concerned with maintaining authenticity in the building as he is with comfort. There is practical information, too, on the restoration of fireplaces and interior masonry construction.

Hutchins, Nigel. **Restoring Old Houses.** New York: Van Nostrand, 1982. 240p. $29.95 (643.7)

Both a contractor and a preservation consultant, the author is lyrical when he discusses the benefits of remodeling an old home. At the same time, he has scores of practical suggestions, and blocks out areas that must be considered by anyone with such a project in mind. The text is supported by excellent photographs, line drawings, and diagrams, some in color. A good basic beginning for anyone, particularly the individual considering buying an older home for restoration.

Johnson, Edwin. **Old House Woodwork Restoration.** Englewood Cliffs, NJ: Prentice-Hall, 1983. 208p. $22.95; pap. $12.95 (694.6)

Here elementary to difficult tasks are explained as the author takes the reader through different processes "to restore doors, windows, walls, stairs, decorative trim, and floors to their original beauty." There are introductory sections on various types of materials, architectural refinements, and the need for accurate restoration. Then the author gets down to the fundamentals of paint removal, refinishing, and the like. Illustrations are adequate, although more diagrams with the text would be helpful. The book should be used with a more general explanation of restoration because the author tends to skip steps from time to time.

Jones, Peter. **Renewing Your Home: A Homeowner's Bible.** New York: Doubleday, 1981. 148p. pap. $4.95 (643.7)

From the ceiling to the floor, and from the floor to the foundation, the author demonstrates the steps (and some of the frustrations) involved in home remodeling. The author's relaxed yet confident writing style is augmented by commonsense suggestions, good illustrations, and easy-to-follow directions. The strong focus is on the interior of the home. Other guides should be used for extensive outside renewal work.

Landry, Arthur. **Restoring Old Houses.** New York: Sterling, 1983. 160p. pap. $8.95 (690.83)

An expert at rebuilding and restoring old houses, Landry offers some firsthand advice on what to do and what to avoid when considering a house for remodeling. The most valuable section is the one on selecting the right house for rehabilitation, and possible resale. There is a detailed plan for examining the building so as to avoid expensive oversights. Once this is done, there is useful although less than unique information on actual remodeling. A final section considers the tools needed. There are adequate illustrations.

Litchfield, Michael. **Renovation: A Complete Guide.** New York: Wiley, 1982. 640p. $29.95 (643.7)

The adjective "complete" is correct. In this massive volume the home owner will find an answer to any question regarding renovation of an old house. Working on the principle that most people cannot or do not wish to tear down all the walls and rip out all the fixtures, the author limits renovation to step-by-step procedures for improving a single wall, reorganizing a single room, or making use of a half basement. All of the instructions are extremely detailed, and most have good-to-excellent illustrations. Specific product information, from cement blocks to types of lumber, is given for each of the projects. While the more involved remodeling projects assume some knowledge of carpentry and plumbing, the easier ones are explained in such a way that a beginner will have no problems. There is a good section on how to plan to remodel, and what to do and not to do based on the intrinsic structure of the house.

U.S. Department of the Interior. **Respectful Rehabilitation: Answers to Your Questions about Old Buildings.** Washington, DC: Preservation Pr., 1982. 192p. pap. $9.95 (720.28)

Prepared by the Technical Preservation Services Division of the National Park Service, this employs a question-and-answer format for common questions on how to preserve and renovate a historic building. The focus is primarily on remodeling problems, although there is a chapter on historic preservation guidelines, and interest in all types of old buildings that should be saved. Numerous photographs and line drawings are included. *Note:* This is published by a nonprofit organization.

Vila, Bob, and Anne Henry. **Bob Vila's This Old House.** New York: Dutton, 1981. 284p. $21; pap. $13.50 (690.3)

Another addition to the growing number of titles by Bob Vila, this follows the pattern of *This Old House* (Little, 1980). The difference is that here the concentration is on a single complex, which Vila and his group turn into condominiums. There are also a number of historic outbuildings that are repaired. Throughout the job, Vila offers a distinct approach in everything from heating plants to arrangement of rooms. What it amounts to is that while only one basic structure is considered in detail, there are so many variations that the reader will gain scores of ideas on remodeling almost any type of home. Then, too, there are excellent color photographs documenting the procedures. An added feature is the photographs of historic buildings that have been remodeled for contemporary use.

HORSES

Amaral, Anthony. **How to Train Your Horse: A Complete Guide to Making an Honest Horse.** New York: Winchester, 1977. 221p. $8.95 (636.1)

After instructions on how to buy a horse, the author, an experienced horse trainer, turns to the steps involved in training them. He next talks about equipment and concludes with an excellent bibliography of horse books he has enjoyed reading. The illustrations are useful and nicely placed. The book can be read by both young people and adults and remains one of the best basic books in the field.

Baker, Jennifer. **Saddlery and Horse Equipment. A Practical Horse Guide.** New York: Arco, 1982. 96p. $7.95 (685.1)

The first assumption that the author makes is that the reader owns a horse or has access to one and is therefore interested in knowing about the best equipment for riding. The primary focus is on selecting the right saddle through a process of ascertaining its probable use and determining the fit. Beyond that, there is similar advice on purchasing accessories. The author's obvious love for her subject shines through her prose. Her style is lively and informative, and she provides excellent illustrations to clarify her points. While the book is aimed at the rider, it has a wider appeal. For example, the opening provides a brief history of riding and the development of such advances as the saddle.

Condaz, Kate. **Riding: An Illustrated Guide.** New York: Arco, 1983. 221p. $14.95 (798.2)

How does one learn to ride? Well, according to this British expert, the first move should be locating a good teacher. She tells how to do this, and describes the elements of basic and advanced riding, which are part of a good instruction program. Beyond that are hints on safety, equipment, the purchase or rental of a horse, and a general discussion of the joys of the sport. Particularly helpful are over 100 drawings and diagrams illustrating major riding points. This is primarily for beginners, but would-be experts will find much of value.

Corley, G. F. **Riding and Schooling the Western Performance Horse.** New York: Arco, 1982. 241p. $19.95 (798.2)

While written for the experienced rider, this should be of value to the enthusiastic beginner who wishes to have a model to follow. The focus is on Western riding and horse shows that feature this style. Corley does start with basics, yet he moves quickly into precise riding procedures and schooling. The detail and the directions presuppose careful study. The excellent and well-captioned photographs underline the author's main points.

Edwards, Elwyn, ed. **The Complete Book of the Horse.** New York: Larousse, 1982. 334p. $17.95 (636.1)

First published in England, this is an illustrated general guidebook to horses. One impressive section includes a detailed text and illustration of breeds native to various parts of the world. This is the best part of what is a somewhat too general treatment. Still, for browsing and some reference purposes it is useful enough in that the coverage is wide, although sometimes less than thorough, and it concerns almost everything connected with horses from health care to breeding and various sporting events.

Foster, Carol, ed. **The Complete Book of the Horse.** New York: Crown, 1984. 208p. $12.95 (798)

Over 300 color photographs make this a book to look at as much as to read. Each of the pictures is briefly described and the book is divided into sections that carry the novice from the point of purchasing a horse to long-distance riding. The sections on veterinary practices and the care of the horse are excellent, and matched only by the marvelous pictures of what the editors call the 40 most popular breeds of horses in the world. Here each type is explained in terms of size, habits, riding, etc. The book ends with a section on different advanced activities, from standard jumping procedures to showing horses.

Gordon, Sally. **The Rider's Handbook.** New York: Putnam's, 1980. 224p. $19.95 (798.2)

This is a basic guide for beginners and it covers such topics as the purchase, care, feeding, grooming, exercising, and health of horses, as well as equipment, competitions, and European, Western, and sidesaddle styles of riding. The illustrations are adequate and the text is clear, but there are several editing errors. This work has the advantage of being thorough, but should be considered supplementary to other books in this category.

Gordon-Watson, Mary. **The Handbook of Riding.** New York: Knopf, 1982. 288p. $22.50 (798.2)

An Olympian gold medalist draws on her appreciation and understanding of horses and riding to offer both beginners and experienced riders an excellent guide to the subject. Riding is discussed in a clear, lively prose style. There are two or three color pictures, drawings, or charts on almost every page to support the text. In addition to the valuable material on riding, the author considers more briefly the training of the horse and how it should be maintained in top condition. While some of the book is on competition, much of it is concerned with average problems associated with pleasure riding.

Hawcroft, Tim. **The Complete Book of Horse Care.** New York: Howell, 1983. 208p. $17.95 (636.10)

From buying the horse to treating the animal for minor illnesses, the author explains it all. This is about as basic as one can get, and is ideal for the beginner. There is particular emphasis on the care of the horse, and here the author is wise in the ways of shortcuts to save time and energy for the owner. The commonsense rules on safety are excellent and the diagrams and illustrations support the down-to-earth text.

Kays, John. **The Horse.** 3rd ed. New York: Arco, 1982. 402p. $19.95 (636.1)

A classic, and now in its third edition, this is a basic book on horses covering everything from how to ride to how to buy a horse. Background information includes such topics as feeding, breeding, judging, and even selling horses. There are excellent sections on the history of the animal. The text includes numerous photographs of famous horses, usually with their riders. The manual is factual and free of jargon. This will appeal to anyone, of any age group, who is interested in horses.

Saunders, Ray. **Riding and Training.** Horsekeeping Series. New York: Sterling, 1983. 112p. $12.95; pap. $6.95 (636.1)

Assuming that the reader is a rider and wants to know more about the finer points of the art, Saunders begins with basics, yet quickly moves into a discussion of qualities needed to become a first-rate horseperson. In fact, he has little time for beginners, and the very tone of the text suggests he is interested primarily in reaching people who take riding as a serious activity, not a passing fancy. For this audience, he discusses how one schools a horse in various techniques. The training is accompanied by numerous photographs, some in color. Instructions are precise, and easy enough to follow if one appreciates the riding-training syndrome.

Smythe, Heather. **Basic Horse Training: A Practical Guide.** New York: Stein & Day, 1983. 144p. $18.95 (636.1)

Written by a British expert who is at home on a horse and judging various events, this short guide is for someone familiar with horses and now interested in training. After a section on the basics of training and, equally important, the attributes of a trainer, the author offers specific advice. Smythe has a relaxed, confident style that carries the reader through the selection of a good horse right to riding in shows. The basics of balance and the early things to watch for in riding are explained, not only in words, but with adequate illustrations. There are advanced sections on hacking, dressage, and even hunting.

Twelveponies, Mary. **There Are No Problem Horses, Only Problem Riders.** Boston: Houghton, 1982. 228p. $13.95; pap. $8.95 (798.2)

Given a name like that of the author, one can only expect a thorough and winning treatment of horses. The reader is not disappointed. Here the focus is on the difficult, hard-to-appreciate horse who tends to want to do anything but assist the rider. The author begins with the real problem—the trainer. She surveys the right and wrong approaches in various steps normally taken to develop a good riding horse. There is a continual plea to try to understand the horse and not to break it. While hardly for the beginner, this is an excellent, unique manual that will be of help to trainers and owners of spirited horses.

Williams, Dorian, ed. **The Horseman's Companion.** Rev. ed. New York: St. Martin's, 1980. 565p. $15 (636.1)

While not precisely a how-to-do-it book, this is an invaluable, not to mention delightful, reader on horses and riding. The author offers a historical menu from Xenophon to Winston Churchill. In addition, the book is enlivened by snatches from novels, poetry, and other literary sources. There are over 100 famous horse lovers represented here, so this is an excellent background book for almost anyone, of any age, interested in riding and horses.

HORTICULTURE. *See* Gardening

HOT RODS. *See* Automobiles

HOT TUBS. *See* Bathrooms

HOTELS. *See* Travel

ILLUSTRATION   189

HOUSE PLANTS. *See* Gardening—Indoors; Plants

HOUSECLEANING
See also Home Economics

Aslett, Don. **Is There Life after Housework?** Cincinnati: Writer's Digest, 1981. 170p. pap. $6.95 (648.5)

The president of one of the country's largest cleaning companies offers "a revolutionary approach that will free you from the drudgery of housework." This amounts to basic, ingenious techniques for doing almost anything around the house. The author suggests many fast, uncomplicated ways to clean floors, wash windows, care for bathrooms, etc. This is supplemented by advice on the best cleaning supplies. Less useful is the section on how the reader might start a housecleaning business. The text is supplemented by sketches that are long on humor and short on instruction. The tips are not likely to date.

Chapman, Eugenia, and Jill Major. **Clean Your House & Everything in It.** New York: Grosset, 1982. 159p. pap. $6.95 (646.6)

Yes, there is more to housecleaning than vacuuming and dusting. In fact, so much more that the authors have put together a book that not only explains the easiest and most efficient methods of cleaning almost anything, but demonstrates various approaches that are guaranteed to save time. They even supply information on various cleaning products, including many that can be mixed at home. They whip through the house like that commercial-brand giant, and point out the best way to polish floors, clean hard-to-reach fixtures, vacuum carpets, and clean the dirt off windows. They stop long enough to explore various methods of bringing the furniture and curtains back to life. The best part, at least for some, is the section on when and how to hire professional housecleaners, and how to get the whole family involved. This is as ambitious and useful a book on the subject as one is likely to find.

Guilfoyle, Ann. **Home Free: A No-Nonsense Guide to House Care.** New York: Norton, 1984. 220p. $12.45 (640)

Is there an easy, efficient way to keep the house clean? Yes, says the author and she demonstrates not only strategies for keeping off dust, but shortcuts for cooking, laundering, and other activities around the home. In addition to the useful tips, she explains the benefits and drawbacks of hiring professional housecleaners. Addressing herself to the housewife, she adds that it is useful to have the husband do his share, but that this should not be attempted through confrontation. The wife should diplomatically ease the man into certain jobs. There is even a section on what children can do as part of the cleaning brigade. The material on cooking and nutrition is not all that good, and readers will find better bits of advice in other books, but when it comes to housecleaning, the author is an expert.

HOUSEHOLD APPLIANCES. *See* Appliances

HUNTING. *See* Fishing & Hunting

ILLUSTRATION. *See* Graphic Arts

INDEXES
See also Catalogs

America Buys: The Index to Product Evaluations. Menlo Park, CA: Information Access, 1981– . Annual plus quarterly loose-leaf updates (price varies) (640.7)

This is an index that allows the reader to find information in 375 magazines and three newspapers about particular products or types of products. Arrangement is in two parts. The larger section is a brand-name index. Here one looks for a brand name and is referred to an article. If one is interested only in a type of product, from cosmetics to corn poppers, one can look up the product in another section and be referred to pertinent articles. This publication does not include the brief descriptive notes found in its competitor, *Consumer's Index* (q.v.), but it does index more periodicals and is somewhat easier to use. Both should be consulted when any in-depth research is needed about a particular brand or a type of product.

Consumer's Index to Product Evaluations and Information Sources. Ann Arbor, MI: Pierian, 1973– . Quarterly with annual cumulations. $98 (016.64)

This is an index to reports on products in about 110 different magazines and 200 books each year. The arrangement is under 14 broad categories from family and society to sports and business management, and the subject index is detailed and excellent. Each entry refers the reader to an article where the product is mentioned. Most entries have a brief description of the content of the article or book. There is a most useful section devoted to reviews of books of particular interest to consumers, and an index by keywords (usually the brand name although this is not always the case). *America Buys* (q.v.) serves a similar function.

Index to How to Do It Information. Wooster, OH: Norman Lathrop Enterprises, 1963– . Annual. 1981 Index, pap. $15; Cumulative Index 1963–1969, pap. $15; Cumulative Index 1970–1974, pap. $15 (016.74)

This is an index to 63 popular magazines that contain how-to-do-it information. The arrangement is by subject from AC-DC radios to zoom lenses. One simply turns to the subject and finds articles, news notes, etc. The entry is clear enough so that one can find the precise magazine by date and the piece needed by page number. An advantage is the in-depth indexing and the meticulous attention to subject coverage, which is good although variably current, as this is published annually. *Note:* More up-to-date information can be found by consulting the *Magazine Index,* available on microform in many libraries. This index includes how-to-do-it and self-help citations by subject, and is updated once a month. See also *Readers' Guide to Periodical Literature* found in libraries.

Torgeson, Kathryn, and Sylvia Weinstein. **The Garland Recipe Index.** New York: Garland, 1984. 312p. $35 (016.6)

As the title promises, this indexes recipes. The authors analyze the contents of 48 current standard cookbooks from Julia Child and James Beard to Craig Claiborne (many of which are included in this volume—see Cooking section). Index entries are by name, type, and ingredients. Keys make it possible to differentiate between several recipes for the same dish.

INSECTS
See also Cockroaches

Arnett, Ross. **Simon & Schuster's Guide to Insects.** New York: Simon & Schuster, 1981. 511p. pap. $9.95 (595.7)

Limited to North America, this guide describes and illustrates 350 insects. Each of the species is carefully considered in terms of habitat, environmental influences, organization, etc. There is a good section on collecting and mounting insects, and a breezy history of the avocation. This is useful for both beginners and experts.

Milne, Lorus, and Margery Milne. **The Audubon Society Field Guide to North American Insects and Spiders.** New York: Knopf, 1980. 1,008p. pap. $9.95 (595.7)

Following the pattern of other Audubon guides, this opens with a mass of color plates showing spiders and insects in their natural habitat. There is a shape index that allows easy reference between text and illustrations, and provides quick identification. Once identified, the insect is described in enough detail to establish its distinctiveness from its close relatives.

Pyle, Robert. **The Audubon Society Field Guide to North American Butterflies.** New York: Knopf, 1981. 916p. pap. $12.95 (595.78)

Following the approach of other Audubon Society guides, there is a section of over 1,000 beautifully colored plates showing butterflies in their natural habitat. This is followed by a general introduction and specific data on more than 600 species of North American butterflies. The difficulty in this volume is that one must turn back and forth from the descriptions to the illustrations, but this is a small price to pay for an otherwise superb work. There is the usual glossary and detailed index.

White, Richard, and Donald J. Borror. **A Field Guide to the Insects of America North of Mexico.** New York: Houghton, 1974. 404p. $9.95 (595.7)

One of the familiar Peterson Field Guide Series, this is a definitive work on the subject. Unfortunately, it does require some knowledge of entomology for full appreciation. This is particularly true where there are no illustrations for an insect, or only one pictorial key for a group. Despite this drawback, the information is complete, the data accurate, and the identification to the family level quite superior. Because this covers so many more species in an equally more thorough manner, it is recommended over the more recent *Audubon Society Field Guide to North American Insects and Spiders* (q.v.), in which about 600 species are covered.

INSECTS, GARDEN

U.S. Department of Agriculture. **Control of Insects on Deciduous Fruits and Trees in the Home Orchard—Without Insecticides.** Washington, DC: GPO, 1981. 36p. $2.75 (A1.77:211/3)

Most of the information here is useful for almost any home garden in any part of the United States. General information is given on methods of killing or eliminating bugs and other pests without using chemicals. The focus of the pamphlet is on fruit and nut trees, but much of what is said will be of value in other parts of the garden.

U.S. Department of Agriculture. **Insects and Diseases of Vegetables in the Home Garden.** Washington, DC: GPO, 1980. 54p. $3.75 (A1.75:380/2)

Basic information is provided on how to maintain a healthy garden. Specifics are given as to how to identify diseases and insects that harm vegetables, and there is even a bit on insects that help. Suggested checks to the bugs and diseases are spelled out.

U.S. Department of Agriculture. **Insects on Trees and Shrubs around the Home.** Washington, DC: GPO, 1980. 52p. $3.50 (A1.77:214/2)

This covers the whole of the United States. The title is self-descriptive of the content, which is easy to follow. A plus is the sure way of identifying various types of insects.

U.S. Department of Agriculture. **Lawn Insects: How to Control Them.** Rev. ed. Washington, DC: GPO, 1980. 20p. $2.75 (A1.77:53/8)

One sure way to produce a green, lasting lawn is to get rid of pests. This bulletin explains how it is done. Identification of various insects and bugs is quite clear, as are instructions on the application of pesticides.

Yepsen, Roger, ed. **The Encyclopedia of Natural Insect and Disease Control.** Emmaus, PA: Rodale, 1984. 465p. $21.95 (635.04)

There are numerous ways to control pests in a garden without using chemicals. For example, in this exhaustive guide there are suggestions on how to develop biological controls. These are simple and more effective than many man-made chemicals. The guide offers plant-by-plant, variety-by-variety coverage. Arrangement is by type of plant, and for each there is a discussion of common insect and disease problems. There is enough information for the layperson to recognize the symptoms and the specific cure, plus explanations of how to keep plants healthy and pest- and disease-free. In addition to the main part, there are sections devoted to common pests and problems and what to do in each case. There are numerous, well-placed illustrations, some in color. *Note:* This replaces the publisher's *Organic Plant Protection* (1976).

INSULATION. *See* Homes—Energy Conservation

INTERIOR DECORATION
See also Homes—Additions; Homes—Remodeling

Almeida, Philip. **How to Decorate a Dump.** New York: Stuart, 1983. 143p. $17.95 (747)

Too many interior decorating guides assume that the reader is living in a mansion or a 15-room apartment, and has unlimited funds. Not this one. Here "dump" is a reference to the typical overpriced, too-small apartment in an average urban center. The author sets out to show how the place may be made not only livable, but actually quite attractive. His ideas are illustrated with line drawings and photographs, and even the most inept reader should be able to garner enough to help to put the chair or table in the right place. A nice added feature is the advice on how to find inexpensive furniture from such places as the Salvation Army. There is even a useful list of suppliers. All in all, this is a basic title for people with limited funds, limited space, and a need for extending a limited view of decoration.

Better Homes and Gardens New Decorating Book. Des Moines, IA: Meredith, 1981. 432p. $29.95 (747)

The coverage here is according to style and preference for certain types of interior decorating. The book is divided into sections such as country, traditional, etc. All aspects of decoration are considered, including floors, ceilings, furniture, and lighting. There is a section devoted to exterior decoration, but this is less than satisfactory and only hints at possibilities. The real strength of the volume, as in other *Better Homes and Gardens* titles, is in the illustrations. They are found on almost every page, usually in color, and they nicely augment the brief yet informative text.

Better Homes and Gardens Stretching Living Space. Des Moines, IA: Meredith, 1983. 160p. $9.95 (728.3)

This is a volume in the All about Your House Series, which is notable for its clear photographs, clearly written instructions, and good format. By "stretching" the authors mean not adding space but making a space look larger. Each primary room is analyzed in terms of furnishings, adding a window, lowering a ceiling, taking out a wall, etc. Suggestions on everything from new approaches to paint and wallpaper to camouflaging problem areas are included. With this, they then turn to vacant space—from an attic to a garage—and explain how the unused areas might be converted into rooms for living.

Better Homes and Gardens Your Family Centers. Des Moines, IA: Meredith, 1983. 160p. $9.95 (643.7)

In this member of the All about Your House Series, the writers and photographers turn to a careful study of the traditional and not so traditional living room, dining room, and family room—which may or may not be neatly separated. The emphasis here is more on interior decorating to reflect personal taste than it is on creating space. At the same time, much of the focus is on building simple furniture, from tables to storage units. There are tips, too, on where to purchase various items and what to look for in, for example, a good wood-burning stove. Still, the primary value is the illustrations, which give notions of possibilities on decorating this or that room.

Brown, Erica. **Interior Views: Design at Its Best.** New York: Viking, 1980. 173p. $25 (729)

Here some 40 international designers briefly explain how to improve a room, and their individual ideas are then illustrated by two to three pages of color photographs. While the overall impression is one of mass disagreement, the book is useful for the reader who is looking for ideas. Here is everything from the traditional to European modern, and while no directions are given on how to actually improve a given space, anyone with a good eye and an aesthetic response to one or more of the decorators is likely to be grateful for this book.

Carry, Virginia. **Double-Duty Decorating: Design Ideas to Help You Get the Most Out of Your Limited Space.** New York: Scribner's, 1983. 177p. $17.95 (747.21)

This is written for the person on a budget, and is ideal for the occupant of a studio or a one-bedroom apartment. The text, supported by superior line drawings, is addressed to the amateur—few of the projects are very difficult. The idea is to show the reader how a bit of paint, cloth, screen, or shelving may transform a room. The presentation is practical, and the information can be used to make a small room appear larger.

Dickson, Elizabeth, and Margaret Colvin. **The Laura Ashley Book of Home Decorating.** New York: Harmony, 1982. 160p. $24.95 (747)

Laura Ashley is well known for her fresh, modernized Victorian approach to clothing and furnishings. Here one finds startling color photographs of the British designer's best efforts in decorating various kinds of rooms in dwellings from simple apartments to châteaux. The emphasis is on the photographs, and there is plenty to inspire anyone—at least anyone with a greater than average budget for interior decorating. Beyond the pictures, though, is excellent although brief text. The author goes from room to room in the home and explains what basics to consider when decorating. The second part of the book considers, somewhat less usefully, the decorating of furniture, usually with Ashley's print patterns.

Eiseman, Leatrice. **Alive with Color: The Total Color System for Women & Men.** Washington, DC: Acropolis, 1983. 242p. $18.95 (155.9)

Not all walls have to be painted white or landlord green. There are thousands of more imaginative choices, and many of these are explained here, along with color illustrations, by an expert on the subject who also manages to convey information about the tastes of the international set. Gossip aside, the advice is useful, even for those who are on a somewhat more limited budget than the author's. There are excellent sections on how certain colors enliven or deaden a room, and how color reflects the personality of the occupant. There is probably too much material on matching colors to the time of day—from sunrise to sunset—but this is a convenient device for making the book provocative and lively.

Gilliatt, Mary. **The Decorating Book.** New York: Pantheon, 1981. 404p. $39.95 (747)

Thanks to excellent drawings, color photographs, and the author's fine sense of organization, this is a splendid guide to almost any question concerning interior decoration. Aimed at the layperson, the guide goes into considerable detail in explanations of different approaches to color, lighting, texture, space use, etc. Each room is given separate treatment, and problems of size, shape, and location are considered. There are two unusual features: The last section offers the reader a step-by-step design kit, including graph tear-out paper and furniture cutouts; another section shows samples of everything from paints and fabrics to different types of shades.

Grow, Lawrence. **The Catalogue of Contemporary Design: A Complete Style & Resource Book of Interior Design from 30's Modern to Post Modern.** New York: Collier, 1983. 256p. pap. $10.95 (728.3)

In some 500 black-and-white photographs, and a minimum of text, the author offers the work of outstanding designers of furniture, lighting, textiles, hardware, and other elements of the stylish home. This book is directed to the person with taste, money, and a will to be different. The primary text is concerned with how to use all of these elements in the home, and here Grow is particularly perceptive. A useful addition is the list of 3,000 suppliers. *Note:* This is to be updated every two years.

Kangas, Robert. **By Hand: Low-Cost, No-Cost Decorating.** Englewood Cliffs, NJ: Reston/Prentice-Hall, 1983. 256p. $16.95; pap. $12.95 (684)

Few people can afford or, for that matter, want to employ an interior decorator. Few can afford expensive refurbishings of a house. What is to be done? Turn to Kangas, who offers practical, easy-to-follow methods of turning an otherwise undistinguished home into a fascinating place to live. (The advice is as applicable to a one-room apartment as to a house.) The trick involves imagination, good tools, and an ability to employ standard items—from lighting fixtures to furniture—in an unusual way. There are about 70 to 80 different basic ideas here, including instructions on what tools are needed, types of materials, and simple mechanical instructions. The author moves from the simple job of stripping furniture to more complex carpentry projects. Some of the notions are not all that tasteful, but the majority are considerably better than those found in other, more expensive books of this type.

Kent, Kathryn. **The Good Housekeeping Complete Guide to Traditional American Decorating.** New York: Hearst, 1982. 255p. $27.95 (747.21)

Here "traditional" is underlined and reinforced by striking colored photographs of various rooms of the home. By traditional the author means almost anything that is not modern, which is to say that she encompasses numerous styles of many periods. She lists the telling points of each and then proceeds to explain what is needed to pull a room together in a particular style. This means taking a careful look at the complete space, from paint on the walls to minor accessories. As everything is covered, as everything is explained by picture and prose, this is an ideal work for the reader who wants ideas, wants to dream, or wants to carry out some of the projects.

Kron, Joan. **Home-Psych: The Social Psychology of Home and Decoration.** New York: Crown, 1983. 327p. $14.95 (747.01)

The author of the famous book on how to use metal and modern business/warehouse furniture to furnish a home (*High-Tech,* 1979) turns to why some people decorate in one fashion, others in a completely different way. It all has to do with mind set, social reactions, and behavior, as well as education and class. Analytical and descriptive, rather than prescriptive, the author offers controversial points that may influence the reader's decorating plans. Most of this is obvious to anyone who has considered taste, class, and money as discussed in scores of books on the subject. Still, Kron's viewpoint is different and witty enough to warrant consideration. She is especially good at explaining how tastes are shaped and formed by advertising and sex roles.

Mejetta, Mirko, and Simonetta Spada. **Interiors in Color: Creating Space, Personality and Atmosphere.** New York: Watson-Guptill, 1983. 95p. $27.50 (747)

Originally published in Italy, this is a cool, modern, and highly sophisticated oversized collection of marvelous colored photographs. The focus is on using color to shape mood and design in the home—with some consideration of commercial space. It is divided into four parts: color as decoration, designing in white, color and technology, and new directions. There are usually three to four pictures on each page, and no more than a cutline of explanation, although that is quite enough. A book guaranteed to inspire, this provides a wealth of ideas. There are *no* how-to-to-it directions.

Phipps, Diana. **Diana Phipps' Affordable Splendor: An Ingenious Guide to Decorating Elegantly, Inexpensively & Doing Most of It Yourself.** New York: Random House, 1982. 320p. $20 (747)

The "inexpensive," as noted in the subtitle, is more expensive now, but the elements of design that are so enthusiastically explained and illustrated remain the same. The primary approach is to use less-costly materials to cover construction horrors; e.g., a staple gun and fabric will do wonders with walls, and paint can hide mistakes. All of this is explained in detail. The emphasis is on the smaller home or apartment, with every room covered. There are scores of easy-to-follow projects from slipcovers to adding storage space. While all of this may not suit the person who wants the perfect kind of interior decorating that will last forever, it is a remarkably imaginative guide for the individual trying to make a place livable and remain within a budget.

Slesin, Suzanne. **The New York Times Home Book of Modern Design: Styles, Problems and Solutions.** New York: Times Books, 1982. 269p. $35 (747)

Anyone familiar with the Home section of the *New York Times* will recognize the numerous features reprinted in this handy, easy-to-use volume. The emphasis is on contemporary design, and the author points out trends, innovations, and even, if only by implication, mistakes in planning over the past decade or so. Coverage ranges from discussions of individual pieces of furniture to complete rooms. Particularly useful are the numerous solutions to problem areas such as small, awkward spaces, or those with insufficient lighting. There is a great deal of information, too, on individual products. Numerous black-and-white photographs are included as well as a useful list of sources where many of the products and services may be purchased.

Slesin, Suzanne, and Stafford Cliff. **French Style.** New York: Potter, 1982. 288p. $35 (747.24)

Thanks to a combination of striking color photographs and a lucid, witty text, this captures the meaning of the "French style" of architecture and interior design at all economic levels. The authors investigate a garret or a château, and succeed in showing what is truly distinctive about each. Both contemporary and older settings are shown, and there is a handy list of American suppliers of many of the items.

Sunset Decorating with Indoor Plants. Menlo Park, CA: Lane, 1980. 80p. pap. $3.95 (747.98)

Written for the individual with a limited decorating budget, this follows the usual pattern of Sunset books. It is heavily illustrated with color photographs accompanied by brief, yet illuminating, advice on how to make the most of plants in a home or apartment. The twist, as indicated by the title, is how to improve the quality of a room with plants. Numerous examples are given such as using plants to hide a gaffe in a building's plan, or grouping plants to bring out the decor. Useful advice is provided, too, on miniature greenhouses, plant care, and related matters.

Varney, Carleton. **Carleton Varney's ABCs of Decorating.** New York: Dutton, 1983. 295p. pap. $12.95 (747.03)

Arranged in ABC order, with each definition or topic thoroughly explored in terms of decorating wisdom, this is a breezy, helpful guide for the layperson. The author is a columnist who has a somewhat overblown notion of interior decorating, but it is one that appeals to many. In addition to decorating ideas, there are basic definitions and explanations of terms. The photographs are adequate.

Von Furstenburg, Egon. **The Power Look at Home: Decorating for Men.** New York: Morrow, o.p. 247p. $19.95 (747.8)

Working on the premise that many men are interested in translating the "power" look to their living quarters, the noted clothes designer offers suggestions for single men's homes and apartments. Despite the debatable basis of his idea, the actual advice is sound and useful not only for single men, but for many others. The author goes over all the basics—from planning space to painting and furnishing—with a flair not often found in other books of this type. There is an excellent section on the vital matter of costs and budgets.

Yagi, Kogi. **A Japanese Touch for Your Home.** New York: Harper, 1982. 84p. $15.95 (729)

This is an invaluable guide to what constitutes the ideal, if not the cramped reality, of the Japanese home. The author is an experienced architect who offers a careful look at both inner and outer space. There are superior colored plates and over 200 black-and-white drawings to punctuate his points about such things as shoji doors or tatami mat arrangement. He even offers plans for the doors as well as simple lamps. There is a brief section on the tea ceremony.

INVENTIONS

Kivenson, Gilbert. **The Art and Science of Inventing.** 2nd ed. New York: Van Nostrand, 1982. 239p. $17.95 (600)

Now in its second edition, and likely to go into several more, this is a basic guide for the inventor. The author offers considerably more than the expected coverage, such as the securing of a patent. He begins with a general discussion of inventing, then moves on to the various methods of experimentation and shows how to finance a discovery. This industrial researcher's book is noteworthy for the practical advice it gives, supported by actual examples.

MacCracken, Calvin. **A Handbook for Inventors: How to Protect, Patent, Finance, Develop, Manufacture & Market Your Ideas.** New York: Scribner's, 1983. 211p. $14.95 (608)

The author, an inventor himself, delivers all that he promises. He explains everything from protecting research ideas to gaining licensing rights. It is all done in an easy-to-understand, jargon-free style. There are numerous books on patents, but this goes beyond the patent and considers how to carry the idea through to the finished product. Note the good bibliography and numerous lists, which range from inventors' organizations to names of patent searchers.

JEWELRY
See also Antiques

Evans, Chuck. **Jewelry: Contemporary Design and Techniques.** Worcester, MA: Davis, 1983. 267p. $21.95 (739.27)

Written for all kinds of jewelry makers, from beginners to those who are proficient, this is a definitive guide to the topic by an Iowa professor. The title indicates a wider interest in design than is actually found here, but the real value of the work lies in its focus on technique. The author begins with basic procedures that are practiced at the jeweler's bench, and then he carefully, and in great detail, explains the finer points of the art from forging to various methods of lamination and inlay. The manual concludes with valuable information on weights and measures, hardening, shop safety, etc. Throughout there are numerous illustrations, some in color, that support the fine, informative text.

Goldemberg, Rose. **All about Jewelry: The One Indispensable Guide for Buyers, Wearers, Lovers, and Investors.** New York: Arbor, 1982. 162p. $15.95; pap. $6.95 (739.27)

Written for the collector, and to a lesser extent the seller, the subtitle says it all. The concentration is on how to determine the value of precious stones in jewelry as well as that of gold, silver, and other metal settings. Value is more than monetary, and this is pointed up by a clear discussion of the history of certain types of jewelry and how the piece or pieces are properly worn. There is a good section on determining authenticity.

Sprintzen, Alice. **Jewelry: Basic Techniques and Design.** Radnor, PA: Chilton, 1980. 222p. $15.95; pap. $9.95 (739.27)

Useful for essential steps in creating jewelry, this guide offers instructions for employing stones, ceramics, metal, and even wood in jewelry making. There are numerous illustrations showing good examples of each type of jewelry. The sections on equipment and safety are particularly valuable.

Untracht, Oppi. **Jewelry Concepts and Technology.** New York: Doubleday, 1982. 840p. $60 (739.27)

An expensive, beautiful book, this is dedicated to the principle that crafted jewelry can and indeed should be handsome and imaginative. The author makes her point in two ways. A valuable historical background on jewelry sets the stage. Following the history of a particular technique or procedure, she shows how it is modified for today's jewelry making. Sections are divided into special processes and materials and include the history and step-by-step instructions, most of which are well illustrated. There is the usual list of sources of supply, glossaries, and a better-than-average reading list. As comprehensive as it is well organized and written, this is required for any would-be jewelry maker, and is of equal value for the experienced craftsperson.

JUDO & KARATE & AIKIDO

Fromm, Alan, and Nicolas Soames. **Judo: The Gentle Way.** Boston, Routledge, 1982. 117p. pap. $10.95 (796.8)

One of the best books on judo, this will appeal to both adults and teenagers. The teacher-authors stress the noncombative aspects of judo and demonstrate how it is a discipline that helps the individual to exercise both mind and body. Although they assume that the reader has some knowledge of the art, they do offer quite basic beginning steps. Specifics are given on various movements, and on the necessity for total control of mind and body. A well-written, serious, and highly informative text, this is a pleasant change from many newsstand "hit and kill 'em" judo titles.

Sung Son, Duk, and Robert Clark. **Black Belt Korean Karate.** Englewood Cliffs, NJ: Prentice-Hall, 1983. 233p. $12 (796.8)

Using this guide, the amateur should be able to master at least the basic karate movements. The good points about this guide are that the explanations are easy to follow and the illustrations fit nicely into the text. A less desirable aspect is the worshipful tone of the author toward the glories of karate, which is tiresome.

Tegner, Bruce. **Judo: Beginner to Black Belt.** Rev. ed. Ventura, CA: Thor, 1982. 207p. $10.95; pap. $6.95 (796.8)

One of the best basic judo books, this covers all of the beginning and intermediate and some advanced steps in a carefully illustrated text. The photographs clearly show each of the movements described, and while coaching is still necessary, the book is a fine guide for the person trying to brush up or practice. Most of the focus is on the early stages of judo, although there are sections explaining how one moves from the beginning (white belt) to the senior level (black belt). The stress on health and safety, as well as the joys of judo for exercise, is a welcome addition. One of the better, more popular titles in this area, this guide is often updated. It was first published in 1967.

Tegner, Bruce. **Karate: Beginner to Black Belt.** Ventura, CA: Thor, 1982. 220p. $10.95; pap. $6.95 (796.8)

As in *Judo,* the companion book by the same author (q.v.), this covers the basics and the intermediate steps of karate. There is material, too, on more advanced training. The makeup and illustrations are first rate. The focus on exercise and health, rather than on destruction, sets this guide apart from others. A related title is the author's *Karate and Judo Exercise* (1981), which stresses conditioning.

Yamada, Yoshimitsu, and Steven Pimsler. **The New Aikido Complete: The Arts of Power and Movement.** New York: Stuart, 1981. 212p. $25 (796.8)

Used as much for exercise and peace of mind as for self-defense, this Japanese art of using locks and holds, matched with no resistance, is an accepted, even honored, sport in the East. Here the activity is covered in full, with the basic techniques and movements clearly explained. From the relatively simple to the sophisticated, there are excellent photographs and diagrams to make the action clear. Test requirements and a list of aikido schools are included.

JUGGLING

Cohen, Steve. **Just Juggle.** New York: McGraw-Hill, 1982. 177p. pap. $7.95 (793.8)

The author's primary piece of advice on the art of juggling is found in the title. But there really is more to it than tossing balls or plates into the air. Just how much more is explained in loving detail, and in such a way that even the most awkward adult or youngster should be able to astonish friends and foes alike by keeping three balls in movement. After that triumph, Cohen, in the last section, goes on to explain more difficult problems. Well written, nicely illustrated (there is even a flip-picture section), this is by far the best book on the subject.

KARATE. *See* Judo & Karate & Aikido

KAYAKS. *See* Canoes & Kayaks

KITCHENS
  See also Homes—Remodeling

Better Homes and Gardens Your Kitchen. Des Moines, IA: Meredith, 1983. 160p. $9.95 (728)
  Another in the All about Your House Series, which features photographs and a good format. The first assumption here is that the kitchen needs to be improved, probably through drastic redesign. To this end an ideal kitchen is pictured and explained. After this come points on what to consider when reworking the kitchen layout. Everything from cabinets to floors is dutifully explained, and handsomely illustrated. Not, however, a do-it-yourself approach; the focus here is on ideas.

Brett, James. **The Kitchen: 100 Design Solutions.** Rev. ed. New York: Watson-Guptill, 1983. 208p. $32.50 (728)
  Consisting primarily of black-and-white photographs, with some in color, this oversized book is an invitation to consider the possible appearance of a new or remodeled kitchen. The text is minimal, and there are no how-to-do-it directions. Conversely, the hundreds of superb photos depict a wide variety of architect-designed kitchens in various budget categories, although most are rather expensive. The greatest emphasis is on the kitchen as part of the living space in a home. There is a short section on office cooking space and on bars and barbecues. *Note:* The original edition (1977) is still useful, particularly as it stresses designs and approaches not found in the revision. Both books are good-to-excellent sources for ideas.

Cary, Jere. **Building Your Own Kitchen Cabinets: Layout, Materials, Construction, Installation.** Newtown, CT: Taunton, 1983. 143p. pap. $11.95 (684.16)
  Precise drawings, clear explanations, and excellent organization combine to make up one of the best current books on the construction of kitchen cabinets. The author presupposes that the reader has a basic knowledge of woodworking. There are clear instructions on how to measure and fit various types of frames and case assemblies, how to construct drawers, etc. The book is written in such a way that the instructions may be adapted to any personal design or set of architectural drawings. It does not stress particular objects, but opens the kitchen door to different approaches.

Clark, Sam. **The Motion Minded Kitchen: Step-by-Step Procedures for Designing and Building the Kitchen You Want with the Space and the Money You Have.** Boston: Houghton, 1983. 138p. $19.95; pap. $9.95 (643.3)
  The author's precise explanations and apt illustrations measure up to the promise of the subtitle. The twist is the book's focus on the number of steps one takes in a kitchen, and how energy and time can be saved by careful planning to eliminate

excess motion. This focus makes the book a particularly good source for early planning for a new or remodeled kitchen. Most of the advice is practical although some of the results may cost more in money than they save in time. In addition, there is a good section on how to build cabinets, shelves, drawers, counters, etc.— all in such a way as to save the expense of buying ready-made equipment. Kitchen templates are part of the extensive list of items in the appendixes.

Harrison, Rick. **Kitchens: How to Plan, Install & Remodel.** Tucson, AZ: HP Books, 1983. 192p. pap. $9.95 (643.3)

The author offers a twofold attack on the kitchen. First, through illustrations, including many colored photographs, he shows the numerous possibilities of various sizes and types of kitchens. Directions are given on how to modify existing plans and make original ones. Second, he demonstrates what has to be done in the remodeling, or the new house construction, to make such a kitchen possible. Here he meticulously explores the fundamentals from wiring to cabinets. The guide can be used by the experienced carpenter for how-to-do-it directions, but it will more likely be of interest to the average layperson who is looking for practical approaches to a kitchen.

Shapiro, Cecile, et al. **Better Kitchens.** Passaic, NJ: Creative Homeowner, 1981. 160p. $16.95; pap. $6.95 (643.3)

The strength, indeed the focus, of this kitchen book is on color. Thanks to the imaginative, colorful illustrations one gets a new grasp of what a kitchen can look like, without costing more than the house itself. In other words, the text is as practical as the general approach, which suggests reasonable methods of planning a new kitchen or remodeling an old one. The catch is that the how-to-do-it aspects are less exact than the illustrations. Still, for ideas it is a most useful work.

KNITTING & CROCHETING
See also Needlecrafts

American School of Needlework Presents the Great Knitting Book. New York: Columbia House, 1980. 160p. $15.95 (746.43)

This may not be the "great" knitting book claimed in the title, but it certainly is a useful one for anyone devoted to the art. The book opens with ten refresher knitting lessons that may be skipped by everyone but the true beginner. (Even beginners would be better off with more basic guides, at least at this stage. See other titles in this section.) With that, though, the book begins to make its mark in that it offers 75 quite excellent patterns neatly arranged by broad subject headings such as "All Time Favorites" (raglan sweaters, etc.) and "Fashion Show," which concentrates on more difficult, although certainly not always more fashionable, designs. Less successful, from an aesthetic point of view, are the suggestions for projects to brighten up the home. Photographs, several in color, show the completed project and all the needed instructions are there.

Compton, Rae. **The Complete Book of Traditional Knitting.** New York: Scribner's, 1983. 192p. $19.95 (746.4)

While "complete" is an exaggeration, this does include the basic approaches to traditional knitting. A real plus is that it considers knitting not only from England

and the United States but from most of western Europe. Each type of knitting is explained carefully, and in such a way that the beginner or the expert may learn how to use the particular method. While the color illustrations are less than adequate in number, at least the photographs are clear and useful. The book ends with details for 13 different types of wear, U.S. and English suppliers, a metric chart, a needle size chart, and a glossary.

Gerrard, Mady. **Mady Gerrard's Knitwear Designs.** New York: Perigee, 1983. 150p. $19.95; pap. $11.95 (746.92)

The author suggests striking knitwear designs for today's woman, and within that scope does her best to be sure the reader will understand each and every point in the process of making the clothes. Instead of offering esoteric, exotic, or too-simple patterns, Gerrard describes close to 30 designs that can be distinguished by their good taste and attention to detail. Each is described in terms of what can or cannot be done by a beginner, an intermediate, or an advanced master of knitting. The designs are examined from every angle, including problem areas. These are accompanied by step-by-step instructions and detailed photographs, many in color.

Linsley, Leslie. **Quick & Easy Knit & Crochet.** New York: St. Martin's, 1983. 160p. $18.95 (746.43)

Anyone with a basic knowledge of knitting and crocheting will find this book of projects valuable on two counts. First, there are numerous, imaginative projects included. Second, there are full-page illustrations that make it relatively easy to follow directions and get a good idea of the pattern described. Patterns are for various types of knitting and crocheting, but all are, as the author claims, "quick and easy."

McCall's Big Book of Knits and Crochet for Home and Family. Radnor, PA: Chilton, 1982. 304p. $12.95 (746.43)

This is a collection of patterns, illustrations, and detailed instructions from the pages of *McCall's Needlework & Crafts*. It is a grab bag of knitting and crochet ideas that range from the bold to the subtle. Most of the material is addressed to the beginner or near beginner.

Meyers, Belle. **Knitting Know-How: An Illustrated Encyclopedia.** New York: Harper, 1981. 191p. $9.95 (746.9)

Here is a clear, concise, and illustrated explanation of knitting techniques. Prepared for both the beginner and the semi-expert, the alphabetically arranged entries show how to plan and execute designs. There are explanations of such things as needle sizes, American and English crochet hooks, and the like. It is the best specialized work of its kind now available.

Schraffenberger, Nancy, ed. **Woman's Day Crochet Showcase.** New York: Van Nostrand, 1982. 175p. $15.95 (746.43)

Taken from past issues of *Woman's Day*, this is a compendium of nearly 100 crochet projects featured in that magazine. Two or three things make the book outstanding. First, the illustrations are good and there is a designation system that clearly identifies the easy and the more difficult works. Second, the instructions are clear and full. Third, the range of the subjects—from pot holders to an actual wedding dress—is remarkable and such that anyone can find one or a dozen applicable ideas.

KNOTS & SPLICES

Bigon, Mario, and Guido Regazzoni. **The Morrow Guide to Knots: For Sailing, Fishing, Camping, Climbing.** New York: Morrow, 1982. 255p. $14.50; pap. $9.45 (623.88)

Knots of all types, varieties, and shapes are considered here, with clear instructions (usually accompanied by illustrations), on how they are tied. Where the knot is truly complicated, where more than two ropes are involved, the explanation is accompanied by photographs showing each rope in a different color. The explanations are surprisingly easy to follow, even for the most difficult project. There are discussions of various types of ropes and decorative knots. Still, most of the book is for the audience suggested in the subtitle, those interested in knots for sailing, fishing, camping, and climbing.

Russell, John. **The Arco Book of Useful Knots.** New York: Arco, 1981. 79p. pap. $4.95 (623.88)

This explains, in words and illustrations, the basic methods of making useful knots. More than 25 knots are discussed in detail—in such detail, in fact, that even people who are all thumbs should manage. In addition, there are definitions, general words of advice, and a good writing style. First issued in England, this book is of equal value here. Note: There are no permanent decorative knots shown.

LANDSCAPE GARDENING
See also Gardening

Ball, Jeff. **The Self-Sufficient Suburban Garden.** Emmaus, PA: Rodale, 1983. 256p. $14.95 (635)

If the Russians have their five-year plans, so can numerous suburban and small-town residents who, according to the author, can turn their backyards into small, self-sufficient farms in five years' time. For those who have the energy and the inclination, Ball demonstrates a project that results in a flourishing garden in the fifth year. He begins, for example, with ten vegetables and ends with a garden that has grown to include almost all basic nuts, fruits, and berries. His somewhat leisurely approach to self-sufficiency is explained with zest and perhaps a bit too much philosophical musing. He includes little or no specific information on how to grow particular things. Still, the general advice is good, the suggestions on how to diagram and plan excellent, and the overall project stimulating. The book is written to take into account various climatic and growing conditions. There are, as well, good illustrations and numerous charts and summary tables.

Beckett, Kenneth; David Carr; and David Stevens. **The Contained Garden.** New York: Viking, 1983. 168p. $26; pap. $12.95 (635.98)

For a number of reasons, from lack of space to aesthetic considerations, many gardeners prefer to limit planting to containers. This is a rigorous form of gardening that is too little appreciated. To get an idea of what is involved, to become an expert in growing a plant in a pot, this is the ideal guide. In addition to easy-to-follow, intelligent explanations and directions, the author provides numerous color illustrations, usually of container gardens, not just single plants. Aside from the expected advice on types of containers, soil, and diseases, there is a good section on the varieties of plants that do well in this type of gardening.

Damroch, Barbara. **Theme Gardens.** New York: Workman, 1982. 224p. $19.95; pap. $10.95 (635.9)

Within the scope of the average home plot, it is possible to develop and maintain a Zen-type garden, or, at the other extreme, a profuse Colonial one. Here an expert landscape specialist tells how to turn a plot of ground into something quite special with a minimum of expense and time. There are 16 basic types of gardens described, and specific instructions are given to make each one a reality. An added bonus: Not only are the plants carefully described, but in most cases historic background is given. While the settings are primarily for the Northeast, the author suggests enough substitute plants and flowers so that the basic plans can be used in almost any climate.

Davidson, A. K. **The Art of Zen Gardens: A Guide to Their Creation and Enjoyment.** New York: Houghton, 1983. 192p. $15.95; pap. $9.95 (712.2)

Anyone looking for a magnificently simple layout for a garden should turn here first. Precise instructions are given on how to create a Zen garden masterpiece, and, as the method calls for more time and patience than money, the manual can be used by almost anyone. There are numerous illustrations of historic Japanese gardens (which may include waterfalls, bridges, and ponds). These are somewhat irrelevant and seem to be provided more for their beauty than as a fund of ideas. A further drawback is that individual plants are not really considered, except in the appendix, and there only briefly. An artful blend of Haiku poetry and Zen history runs through the book. Even those who have no plans to construct such a garden will enjoy this exceptional book.

Diekelmann, John, and Robert Schuster. **Natural Landscaping.** New York: McGraw-Hill, 1982. 276p. $24.95 (715)

Where conditions allow, why not landscape a property by using existing trees, plants, and wildflowers? The positive answer to that rhetorical question is examined here with specific instructions on how to incorporate the natural beauty of a setting into a backyard or around an entire house. The authors explain which plants and flowers are native to what regions and how these may be cultivated. There is a less useful section on the landscaping of parks and school grounds. Numerous black-and-white and color illustrations are provided.

McHoy, Peter. **Garden Construction.** New York: Blandford Pr./Sterling, 1984. 128p. pap. $6.95 (635)

Materials with which to plan and make a garden grow are the primary focus of this three-pronged attack. The first section discusses a wide variety of tools and other garden equipment. The second considers how to lay out pleasing plots and landscapes—with particular emphasis on how to place fences, walls, patios, and sheds. The last section is concerned with the actual planting of the garden, with advice on what to use or not to use for certain effects. Most of the focus is on items that make the garden a delight, not on gardening per se. The text is illustrated with fine and useful drawings as well as color and black-and-white photographs. First published in England, this book has a definite British bias, but it can be used by most dedicated American gardeners.

Michel, Timothy. **Homeowner's Guide to Landscape Design.** Rev. ed. Woodstock, VT: Countryman, 1983. 180p. pap. $10.95 (712.6)

A landscape architect explains how the fundamentals of good design may be used by the average homeowner to improve the appearance of the home and the surrounding land. There are step-by-step directions, including methods of drawing plans based on an objective evaluation of conditions. The focus is not only on the aesthetics of design, but on energy conservation through erosion control, windbreaks, etc. The manual puts particular emphasis on low-cost, practical approaches that can be carried out by the individual. There are also suggestions for the mobile home owner. Numerous illustrations and drawings make each step clear, and there are useful lists such as the one of plant material organized by type and region.

Schenk, George. **The Complete Shade Gardener.** Boston: Houghton, 1984. 285p. $24.95 (635.9)

What can be done with a garden area that receives little or no sunshine? Drawing from his own experience, the author opens this useful guide with a demonstration of how he turned a hopeless area into a splendid garden. The secret is soil preparation and, most important, knowing the types of plants to grow. Using photographs and clear, detailed explanations, the author suggests various plants that thrive in the shade. Actually, almost half of the work is devoted to descriptions of such plants and how they grow in different climates. Some vegetables are included. There are sections on maintenance and care of a garden, including pruning and how to handle plant diseases. The book ends with a list of nurseries that carry some of the specialized plants Schenk recommends. Most of the plants, however, are available in the average garden store.

Stephenson, Ashley. **The Garden Planner.** New York: St. Martin's, 1983. 247p. $25; pap. $12.95 (712.6)

Due consideration is given here to the unusual as well as the usual. It is not, for example, assumed that all soils are good or that all places are ideally lighted by the sun. The author has ideas for solving gardening problems in areas from small urban plots to forest-dominated country sites. For each situation, the planner offers suggestions and specific ideas on how to overcome the impossible and develop—usually over a period of several years—a suitable garden. By "garden" the author means not only flower beds but greenhouses, lawns, and arbors. There are many photographs and line drawings to emphasize the points, and the text is a model of good writing. A section on flower arrangement is also included. *Note:* This was first published in England, and it has a British bias, but that is minimal and in no way detracts from its worth for American gardeners.

Wirth, Thomas, and Jay Howland. **The Victory Garden Landscape Guide.** Boston: Little, 1984. 358p. $29.50; pap. $16.50 (635.9)

Based on the Public Broadcasting Service (PBS) Victory Garden Series, this is an extremely useful guide for the person who has bought a new house without any landscaping, or who has an older home and wishes to change the landscape plan.

Wirth shows how to work out a plan suitable for the type of home, the size of the lot, and the needs of the occupants—not to mention the growing conditions of a particular part of the country. In fact, there is a month-by-month program that takes the seasons (and the working habits of the reader) into account. Numerous illustrations, many in color, augment the well-written text, which also considers other aspects of landscaping from furniture to patios, if only in a skimpy way.

LAPIDARY. *See* Precious Stones

LAWNS. *See* Gardening; Landscape Gardening

LETTERING. *See* Calligraphy; Graphic Arts

LITHOGRAPHY. *See* Graphic Arts

LOCKS. *See* Burglary Protection; Crime Protection

LOG CABINS. *See* Homes—Building & Construction

MAGIC
   See also Games; Puzzles

Blackstone, Harry. **Blackstone's Tricks Anyone Can Do.** Secaucus, NJ: Citadel, 1983. 240p. pap. $4.95 (793.8)
   Although now dead, Blackstone lives on in legend as one of the world's great magicians. This guide was first published in the 1950s, and is now slightly revised by Blackstone's son. There is an introduction by Walter B. Gibson (well known in the field of magic). It has the advantage of explaining tricks most people can do without expensive props or extensive knowledge of magic. Each trick, from the simple card maneuver to those with ropes, is clearly discussed and takes the reader step by step through the complete process. This should be of particular interest to younger people, and to others who may simply wish to entertain themselves and learn new uses for their agility.

Gibson, Walter. **Walter Gibson's Big Book of Magic for All Ages.** Garden City, NY: Doubleday, 1980. 240p. $12.95 (793.8)
   Gibson is well known as an expert in magic and tricks, hence his confidence in putting his own name in the title. The man's reputation is well earned. Here the beginner, or even the individual with some experience in the field, will find much to enjoy. The directions are quite specific, often accompanied by useful illustrations, and Gibson never leaves one wondering how to get out of a trick gracefully. He sticks with easily available items such as coins and rope, and rarely advises the use of specialized equipment or materials. A nice touch is that the various chapter openings are written by expert magicians who pass on easy-to-follow hints on their particular skills. For more magic and tricks, simply look for other titles by Gibson.

Hay, Henry. **The Amateur Magician's Handbook.** 4th ed. New York: Harper, 1982. 414p. $16.95 (793.8)

Frequently updated, this is a basic guide to magic for the interested amateur of any age. It is suitable for children as well as adults, although some of the more complex tricks may be too sophisticated for youngsters. Illustrations help the beginner move from simple performances to those that are more complicated. There is a section on videotape as a method of self-coaching that may not be of great interest, but there is a good section on magic that is geared specifically to children. The guide ends with biographical sketches of magicians and a useful bibliography.

Lanners, Edi. **Secrets of 123 Old Time Science Tricks & Experiments.** Blue Ridge Summit, PA: TAB, 1981. 192p. $12.95; pap. $7.95 (507)

A plate or a spoon can be turned into evidence of a scientific law, i.e., it can be used for magic tricks that demonstrate scientific truth. These 123 tricks are taken primarily from nineteenth-century books and are nicely illustrated with vintage cuts. Instructions are complete for each of the experiments. While most of the tricks can be performed by youngsters, they all require careful reading of the instructions and a great deal of patience, particularly as the line between success and failure may be no more than a careful measurement or a balancing skill.

MAIL

U.S. Postal Service. **Domestic Mail Manual.** Washington, DC: GPO, 1981. Approx. 360p. $28 (P.1.12/22:trans.6)

Hundreds of regulations governing all aspects of the U.S. mail are provided, often in language that is hard to follow. For example, the delineation of what constitutes third-class and fourth-class mail is clear, but only after careful reading. Still, it is the single most reliable guide available. Regulations are from late 1981, but the guide often is updated so look for the most recent issue.

U.S. Postal Service. **National Zip Code Directory.** Washington, DC: GPO, 1981– . Annual. Approx. 2,000p. $9 (P1.10/8)

This is the definitive place to find zip code data. It is updated each year. This book is essential for discovering a hard-to-find zip code, e.g., one for a very small town. It has other uses, too, such as information on parcel weight and size limits, proper addressing, and a state-by-state list of post offices. *Note:* Zip codes are found in many sources, including general almanacs.

MAIL ORDER CATALOGS. *See* Catalogs

MAPS & MAP READING

U.S. Department of Defense. **Map Reading.** Washington, DC: GPO, 1980. 152p. $6.50 (D101.20:21–26)

An army field manual used in training recruits, this is an ideal introduction to the subject of map reading for the layperson as well. The early chapters include fundamentals of reading and using a map, followed by detailed information on the use of aerial photographs, pictographs, and more. The overall presentation is ideal, and the reader can take what is useful and leave the rest.

U.S. Department of Interior. **Map Data Catalog.** Washington, DC: U.S. Geological Survey, 1981. 48p. $3.50 (I19.2:M32/13)

The government issues thousands of maps and related materials, most of which can be purchased at a reasonable price. Here the reader will find information on maps and "mapping byproducts" such as color separates, digital terrain tapes, and slides. There is a large section on aerial and space imagery.

A related item by the Library of Congress is *Facsimiles of Maps, and Atlases: A List of Reproductions for Sale by Various Publishers and Distributors* (Washington, DC: GPO, 1981, 35p., $2.50). Maps are listed by publisher. Frequently updated, the list normally includes about 500 to 550 maps from about 150 publishers.

MARINE ENGINES. *See* Boats

MARINE LIFE
See also Animals—Field Guides; Nature Study

Boschung, Herbert T., et al. **The Audubon Society Field Guide to North American Fishes, Whales, and Dolphins.** New York: Knopf, 1983. 848p. pap. $12.50 (597.09)

Here is an authoritative, handy guide for fishing enthusiasts, people who like to study fish in aquariums, and the curious. There are some 500 fishes illustrated in full color and described in enough detail that the observer will be able to tell one from the other. The text is useful because the pictures, while generally acceptable, are not always clear and the line drawings may not be so helpful, either. There is a good index, and the arrangement makes it easy enough to use. Following as it does the other Audubon guide formats the book is a compact manual for identifying and understanding fishes. *Note:* Most of the emphasis is on fishes, although, as the title suggests, there are sections on dolphins and whales.

McIntyre, Joan. **The Delicate Art of Whale Watching.** New York: Random House, 1982. 144p. $12.50 (599.5)

The title barely suggests the scope of this intriguing book. The author does explain the process of watching whales, and, in basic guidebook fashion, makes it possible for the beginner to understand the delights of looking at the seas. As much poet as scientist, however, she is more concerned with observing all of nature. This report of her adventure on a distant Pacific Island includes thoughts and observations on almost every aspect of the human condition. It is, then, a book on learning how to see not only the exterior world, but the interior as well.

Meinkoth, Norman. **The Audubon Society Field Guide to North American Seashore Creatures.** New York: Knopf, 1981. 799p. pap. $12.50 (574.90)

Slightly over 650 species of seashore creatures are described, often with full-color illustrations, in this guide for laypersons. The invertebrates that are covered include urchins, anemones, sponges, corals, etc., shown in the pictures in their natural setting. There are easy-to-understand notes on how to recognize specific creatures, where they live, and their particular habits. There is also a useful glossary and index.

Rehder, Harold. **The Audubon Society Field Guide to North American Seashells.** New York: Knopf, 1981. 894p. pap. $11.95 (594)

Some 700 seashells found on both the Atlantic and Pacific coasts of the United

States are described here, and shown in as many good color plates. The arrangement is by shape and color, and this helps the amateur make identifications much faster than if the shells were arranged by family or genus. The shell is identified, too, by a representative family silhouette and a brief yet accurate descriptive text. The first half of the volume is made up of photographs, the second of descriptive matter.

MARTIAL ARTS. *See* Judo & Karate & Aikido; Self-Defense

MASONRY & BRICKWORK

Alth, Max. **Masonry.** Homeowner's Bible Series. New York: Doubleday, 1982. 135p. pap. $4.95 (693.1)

Easy to follow and well illustrated, this is a basic approach to all aspects of masonry work from cement and bricks to concrete and stone. The author does three things: He gives instructions on the methods of masonry, indicates the necessary tools, and offers several projects—for the most part rather easy ones, from steps to patios. An added feature is the information on when and where to apply for building permits. While more advanced masonry work requires advanced books, this is a good beginning for anyone.

Better Homes and Gardens Step-by-Step Masonry & Concrete. Des Moines, IA: Meredith, 1982. 96p. pap. $5.95 (693.1)

A brief yet thorough approach, this is for the amateur who is about to undertake a masonry or concrete project. There is good advice on tools and materials, and, as the title says, step-by-step instructions for specific types of projects such as a planter wall. The book also covers brick and stone, and as with all the *Better Homes and Gardens* manuals, it is heavily illustrated.

Self, Charles. **The Brickworker's Bible.** Blue Ridge Summit, PA: TAB, 1980. 378p. $15.95; pap. $8.95 (693.21)

This is written for the layperson who has modest plans for bricklaying, such as the repair of walls, paths, and patios. The author, who draws from his own professional experience, writes clearly and explains each and every step. He begins with the essentials, from the tools to the types of bonding materials and bricks needed for certain jobs. Tasks are graduated in difficulty from the easy to the complex. The latter include archways, which try the skills of even the experienced hand. There is a glossary and a directory of manufacturers.

U.S. Department of Defense. **Concrete and Masonry.** Washington, DC: GPO, 1979. 201p. $7 (D101.11:5—742)

This book explains the physical characteristics and properties of concrete, brick, and tile. It is an army technical and field manual, and is ideal for someone familiar with the basics of masonry and concrete.

MATHEMATICS
See also Puzzles

Ellis, Keith. **Number Power in Nature, Art and Everyday Life.** New York: St. Martin's, 1978. 236p. $10 (133.3)

This is both a basic reference book and a book of fun for the individual in love with mathematics. The author sets out to examine the role of numbers in myth, nature, science, and popular culture. He poses questions and then gives the answers, usually in the form of short discursive essays. For example, how did the superstition about the number 13 begin, and does it have any meaning today? Some of the data are trite, but much is fascinating and even useful. Among scores of books about numbers, this is one of the best. It is not dated, nor is it likely to be so in years to come.

Gowar, Norman. **An Invitation to Mathematics.** New York: Oxford, 1979. 206p. $26; pap. $11 (510.21)

An expert mathematician explains that it really is not hard to understand basic mathematics. The author has a witty, intelligent approach that makes it possible to follow his discussions with pleasure. The requirement is that the reader must have an understanding of basic mathematics. Once that hurdle is passed, one can enjoy these brilliant, even exciting, discussions of everything from algebra to calculus and geometry.

Hershey, Robert. **How to Think with Numbers.** Los Altos, CA: Kaufmann, 1982. 176p. pap. $7.95 (510)

Laid out for the reader who has difficulty counting even when using fingers and toes, this is an anecdotal, skillfully planned approach to mastering basic mathematics. The procedures are carefully explained and there are storylike problems—none of which should insult the reader's intelligence—indicating how mathematical principles can be applied. For those who cannot appreciate numbers, Hershey offers practical advice on the selection and use of a pocket calculator.

Hilton, Peter, and Jean Pedersen. **Fear No More: An Adult Approach to Mathematics.** Reading, MA: Addison-Wesley, 1983. 281p. $18.60 (513)

As the title suggests, this is a guide for the adult or high school student who either fears mathematics or simply fails to understand its basics. Working from the beginning, the authors stress shortcuts to understanding math and use numerous illustrations and examples to make sometimes difficult techniques and ideas easier to comprehend. From negative numbers to fractions and algorithms, the writing style is easy to follow. The reliance on text as much as on symbols does a lot to remove the mystery of mathematics for the bewildered layperson.

Hogben, Lancelot. **Mathematics for the Millions.** 4th ed. New York: Norton, 1983. 648p. pap. $8.95 (510)

First published in 1937, this is now a classic. It sets out to show that one need not fear mathematics, and at the same time offers the reader a historic background and a practical point of departure for understanding the science. There are specific examples, problems, and solutions throughout the guide that demonstrate how mathematics is used in everyday situations. Everything, from simple addition to ratios, is explained in enough detail, and in such a winning way, that the book is an ideal beginning for even the most mathematically disabled. A first choice in this area.

Jacobs, Harold. **Mathematics: A Human Endeavor.** San Francisco: Freeman, 1982. 649p. $17.95 (510)

In demonstrating that mathematics need not be a major headache, the author goes a long way toward showing laypersons how to master basic math. The particular fascination is that from there it is only a small step to an understanding of logarithms and statistical data. Jacobs carries off what is primarily a work of instruction by turning it all into a game. There are delightful illustrations, diagrams, and photographs to underline his various teaching points. The author has a marvelous writing style that is clear and witty. The result is a superior mathematics text neatly hidden under a bushel of games and delights.

Sperling, Abraham. **Mathematics Made Simple.** New York: Doubleday, 1981. 192p. pap. $4.50 (510)

This is a direct, easy-to-follow explanation of basic mathematics, and, more particularly, the mathematics employed in everyday life. The primary approach is to present a question and then to give the answer, usually in enough detail to help the reader master the principles involved.

Thompson, James. **Arithmetic for the Practical Worker.** 4th ed. New York: Van Nostrand, 1982. 266p. pap. $6.95 (513)

Directed toward those who use mathematics in their everyday work, this begins with fundamentals and gradually works up to more difficult concepts and problems. It is ideal for the individual who is either studying for an examination or needs basic instruction (or a memory refresher) for mathematics on the job. The basics are covered, from addition to particular methods of figuring and calculation.

MEATS. *See* Cooking—Meats & Chicken; Food

METALWORK

Lindsley, E. F. **Metalworking in the Home Shop.** New York: Van Nostrand, 1983. 310p. $30.50 (684.09)

There are not that many good manuals for metalworking, so this is all the more welcome for its thorough, easy-to-understand approach to the subject. The author presupposes that the reader has an interest in metalworking, but knows little about the tools, equipment, and materials. The basics are covered in early sections and then, with numerous illustrations, specific activities such as pattern cutting, layout, various types of drills, attaching, etc., are introduced. There are chapters, too, on working with various types of lathes, saws, and other tools that one could use in related areas such as making jewelry settings. The author ends by offering several projects, although by this point most readers will want to try their own patterns.

MICROCOMPUTERS. *See* Computers

MINERALOGY. *See* Precious Stones; Rock Collecting

MODELS & MODELMAKING

Ellis, Chris. **How to Make Model Aircraft.** New York: Arco, 1974. 80p. $5.95 (629.133)

The best methods of assembling, painting, and adding details to plastic airplane kits are explained here clearly and with attention to the needs of beginners. The attractive illustrations help the user follow the author in his step-by-step approach. While purists may object to the focus on plastic kits, the book is directed to the average enthusiast, not the expert. Originally published in England, this work has been modified for American readers. The author's enthusiasm and knowledge make this an excellent guide.

Jackson, Albert, and David Day. **The Modelmaker's Handbook.** New York: Knopf, 1981. 352p. $19.95 (745.59)

A basic guide for the most popular types of models, this has three unusual features. First, there are some 1,500 superior photographs and drawings. Second, it offers a fine survey of models, particularly those of interest to adults. Third, the authors give specific techniques and instructions applicable to the building of model boats, military miniatures, cars, trains, and airplanes. Most of the basics could be carried over into other types of model building. The explanations are precise, yet sometimes they do require a basic appreciation of technical writing and an understanding of models. The book has a British bias, but this is incidental to the excellent treatment.

Jensen, Gerald. **Building in Miniature.** Radnor, PA: Chilton, 1982. 221p. $14.95; pap. $9.95 (745.59)

The assumption here is that the reader has some experience in miniature building, particularly of individual rooms. The author is more involved with the overall structure, and offers detailed plans on the construction of various types of buildings. Full information is given on everything from the tools needed to various types of materials. In addition to set patterns, he gives helpful suggestions on how to design one's own miniature structures. There are good black-and-white photographs to supplement the instructions.

Paust, Gil. **Model Railroading: How to Plan, Build, and Maintain Your Trains and Pikes.** Garden City, NY: Doubleday, 1981. 146p. $9.95 (625.1)

This is a good, basic beginner's guide for any age group. Enthusiastic as he is informative, the author explains the joys of the hobby and how to make it even more fascinating. His points are accented by good photographs and diagrams. Exact instructions are given on how to set up a model railroad—from buying the engine to fashioning realistic bits of terrain. There is a good section on wiring and another on basic techniques for improving the appearance of the model. The usual names of associations, magazines, etc., are included.

Price, Brick. **Model-Building Handbook.** Radnor, PA: Chilton, 1981. 176p. $13.95; pap. $8.95 (745.59)

Starting at a movie set where he is an expert on model building, Price opens his exposition with a good description of the basic tools needed and the various types of materials, from kits to casting. He explains how many techniques and materials can be used by the beginner. While most of these are suitable for all types of models, Price is particularly interested in vehicles. The explanations are clear and the illustrations apt. The result is one of the best basic model books available.

Price, Brick. **The Model Shipbuilding Handbook.** Radnor, PA: Chilton, 1983. 187p. $19.95; pap. $12.95 (623.8)

There are not many guides to building model ships, but this one is an excellent, basic point of departure for the beginner. Price explains all, from what tools and materials are needed to how to borrow odds and ends from various kits in order to construct a superior, original model. Each detail of construction is considered, and the step-by-step directions are supported with good illustrations, including photographs.

Schleicher, Robert. **Building and Displaying Model Aircraft.** Radnor, PA: Chilton, 1981. 158p. $13.95; pap. $8.95 (629.13)

Using photographs and a commonsense text, this expert model maker shows the reader how to make a plastic model airplane look its best. The concern is with displaying as well as building models. He moves from the first steps of construction to the final setting. In the latter category are such things as simple dioramas. A novel twist is his suggestion for using models in war games. The author includes a good bibliography of both books and magazines.

Schleicher, Robert. **The HO Model Railroading Handbook.** Rev. ed. Radnor, PA: Chilton, 1983. 220p. $10.95 (625.1)

Primarily for beginners, this is a good introduction to HO railroad models. There is background material on the history of the form and how the small-scale models became popular. The heart of the guide is the information on how to purchase equipment or build it from kits; layouts and constructing landscapes; and data on track, switching, power, wiring, etc. There is an overview, too, of the types of equipment available, although only a modest effort is made to indicate which is best. There are adequate illustrations.

Schleicher, Robert. **The Modeler's Manual: Trains, Planes, Ships, Military Vehicles, Cars, Rockets.** Radnor, PA: Chilton, 1981. 184p. $14.95; pap. $10.95 (629.04)

A thoughtful, useful overview of various types of models and how they are built, this book excels in its imaginative approach to the subject. For the most part the author encourages readers to avoid ready-made kits, or, at best, to modify them for particular purposes. He encourages readers to build from scratch. To this end, there are illustrated instructions for numerous projects. In addition, there are good sections on basic tools, finishing processes, problems with dealing with small parts, etc.

Schleicher, Robert, and James Barr. **Building and Flying Model Aircraft.** Radnor, PA: Chilton, 1980. 166p. $13.95; pap. $6.95 (629.13)

For anyone who wants to begin building model aircraft, this is the place to start. The fundamental directions are as clear and precise as the illustrations. The authors are particularly helpful in that they offer a good introduction to the hobby. They also indicate that it can be quite expensive and time consuming, then go on to introduce the reader to basic materials and equipment, including kits.

Smeed, Vic, ed. **Complete Railway Modelling.** Radnor, PA: Chilton, 1983. 191p. pap. $12.95 (625.19)

There are various levels of difficulty and sophistication in this guide to railway modeling. Contributing experts explain how to lay out tracks, and then how to construct different elements from scenery to buildings. More difficult is the actual building of stock equipment such as locomotives and cars. Some of this, to be sure, is from kits, but some of it is from separate parts. Well illustrated, this is relatively easy to follow.

Stine, Harry. **Handbook of Model Rocketry.** 5th ed. New York: Arco, 1983. 367p. $10.95 (629.46)

Now in its fifth edition, this is the basic guide for the home rocket enthusiast— junior high school age to adult. The author's general introduction covers the types of skills needed and the tools required. Instructions are given on how to select the best type of rocket motors and recovery devices. The appendixes include three computer programs.

Wesolowski, Wayne. **Model Railroad Scratchbuilding.** Blue Ridge Summit, PA: TAB, 1981. $16.95; pap. $9.95 (625.1)

Whether the hobbyist is working with wood, paper, or plaster, this is the source for reliable information on the construction of buildings and backgrounds associated with model railroad layouts. In addition to specific, easy-to-follow directions, there are some 200 illustrations. For each of the media, the author carefully describes advantages and limitations and how it is employed. The writing is as enthusiastic as the instructions are precise.

Winter, William J. **The World of Model Airplanes.** New York: Scribner's, 1983. 294p. $19.95 (629.13)

Winter, together with writers for the periodical *Model Aviation,* offers the essentials of building model airplanes. In addition to good instructions, there is enthusiasm and interest in a fascinating subject evident on every page. The advice itself is current and takes into consideration almost every budget, every level of ability. General sections range from basics of aeronautics to competitions. Specific chapters deal with various techniques of construction and flying. This is a first choice in the field.

MOTELS. *See* Travel

MOTION PICTURE & TELEVISION PHOTOGRAPHY. *See* Photography—Motion Pictures & Television

MOTORCYCLES

Carric, Peter, ed. **Encyclopaedia of Motor-Cycle Sport.** 2nd ed. New York: St. Martin's, 1982. 240p. $14.95 (796.75)

This is a background book on motorcycles, not a how-to-do-it manual. Articles of various length are arranged in alphabetical order to cover the history of motorcycle sport from the turn of the century to the late 1970s. It excels in three areas: extensive and detailed race results, biographical sketches, and hard-to-find material on famous and not-so-famous events, races, and contests. As a background guide it is useful. The photographs are grouped together and not tied to the text.

Minton, David. **The Complete Motorcyclist's Handbook.** New York: Simon & Schuster, 1981. 239p. $10.95 (796.7)

The "complete" in the title is correct. This is one of the best books for the dedicated motorcyclist in that it covers almost every conceivable topic of interest. Sections deal with the selection of bikes, clothing and other equipment needed, riding skills, and even first-aid procedures. One part covers racing events and biographical sketches of famous riders, and there is a fine section on safety. Numerous illustrations add to the usefulness of the guide. Information is given on maintenance, although the bike owner will want a manual specific to the kind of cycle owned. This guide will be of use to both beginners and experts. Note: While this was first published in England, it has been revised and updated for American readers.

Stermer, Bill. **Motorcycle Touring.** Tucson, AZ: HP Books, 1982. 144p. pap. $7.95 (796.7)

Riders other than the Hell's Angels go on motorcycle tours, but there is not much published to help this type of tourist. This is one of the few guides of its type. Stermer discusses the obvious (maintenance of the bike, clothing and other gear) and the not so obvious (the various types of equipment that can make or break a trip). The writing style is a bit rough (particularly as there is included an unwarranted piece of fiction).

Tragatsch, Erwin, ed. **The Complete Illustrated Encyclopedia of the World's Motorcycles.** New York: Holt, 1977. 320p. $22.95 (629.22)

This is *the* reference book on motorcycles. There are over 2,500 bikes from all places and all periods dutifully listed, with detailed descriptions. About one-half of the entries are illustrated, some in color. In addition to the descriptive listings, the author provides a short history of motorcycles up to World War II, and a good section on famous designers. As an invaluable reference source it has no peer; it is useful too for the collector or motorcycle fan who wants to know more about a particular model.

MOUNTAINEERING

See also Hiking & Backpacking; Survival Techniques (Wilderness)

Foster, Lynne. **Mountaineering Basics.** San Diego: Avant Books, 1983. 240p. pap. $9.95 (796.5)

As the title says, this is basic, and the one book everyone interested in mountain climbing should own. The book is divided into two main sections. The first part is an introduction not only to climbing, but to hiking and camping. Here one finds the needed information on planning a trip, equipment, dangers to avoid, training, etc. The next section is on the climb itself, with precise drills on rock climbing, safety, and all of the factors involved in mountaineering. The appendixes include the addresses of sources of supplies. Well organized and nicely illustrated, this is a starting point for amateur and expert alike. Note: This updates the first edition, published as *Basic Mountaineering,* and is different enough to warrant ordering.

Loughman, Michael. **Learning to Rock Climb.** San Francisco: Sierra Club, 1981. 141p. $17.95; pap. $9.95 (796.5)

Using photographs of himself and his wife on the rock face, as well as sketches, the author stresses basic techniques for getting from the bottom of rocks to the top without danger or overexertion. Directed to the beginner, the guide focuses on basic skills, and offers step-by-step (here, quite literally) instructions. There are sections on equipment and various elementary and semi-advanced techniques. The writing style is as clear as the instructions.

Mitchell, Richard. **Mountain Experience: The Psychology and Sociology of Adventure.** Chicago: University of Chicago Pr., 1983. 272p. $27 (796.22)

Why does one court danger in sports, and most particularly in mountain climbing? There are almost as many answers as there are individuals engaging in the activity, but here a sociologist traces what seem to be the common elements. For example, most mountaineers are employed in work that requires little or no risk, and is likely to be much the same day in and day out. Looking for almost anything to break the pattern, the individual climbs a mountain. The author analyzes such things as how equipment is selected and what type is chosen as an explanation of the danger factor. He moves into a discussion of the choice of climbing companions, or when one goes on a climb alone. There are about half a dozen other areas explored by way of explanation other than the traditional one for climbing a mountain, i.e., "It is there." While some of this is technical and of interest only to a scholar, most of it will do much to explain the lure of danger in sports.

MUSHROOMS

Christensen, Clyde. **Edible Mushrooms.** 2nd ed. Minneapolis: University of Minnesota Pr., 1981. 118p. $12.95; pap. $6.95 (589.2)

Is this mushroom safe to eat? The answer to that question is the primary, although not the only, objective of this guide. Some 55 different North American mushrooms are clearly described. Each is shown in a good photograph. The book opens with an explanation of the four easy-to-recognize, totally safe species. From that point, the guide moves to species that are more difficult to identify. The book closes with some recipes (only six or seven pages), and a short bibliography.

Lincoff, Gary. **Audubon Society Field Guide to North American Mushrooms.** New York: Knopf, 1981. 926p. pap. $12.50 (589.2)

Although this is a trifle too large to carry around, it is an invaluable guide to identifying mushrooms. Each is shown in its natural habitat. The publisher claims that there are 762 full-color photographs. Edibility is clearly marked, and there is an x for poisonous varieties. The great mystery is the group with neither poisonous nor recommendation labels. Here readers are on their own. Material is arranged and keyed by name, size, color, etc. Descriptions are ample and while this may be too complicated for casual mushroom hunters, it is a basic guide for others.

Miller, Orson. **Mushrooms in Color.** New York: Dutton, 1981. 286p. $11.50 (589.2)

Just about everything the beginner needs to know about mushrooms is to be found in this volume, one of the best guides of its type. The author limits the hunt to 90 species likely to be found in North America. He then carefully explains, with detailed descriptions and keyed illustrations in color, what to eat and what to avoid. The guide is practical. It opens with a discussion of how to isolate a particular species, and throughout the author relies on a nontechnical, nonscientific vocabulary. The pocket-size format makes it ideal for carrying about when on a quest for mushrooms. Miller also wrote *Mushrooms of North America* (1979).

MUSIC

Harris, Kenn. **The Ultimate Opera Quiz Book** New York: Penguin, 1982. 256p. pap. $7.95 (782.1)

The Texaco opera on-the-air series is as well known for its intermission quizzes as it is for the operas. Here are over 100 such quizzes, and while not from the Texaco program, they follow the same pattern. The reader is asked to identify composers, operas, performers, and recordings. Harris even includes pictorial puzzles and there are scores of anecdotes that enliven his already enjoyable and witty discourse. A similar title is James Camner's *Operatic Quiz Book* (St. Martin's, 1982).

Hines, Chet. **How to Make and Play the Dulcimore.** Harrisburg, PA: Stackpole, 1973. 157p. $9.95 (787.9)

The author is a founder of the Mountain Dulcimore Society of America. (He favors the spelling dulcimore to dulcimer, and in a brief history of the instrument, he explains why.) Hines shows a step-by-step method for its construction. There is a pattern inserted in the book, as well as numerous illustrations. The author ends with some fundamental information on playing, but his work is primarily useful for its instructions on building the dulcimore. While ideal for the beginner, it is not the book for an expert. Someone who wishes various patterns, various approaches to construction, should use other, more advanced titles.

Hurd, Michael. **The Orchestra.** New York: Facts on File, 1980. 224p. $24.95 (785.06)

In many ways, this is an ideal book for anyone who wants to know how an orchestra functions, the difference between instruments, and who the best conductors are. While hardly a how-to-do-it book in the usual sense, it is a necessary one for the person who claims some knowledge of serious music. The text is extensively illustrated, and the most valuable section is that devoted to instruments. Each type (from string to percussion) is considered, as is the individual piece within the orchestra. The author explains how each instrument functions and concludes with a section on musical scores. Somewhat less useful for the reader seeking basic information, yet certainly of value, are the sections on the history of the orchestra, and on current orchestras and outstanding conductors.

Linton, Stanley. **Music Fundamentals and Functional Skills.** Englewood Cliffs, NJ: Prentice-Hall, 1984. 255p. pap. $19.95 (780.1)

Although primarily a textbook for college students, this is of invaluable assistance to anyone who wishes to master the fundamentals of music. Here "fundamentals" include detailed explanations of rhythm, scales, music notation, etc. With each explanation there usually are examples and do-it-yourself exercises. There is a special focus on the keyboard and the guitar. Nothing in the realm of basic music is missed, and this is both a reference work and a self-help guide.

Pareles, Jon, and Patricia Romanowski, eds. **The Rolling Stone Encyclopedia of Rock & Roll.** New York: Summit, 1983. 704p. $19.95; pap. $11.95 (784.5)

From punk, to funk, to rock and roll, to—well, name it, and if it has anything to do with modern music it will be found in this fine encyclopedia. Treating individuals and topics, movements and fads, as well as select discographies, this is about as complete a coverage of the topic as is available. Definitions are clear and the biographical sketches are accurate, and even those with little or no knowledge of MTV will find they are able to cope with the material. *Note:* This is one of the few such works that strikes a good balance between contributions of blacks and whites to rock and roll.

Previn, Andre. **Andre Previn's Guide to the Orchestra.** New York: Putnam's, 1983. 192p. $16.95 (785)

This well-known orchestra conductor takes the reader on a tour of his province, and in doing so nicely explains what every member of the orchestra does. The treatment is simple, direct, and easy to understand, and there are numerous illustrations. At the same time, the book is thorough in that Previn gives a good history of every instrument and then explains why a harp, for example, gives off its particular sound. There is a part, too, devoted to electronic instruments and the use of the computer in music. Each section of the orchestra is explained, and then the author moves on to the human voice—an unexpected bonus. Here is a delightful and instructive account of the voice in solo, operatic, and musical comedy performances. The book ends with a section on the roles of the conductor and the composer, and how music is recorded.

Waring, Dennis. **Making Folk Instruments in Wood.** New York: Sterling, 1981. 160p. pap. $7.95 (781.9)

The dulcimer is one of some 50 different types of instruments discussed, and while it is probably the most popular of the group, it is also one of the more difficult to make. For easier folk instruments, which may not sound so good but certainly carry a tune, the author offers detailed instructions. The procedure is to give a short history of the instrument and then explain what is needed in terms of materials and working skills. There are step-by-step instructions, usually with good illustrations. Less useful, although certainly a help, are the basic instructions on how to play each of the instruments.

Yehudi Menuhin Music Guides, The. New York: G. Schirmer/Macmillan, 1983– . 200–300p. ea. $19.95 ea.; pap. $9.95 ea. (788.41)

Titles in the series include William Pleeth, *Cello* (1983); James Galway, *Flute* (1983); and Barry Tuckwell, *Horn* (1983). Each of these guides has several missions—although the most important, for purposes of the majority of readers, is its introduction to instruction on playing the various instruments. Under the guidance of world-renowned experts, the reader is given background information on the history of the instrument, shown how it operates from a mechanical/technological point of view, and then shown various techniques for learning how to play it and improve one's playing. The musicians vary in their specific approaches, although almost all give tips on how to practice, face an audience, and interpret music. There are numerous drawings and diagrams throughout the volumes.

NATIONAL PARKS. *See* Camping; Travel

NATURAL FOODS. *See* Cooking—Natural Foods; Organic Gardening

NATURE STUDY
  See also Animals—Field Guides; Camping; Marine Life

Brown, Vinson. **Investigating Nature through Outdoor Projects: 36 Strategies for Turning the Natural Environment into Your Own Laboratory.** Harrisburg, PA: Stackpole, 1983. 254p. pap. $12.95 (574.07)
  This is a fascinating guide to nature appreciation through active participation. Brown explains everything, from how to capture and study various common animals and insects, to methods of watching them in their natural surroundings. The projects involve the construction of birdhouses and simple experimental objects. Directions for these are interspersed with snatches of natural environmental information, facts, and tips on how to enjoy the out-of-doors. Unfortunately, the illustrations are not up to the text, but at least they indicate the general shape of the points the author is making in his lucid discussion.

Durrell, Gerald, and Lee Durrell. **The Amateur Naturalist.** New York: Knopf, 1983. 192p. $22.50 (574)
  This is a how-to-do-it guide to nature with an emphasis rarely found in books of this type. Between anecdotes and basic scientific lessons, the authors explain what to look for when walking in various places—including the backyard. In addition to training the eye, the Durrells suggest various simple projects and experiments that can be carried out to improve one's enjoyment and understanding. These range from methods of cataloging plants to butterfly collecting. Particular attention is paid to preserving specimens. All of this is told in a delightful yet instructive fashion that sets this apart as one of the best books of its type. Good illustrations, too.

Sisson, Edith. **Nature with Children of All Ages: Adventures for Exploring, Learning, and Enjoying the World around Us.** Englewood Cliffs, NJ: Prentice-Hall, 1982. 195p. $19.95; pap. $10.95 (372.3)
  How do parents teach children a love and respect for nature? The answer is to organize activities that will make them aware of their world. The author takes the child and the guide on a chapter-by-chapter trip through various aspects of natural history. She brings excitement and interest to their quest by proposing numerous games and activities in the particular settings. Thanks to a vivid imagination, a fine writing style, and a real appreciation for the interests of children, she can make even the most difficult scientific proposition understandable. The book's activities are illustrated and there are suggested readings and explanations of various natural history crafts.

Thompson, Gerald, and Jennifer Coldrey. **The Pond.** Cambridge, MA: MIT, 1984. 256p. $25 (574.5)
  There is more life in a drop of water than . . . This old saw is magnified here to include an average pond, and the authors demonstrate the masses of wildlife one can find by careful observation. This work offers several exceptional advantages over many nature books. First, the more than 400 color photographs are worth the

price of the book in themselves. The pictures are enlargements of the jungle life found in the pond, and appear ten times as fierce. Second, the scope covers not just common plants and animals, but pond life in various parts of the world. Third, the prose is easy to understand, and free of technical jargon. Finally, the captivated reader is shown how to construct his or her own pond, and see some of the things shown and explained in this marvelous book.

NAVIGATION
   See also Airplanes—Piloting; Boats; Sailing

Dashew, Steve, and Linda Dashew. **The Circumnavigator's Handbook.** New York: Norton, 1983. 498p. $35 (623.88)
   Some how-to-do-it books are an invitation to dream, and this is one of them. Here, two experienced navigators give detailed information on how to take a long sea voyage in a small craft. There are the obvious points made about the type of boat needed, navigational aids, and food requirements, but there are imaginative points of departure as well, such as what to do about pirates and how to stay fit and attractive while on the waves. This is a meticulous, extremely detailed work (with many good illustrations) that will be of considerable value not only to the voyager of several months, but to almost anyone with a boat.

Duxbury, Ken. **Coastal Navigation for Yachtsmen.** Rev. ed. New York: Van Nostrand, 1982. 128p. $13.95 (623.8)
   While there are more detailed navigation books published, this is ideal for the beginner in that it assumes the reader knows nothing about navigation. Every step, every instrument, is completely and fully explained. This is done to the point that someone conversant with basics will be upset by the elementary style, but it cannot be too basic for the individual who would be lost in more advanced guides. There are self-testing problems (along with answers) throughout, and most points are quite well illustrated.

Fraser, Bruce. **Weekend Navigator.** Camden, ME: International Marine, 1982. 308p. $18.50 (798.17)
   While this presupposes an ability to do simple mathematics (and "simple" should be stressed), the explanations, charts, diagrams, and illustrations are such that even the person lost between the house and the garage should be able to master navigation in a boat. Everything is clearly explained, from map reading and the use of basic navigational instruments to setting out a course for the day's activities.

Rousmaniere, John. **The Annapolis Book of Seamanship.** New York: Simon & Schuster, 1983. 347p. $19.95 (623.88)
   Drawing on the U.S. Naval Academy's curriculum and his experience as a coach, the author offers answers to almost any question the person who sails is likely to ask. It is all here, in logical order, from how to tell one side of a boat from the other (basic) to complex points of navigation (advanced). This movement from the elementary to the complex is the way most of the material is organized. Clarity is further ensured by the use of numerous easy-to-follow diagrams and illustrations, which seem to be on every page. The book does not have an index, although the extremely detailed and well-thought-out table of contents serves almost as well. A

basic reference work that should be found in any library where there is an interest in seamanship.

Saunders, A. E. **Small Craft Piloting and Coastal Navigation.** New York: Van Nostrand, 1982. 287p. $19.95 (623.89)

Specifically written for the beginner, this is a good basic guide to navigation for the small-craft owner. The early parts of the work are concerned with reading a compass and understanding a navigational chart. The lessons then advance to the more sophisticated areas of figuring distance and time, charting a course, and the difficult matters of understanding a sextant, getting a fix on a position, etc. The book is well illustrated and easy to follow.

Tate, William. **A Mariner's Guide to the Rules of the Road.** 2nd ed. Annapolis, MD: Naval Institute Pr., 1982. 169p. $12.95 (623.88)

This is a definitive guide to rules of navigation both on the high seas and on inland waters. It is not for the beginner, but is required for anyone, either professional or amateur, who is deeply involved with maritime activities.

U.S. Coast and Geodetic Survey. **United States Coast Pilot.** Washington, DC: GPO, 1959– . Irreg. (C55:422-7)

Updated every year or so, this is a series of nine books covering the coastal waters of the United States, e.g., one volume is devoted to the Atlantic Coast, Eastport to Cape Cod; another to the Pacific and Arctic coasts, etc. The books offer standard data on a wide variety of subjects from pilot routes and portage to navigation regulations.

U.S. Department of Defense. **Nautical Almanac for the Year . . .** Washington, DC: GPO, 1981– . Annual. 3rd. ed., 1983. 311p. $11 (D213.11:983)

This basic handbook for navigation at sea contains ephemeral and other data as well as basic charts. While specifically for navigation and astronomy, it can be and is used by astrologers. It is of equal interest to anyone who is involved with astronomy and offers an accurate annual summation of new findings and changes in the heavens.

NEEDLECRAFTS

See also Knitting & Crocheting; Quilts; Sewing; Weaving

Ambuter, Carolyn. **The Open Canvas.** New York: Workman, 1982. 271p. $22.50; pap. $12.95 (746.44)

The author of several basic works on needlepoint offers a relatively complete overview of what can be done with the process commonly called "open work." The sections carry the beginner (as well as the more experienced) through the steps, from choice of fabric to various approaches to embroidery. There is a sampler in each chapter, plus clear descriptions of tools and materials needed, and illustrations of the various stitches.

Better Homes and Gardens Treasury of Needlecrafts. Des Moines, IA: Meredith, 1982. 480p. $24.95 (746)

In the usual fashion of *Better Homes and Gardens* books, this is a well-constructed guide to all aspects of needlework, and is as useful to the beginner as it is to the near expert. Each section is heavily illustrated, usually with color photographs and patterns. There are clear instructions for quilting, appliqué, knitting, needlepoint, embroidery, rug making, etc. Techniques, materials, equipment, and problems are considered in considerable detail. Thanks to the clear style and the fine illustrations, this is a basic book that should be consulted before going on to more detailed guides.

Davis, Mary. **The Needlework Doctor: How to Solve Every Kind of Needlework Problem.** Englewood Cliffs, NJ: Prentice-Hall, 1983. 288p. $24.95; pap. $13.95 (746.4)

Employing charts, illustrations, and an easy-to-use format, the author offers answers to common questions likely to occur both to beginners and experts in needlework. The 20 chapters consist of questions and answers covering every conceivable needlework situation. Here are answers to such puzzlers as the amount of yarn or other material that is required for a given type of work, the kinds of designs available and where they can be located, and technical questions both simple and difficult. As a reference book, not a step-by-step guide, this is excellent.

Hurt, Zuelia. **Country Samplers.** Birmingham, AL: Oxmoor House, 1984. 128p. $18.95 (746.44)

Primarily an idea book, filled with sampler illustrations, this is written for someone with a basic knowledge of needlework. The samplers are divided into 350 motifs, borders, alphabets, etc., which require some knowledge of layouts, particularly as the author encourages the reader not to be slavish and copy the samplers. Instructions are full and precise and the various illustrations, including color photographs, are good to excellent.

Hutchins, Jeane, ed. **The Fiberarts Design Book II.** Asheville, NC: Lark, 1983. 208p. $27.95; pap. $18.95 (746)

In 1981 the first of the "fiberarts" design books was published, and this is the second. A third is likely in the future. The reason for the books' success is that each volume captures the work of various artists in the medium. Here are over 500 different people and their work. True, there are no specific instructions on how to make any of the handiwork, although credit is dutifully given and there is a note on what materials are employed and the overall size of the piece. At the same time, due to the excellent photographs, divided between color and black and white, one gets a good impression of what each artist is about. Hence, the book serves as inspiration, a model for those in needlework, soft sculpture, weaving, quilt making, and other work that is described as fiberarts.

Longhurst, Denise. **Vanishing American Needle Arts.** New York: Putnam's, 1983. 155p. $17.95 (746.4)

There is much to be faulted here, but because the author is concerned with disappearing needlework techniques, it is worth considering. It is for the relative expert in the craft, not the beginner. The assumption is that the reader understands the terminology and is capable of carrying on some of the more difficult how-to-do-it suggestions. The problem is focus. The author tends to go over fairly well-known methods (tatting, for example) but does not give enough attention to disappearing approaches such as netting. Among the eight different arts discussed, only about one-half can really be termed "lost" in the sense they are not that often employed. Add to this the poor illustrations and the less-than-explicit instructions, and the book is more a reminder than a basic text. For what it does, though, it succeeds well enough.

McCall's Big Book of Country Needlecrafts. Radnor, PA: Chilton, 1983. 312p. pap. $12.95 (746)

Following the pattern of presentation in the magazine McCall's Needlework & Crafts, here are about 150 patterns, projects, and ideas for the person with some training in needlecraft (beginners might want to start with a more general approach). Coverage ranges from seventeenth- to early nineteenth-century designs, accompanied by fairly indifferent photographs. There is added material on accessories, crocheting, etc., and a good description of floor stenciling. There are sections, too, on quilts and rugs. As an overview and as an inspiration to the craftsperson, this is a useful work.

McCall's Big Book of Cross Stitch. Radnor, PA: Chilton, 1984. 312p. pap. $12.95 (746)

Ranging from traditional to modern styles, here are design ideas for various types of cross-stitch work. Almost every room of the house is the target, i.e., there are items for use in the bedroom, bathroom, living room, or kitchen. Directions on making everything from placemats to baby bibs are given in full, and usually illustrated. Basic and easy enough to follow, this is for both the beginner and the intermediate-level sewer.

McCall's Big Book of Needlecrafts. Radnor, PA: Chilton, 1982. 304p. $12.95 (746.44)

The text and illustrations are from past issues of McCall's, and they follow the traditional, easy-to-understand instructions so familiar to readers. All the basics of needlework are considered, e.g., quilting, appliqué, patchwork, needlepoint, embroidery. The various processes are explained, and the supposition is that the reader knows nothing about any of them. The explanations even include a brief history of the art. The heart of the book is the patterns, accompanied by photographs, graphs, and diagrams to reinforce the careful instructions.

Petersen, Grete. **Stitches and Decorative Seams.** New York: Van Nostrand, 1983. 95p. pap. $6 (746.44)

Embroidery stitching is clearly illustrated here, with line drawings that take the reader from borders and seams to hems. The more complex work is explained in some detail. In addition to the drawings, there are photographs that underscore the points made. There are sections as well on the history of stitching and on various types of threads and fabrics. Some attention is given to decorative techniques. This is for intermediate-level sewers.

Reader's Digest Complete Guide to Needlework. Pleasantville, NY: Reader's Digest, 1979. 504p. $19.50 (746.4)

With step-by-step instructions and full illustrations, this is a good introductory guide to the basics of needlework. Separate sections cover needlepoint, patchwork, quilting, rug making, appliqué, crochet, embroidery, knitting, lacework, and macrame.

Wilson, Erica. **Erica Wilson's Children's World.** New York: Scribner's, 1983. 160p. pap. $11.95 (746.4)

A collection of designs particularly suitable for children, this book offers suggestions on how to embroider figures on clothing, quilts, pillows, wall hangings, etc. After writing a number of books on needlework, Wilson turns to everyone's favorite creatures such as Peter Rabbit, Babar the Elephant, Winnie the Pooh, and Miss Piggy. Also included is the usual method, which Wilson pioneered, for transferring designs onto fabric. The patterns are clearly illustrated and there are specific directions on each page, as well as suggestions, on where to apply the patterns.

Wilson, Erica. **Erica Wilson's Needlework to Wear.** New York: Harper, 1982. 154p. $17.95 (746.4)

One of the best-known authors on the subject, Wilson is an expert with a stitch. She is equally expert at explaining how to turn a piece of ordinary clothing into a striking garment, or how to work wonders with belts, sweaters, handbags, etc. Here she combines traditional designs and patterns with her own innovative ideas. There are numerous color photographs and other illustrations throughout the book. While this is not written for the beginner, the directions are so clear that anyone with the slightest interest in the subject should be able to complete most of the items described. There are numerous special features appended, including a list of suppliers and a chart showing various types of stitches.

OCEAN. *See* Marine Life; Navigation

OFFICE DECORATION
See also Interior Decoration

Becker, Franklin. **The Successful Office: How to Create a Workspace That's Right for You.** Reading, MA: Addison-Wesley, 1982. 212p. $19.95; pap. $9.95 (747.85)

While the primary focus here is on the larger office, most of the suggestions are applicable to the home office as well. As more and more people are working out of their homes on computer terminals, the guide suggests a wider audience than the title might imply. Within the framework of the office, this Cornell professor considers such things as lighting, colors, placement of furniture, and kinds of space for particular types of work. In the final part, he demonstrates how different working styles require different office arrangements.

Klein, Judy. **The Office Book: Ideas and Designs for Contemporary Work Space.** New York: Facts on File, 1982. 288p. $40 (725.23)

While the author examines office space on a medium-to-large scale, many of the ideas are applicable to the design of smaller offices, even those in the home. This is particularly true in the discussion of space. There are several hundred color photographs of offices from their early beginnings to today. The best representative designs, both here and abroad, are considered, and there is practical information on everything from lighting to room for eating. The appendix lists manufacturers and sources of office supplies.

ORCHARDS. *See* Gardening; Trees & Shrubs

ORCHESTRAS. *See* Music

ORGANIC GARDENING
See also Gardening

Catton, Chris, and James Gray. **The Incredible Heap: A Guide to Compost Gardening.** New York: St. Martin's, 1984. 64p. pap. $7.95 (635.04)

A brief, carefully written and illustrated guide to the old fashioned compost heap, this is an ideal book for a gardener with almost any type or size of garden. There is a good introduction on the value of composts and organic gardening. The promise is for better lawns, flowers, and crops when the "incredible heap" is mature. Specific step-by-step instructions are given for starting and maintaining the compost pile, as well as good sections on what should and should not be included in its ever growing makeup. The diagrams and photographs are useful, but the writing style is even better.

Fryer, Lee. **The Bio-Gardener's Bible.** Radnor, PA: Chilton, 1982. 288p. $14.95; pap. $9.95 (635.04)

Whether one can call this a "bible" is debatable, but it certainly does cover most aspects of nonchemical gardening. Drawing on a wide knowledge of organic gardening, the author gives specific directions on how to make the garden grow sans Dow Chemical. For example, he spends considerable time and effort on release factors for nitrogen. There are easy-to-follow directions for eliminating insect pests, and a less full, yet useful, discussion of various things to grow. Natural methods (from soil bacteria to earthworms) are considered in detail. The writing style, despite the technical aspects of the subject, is relaxed and the content is easy to understand. This is a fine guide for the organic gardener.

Rodale Press Editors. **The Organic Gardener's Complete Guide to Vegetables and Fruits.** Emmaus, PA: Rodale, 1982. 528p. $21.95 (635.04)

There are several advantages to this guide. First, it is encyclopedic in scope and is divided into two sections: vegetables and fruits. Second, the authors offer good, general information on gardening that can be used by anyone, not just those who rely on the organic approach. Third, specific details are given for individual vegetables and fruits as to planting times, soil preparation, caring for the new plants, when to pick them, and just about everything needed to ensure success. "Tricks of the trade" dot the book, and these are tips on such things as weeding and the best way to tie back tomatoes. The illustrations, while useful, might have been better, and sometimes the writing style is a bit precious. Otherwise, this is one of the best books available on the subject, certainly one of the most comprehensive.

ORIENTAL RUGS. *See* Rugs

ORNITHOLOGY. *See* Birds

OUTDOORS. *See* Camping; Nature Study

PAINTING (ART)

Blockley, John. **How to Paint with Pastels.** Tucson, AZ: HP Books, 1982. 64p. pap. $5.95 (741.235)

Dedicated to the amateur painter, this is an excellent, elementary guide. Originally published in England, it begins with a justification of painting as a hobby. The various peculiar qualities of the medium—in this case pastels—are considered in an early chapter. Then (and this takes up most of the book) there are steps—almost too elementary, some might say—on how to carry out various types of painting from landscapes to portraits. The instructions are reinforced with color photographs on almost every page. Finally there is a section on main points to remember when approaching pastels. *Note:* This is one of a series of books with titles beginning *How to Paint with . . .* that follow the same basic pattern. Others will be found elsewhere in this section.

Crawshaw, Alwyn. **How to Paint with Acrylics.** Tucson, AZ: HP Books, 1982. 64p. pap. $5.95 (751.42)

This follows the same format and presentation as Blockley's guide to pastels (q.v.). It is an ideal starting point for the amateur painter who wishes to use acrylics.

Crawshaw, Alwyn. **How to Paint with Watercolors.** Tucson, AZ: HP Books, 1982. 64p. pap. $5.95 (751.42)

This follows the same format and presentation as Blockley's guide to pastels (q.v.). It is an ideal beginning for the amateur painter who wishes to use watercolors.

Garrard, Peter. **How to Paint with Oils.** Tucson, AZ: HP Books, 1982. 64p. pap. $5.95 (751.45)

This book is an ideal beginning for the amateur painter who wishes to use oils. Garrard's book follows the same format and presentation as Blockley's guide to pastels (q.v.).

Griffith, Thomas. **A Practical Guide for Beginning Painters.** Englewood Cliffs, NJ: Prentice-Hall, 1981. 145p. $11.95 (750.28)

If painting as an art form can be taught via a book, this certainly is one of the best guides. Even for the experienced painter, the numerous illustrations and specific instructions may be useful. The author begins with small, simple exercises, often the kind readers may remember from their childhood. Once confidence is acquired, the material increases in difficulty from portrait and landscape to still life. Various types of media are considered, including pastels and charcoal, as well as major forms. Composition is discussed, as is the proper use of color. The exercises, from the easy to the difficult, are carefully chosen and in each case nicely illustrated.

Leslie, Clare. **Nature Drawing: A Tool for Learning.** Englewood Cliffs, NJ: Prentice-Hall, 1980. 206p. $19.95; pap. $10.95 (743.83)

For the individual who longs to draw a bird or capture a plant on paper, this is an excellent beginning. While it presupposes that the reader has some talent as well as interest, the author leaves very little to chance. Through a wide number of exercises, which move from the simple to the complex, the basic techniques and methods of drawing are carefully explained. There is a good reading list at the end of the book.

Porter, Albert. **Expressive Watercolor Techniques.** Worcester, MA: Davis, 1982. 128p. $17.95 (751.42)

A precise manual for the student of watercolor, this has the advantage of using examples from great painters. At the same time, the instructions are step by step and easy to follow. The combination of the practical and the inspirational is useful and goes well with the sensible style of the author, himself a teacher of watercolor. Porter is adventurous in that he goes beyond the basics and demonstrates how even a beginner can draw on imagination to produce acceptable abstracts and other forms.

Rubelmann, Stephen D. **Encyclopedia of the Airbrush.** 2 vols. New York: Art Direction, 1982. $39.50 (751.4)

The two volumes cover every conceivable aspect of the airbrush and its employment in graphic arts. As such, it is for both expert and beginner. The first volume concentrates on various types of equipment, basics of use, and the problems (and solutions) associated with the form. The second volume focuses on maintenance and more technical aspects. It concludes with a directory of manufacturers and suppliers.

Simpson, Ian, et al. **Painter's Progress: An Art School Year in Twelve Lessons.** New York: Van Nostrand, 1984. 520p. $35.50 (750.2)

This book offers the student just about every aspect of instruction in painting. Whether one wants to know the fundamentals of oils, watercolors, drawing, or pastels, it is all here. Each lesson is supported with types and forms of painting from portraits and landscapes to still lifes and seascapes. Specific instructions, backed by excellent illustrations (many in color), allow even the amateur to pick up the guide and progress with ease. The book is arranged so that the reader may use it for a step-by-step course in painting, or as a reference work to study some particular type of artistic method. It is clearly written and a fine manual for all would-be artists.

Smith, Ray. **How to Draw and Paint What You See.** New York: Knopf, 1984. 256p. pap. $15.95 (750.28)

Actually, the focus here is on the simple rules of how to paint. Drawing is used as the beginning step for the finished painting. The author follows the familiar grid system. Not a first choice, but a useful one for those who appreciate the step-by-step style of painting instruction.

Tombs, Curtis. **The Airbrush Book: Art, History and Technique.** New York: Van Nostrand, 1980. 160p. $24.95 (741.2)

The best techniques for the use of the airbrush are carefully and precisely explained, and while the author expects the reader to have some understanding of the process, this understanding need only be minimal. Various types of airbrush equipment are explained, and the advantages and disadvantages of each brush weighed and considered. The strength of the manual is in its numerous exercises, which are well illustrated. There is an appendix, which focuses on products and the care of equipment. Less successful: the history and background of the technique.

PAINTING & WALLPAPERING
See also Homes—Remodeling

Better Homes and Gardens Your Walls & Ceilings. Des Moines, IA: Meredith, 1983. 160p. $9.95 (643.7)

Clear photographs, carefully written instructions, and a pleasing format characterize the All about Your House Series, of which this is one volume. Here are the usual instructions on painting to improve the appearance of the room, but there is much more on other treatments—from tile and brick to wallpaper and insulation. In addition, there are tips on where and how to hang pictures, and even on making stenciling designs. This is an extremely practical, useful book.

Hand, Jackson. **How to Do Your Own Painting and Wallpapering.** 2nd ed. New York: Harper, 1976. 170p. pap. $3.95 (698.1)

Beginning with the basic equipment needed to paint or wallpaper, the author explains what you do and do not need, and what is best for your particular purposes. There is some emphasis on preparation of surfaces for the work, that is to say, the reader is strongly advised against just slapping wallpaper or paint over an old wall. With that, the discussion moves to time-saving techniques in painting and wallpapering, and what to do when certain problems—such as getting in and out of difficult places—arise. Both interior and exterior painting are considered, and there are useful illustrations.

Innes, Jocasta. **Paint Magic: The Home Decorator's Guide to Painted Finishes.** New York: Van Nostrand, 1981. 239p. $29.95 (698.14)

Drawing on high-style eighteenth- and nineteenth-century English and American examples, this British author gives definitive instructions on how to re-create various decorations and finishes. All parts of the home are considered, from floors and woodwork to walls and furniture. The instructions move from the relatively easy (marbling and graining) to the much more sophisticated (creation of a trompe l'oeil). Complete lists of materials (including sources of supply), techniques, and methods of preparation are given. The author presupposes an interest in more difficult than average redecorating projects, and her guide is only for the skilled craftsperson.

Percival, Bob. **Encyclopedia of Painting & Wallcovering.** Rev. ed. Blue Ridge Summit, PA: TAB, 1984. 263p. pap. $12.95 (698)

Divided into two sections—painting and wallcoverings—this is a dictionary arrangement of information on both. The entries may be brief or lengthy. The arrangement leaves much to be desired because there is no index and few cross-references. Therefore, one must know the precise subject heading in order to find what is needed. The expected terms are discussed, from types of brushes to how to use a wallpaper table. The writing is clear, and there are well-placed photographs and line drawings. This may be too general for many, but it does offer a good overview.

PAPER CRAFTS. *See* Handicrafts

PAPERMAKING

Barrett, Timothy. **Japanese Papermaking: Traditions, Tools, and Techniques.** New York: Weatherhill, 1983. 320p. $32.50 (676.2)

Here is the basic book on the subject of handmade Japanese paper, and it can be used by both the beginner and the more involved amateur. This is *how* to make paper, not the art of folding paper. There is a good history of the art and detailed notes on adapting Japanese methods to American ways. There are instructions on handmade paper, including basic information on the tools needed, and a simplified approach for those who simply want to experiment. The text is supported with excellent illustrations. Specialized, but a model of its kind in that many of the instructions would be applicable to general papermaking.

Toale, Bernard. **The Art of Papermaking.** Worcester, MA: Davis, 1983. 119p. $16.95 (676.22)
For those who want to make their own paper, and long for some artistic direction, this is the ideal guide. Combining basics with advanced techniques in the art and craft of papermaking from the Orient to the modern West, Toale offers a well-balanced approach. All types of papermaking are considered from using cloth to plants. A good directory of sources is included.

PARTIES. *See* Entertaining & Parties

PASTA. *See* Cooking—Pasta

PEST CONTROL
   See also Cockroaches; Insects, Garden

U.S. Department of Agriculture. **Subterranean Termites.** Washington, DC: GPO, 1983. 36p. pap. $2.50 (A1.77:64/8)
This is an easy-to-follow bulletin that shows the reader how to identify the tracks of a termite and, essentially, determine if termite control is necessary. The preferred chemical method of elimination is explained, and there are sections on how to prevent termites when first putting up a structure.

PETS
   See also Birds; Cats; Dogs; Fish (Pets); Horses; Rabbits

Beck, Alan, and Aaron Katcher. **Between Pets and People: The Importance of Animal Companionship.** New York: Putnam's, 1983. 317p. $14.95 (615.85)
Pets are good companions, and just how valuable they are is explained by two University of Pennsylvania professors who are experts in such matters. From a basis in research, not simply hunches, they explain that most people with mental problems, or those who are growing old or are simply lonely, will be well advised to acquire a pet. Animals provide a good outlet for affection and offer subtle relationships that can do nothing but good for the individual. Actually, most of this is known to pet owners, but the book documents the natural feelings that people have about animals. There is a good chapter explaining how, on occasion, an animal may turn on its master—but it is clear that this is the exception, not the rule.

Fogle, Bruce. **Pets and Their People.** New York: Viking, 1984. 227p. $14.95 (636.08)
The close relationship between pets and people is rarely well understood, but

here a London veterinarian succeeds in showing the various facets of that unique companionship. Basing his discussion both on his own experience and on scientific research, the author focuses on dogs and cats, and examines why people buy pets. Reasons differ with the needs and personalities of the owners, and may spring from neurotic as well as healthy needs. Enough examples are given so that the reader can test his or her own position in the relationship. There are sections on everything from the place of a pet when the owner is ill to how to get over the death of an animal. All of this is related with common sense and in good prose—no cuteness or oversentimentality. The realistic and analytical approach will be appreciated by anyone who owns a pet and is the least bit curious about interactions. Note, too, that the book is nicely illustrated.

Whiteside, Robert. **Animal Language: How to Understand Your Pets.** New York: Fell, 1981. 152p. $9.95 (636.08)

While critics generally dismiss this as a book that draws more on popular psychology than science, more on wishful thinking than fact, some animal owners claim the author is on target. The final decision must be made by the reader—and, if you wish to go along with the author, by the animal. He divides animals such as cats, dogs, and horses by certain personality characteristics and then matches these to owner characteristics. When you get a nearly perfect match, you have the nearly perfect pet. The author appears to be quite serious. At any rate, it is great fun to read.

PHOTOGRAPHY

Adams, Ansel. **Examples: The Making of 40 Photographs.** Boston: Little Graphic Society, 1983. 177p. $34.50 (770.92)

This late master explains, usually in considerable detail, how he took 40 photographs over a time period from 1921 to 1982. The book is not a manual, but a combination of anecdotes, personal history, and artistic observations. Yet, thanks to particular attention to such things as location, exposure, and problems involved with taking the photographs, Adams reveals considerable technical data that will be of help to both the beginner and the expert. The secret of his genius was patience and a love of detail. This is never so evident as when he explains precisely the qualities he sought in a given photograph, and then proceeds to the steps taken to achieve the desired effect. There is a good deal of talk about famous contemporaries, most of whom were Adams's friends, and the relaxed, authoritative style nicely matches the superb photographs. An unusual, highly valuable book for anyone seriously concerned with the art.

Angel, Heather. **The Book of Close-up Photography.** New York: Knopf, 1983. 168p. $17.95 (778.3)

Thanks to better lenses and cameras, close-up work is now common among photographers. So common, in fact, that few stop to think how it might be improved. Angel takes the reader from beginning techniques right up to those used by experts. For the most part, normal equipment is adequate, although as the text progresses so do the requirements for more sophisticated equipment. The work is augmented by an appendix that provides information on how to establish a close-up studio. The format is unique: The text runs across two pages in such a way that each topic is covered under a heading or subheading. And there are, as would be expected, numerous supporting photographs.

Angeloglou, Christopher, ed. **Successful Nature Photography: How to Take Beautiful Pictures of the Living World.** New York: Amphoto, 1983. 240p. $24.95 (778.9)

Take a 35mm camera, go out of doors, and take a good picture—at any rate, that is a possibility when following the specific directions given in this heavily illustrated manual. Basics are explained for everything from taking a picture of a domestic animal to underwater setups. The drawback for some is that this is limited to 35mm cameras. Otherwise, the instructions are uncomplicated and the book is good for the beginner. It may be a trifle too elementary, though, for the more expert.

Bailey, James. **How to Select & Use an Electronic Flash.** Tucson, AZ: HP Books, 1983. 143p. pap. $9.95 (778.3)

Almost all photographers are now in possession of electronic flash systems, but how are they used most effectively? The author answers the question in a manner that serves both the amateur and professional photographer. There may be too much about the technology of the electronic flash for some tastes, but the interested reader will not leave the book with any unanswered queries. The advice is practical and covers a variety of situations, and there is a particularly good section, at least for amateurs, on the proper use of the flash.

Bailey, Rick, ed. **Learn Photography Series.** Tucson, AZ: HP Books, 1982. 93–96p. pap. $5.95 ea. (770.2)

These brief photography guides are among the best available for the beginner. The reason is that each step, fittingly enough, is accompanied by explanatory illustrations and an especially easy-to-follow text. As a consequence, a beginner might enter a darkroom with the proper guide in hand and come out with a good-to-excellent print. Before that, he or she might want to turn to the first work in the series, which explains everything one needs to know about a camera and how to set the lens for a picture. This is *SLR Tips and Techniques.* One might then want to take up the self-explanatory *How to Take Pictures Like a Pro,* which concentrates on candid and studio work. There are two darkroom manuals, *Basic Guide to B&W Darkroom Techniques* and *Basic Guide to Creative Darkroom Techniques.* The series was first published in England, but the advice is presented in such a way as to be of equal value to Americans.

Bodin, Fredrik. **How to Get the Best Travel Photographs.** New York: Van Nostrand, 1982. 150p. pap. $14.95 (778.9)

The title is a bit deceptive, in that the photography is limited to the use of a 35mm camera and the guide is as much a manual on that camera as it is on travel. At the same time, the extremely well written text (and fine photographs and illustrations) makes this an ideal book for the amateur who is seeking professional advice on how to capture a vacation on film. There is the usual opening section on equipment, followed by an unusual section on how to pack and unpack a camera quickly. From place to place, area to area, the author suggests the best types of shots to take, and there is practical advice on such things as getting permission to photograph subjects at play or work. The book ends on what to do with the pictures once they are developed—including a short discussion of sales.

Cermak, Lanny. **How to Repair Your Own 35mm Camera.** Blue Ridge Summit, PA: TAB, 1981. 224p. $14.95; pap. $8.95 (771.3)

Despite the title, the real value of this carefully written and illustrated manual is to help the photographer decide whether the needed repair is major or minor. By pointing out precisely what is wrong, the author indicates the relative complexity of the trouble. Given that data, one may then proceed either to fix a minor problem or, more likely, to send the camera back to the dealer (or in extreme cases to junk it). Emphasis here is on the manual 35mm SLR.

Curtin & London, Inc. **The Book of 35mm Photography.** New York: Van Nostrand, 1983. 176p. pap. $17.95 (770.28)

Among numerous beginner's guides to 35mm photography, this is one of the best because of its effective format and clear approach. Almost every page on which there are instructions about the camera or photographic techniques carries diagrams and illustrative photographs. All of this makes for a handsome book that includes tables and pictorial examples. The writing is direct and the instructions easy to follow. While darkroom procedures are not considered, all other basics are discussed from correct exposures to types of lenses and kinds of film. This is an excellent beginning guide for anyone interested in 35mm cameras.

Diamonstein, Barbaralee. **Visions and Images.** New York: Rizzoli, 1982. 190p. $30; pap. $17.50 (770)

The ABC-TV arts and entertainment commentator interviews 15 of the world's leading photographers. The result provides insights into the art if not precise how-to-do-it instructions. The combination of reminiscence with sharp aesthetic and, sometimes, commercial points makes this an invaluable guide for beginner and expert alike. It is marvelous reading.

Eastman Kodak Company. **The Joy of Photographing People.** Reading, MA: Addison-Wesley, 1983. 240p. $29.95; pap. $14.95 (778.9)

Put together by the people at Eastman Kodak Company, this is a guide with wide appeal to amateur photographers. It is not for the intermediate or the expert. The assumption is that the reader knows little or nothing about snapping pictures of people, and the writers give basic instructions on everything from how to hold the camera to types of film to employ. There are numerous illustrations, many in color, to make each and every point. The combination of photographs and text is such that there is little reading and much viewing. While less than sophisticated, the guide is quite thorough at the elementary level. It is suitable for young people.

The Eastman-Kodak company publishes a number of individual camera guides, but those of a more ambitious and general nature (all distributed by Addison-Wesley) include *The Joy of Photography* (1979), which is an introduction to basics for the beginner and the intermediate-level photographer, and *More Joy of Photography* (1981), an update of the earlier work.

Freeman, Michael. **The Wildlife and Nature Photographer's Field Guide.** Cincinnati: Writer's Digest, 1984. 230p. $14.95 (778.9)

Although the author does have a section on basics—such as the selection of the right camera—this really is a handy guide for the experienced photographer. The assumption is that the reader wants to know how to track various animals and how to shoot them from concealed areas. There is specific information as to what kinds of lenses and lighting are required, and even methods of repairing the camera in the wilderness. Along with that come hints on how to prepare a place from which to observe the animals and how to lure the animals to you, and even a section on underwater work. The technical aspects are laced with information on natural history. Illustrations and diagrams are carefully placed throughout the compact text. Written in an easy-to-follow style and packaged as a sturdy pocket manual, this is a superior work on the subject.

Grill, Tom, and Mark Scanlon. **Photographic Composition.** New York: Amphoto, 1983. 144p. $22.50 (770.1)

While it is doubtful that brilliant composition can be taught, one can at least teach the basics in such a way that even the least artistic individual can produce good photographs. That is what is attempted here, and while the early discussion of the principles of composition may be a trifle too rudimentary even for amateurs, the specifics are another matter. When it comes to instruction in perspective, color, and the use of patterns and contrast, the authors are excellent. They excel, too, in the final part of the book, where they use two projects to illustrate their points. All of this is accompanied by illustrations, many in color.

Hedgecoe, John. **John Hedgecoe's Advanced Photography.** New York: Simon & Schuster, 1982. 304p. $35.95 (770)

Advanced photographers, for whom this manual is written, will recognize the author as an old hand at the art. Drawing on his practical experience, he suggests shortcuts, new technological methods and equipment, and various special approaches to everything from planning the photograph to working it up in development and enlargement. Each discussion is supported by numerous photographs, usually in full color. In fact, there are so many photos that this can be enjoyed simply as a picture book.

Hedgecoe, John. **The Photographer's Handbook: A Complete Reference Manual of Techniques, Procedures, Equipment and Style.** 2nd ed. New York: Knopf, 1982. 352p. $18.95 (770.2)

This is written particularly for beginning and intermediate-level photographers. Each section begins with a clear explanation of what is involved with, for example, the darkroom or the selection of a camera, and then takes the reader step by step (often, illustration by illustration) through the various techniques and processes. It is clear and well organized, and covers almost any question likely to arise. It is somewhat dated, particularly in its discussion of "current" equipment and film, but the procedures are valid. Note: Now in its second edition, it is due for revision soon.

Holloway, Adrian. **The Handbook of Photographic Equipment.** New York: Knopf, 1981. 215p. $15.95 (771)

Because of rapid technological change in the development of photographic equipment, this handbook is only relatively useful. It does, however, provide a thorough coverage of basics. When one considers general equipment, it is only slightly out of tune with the times. The author offers a clear and accurate explanation of the basic camera and the use of lenses. Accessories are considered in detail, and there is a complete rundown of darkroom equipment and supplies. This is augmented by excellent illustrations, and a summary of the basic points to watch for in each type of equipment. The list of best brands is still sound, although the prices are out of date.

Kirkman, David. **How to Use & Display Your Pictures.** Tucson, AZ: HP Books, 1983. 144p. pap. $9.95 (770.28)

While there are many books on photography, few tell the amateur what to do with the pictures once they are developed. Kirkman solves this problem by suggesting numerous methods of display, from conventional framing to the use of fabric as a base for the picture. There are good sections on lighting, coloring, and, of course, the use of slides. The text is illustrated, and the author lists sources of necessary materials.

Langford, Michael. **The Book of Special Effects Photography.** New York: Knopf, 1982. 168p. $16.50 (778.8)

Here a well-known writer on photography turns to an area that is primarily of interest to the expert. Special effects can be achieved in a number of ways—from the type of camera and lighting used to the photograph's development and cropping. Each is explained and variations are explored. There are both color and black-and-white photographs to support the text.

Langford, Michael. **The Master Guide to Photography.** New York: Knopf, 1982. 432p. $35 (770)

Still photography is considered here the way it should be, i.e., for each short descriptive piece about some aspect of the art there are numerous photographs to illustrate the point. Where a photograph is not enough, a diagram or chart is inserted to make the point clear. Aside from the striking format, the general coverage is similar to other works of this type. This experienced author is concerned with techniques and equipment, but there is particular emphasis on composition and treating photography as an art form, even when taking a picture of the family or a conventional landscape. All of the terms are adequately defined and there are numerous cross-references and a good index. While this is only of passing interest to a veteran, for the beginner it is as useful as it is inspirational. An excellent introduction for the serious beginner is the author's *The Step-by-Step Guide to Photography* (1979), from the same publisher.

Pinkard, Bruce. **The Photographer's Bible.** New York: Arco, 1983. 352p. $24.95 (770.3)

A dictionary/encyclopedia approach to photography, this moves from a to z with entries that range from only a few lines to many pages. All basics are covered, and there are numerous cross-references. In addition to the usual information on cameras, developing processes, printing, filters, etc., there are useful entries on individual photographers and others who have contributed to the art. The book features numerous tables and charts as well as diagrams and photographs. In the appendix one finds useful lists of photography magazines, galleries, suppliers, and schools.

Note: While this was written by a London photographer, almost all of the data are applicable in the United States.

Sahadi, Lou, and Mickey Palmer. **The Complete Book of Sports Photography.** New York: Watson-Guptill, 1982. 160p. $21.95; pap. $14.95 (778.9)

Two successful photojournalists combine their talents here to explain the combinations necessary for outstanding sports photography. Vital items include better-than-average equipment and a thorough understanding of film. With that, the authors move to specific games and equally specific problems associated with shooting action pictures and stills. There are separate sections on football, basketball, boxing, golf, etc. The advice is peppered with sometimes unexciting anecdotes, but no matter. The two authors are authentic experts who explain fundamentals in such a manner that even the beginner will have no problem following instructions. At the same time, this is a fine guide for would-be professionals. The photographs are good to excellent, and there are close to 200 of them, of which about 30 are in color.

Sanders, Norman. **Photographing for Publication.** New York: Bowker, 1983. 112p. $34.95; pap. $24.95 (686.2)

The title is another way of saying that in order to get a photograph published in a satisfactory fashion, it is essential that the photographer know the basics of printing processes. If one delivers the wrong type of photograph, no matter how well it is done, to a lithographer, the result is going to be a disaster. The author, who is trained in photography and printing, carefully explains how one art complements the other. Both the text and the beautiful and practical illustrations make the point that, for example, the photographer must appreciate what goes on in offset in order to deliver the kind of work necessary for that process. Both color and black-and-white photography are considered, and Sanders demonstrates a fine sensibility as well as a command of technology. While all of this is technical, it is easy enough to understand. A vital, major work for the commercial photographer, it will be of almost equal interest to the amateur and the printer.

Thompson, Bill. **How to Create Great Informal Portraits.** New York: Watson-Guptill, 1982. 143p. $14.95; pap. $8.95 (778.9)

Here is a practical guide for the beginner. The author starts with fundamentals of composition and emphasizes his points through the technique he calls "portrait workshop." This is a group of single and group portraits that are thoroughly analyzed, photo by photo. As the teacher explains what does or does not make the portrait acceptable, the reader picks up a great deal of useful information. All of this is done in a relaxed yet technically thorough style that gives even the most unsure photographer some degree of confidence. The photographs used to illustrate the text are useful and well placed.

Thwaites, Jeanne. **Starting—and Succeeding In—Your Own Photography Business.** Cincinnati: Writer's Digest, 1984. 380p. $17.95 (770.68)

A successful photographer points the way for others with limited budgets to start a freelance or studio business. Based on her own experience, Thwaites offers a highly practical guide that is within the reach of almost anyone who has a good camera and a darkroom. Of course, equipment is considered, but the primary value is in the day-by-day suggestions for getting started and making the business flourish. There are excellent sections on simplified accounting, pricing, and advertising.

Time-Life Books. **Life Library of Photography.** New York: Time-Life, 1980– .
Approx. 224p. ea. $15.95 ea.

The series includes *Color* (1981); *The Camera* (1981); *Photographing Nature* (1981); *The Print* (1982); *Light and Film* (1982); *The Art of Photography* (1982); *Special Problems* (1982); *Travel Photography* (1982); *Photography as a Tool* (1982); *The Great Themes* (1982); *The Studio* (1982); *Caring for Photographs* (1983); *Photographing Children* (1983); *Photojournalism* (1983); *Documentary Photography* (1983); *Great Photographers* (1983).

These follow the pattern of other Time-Life manuals in that there is considerable emphasis on illustrations and a clear text to clarify even the most basic steps for the beginning and, sometimes, the intermediate-level photographer. Under each of the titles, one can be sure that all of the fundamentals of the particular process or subject will be discussed and fully illustrated. In this particular series much of the data is from professional photographers, and, probably thanks to careful editing, the explanations are extremely easy to follow. The series can be recommended for almost anyone, and it is a basic purchase for most home libraries. *Note:* While most of the titles are self-explanatory, for those that are not, a few words. *The Art of Photography* discusses the aesthetics of photography, not basic how-to-do-it information. *Special Problems* concerns difficulties of taking pictures under unusual circumstances. *The Studio* is focused on studio photography, and *Photography as a Tool* is an explanation of how to use the camera in technology.

PHOTOGRAPHY—MOTION PICTURES & TELEVISION

Courter, Philip. **The Filmmaker's Craft: 16mm Cinematography.** New York: Van Nostrand, 1983. 309p. $29.95 (778.5)

Written for the serious beginner (not the home-movie maker), this covers all aspects of making a 16mm film. The text moves from idea generation to script preparation, then to casting, directing, and actually shooting the picture. Obviously any one of these parts is worthy of a book or several books, but Courter has the ability to cover the high points and most questions the reader would have with authority and ease. He is equally knowledgeable about equipment, which he describes in the appendix. The text has excellent illustrations. This would be a first choice for anyone who wants a quick introduction to the subject.

Fuller, Barry; Steve Kanaba; and Janyce Brisch-Kanaba. **Single-Camera Video Production.** Englewood Cliffs, NJ: Prentice-Hall, 1982. 241p. $26.95; pap. $16.95 (778.59)

The single camera television film now brings the potentials of Hollywood to almost anyone who has patience and skill. What the new equipment means is that the individual can shoot and edit in the manner of regular filming. Here is a complete guide to the art, from the type of equipment needed to editing and even set design. While the authors expect the reader to have had some experience with photography and film, the book can be used by the beginner who is willing to follow the detailed instructions.

Monaco, James. **How to Read a Film: The Art, Technology, Language, History, and Theory of Film and Media.** Rev. ed. New York: Oxford, 1981. 502p. $25; pap. $12.95 (791.43)

Everything you ever wanted to know about film is presented here in a thorough yet understandable fashion. There is a superior overview of film theory, a history of motion picture technology, and chapters on criticism that discuss topics from basic assumptions to critical examinations of modern philosophical concerns with film. The most impressive section of this well-illustrated book is on film-related technology. The ability of the author to explain otherwise difficult theories is matched only by his superior command of history. He takes nothing for granted, and even includes a glossary. For both the beginner and the expert, this is one of the finest manuals on movies available.

Norris, R. C. **The Complete Handbook of Super 8 Film Making.** Blue Ridge Summit, PA: TAB, 1982. 368p. $14.95 (778.5)

This is a basic handbook that carries the beginner through a general discussion of filmmaking to the selection of a camera and on to the final screening. Each step is thoroughly explained and often illustrated. There is particular interest in the technical aspects of filmmaking, so this should be used with another work when additional information is needed on script and direction.

PHOTOGRAPHY—PROCESSING

Adams, Ansel, and Robert Baker. **The Print.** Boston: Little Graphic Society, 1983. 210p. $19.95 (770.28)

Updating his 1968 work on the same subject, this master of photography explains the basics of the print and darkroom procedures and equipment. The writing style, illustrations, and directions are up to the best of Adams's work, and this is about as basic as one can get for a collection of how-to-do-it books on photography. Adams not only offers specific directions, but, more important, he laces everything with his philosophy and attitude about the art. This should be a first stop for everyone from beginners to near experts.

Arnow, Jan. **Handbook of Alternative Photographic Processes.** New York: Van Nostrand, 1982. 256p. $35 (770.28)

Here "alternative" means basic photographic darkroom processes with variations. The scope is wide enough to include almost forgotten early steps as well as quite advanced processes. The assumption is that the reader has some knowledge of the subject; the guide is not for the beginner, but even amateurs will benefit from its treatment of the historical background. Each of the darkroom approaches is divided into chapters, and there is detailed information on materials, processes, and potential problems. Thanks to the writer's clear style and meticulous attention to detail, this is one of the best guides of its type now available.

Carroll, John. **Photographic Lab Handbook.** 5th ed. Englewood Cliffs, NJ: Prentice-Hall, 1979. 556p. $24.95; pap. $12.95 (770.28)

Frequently revised (look for the latest edition), this gives detailed instructions to anyone—professional or amateur—concerned with serious photography. The book's ten sections cover topics from black-and-white films to motion pictures and slides. There are numerous tables and reference aids, including a methodical coverage of film stock available in the United States. This is the place to turn when trying to find the precise fixer or toner for a particular film, situation, or effect.

Crawford, William. **The Keepers of Light: A History & Working Guide to Early Photographic Processes.** Dobbs Ferry, NY: Morgan & Morgan, 1979. 320p. $25; pap. $16.95 (770.2)

Here the reader will find some of the material in Arnow's book (q.v.), but with considerably more attention to the historical development of photography. The particular strength of the work is its total devotion to old photographic processes, from ambrotype to tintype. The text is divided into two sections. The first part considers how the various techniques influenced the photographer and the final picture. The second part details various methods by which the modern photographer can duplicate some of the early (1850 to about 1915) processes. The directions are precise, and there is a directory of supply houses for some of the difficult-to-find chemicals.

Croy, O. R. **The Complete Art of Printing and Enlarging.** Woburn, MA: Focal, 1950– . Irreg. 1983 ed., $19.95 (770.2)

Often updated, this is considered by many to be one of the better guides to printing and enlarging. It is specialized, and there is very little about general darkroom practices, the supposition being that the reader has at least a passing knowledge of the basic processes. Given that, the author offers ingenious approaches to printing and enlarging. He has numerous methods of changing the basic photo, and even includes over 50 different formulas for as many different types of solutions. There are excellent parts on retouching and otherwise altering the picture. Nicely illustrated, this is a well-written, although technical, approach to the subject.

Curtin, Dennis, and Steve Musselman. **Into Your Darkroom Step by Step.** New York: Van Nostrand, 1981. 90p. $11.95 (770.28)

The format, a spiral-bound handbook, makes this suitable for use in the darkroom, where the beginner may want to consult it for information on developing and printing. There are numerous step-by-step demonstrations of basic techniques, usually with extremely detailed photographs and scale drawings to supplement the text. One helpful feature is the "before" and "after" example of what it takes to turn a bad print into a superior one. In addition, there are good sections on designing and equipping a darkroom.

Hattersley, Ralph. **Beginner's Guide to Color Darkroom Techniques.** New York: Doubleday, 1982. 200p. pap. $12.95 (778.6)

After an introductory part on the conventions of printing and developing, which is clearly written and carefully illustrated, the author moves into more technical areas. What it amounts to is a book for beginners (the first section), and a book for intermediates (roughly the second part). In somewhat complex sections, Hattersley considers various types of equipment, materials, solutions, etc. Little is left out, and this is the best guide of its type. Incidentally, the illustrations are usually in color, but for more basic directions they are in black and white.

Langford, Michael. **The Darkroom Handbook.** New York: Knopf, 1981. 352p. $25; pap. $12.95 (770.28)

Divided into two basic sections, this is concerned first with darkroom equipment, the processing of film, and both color and black-and-white printing. The second part assumes that the user is by now experienced enough to be interested in rather sophisticated methods of developing and printing. Written for both the serious amateur and the expert, this manual covers almost every conceivable aspect of the subject. An excellent feature is the numerous photographs, which are closely tied to the text.

Nadler, Bob. **The Basic Illustrated Color Darkroom Book.** Englewood Cliffs, NJ: Prentice-Hall, 1982. 300p. $24.95 (778.6)

By "basic" the author means for the beginner, and this is a guide for the person who knows nothing about color processing. Nadler relies on photographs, with brief explanations, to literally carry the reader step by step through the various processes. If one simply puts things in place in the way they are illustrated, the results are bound to be superior. The catch, of course, is that this will drive the less-than-orderly person mad. If the reader is willing to follow precise instructions, this is the ideal guide.

Wall, E. J., and Franklin Jordan. **Photographic Facts and Formulas.** Englewood Cliffs, NJ: Prentice-Hall, 1903– . Irreg. 1975 ed., 480p. $19.95 (770.28)

The oldest and best known of the photographic laboratory manuals, this is for the expert and the dedicated amateur. Every formula needed is described in precise detail. There are numerous tables, charts, weights and measurements—in metric and U.S. style. This is a standard guide.

PIANO
See also Music

Bernstein, Seymour. **With Your Own Two Hands: Self-Discovery through Music.** New York: Schirmer, 1981. 300p. $16.95 (786.3)

The "discovery" is in how to play the piano more effectively. Assuming that the reader has a basic knowledge of the keyboard, the author shows how to sharpen practice skills and how to memorize scores. He assures the patient reader that nothing is beyond possibility, at least with exercise and concentration. Numerous examples are offered in an exhilarating writing style in this clear and useful text.

Stormer, Win. **Popular Piano Self Taught.** New York: Arco, 1982. 137p. $11.95; pap. $6 (786.3)

This is for the person who thinks that piano can be self-taught. Actually, most people realize that a teacher helps, but this is still an extremely helpful guide. The exercises begin with an explanation of the keyboard and move into more sophisticated areas and theory. The fundamentals of piano improvisation are considered. There are adequate illustrations, and, as one might expect, the music is popular, not classical.

PICTURE FRAMES

Brown, Raymond. **How to Do Your Own Professional Picture Framing.** Blue Ridge Summit, PA: TAB, 1981. 160p. $11.95; pap. $6.95 (749.7)

A basic approach, this offers detailed instructions on the construction of wooden and builder's frame molding. Each set of instructions is accompanied by photographs, which unfortunately are sometimes blurred and not terribly useful for details. Despite this fault, the instructions are clear and most have easy-to-follow diagrams.

Duren, Lista. **Frame It: A Complete Do-It-Yourself Guide to Picture Framing.** Boston: Houghton, 1976. 216p. $12.95; pap. $5.95 (749.7)

Although published several years ago, this remains one of the best basic books on framing. Written for the average workshop fan, it is long on how-to-do-it, but much shorter on history and aesthetics. Everything is carefully illustrated and the section on assembling frames provides step-by-step directions. Three other parts include materials and skills required, how to hang and display artwork, and how to select the proper frame for the particular picture. There is a short list of suppliers, but this is fairly dated.

U.S. Library of Congress. **Matting and Hinging Works of Art on Paper.** Washington, DC: GPO, 1981. 32p. pap. $2.75 (LC1.2:Ar7)

Based on conservation methods at the Library of Congress, the concise instructions given here will help the layperson in matting a print or other work of art. Various techniques are clearly explained and usually supported with illustrations. A list of suppliers is included.

Wright-Smith, Rosamund. **Picture Framing.** New York: Van Nostrand, 1981. 128p. $16.95; pap. $9.95 (749.7)

Combining history, aesthetics and how-to-do-it, this British author offers the reader a thorough introduction to the art of picture framing. She stresses the importance of using the right frame for the right picture, and in this respect has by far the best explanation of the frame as something more than a holder—a notion too often missing from other books of this type. At the same time, she has ten basic patterns the beginner can follow to make a successful frame. These vary in difficulty, but each is accompanied by good illustrations and directions. There are good sections, too, on the restoration of old frames. Excellent line drawings and color photographs underline and support the easy-to-follow directions.

PLANTS

See also Gardening—Indoors

Baumgardt, John. **How to Identify Flowering Plant Families: A Practical Guide for Horticulturists and Plant Lovers.** Beaverton, OR: Timber Press, 1983. 270p. $22.95 (582.13)

Basic characteristics of plant families are carefully explained, and the author gives detailed descriptions of individual plants accompanied by specific line drawings. There is also a limited number of color photographs. The arrangement is such that it is relatively easy to locate the general attributes and go from there to specific plant identification.

Benson, Lyman. **The Cacti of the United States and Canada.** Stanford, CA: Stanford University Pr., 1982. 1,044p. $85 (583.47)

The ultimate encyclopedic work on cacti, this is the perfect and complete guide for expert and amateur alike. The second part will be of most interest to average readers. This consists of coverage of all the cacti species of the United States and Canada. Each is carefully described and equally well illustrated. There are identification aids that indicate the precise place the plant is to be found, and exactly what to look for when trying to identify it. The first section covers broader matters, including some excellent chapters on classification and a good section on various methods of using the plants. For true believers, there is a list of associations involved with cacti in the United States and Canada.

Browse, Philip. **Plant Propagation.** New York: Simon & Schuster, 1979. 96p. pap. $7.95 (635.04)

One of the best practical guides to propagation, this is part of the Royal Horticultural Society series on gardening. Each of the numerous sets of instructions is clearly illustrated, and the directions are easy to follow. Various types of propagation are explained. Browse moves from the usual stem cuttings and leaf cuttings to seeds and bulbs, layering, grafting, and related matters. Each operation is explained in enough detail to allow even an amateur to carry it out successfully. The British bias in no way hinders its appreciation by American gardeners.

Crockett, James. **Crockett's Flower Garden.** Boston: Little, 1981. 311p. $24.95; pap. $14.95 (635.9)

Published after the famed author of the Victory Garden Series died, this is not quite up to those earlier titles, but it has many strong points. Using the same format as the others in the series, he devotes a chapter to each month's tasks in the flower garden. There is an emphasis on annuals and perennials that guarantee color and enjoyment for the gardener. In fact, the strength of this is not so much in the information as in the spirit of the book. Crockett is so enthusiastic that it will make even a lazy urbanite long for a bit of earth. The illustrations are good, and it is a book to be read both for information and for enjoyment.

Fell, Derek. **Annuals: How to Select, Grow and Enjoy.** Tucson, AZ: HP Books, 1983. 160p. pap. $7.95 (635.93)

Useful in any section of the country, this is a detailed guide to annuals. It should be a great help to the gardener seeking unusual plants, particularly as the major ones are nicely illustrated and arranged in such a way that it is easy to find precisely what each is called. There is a good explanation of where different plants will grow best, when to plant them, what to feed them, types of soil to use, etc. Particularly useful is the author's suggestion of how the annual may be used in a garden setting. Each chapter, in fact, opens with a specific design plan. Well written and illustrated, this is a good supplement for the more general garden manual.

Fitz, Franklin. **A Gardener's Guide to Propagating Food Plants.** New York: Scribner's, 1983. 128p. $10.95 (631.5)

How can people save money and at the same time get more enjoyment out of their gardens? The answer to both questions is found in the practice of propagating one's own plants, in this case vegetables, fruits, and more exotic types of edibles from coconuts to horseradish. Precise directions are given after the name of each plant, which is found in the alphabetical listing. Procedures vary from root divisions and grafting to gathering pods. Fitz notes where plants grow best, although anyone reading this book is probably already an experienced gardener who knows the basics. The illustrations help to explain the different propagation methods, and the whole is clear and helpful.

Heywood, Vernon, and Stuart Chant, eds. **Popular Encyclopedia of Plants.** New York: Cambridge University Pr., 1982. 368p. $28 (630.3)

If you have the name of a plant (scientific or common), you simply turn to that name and read about the plant's strengths and drawbacks, and how to care for it under various circumstances. There are over 700 color photographs for the 2,200 entries. Also, there are some 20 sections on the larger plant groups. An encyclopedic approach, this is sometimes overwhelming and too detailed for the average gardener, but for the enthusiast it will be a major aid.

Hickey, Michael, and Clive King. **100 Families of Flowering Plants.** New York: Cambridge University Pr., 1981. 220p. $69.50; pap. $19.95 (582.13)

With a strong English bias (although the text is suitable for American readers), the authors systematically explain and illustrate 100 common flowering plants. The first part of each description is a general background of the plant family, where it is located, and its characteristics. Then there is specific data on the species. Also provided is a chart of flowering times (limited to England, yet applicable to certain areas of the United States) and numerous illustrations. Written for both the student and the serious gardener, this is a good text, but it is not a book for a beginner.

Krussmann, Gerd. **The Complete Book of Roses.** Beaverton, OR: Timber Pr., 1981. 436p. $50 (635.9)

If there is anything you want to know about roses, it can probably be found in this definitive study, the most complete work now available on the subject. Everything is here, from the history of the flower to detailed explanations of how to grow and care for hundreds of varieties. The guide concludes with a brief description—which includes color, year of introduction, parentage, etc.—of over 1,300 commercial roses. The translation from the German is excellent, and the photographs and line drawings, drawn from both recent and historical sources, are up to the quality of the book.

Moggi, Guido, et al. **Simon & Schuster's Guide to Garden Flowers.** New York: Simon & Schuster, 1983. 511p. $19.95 (635.9)

The particular twist here is the heavy dependence on glorious color photographs to identify the approximately 350 flowers described. There is the usual descriptive matter, including history, and solid advice on planting and care. Symbols indicate seasons, areas where particular plants are grown, etc.

Northern, Rebecca. **Miniature Orchids.** New York: Van Nostrand, 1980. 189p. $26.95 (635.93)

Orchids are no longer only a rich person's hobby. Now many Americans grow them. Little wonder—there are countless varieties for almost any situation, from windowsills to impressive greenhouses. Here the author limits herself to the miniature orchid, but this is no more difficult to grow and tend than other types. In fact, a good part of the book is an implied argument that among houseplants the orchid is a rewarding hobby. Each of the varieties suitable for home care is described in full, along with complete instructions on how to make the plant healthy and productive. Various problems are, of course, considered. Anyone even remotely interested in the subject should start here. The author's enthusiasm is contagious.

Perry, Frances, and Roy Hay. **A Field Guide to Tropical and Subtropical Plants.** New York: Van Nostrand, 1982. 136p. $10.95; pap. $6.95 (582.09)

A slim, well-illustrated guide that makes it possible for almost anyone to isolate and identify tropical plants. While the authors go right to the area where the plants are grown, most readers will find the book of more value for determining the name of a particular greenhouse plant. All types of plants are considered in their locations, from swamps to the highlands. There is a complete description for each. If nothing else, the book is an ideal guide for ambitious gardeners to browse in.

Slack, Adrian. **Carnivorous Plants.** Cambridge, MA: MIT, 1980. 240p. $19.95 (583.121)

There are more carnivorous plants than the familiar, much-advertised Venus's-flytrap. In fact there are at least 50 other species that enjoy the same type of food, although some are more refined. A full description is given of each of these plants, and, where appropriate, there is a further section on the use of the plant in the home. There are fine illustrations, many in color. The book draws on scientific research, not the horror flicks, for data.

Stone, Doris. **The Lives of Plants.** New York: Scribner's, 1983. 304p. $14.95 (582.13)

Based on current scientific research, this guide explains how a plant develops from a seed, blossoms, and then returns to earth. All of this is done in an eminently readable style and with well-placed stories and allied data that enhance the general wonder of it all. There are even several experiments offered that allow the careful observer to study the stages of plant development. The illustrations are good and augment the fine text.

U.S. Department of Health. **Common Poisonous and Injurious Plants.** Washington, DC: GPO, 1981. 29p. $3.25 (HE20.4002:P69)

How does one recognize poison ivy and avoid it as well as 25 other injurious species? The plants are illustrated here with specifics on where they are found and how they appear. In addition, there are details on emergency treatment.

Weiner, Michael. **Earth Medicine—Earth Food: Plant Remedies, Drugs, and Natural Foods of the North American Indians.** Rev. ed. New York: Macmillan, 1980. 230p. $18.95; pap. $10.95 (581.6)

This is a fascinating study of early Native American remedies and the plants that were employed in making them. Each of the plants is described fully, including a history of how it was used. Much of the time the plant is still considered acceptable, and when this is the case, it is so noted. An ethnobotanist, Weiner is more involved with describing than prescribing. No effort is made to "sell" the reader on the benefits of this or that cure. The writing style is exciting and factual, and most of the specimens are illustrated.

Wright, Michael. **The Complete Handbook of Garden Plants.** New York: Facts on File, 1984. 544p. $18.95 (635.90)

Here is a handy, pocket-size guide to over 9,000 different species and varieties of garden plants. Each is thoroughly explained and identified, and about 2,500 are illustrated in watercolor paintings. The illustrations are small and sometimes hard to differentiate, but they generally are good enough for identification purposes. Coverage is worldwide, and the focus is on outdoor garden plants, although many of the more exotic types might be grown in the home or greenhouse. The encyclopedic approach is primarily for people seeking to find the proper name for a plant. There are no tips on actual growing of plants, but here one will find exact dimensions and descriptions of each species and variety. As with the illustrations, the text tends to be cramped and sometimes hard to read—but this is not a serious difficulty. This is the definitive guide for the gardener who wants to locate and name almost any of the world's garden plants.

PLASTERING. *See* Homes—Maintenance & Repair; Homes—Remodeling

PLAYING CARDS. *See* Gambling & Betting

PLUMBING
See also Homes—Maintenance & Repair

Brann, Donald. **Plumbing Repairs Simplified.** 12th ed. Briarcliff Manor, NY: Easi Bild Directions, 1983. 226p. pap. $6.95 (696.1)

Whether it is fixing a leaking faucet or an overflowing tub or shower, specific directions are given here on how to make it right again. The key word is "repairs," although information is given on how to replace certain fixtures. As in all titles from this author and publisher, the directions are detailed, easy to follow, and carefully prepared for the beginner. Unfortunately, this is now in the 12th edition and some of the carry-over illustrations lack clarity.

Fredriksson, Don. **Plumbing for Dummies: A Guide to the Maintenance and Repair of Everything Including the Kitchen Sink.** Indianapolis, IN: Bobbs-Merrill, 1983. 256p. pap. $10.95 (643.6)

An ideal book for the man or woman who does not know the difference between a pipe and a socket wrench, this begins at point one and takes the reader through *all* the necessary steps for maintaining and repairing everything including the kitchen sink. The clarity of the author's style is enhanced by good illustrations. Instructions range from a discussion of essential tools to relatively easy jobs such as unplugging a sink, then on to larger, more complex problems such as the installation of piping systems. While most of the book is for "dummies," at least part of it really does depend on some inherent skill that probably cannot be learned even from this book.

Hedden, Jay. **Modern Plumbing for Old and New Houses.** 2nd ed. Passaic, NJ: Creative Homeowner, 1981. 160p. pap. $2.95 (696.1)

A brief yet extremely useful introduction to plumbing fundamentals for the layperson, this is written by the editor of the popular magazine *Workbench*. There are sections on the pros and cons of certain materials and tools, and chapters on complex projects like installing a bathtub and repairing a dishwasher. The most useful advice concerns tips on how to do common repairs around the house, e.g., clogged drains, dripping faucets, blocked toilets, and other matters that may not require the help of a professional plumber.

Jones, Peter. **The Complete Book of Home Plumbing.** New York: Scribner's, 1980. 113p. $13.95 (696.1)

"Complete" is an accurate description. Here an expert on home repairs and plumbing literally offers the amateur a complete guide to the tools, materials, and principles of the trade. (His *Plumbing without a Plumber* [q.v.] is a stripped-down version.) Almost every plumbing topic is covered from installing an entire system in a home to putting a new washer in a faucet. There are useful sections that show the beginner what to look for when a problem arises, and basic steps for basic repairs. The illustrations are clear and nicely augment the text.

Jones, Peter. **Plumbing without a Plumber.** New York: Butterick, 1980. 128p. pap. $4.95 (696.1)

Here are excellent illustrations and charts that clearly demonstrate how to carry out the plumbing projects described in the text. The explanations are straightforward and written in such a way that even the reader who has trouble distinguishing a wrench from a hammer will be home free. The coverage is limited to basic repairs and installations, but what this book treats, it treats well indeed. More extensive coverage is provided in the author's *The Complete Book of Home Plumbing* (q.v.).

Wilson, Scott. **The Plumber's Bible: A Practical Step-by-Step Home Repair Guide.** Garden City, NY: Doubleday, 1981. 146p. pap. $4.95 (644.6)

Thanks to good illustrations and simple, easy-to-follow instructions, this is a useful, inexpensive guide to have around when the sink is plugged up or the basement floods. The author covers all basic plumbing problems and installations that can be carried out by a layperson. While hardly a "bible," it is at least an adequate discussion of the majority of home plumbing situations, and because of its low price can be recommended.

POKER. *See* Gambling & Betting

POLO. *See* Horses

POOL. *See* Billiards

POSTAGE STAMPS. *See* Stamps

POSTAL SERVICE. *See* Mail

POTTERY & PORCELAIN. *See* Antiques

POWER TOOLS. *See* Tools

PRECIOUS STONES
See also Rock Collecting

Matlins, Antoinette, and Antonio Bonanno. **The Complete Guide to Buying Gems.** New York: Crown, 1984. 255p. $17.95 (553.8)

Anyone planning to purchase a gemstone worth more than a few hundred dollars may wish to consult this lucidly written guide. (Others, of course, can short-circuit the process by going to a trusted jeweler.) Subtitled "how to buy diamonds and colored gemstones with confidence and knowledge," the book discusses what to look for in a precious stone. There are illustrated explanations of the basics, from cut and clarity to polishing. Possibly most fascinating is the consideration of how people can be fooled by hard-to-detect imitation stones. The numerous colored photographs and the charts that clearly describe the countless types of gems will be of interest to almost anyone. *Note:* More extensive information can be found in Webster and Anderson (q.v.) and in several older guides published by Van Nostrand, e.g., the two-volume *Gemstones of North America* (1976).

Webster, Robert, and B. W. Anderson. **Gems: Their Sources, Descriptions and Identification.** 4th ed. Woburn, MA: Butterworth, 1983. 1,006p. $79.95 (553.8)

This is a guide to gems—everything from relatively easy-to-find, less-than-desirable stones to the most precious ones. The material is technical, i.e., for the stones and gems there is specific information on physical and chemical properties and there is also a detailed description of devices, tools, and instruments employed in the discovery and recovery of gems. While hardly a basic manual, it is an ideal identification guide and a good work for the history and background of the world of precious and semi-precious gems.

PRESERVATION OF FOODS. *See* Food—Canning & Freezing

PRICE GUIDES. *See* Catalogs; Consumer Education

PRINTING
See also Graphic Arts

Gray, Bill. **Tips on Type.** New York: Van Nostrand, 1983. 128p. pap. $8.25 (686.2)

What is the ideal typeface for a particular kind of stationery, advertisement, label, and so on? Working on the premise that the average layperson knows little or nothing about such matters, the author offers a practical explanation of typographic basics. Each tip is carefully illustrated, and terms are well defined. The guide concludes with current advances in typesetting, from computer to digital.

Treweek, Chris, et al. **The Alternative Printing Handbook.** New York: Penguin, 1984. 110p. pap. $8.95 (686.2)

Written for the person who knows nothing about printing and wants an alternative to a large, commercial printer, this is an ideal guide. The author carefully explains the different printing processes—from offset to stencil—and shows the advantages and disadvantages of each. The types of equipment employed in the various processes are illustrated and fully discussed. Each step and each procedure are explained in simple, direct language and generally illustrated with line drawings.

Van Uchelen, Rod. **Instant Printing Art.** New York: Van Nostrand, 1983. 89p. pap. $10.25 (686.2)

Including the basics of printing, copyright, and typeface selection, the author offers a concise, readable, and imaginative guide to instant printing. Applications include stationery, invitations, and even personal stamps, all well illustrated.

PRINTS. *See* Art—Collecting; Graphic Arts

PROGRAMMING LANGUAGE. *See* Computers—Programming & Software

PROSPECTING

U.S. Department of the Interior. **Suggestions for Prospecting.** Washington, DC: GPO, 1981. 24p. $3.25 (I19.2:P94/978)

Apparently prospecting is a hobby that continues to attract more and more people. This pamphlet, a general introduction to the subject, gives careful attention to techniques, necessary equipment, staking a claim, services available, and what it all may cost.

PRUNING
See also Gardening

Brickell, Christopher. **Pruning.** New York: Simon & Schuster, 1979. 96p. pap. $7.95 (631.5)

Prepared by the Royal Horticultural Society of England, this is a precise, uncomplicated handbook on pruning. The illustrations augment the text in such a way that even a beginner should have no difficulty knowing precisely where to cut or not to cut. All types of garden plants, bushes, trees, etc., are considered. It is one of the best of its type, and is as applicable in the United States as in Great Britain.

Stebbins, Robert, and Michael MacCaskey. **Pruning: How-to Guide for Gardeners.** Tucson, AZ: HP Books, 1983. 160p. pap. $7.95 (631.54)

Thanks to good illustrations and a precise presentation, this is a much better than average guide to pruning. It is for both beginners and experienced gardeners, although the latter will find it particularly useful. Stebbins opens with some basic explanations of plant growth (and nongrowth), plant diseases, and pruning tools. Each section, arranged by type of plant from roses and fruit trees to vines, gives specific instructions on when to cut, what to cut, how much to cut, etc. There is an unnecessary section on bonsai and a detailed list of plants.

Steffek, Edwin. **The Pruning Manual.** 2nd ed. New York: Van Nostrand, 1982. 152p. $9.95; pap. $4.95 (635.91)

First published in 1969 and slightly revised in 1982, this is a basic guide for amateur gardeners. Using simple yet convincing drawings to illustrate his points, Steffek shows how to trim various types of trees, shrubs, hedges, and other plants around the house. The book is organized by groups of plants with a breakdown by specific varieties. The 1982 revision includes a new section on power tools.

PUZZLES
See also Mathematics

Agostini, Franco. **Math and Logic Games.** New York: Facts on File, 1983. 181p. $18.95 (793.7)

Although the Rubik's Cube fad has faded, the challenge lingers and Agostini explains why it does by giving the reader background on the puzzle. Along the way he explains how to quickly solve the Rubik's Cube and numerous other games of mathematics and logic. Younger people will enjoy the "magic" of being able to do everything from guessing someone's age to getting a vest off without first taking off the coat. There are more advanced skills and tests of logic to be mastered by adults. All of this is presented step by step, so that even the individual who has problems with math should be enlightened.

Bryant, Mark. **Riddles: Ancient and Modern.** New York: Bedrick Books, 1984. 205p. $15.45; pap. $6.70 (398.6)

In two parts, this is a reference work for persons interested in the history of riddles, or simply devoted to confounding themselves and their friends. The first, more scholarly, section traces the development of the riddle from classical and biblical times to the present. Along the way, the reader is given a literary history lesson. Bryant uses epics and the works of everyone from Puccini to Shakespeare to make his points and to offer illustrations of the ubiquitous form. With that, he switches over to some 700 examples of riddles, taken from almost every time period and a wide variety of sources. Fortunately, the answers are supplied, although in all honesty most of the riddles can be solved without undue difficulty.

Gardner, Martin. **Mathematical Circus: More Games, Puzzles, Paradoxes & Other Mathematical Entertainments from Scientific American; with Thoughts from Readers, Afterthoughts from the Author, and 105 Drawings and Diagrams.** New York: Vintage, 1981. 272p. pap. $4.95 (793.7)

What is not revealed in the title is the stress on common sense and easy-to-follow instructions. Gardner writes as well as he explains the various fascinating games and the book is filled with enthusiasm and discovery. Suitable for those 12 years old and up, it is one of the best books of its type.

Gardner, Martin. **Science Fiction Puzzle Tales.** New York: Crown, 1981. 128p. $10.95; pap. $4.95 (793.7)

A four-step approach to some 36 fascinating puzzles, this is a book for almost anyone of any age interested in both science fiction and clever problems. The first section offers the puzzle. The second part gives a solution, but goes on from there to an extension of the basic problem. Part three offers more details, and part four gives the final answers. The story form of the puzzles is particularly appealing. *Note:* Some puzzles are drawn from the author's regular column in *Isaac Asimov's Science Fiction Magazine.* See also the author's *Mathematical Circus* (q.v.) and *Wheels, Life and Other Mathematical Amusements* (q.v.).

Gardner, Martin. **Wheels, Life and Other Mathematical Amusements.** San Francisco: Freeman, 1983. 261p. $15.95 (793.7)

Another collection of Gardner's columns from *Scientific American,* this follows the pattern of *Mathematical Circus* (q.v.). There is the usual number of intellectual puzzles and tricks, and the not-so-usual historical background on paradoxes that have puzzled generations. There is an equal number of tricks based on various manual techniques such as paper folding. Fortunately, not only are answers given in detail, but the author usually supplies sources for further reading on the subject.

Hamilton, Ben. **Brainteasers and Mindbenders.** Englewood Cliffs, NJ: Prentice-Hall, 1981. 193p. $10.95; pap. $4.95 (793.7)

While the author does not tell you how to solve a puzzle or riddle, he at least gives answers for all the problems found in this book. These vary in range and difficulty from crossword puzzles to logic exams to mathematical and spelling games. There are even mental tests that purport to distinguish the genius from average folks.

Hoffman, Paul. **Dr. Crypton and His Problems: Mind Benders from Science Digest.** New York: St. Martin's, 1982. 180p. $10.95 (593.73)

A collection of the puzzles by Dr. Crypton found in *Science Digest,* this is much above average in its challenge. At the same time, the columnist has won a wide audience for his uncomplicated presentations and his witty style. The numerous puzzles and mathematical problems presented often include reader reactions.

Jargocki, Christopher. **More Science Braintwisters and Paradoxes.** New York: Van Nostrand, 1982. 192p. $14.95 (793.73)

Through a series of some 200 questions, the author offers an easy-to-understand, usually entertaining entrance into the world of science, and particularly the more fascinating and mysterious side of science. The questions differ in scope and in importance as do the answers. Sometimes the author is a bit flip, e.g., in treating the differences in swimming abilities of men and women; but for the most part he sticks to material that is appropriate to an appreciation of everyday life. While some scientific background is required, at least for the mathematical answers, for the most part the questions and answers can be appreciated by the intelligent and interested layperson.

Kohl, Herbert. **A Book of Puzzlements.** New York: Schocken, 1981. 287p. $14.95 (793.7)

Sweeping over a vast array of games and puzzles, the author picks out the best and brings them together in a book suitable for all ages. The 300 easy-to-follow, although often not easy to solve, braintwisters range from palindromes to codes and standard puzzles. There is a section, too, on the method of developing games. The author concludes by suggesting other books in the field.

Lewis, David. **Eureka: Math Fun from Many Angles.** New York: Putnam's, 1983. 203p. $5.95 (793.74)

If nothing else, this is a guide to conquering the famous and infamous Rubik Cube. The author has a complete section on the puzzle, as well as a lucid explanation of the mathematics involved. That is typical of the things that make this witty, well-written guide to math a joy. Lewis considers the historical and the theoretical aspects of the science, and offers specific puzzles and problems for solution. Readers will amaze their friends when they learn the basics that ensure almost instant calculation of basic mathematical problems. There are nice sections, too, on tricks and various ways to turn geometry into a pastime.

Salny, Abbie. **Brain Busters: The Most Challenging Puzzles You'll Ever Do.** New York: Dodd, 1984. 125p. pap. $6.95 (793.73)

Working on a scale of difficulty, Salny begins with fairly easy puzzles and ends with what he calls "incredibly difficult" problems. Most of the braintwisters, which range from word games to cryptograms, are the author's work. Well written and a real challenge.

Smullyan, Raymond. **The Lady or the Tiger? And Other Logic Puzzles, Including a Mathematical Novel That Features Gödel's Great Discovery.** New York: Knopf, 1982. 226p. $13.95 (793.7)

An unusual approach to the common puzzle or the mathematical game, this guide not only offers problems but shows the reader how to solve them. Along the way the author is teaching logic and mathematical theory, but always in such a manner that even the most unmathematical individual will enjoy the quest. The riddles progress from relatively simple ones in the early chapters to the truly complex later on. The second half of the book is a novel that takes the reader on a trip through the wonders of Gödel's theories. All of this includes a wide cast of characters from vampires to a Scotland Yard inspector.

QUILTS

Bishop, Robert, et al. **Quilts, Coverlets, Rugs & Samplers.** Collectors' Guides to American Antiques. New York: Knopf, 1982. 476p. pap. $13.95 (746.9)

This follows the same format as the Ketchum book on chests (see Antiques section, p. 8 in this book). Some four centuries are covered and so much information is provided that this work is of benefit not only to the beginner but also to the specialist. The latter may occasionally be disappointed because of lack of detail due to the extensive time coverage, but the book is an ideal place to turn for good illustrations and specifics on particular items.

Houston, Julie, ed. **Woman's Day Prize Winning Quilts, Coverlets & Afghans.** New York: Van Nostrand, 1982. 255p. $19.95 (746.9)

This is a collection of 35 prize-winning patterns, selected by the editors of *Woman's Day* magazine. A brief sketch of the designer is given for each, and precise directions follow on how the pattern can be worked into a quilt, coverlet, or afghan. Several illustrations are in color.

Linsley, Leslie. **America's Favorite Quilts.** New York: Delacorte/Doubleday, 1984. 176p. $19.95 (746.9)

An idea book and an inspiration, this is a study of 26 distinctly different types of (primarily) patchwork quilts. These are beautifully illustrated in both black and white and color, and the photographs are good enough to allow the reader to see precisely how the finished quilt should look. Once a design is chosen, there are full instructions on types of material and various techniques, and a complete range of charts, diagrams, and detailed instructions. The book is so constructed that it can be used by both the beginner and intermediate-level quiltmaker, although obviously the latter is likely to find more of interest here.

Martin, Judy. **Patchwork: Easy Lessons for Creative Quilt Design and Construction.** New York: Scribner's, 1983. 170p. pap. $15.95 (746.9)

While at one time the women who made patchwork quilts organized the designs in their own imagination—and often borrowed designs from ancestors—today the art is rapidly dying out. The purpose of this guide is to organize, explain, and detail the various approaches to designing patchwork. Each section or chapter is devoted to a particular set of principles and procedures, from pattern and proportion to fabrics and finishing. The result is a methodical and thorough guide that will be of particular interest to intermediate-level quiltmakers. It is too complicated for beginners, although the information is such that it should at least be examined by all who are interested in quilts.

Sunset Quilting, Patchwork, Appliqué. Rev. ed. Menlo Park, CA: Lane, 1981. 88p. pap. $4.95 (746.46)

Following the familiar Sunset format with a huge number of illustrations (here some 200, with 50 in color), this is both an introduction to quilting and a marvelous overview of its possibilities. Specific instructions, suggestions for types of material, and techniques are combined with the pictures to offer the beginner and the expert paths to success.

RABBITS

Fritzsche, Helga. **Rabbits.** Woodbury, NY: Barron's, 1983. 67p. pap. $3.95 (636.93)

The subtitle to *Rabbits* is "everything about purchase, care, nutrition, and diseases," and that covers the scope of this brief yet substantial guide. The emphasis is on the domestic pet. The author shows what makes for the best kind of housing, what to feed the animals, how to handle them, when to breed or prevent breeding, etc. All of this is illustrated on almost every page with photographs and line drawings. The style is direct, easy to follow, and perfectly suitable for younger people.

RACING. *See* Gambling & Betting; Horses

RADIO

American Radio Relay League Inc. **The Beginner's Guide to Amateur Radio.** - Englewood Cliffs, NJ: Prentice-Hall, 1982. 182p. $16.95; pap. $8.95 (621.38)

Amateur radio remains a thoroughly popular hobby, and in this guide the various staff members of the American Radio Relay League introduce the beginner to basics. Following a general overview of the subject are illustrated chapters and sections on the types of equipment needed (given in a wide price range), principles of communication and engineering, government regulations, processes needed to obtain an amateur radio license, and material on repair and maintenance. The basics are all here for the would-be ham operator.

Gibson, Stephen. **Amateur Radio License Guide.** Reston, VA: Reston, 1982. 246p. $18.95; pap. $12.95 (621.38)

Logically, this guide opens with information on how to obtain the first-level radio license and what legally can be done with such a passport to amateur radio. There is also a rundown on the authority and activities of the Federal Communications Commission (FCC). With this background, the author takes the reader through the various steps necessary to gain a regular license, including learning the Morse Code.

Helms, Harry. **How to Tune the Secret Shortwave Spectrum.** Blue Ridge Summit, PA: TAB, 1981. 182p. pap. $6.95 (384.54)

Here "secret" means shortwave signals that are floating about the airways and come from such sources as the secret government radio stations of various countries. There are also less secret voices about, such as pirate radio (i.e., those operating without a license). How to tune in to these is the message of this guide. After a section on necessary equipment, techniques for tapping the secret sources are given. A good deal of the book is concerned with explaining what is out there and who is sending signals.

Luciani, Vince. **Amateur Radio: Super Hobby.** New York: McGraw-Hill, 1984. 290p. pap. $9.95 (621.38)

From building a radio set to securing an amateur license, the author covers the basics of amateur radio. Perhaps the best news is that everyone, not just electronics experts, can enjoy amateur radio. This theme is reiterated by individuals in separate chapters. They second the notion that amateur radio is a truly satisfying hobby. There are sections and chapters covering everything the beginner must know from equipment needed to contacting authorities in the field.

Sessions, Ken, and W. E. Hood. **How to Be a Ham.** 2nd ed. Blue Ridge Summit, PA: TAB, 1981. 240p. pap. $6.95 (621.38)

This differs from the American Radio Relay League work (q.v.) in that aside from basics, most of the focus is on how to obtain various types of ham licenses. There are sample examinations, study guides, lists of government offices, and FCC rules and regulations. Beyond all of this is basic information on equipment, operations, and even etiquette.

Wells, Andy. **Building Stereo Speakers.** New York: McGraw-Hill, 1983. 192p. $9.95 (621.38)

In the early years of high fidelity, this was the only way to go, i.e., if you wanted true fidelity you had to construct your own speaker cabinet system. Today, of course, there are hundreds of types available, and there is really no need to build your own. Still, for those who want to save money, who want the joy of a finely tuned system, this is an ideal book. Wells offers five basic sets of plans for the construction of speaker cabinets, and then shows how to install the various pieces of electronic equipment, including the speakers, in the enclosure. Complete details are given for each, from materials needed to specific instructions on how to put the parts together. The cabinets are of varying difficulty and cost.

RAILROADS, MODEL. *See* Models & Modelmaking

RECORDS. *See* Music; Radio

RECREATION. *See* Camping; Games; Sports

REMODELING. *See* Homes—Remodeling

REPTILES

Mattison, Christopher. **The Care of Reptiles and Amphibians in Captivity.** New York: Sterling, 1982. 303p. $17.95 (597)
This is basic for the individual seeking reliable information on the care and feeding of snakes, alligators, and other awesome pets. The British author is a professional but his guide is primarily for the amateur. It will be of particular value to teachers and parents who must keep reptiles and amphibians for their small charges. The animals are quickly identified by black-and-white photographs and line drawings throughout the book, and there is a generous section of color photographs. The book gives all the necessary background information on the various types of species likely to be kept at home or in school, and there is guidance on almost everything from feeding to what to do when the pet becomes ill. There is a list of sources and of groups and organizations interested in the subject, as well as an outline of the laws governing the purchase and possession of these creatures.

RESTAURANTS. *See* Food

RIDDLES. *See* Mathematics; Puzzles

RIDING. *See* Horses

ROBOTICS

Aleksander, Igor, and Piers Burnett. **Reinventing Man: The Robot Becomes Reality.** New York: Holt, 1984. 301p. $17.45 (629.89)
Written by a computer designer, this is a definitive history of robotics, as well as a look into the robot's future. While not a how-to-do-it manual, it does supply necessary background for anyone concerned with the construction of robots. There is much, too, of help to programmers. The authors show how programming is essential to a sophisticated robot, but it has to be done very differently from the way it is done for today's computers. It is a matter of the robot's feeding on past programs and making decisions about new ones. The authors then go on to investigate various artifical intelligence theories and programs including one devised by Aleksander. The various methods and ideas are explained in detail.

Berger, Phil. **The State-of-the-Art Robot Catalog.** New York: Dodd, 1984. 162p. pap. $12.95 (629.8)
What promises to be a frequently updated catalog offers the curious reader a wide assortment of robotic machines and hardware. The author has compiled a descriptive list of what is now available to laypersons. The models are fully described, and there is information about the manufacturer as well as price (as of 1984). The robots range in complexity and sophistication from simple toys to involved and highly expensive industrial models. There is adequate background information on robots and some good illustrations.

Krasnoff, Barbara. **Robots: Reel to Real.** New York: Arco, 1982. 154p. $12.95 (629.8)

A basic explanation of robots, this is for the person who has problems understanding scientific writing. The author's style is clear and witty, and she examines various uses of robots in industry, the armed forces, and space, as well as their potential for home deployment. There are numerous illustrations. The title comes from the author's comparison of movie (reel) robots with those in use at the beginning of 1982, and those that will probably be in production by the close of the 1980s.

Safford, Edward. **Handbook of Advanced Robotics.** Blue Ridge Summit, PA: TAB, 1982. 468p. $21.95; pap. $15.95 (629.8)

Most of the information here is as suitable for those who are totally ignorant of robotics as it is for those with some information on the subject. The author does have data for scientists, but this is kept to a minimum. Safford concentrates on the various types of robots in use in such places as factories and homes, as well as their potential development. The explanations are clear and usually accompanied by numerous illustrations. There is also a section on robots that can be built by the beginner who has at least a minimal knowledge of engineering and electronics.

Ullrich, Robert. **The Robotics Primer: The What, Why and How of Robots in the Workplace.** Englewood Cliffs, NJ: Prentice-Hall, 1983. 121p. $17.95; pap. $8.95 (629.8)

While not a how-to-do-it book, this is a good and thorough background on the subject—a background needed by anyone who wants to master robotics. The author is involved with the pragmatic possibilities of automation in the world's industries. He explains the various applications of robots, and how they are presently being used and may be used in the future. There are illustrations of various tasks performed by robots, and Ullrich sees these expanding considerably in the next decade. The problems of the relationship between people and robots are considered, but only in the most optimistic way. Throughout, the author is careful to avoid jargon—although he does get carried away with the great American business ideas about opportunity.

ROCK COLLECTING
See also Precious Stones

Chesterman, Charles. **The Audubon Society Field Guide to North American Rocks and Minerals.** New York: Knopf, 1979. 850p. $12 (549)

This follows the usual pattern of Audubon field guides, i.e., there is a visual key (by color and by description) to help the beginner identify specific rocks and types of mineral formations. There is an approach by rock types and an index to various localities in North America in which specific types are found. The illustrations are excellent color photographs, and the descriptions are accurate. While too large for easy carrying about, it is the ultimate source of identification.

Fay, Gordon. **The Rockhound's Manual.** New York: Harper, 1973. 290p. pap. $4.95 (549)

A basic guide for the beginner, this covers all aspects of collecting rocks. There is detailed information on how to locate and identify specific rocks or minerals. There are adequate to good colored photographs. Of most interest is the detailed information on testing and polishing rocks, mounting gems, photography, and the ins and outs of organizing specific types of collections. All of this is presented in a nontechnical, easy-to-follow fashion. Despite the publication date, the guide is in no way dated and retains its usefulness.

MacFall, Russell. **Rock Hunter's Guide: How to Find and Identify Collectible Rocks.** New York: Crowell, 1980. 247p. $13.50 (552)

Even more basic than Fay (q.v.), this opens with a brief history and summary of the fundamentals of geology and mineralogy. The author quickly turns to basics, and offers an easy-to-follow description of principal types of rocks and how they can be identified. There is a nice section on collecting and displaying the finds, but the heart of the book is the state-by-state list of rock locations. The illustrations are adequate.

Tindall, James, and Roger Thornhill. **The Collector's Guide to Rocks & Minerals.** New York: Van Nostrand, 1975. 256p. $17.95 (549)

Along with Fay (q.v.), this is a basic guide for the rock hound. The difference is that here the information is more technical, and there is additional data on the formation of the earth. In fact, a particular strength of this book is the fine summary and history of the biological and physical aspects of the subject. There is complete coverage of such things as crystallography, chemical tests for various types of minerals, formation and character of rocks, etc. The final part of the book deals with the problems of collecting, and there is a good section on cutting and polishing rocks for exhibit. This is likely to be of more interest to the advanced collector. Beginners will find Fay more helpful.

RUBBER STAMPS. *See* Stamps, Rubber

RUGS
See also Interior Decoration

Amini, Majid. **Oriental Rugs: Care and Repair.** New York: Van Nostrand, 1981. 128p. $19.95 (746.7)

This book is a splendid introduction to flat-woven Oriental rugs. Following the usual history and explanation of terms, the author gives sound advice on what to look for when selecting rugs in different price ranges and for various situations. He devotes a part of the book to the proper care of a rug, including advice on minor repairs. All of this is accompanied by excellent color photographs and well-placed drawings.

Ford, P. R. **The Oriental Carpet: A History and Guide to Traditional Motifs, Patterns and Symbols.** New York: Abrams, 1981. 352p. $75 (746.77)

Organized by design and pattern, this is one of the more complete guides to new Oriental rugs. (Antiques are not considered.) Under each of the major patterns, there is a discussion of the types and variations found within certain areas—primarily Iran, but with a bow to India and China and other countries as well. There are over 800 illustrations, many in color, as well as maps that tell precisely the area in which a given design or pattern originates. The clear text and commonsense approach reveal the author's full understanding of the subject.

Jerrehian, Aram. **Oriental Rug Primer: Buying and Understanding New Oriental Rugs.** New York: Facts on File, 1980. 223p. $12.95; pap. $7.95 (746.7)

A rug dealer with considerable experience explains what to look for when selecting a new Oriental rug. He offers excellent suggestions as to the benefits of certain types of rugs. There is a section on caring for the rug and a good directory that lists major rug types with descriptions of their basic colors, designs, and sizes. The illustrations are numerous and useful.

Quirke, Lillian. **The Rug Book: How to Make All Kinds of Rugs.** Englewood Cliffs, NJ: Prentice-Hall, 1979. 234p. $17.95; pap. $8.95 (746.7)

Intended for the beginning rugmaker, this is much better than many of the manuals and guides in the area. Quirke has an intelligent and clear method of describing the basics, and she assiduously avoids cute phrases and horrible patterns. Her instructions assume that the reader knows nothing about the subject, and for this reason she stays with quite basic approaches to various types of rugs, from woven to braided. The appendixes include varieties of yarns, sources of supplies, and a good glossary.

Rostov, Charles, and Jia Guanyan. **Chinese Carpets.** New York: Abrams, 1983. 223p. $45 (746.7)

A rich, luxurious book with beautiful illustrations in color, this is a basic guide for those who intend to collect Chinese hand-knotted carpets. (It is also valuable for the art historian.) The text provides numerous methods of identifying a carpet, from an analysis of its weaving methods to an identification of its symbols. There is a section, too, on techniques of dating the carpets. The writing style is clear and the text exhaustive.

SAILING
   See also Boats; Knots & Splices; Navigation

Bond, Bob, and Steve Sleight. **Cruising Boat Sailing.** New York: Knopf, 1983. 160p. $14.95 (797.12)
Small Boat Sailing. New York: Knopf, 1983. 160p. $14.95 (797.12)

Written and illustrated for beginners, these are excellent all-around guides to sailing. The instructions are detailed, and there are numerous illustrations to emphasize each and every point. Both regular and emergency sailing situations are considered.

A "cruising boat" is defined as one from 25 to 30 feet, and the catch is obvious: Anyone who owns such a boat probably knows the basics of sailing. Still, this is a useful guide, if only to brush up during the months when one must strike sails. The second in this series is concerned with boats under 25 feet; it follows the same general pattern with generous illustrations and point-by-point instructions.

Farham, Moulton. **Sailing for Beginners.** Rev. ed. New York: Macmillan, 1981. 257p. $14.95 (797.1)

Here is a popular, rudimentary text on sailing. The basic principles are defined and, in an uncomplicated fashion, the author moves from handling a sailboat to rules of navigation. The various methods of sailing the boat are given, as are instructions on handling emergency situations. The photographs fit nicely into the instructional material and there are definitions at the end of each of the chapters. (A single glossary would have been better.) There is a good section on what the individual should look for in purchasing a sailboat.

George, M. B. **Basic Sailing.** Rev. ed. New York: Hearst, 1984. 100p. pap. $8.50 (797.12)

An inexpensive yet thorough manual for teaching the basics of sailing, this is preferred by many who teach the subject. It has the advantage of being simple, emphasizing basics and assuming that the reader knows little or nothing about the subject. The excellent illustrations and diagrams are another large plus. From the explanation of the parts of the boat to that of tacking, the text is a model of easy-to-follow instructions. An excellent start for any would-be sailor.

Herreshoff, Halsey, ed. **The Sailor's Handbook.** Boston: Little, 1983. 224p. $14.95 (797.12)

Everything you wanted to know about sailing, and related topics, is covered in this tightly organized handbook. Types of sails, navigation, safety at sea, and weather and winds are among the subjects considered. Each chapter is written by an expert and the book is divided into logical parts. This is more for the person familiar with sailing than for the beginner, but both will profit from what is a detailed approach to the subject. The book is beautifully illustrated, and there is a section of maps showing—in the editor's view—the best parts of the world for sailing.

Jones, Tristan. **One Hand for Yourself, One for the Ship: The Essentials of Single Handed Sailing.** New York: Macmillan, 1982. 226p. $14.95 (797.1)

After nine solo trips across the Atlantic and many years of working a boat by himself, the author is more than qualified to explain how it is done. He covers almost every conceivable topic from the kind of boat best suited to solo sailing to types of food and clothing needed. He even includes tips on how to cook while sailing alone. The high quality of the writing style is a match for the author's adventures, and the advice is detailed and easy to follow.

Leather, John. **Sail and Oar.** Camden, ME: International Marine, 1982. 143p. $20 (797.1)

Most people begin with small boats, and many stay with canoes, sailboats, and rowboats for a lifetime. Oddly enough, though, there are few books on the small boat. Leather's is an exception. Here he considers various types of boats under 21 feet in length, and for each he discusses its good and bad features, how it is best employed, and even some historical background. There are details on some two dozen boats of different designs. While not enough information is given for the reader to actually build one of the boats, there is enough to help you decide if this kind of boat is for you, and to get you started.

Meisel, Tony, ed. **Under Sail.** New York: Macmillan, 1982. 192p. $24.95 (623.8)

In this basic manual, the authors, both sailing experts, discuss all aspects of the sport from the sails themselves to various electronic navigational systems. There is a good chapter on how to check the boat for possible problems, and a section devoted to repair tools and their use. Good line drawings and photographs are used throughout.

Oakley, John. **This is Down Wind Sailing.** Boston: Sail Books, 1981. 141p. $17.95 (797.12)

Newcomers to sailing will find all the basic information needed in this well-illustrated guide. Written by an experienced sailor, the book covers everything from racing gear to sails. The careful explanations are augmented by detailed pictures, diagrams, and drawings that make clear the differences between various types of equipment and sails. Although racing is the focus, the information is basic enough to be of value to even the most leisurely sailor.

Powledge, Fred. **A Forgiving Wind: On Becoming a Sailor.** New York: Sierra/Random House, 1983. 224p. $12.95 (623.88)

A Sierra Club publication, this has the advantage of a discursive, relaxed style. The lessons of sailing, from beginning to end, are taught by fact and anecdote. The two are woven together in a pleasing conversational fashion that avoids the "see the mast/see the sail" routine. At the same time, the information is accurate and complete. Powledge covers everything from how to identify boats to the jargon of sailors. Instruction on the actual techniques of sailing, which makes up most of the text, is excellent.

Richey, Michael, ed. **The Sailing Encyclopedia.** New York: Lippincott, 1980. 288p. $29.95 (797.1)

A beautiful book, with illustrations (many in color) on almost every page, this is a guide of interest to both seasoned sailors and those who only dream about the subject. The book lives up to its title. Everything is covered—if not always in great depth, at least in an informative way. There are, for example, well-illustrated sections on navigation, racing, safety, boat design, and rigging. The coverage may be too broad for the average sailor but this is a handy reference guide and one that, if used with other titles, can offer considerable enjoyment and data on the joys of sailing. First published in England.

Rosenow, Frank. **Sailing Craft.** Boston: Sail Books, 1982. 128p. $15.95 (623.82)

This is a browser's book, a book for someone looking for ideas and dreaming of unlimited funds. (At the same time, it should be quickly added, there are numerous suggestions, if only by implication, of benefit to the less-than-wealthy boat owner.) The author incorporates autobiographical material into his text in that he describes his own experiences over the years with numerous sailing craft of almost every size (most medium to large) and from almost every country. The text is divided by designers and types of boats. The author writes with charm and verve and this is splendid reading for anyone involved with the sport.

Smith, Terry. **Looking After Your Dinghy.** Salem, NH: Merrimack, 1983. 95p. pap. $10.95 (623.8)

Ideally suited for the individual with a limited budget, a small boat, and a passion for sailing, this book is for the average dinghy owner. The author has wide experience with the craft and makes a point of considering details not often found in such manuals—for example, how to store a small boat over the winter months. The instructions are supported by line drawings, which prove valuable when the author is discussing repair and maintenance. First published in England, but the slight English bias does not interfere with use in the United States.

Ulian, Richard. **Sailing: An Informal Primer.** New York: Van Nostrand, 1982. 160p. $12.95 (797.1)

A man in love with sailing explains the joys of the sport and what it can do to lift a tired spirit. In the wake of his adventures as related in anecdotes collected over some 40 years, Ulian explains the basics of sailing. The approach is unconventional, but when one puts the book down it is a poor reader, indeed, who will not be more confident about hoisting a sail. True, other books (see other titles in this section) give more specific advice on step-by-step procedures, but Ulian simply cannot be topped for a sense of what it means to enjoy the sport.

SALADS. See Cooking; Cooking—Vegetables

SANDWICHES
See also Food

DeGouy, Louis, et al. **The Ultimate Sandwich Book.** Philadelphia, PA: Running Pr., 1982. 155p. $12.90; pap. $5.95 (641.8)

First published in 1929, this is a kind of classic for the sandwich fancier. It is now revised and updated to include over 700 variations. The book is enthusiastic in its praise and descriptions, well illustrated, and certainly easy to understand.

Harris, Diane. **The Woman's Day Book of Great Sandwiches.** New York: Holt, 1982. 180p. $16.45; pap. $9.70 (641.8)

Americans who love sandwiches will find 230 different varieties explained here, often in detail. Arranged by cold and hot varieties, there is a further division by regional favorites and, finally, international delights. Each type is explained, often with an indication of what is suitable to serve at a table and, by implication, the type of person likely to enjoy the flavor. Along the way the author shows the reader how to bake bread and rolls and make a variety of sauces and garnishes.

SCIENCE & TECHNOLOGY

Hess, Fred, and Arthur Thomas. **Chemistry Made Simple.** Rev. ed. New York: Doubleday, 1984. 210p. pap. $4.95 (540)

Written as a general introduction to chemistry for the layperson, this book explains chemistry in terms the average reader can understand. There is a minimum of jargon and technical language, a maximum of a concerted effort to clarify sometimes difficult concepts. The revised version (it was first issued in 1955) considers matters of current interest such as the environment and space.

LeShan, Lawrence, and Henry Margenau. **Einstein's Space and Van Gogh's Sky: Physical Reality and Beyond.** New York: Macmillan, 1982. 268p. $14.95 (110)

For anyone trying to understand the role of the individual in the universe, this is an excellent and highly imaginative guide. It is also controversial. The psychologist (LeShan) and the physicist (Margenau) set out to explain what reality is, particularly in terms of what is now known about quantum mechanics. This part is difficult to challenge, but in the earlier chapters, where such things as the definitions of art and the explanations of parapsychology are considered, one may take issue with both the discussions and the conclusions. Nevertheless, thanks to the clear writing style and the well-defined concepts, the guide is a good introduction for interested laypersons to the world around them and to the place the individual occupies in that world. In one sense, it is a first step in any self-help program.

Rheingold, Howard. **Talking Tech: A Conversational Guide to Science and Technology.** New York: Morrow, 1982. 324p. $13.50 (603)

How can nonscientists hold their own in conversations about modern technology? One aid is this guide, which defines and explains 70 topics likely to be the focus of conversation in living and dining rooms. For each subject, the terminology is explained and the history or background of the concept is concisely given. There are references to related topics and a reading list. Much is made of the enjoyable aspect of being able to speak intelligently, if not in great depth, about such things as acid rain, optics, computers, and clones. At the same time, the information is accurate and serves to give the reader, student and nonstudent, some background for term papers and intelligent conversation.

Sutton, Caroline. **How Did They Do That?** New York: Morrow, 1984. 350p. $14.45 (032.02)

This book follows the pattern of the earlier Sutton and Anderson How Do They Do That? (q.v.). Here the author takes a historical look at what are now fixed customs and procedures, such as the elevation of champagne to its status as the drink for celebrations. There are explanations, of topics of common interest, such as how the pyramids were constructed, and sections on historical figures, events, technology, etc. Answers vary in length, and the book can be used both for reference and for inspiration for the how-to-do-it fan.

Sutton, Caroline, and Duncan Anderson. **How Do They Do That? Wonders of the Modern World Explained.** New York: Quill, 1982. 292p. pap. $7.50 (032.02)

This is not a how-to-do-it book for the layperson, but an explanation of how it is done by experts. Queries range from how experts measure the heat of the sun to their capacity to estimate the speed of a fastball. The focus is on science and technology, and while the material can be classed in the genre of trivia, it is basically educational, and usually entertaining. There are 150 questions with sometimes lengthy answers, although many of the explanations are no more than a paragraph or two.

SCUBA DIVING

Taylor, Herb. **The Sport Diving Catalog.** New York: St. Martin's, 1982. 320p. $24.95; pap. $12.95 (797.2)

It is important to stress two things about this useful guide. First, its concern is with scuba diving not only as a sport but as a method of exploration. Second, it is a collection of material, not a consistent presentation of data about diving. As a catalog it offers, under appropriate subject sections, articles, annotations, and comments about diving, as well as useful notes on a vast amount of equipment. Subjects range from underwater photography to the use of diving boats. There are sections of a how-to-do nature that are concerned with selecting the right type of equipment, rather than with the actual talents required for scuba diving. It is fascinating reading, and will be of great value to both the beginner and the expert.

SCULPTURE

Andrews, Oliver. **Living Materials: A Sculptor's Handbook.** Berkeley: University of California Pr., 1983. 348p. $45 (731.2)

There are few really worthwhile books on the art of sculpture, most of them being too simplified or plagued with terrible taste. Not so here, as an experienced teacher takes the novice through the various steps from the materials to use to the finished artwork. There are unobtrusive lessons on the aesthetics of both traditional and avant-garde styles, and good advice on tools, materials, and space requirements. Moving from clay through stone, the author opens avenues for exploration. The basic instructions are accompanied by black-and-white illustrations.

Padovano, Anthony. **The Process of Sculpture.** New York: Doubleday, 1981. 331p. $19.95 (731.4)

There are few good guides to teaching sculpture. Here is an exception. An experienced artist demonstrates the basics of working in metal, stone, wood, clay, bronze, and plastic. The author takes the beginner from the moment an idea is conceived through to the finished piece of work. Each of the basic steps is carefully explained and illustrated. There are numerous charts and diagrams to help in the selection and use of the various media. All of this is done with a gracious style and a confidence that will inspire. Thanks to the wide coverage and the intelligent approach, it is a book that will be of some value to intermediate-level as well as beginning artists.

SEAMANSHIP. *See* Boats; Knots & Splices; Navigation; Sailing

SECONDHAND TRADE

Gould, Joe. **Don't Throw It Out—Sell It.** Englewood Cliffs, NJ: Prentice-Hall, 1983. 138p. $14.95; pap. $6.95 (658.87)

The idea behind this book is to encourage the reader to find material in the closet, attic, or basement that someone else will find valuable. With that accomplished, how does one go about finding customers? Gould supplies the answers by outlining numerous approaches to selling secondhand merchandise. These range from garage sales to selling the material to secondhand dealers or thrift shops. The step-by-step instructions are paralleled by a good explanation of what is and is not commercially valuable. The author is particularly helpful in explaining that what may appear to be junk to some is gold to others. The book is well written; there are some indifferent illustrations.

Hyman, Henry. **The Where to Sell Anything and Everything Book.** New York: Ballantine, 1981. 400p. pap. $7.95 (790.1)

Having something to sell, how does one find a market? The answer, which may range from a classified advertisement in the local paper to going to an antique dealer, is outlined here. Not only does the author explain where to find outlets, but he goes into considerable detail showing how to determine the probable value of the item and why it may or may not be difficult to sell. With that, there is a list, under 17 broad subject headings, of over 500 major buyers in the United States and Canada. This may date, but it at least indicates the wide range of possibilities and suggests that there is always a market for almost anything.

Wasserstein, Susan. **Collectors' Guide to U.S. Auctions & Flea Markets.** New York: Penguin, 1981. 296p. pap. $7.95 (658.84)

Although a bit dated, this guide remains useful for pinpointing the larger, better auctions and flea markets in the United States. The arrangement is by six major areas of the country, with states alphabetically arranged within region. Entries include complete information, from addresses to kinds of merchandise sold. (For those interested in participating, the rental price for booth or stand is given.) There are three indexes: a subject guide to auctions, and the names of auctions and flea markets.

SELF-DEFENSE
See also Judo & Karate & Aikido

Heyden, Margaret, and Allen V. Tarpenning. **Personal Defense for Women.** Belmont, CA: Wadsworth, 1970. 94p. $1.95 (796.8)

Complete descriptions are given of basic self-defense techniques, which may also be useful as exercise. Each situation is illustrated with drawings. After the basics, there are instructions on how to maintain the level of skill. Sections on equipment and a final chapter on testing and evaluation add up to the best book of its type available. While this was published in 1970, the information is still current. *Note:* Although this is written for women, much of the material is applicable to men.

McGurn, Thomas, and Christine Kelly. **The Woman's Bible for Survival in a Violent Society.** New York: Stein & Day, 1984. 212p. $16.95 (362.2)

The authors team up to show a woman how to defend herself under a variety of circumstances and in locations from the home to the street. They explain different methods that can be employed, and are careful to point out the fallacy of many self-defense myths. It is not a good idea, for example, to head for the throat or the groin of a male attacker. It is refreshing to find that self-defense does not depend entirely on such things as karate. Much of it is more a matter of attitude than actual force.

Van Clief, Ron. **The Manual of the Martial Arts.** New York: Rawson, 1982. 188p. $14.95; pap. $10.95 (796.8)

Illustrated instructions on self-defense, or, if you will, the martial arts, are divided here between the needs of the average young man or woman and the older person, as well as children. Specific advice is given for each group, and basic moves are explained. The guide has a fine introduction to karate, aikido, jujitsu, kung fu, etc. It is not, however, more than that, and anyone seriously involved will need specific guides and, of course, personal instruction.

SEWING
See also Needlecrafts

Boyd, Margaret. **The Sew & Save Source Book: Your Guide to Supplies for Creative Sewing.** White Hall, VA: Betterway, 1984. 200p. $9.95 (646.1)
The title tells it all. The author simply divides sewing skills into 16 categories and, under each, lists the primary sources of supply of materials and services. For each of the some 1,500 listings, there is a name, address, and brief description of what is offered.

Cabrera, Roberto, and Patricia Meyers. **Classic Tailoring Techniques: A Construction Guide for Men's Wear.** New York: Fairchild, 1983. 245p. $20 (646.4)
By "classic" the authors mean traditional tailoring by professionals. It is their contention that anyone with a command of sewing techniques can become a passable tailor by following their precise instructions, which are usually accompanied by good illustrations and photographs. They provide instruction in the technique of making sleeves and sleeve finishing, stitches and seams, zippers, collars, darts, and the basics of sewing. Every point is covered in detail from patterns to final fitting. The text is clear, the presentation logical, and the result is one of the best books on the subject.

Godsworthy, Maureen. **Mend It: A Complete Guide to Clothes Repair.** New York: Stein & Day, 1980. 127p. $5.95 (646.2)
While the art of mending socks went out years ago, the author seems at least to indicate that it can come back. More to the point, she gives specific instruction on mending and repairing more expensive pieces of clothing. She is particularly good in her step-by-step approach to reweaving and to making invisible patches. Illustrations liberally augment the well-written text.

Hutchison, Howard. **The Complete Handbook of Sewing Machine Repair.** Blue Ridge Summit, PA: TAB, 1980. 308p. $14.95; pap. $8.95 (646.2)
While most sewing machine owners are likely to send for a repairman or take the faulty machine to a shop, there are others who want to know what is wrong, and what can be done. It is to these that Hutchison addresses his guide, as well as, incidentally, to others who may simply want to know more about maintenance and simple adjustments than can be found in the standard product handbook. The first part of the book demonstrates the basics of the machine's operation and equally basic repairs and adjustments. The author then turns to specific makes. While the latter part may become dated, the author says the changes in machines are so minimal that this is not likely.

Ladbury, Ann. **The Dressmaker's Dictionary.** New York: Arco, 1982. 358p. $19.95 (646.4)
In a dictionary format, the author explains just about everything that needs to be known about dressmaking. The definitions and discussions run from a few words to several pages. There are, for example, some 15 pages devoted to collars. A vast amount of material is covered, from various types of sewing techniques, to fabrics, to equipment and patterns. There are numerous, detailed illustrations, which are well placed throughout the dictionary. While originally a British publication, there

are enough cross-references to overcome the occasional differences in words and expressions. This is preferred to the less detailed Meyer's *Sewing Dictionary* (1980).

Reader's Digest Complete Guide to Sewing. Pleasantville, NY: Reader's Digest, 1976. 528p. $20.50 (646.2)

The basic steps in sewing are covered in this book, accompanied by excellent illustrations. The topics discussed include 82 different projects that range from those requiring beginning skills to more difficult ones. The book is arranged in a logical, easy-to-follow way, with summaries of each chapter's content at the head of the chapter. Numerous cross-references and name tabs aid in finding one's way through the work, and there is a detailed index.

Shaeffer, Claire. **The Complete Book of Sewing Shortcuts.** New York: Sterling, 1981. 256p. $17.95 (646.4)

An excellent and, as the title says, complete book on general sewing, this can be recommended for both beginning and intermediate-level sewers. All basic sewing matters are considered from finishing to equipment, and most of the steps and directions are supplemented with excellent drawings. Little is left to chance, and there is even a glossary of common terms. The heart of the guide consists in the detailed techniques, which range in difficulty from simple to complex. Symbols indicate precisely what is to be done and where to do it. There is, however, no particular attention given to styles, cuts, garments as a whole, etc. The author concentrates, instead, on the basics.

Sunset Children's Clothes & Toys. Menlo Park, CA: Lane, 1983. 96p. pap. $4.95 (646.4)

Following the usual highly illustrated Sunset approach to projects, this book offers directions for making various kinds of children's clothing. Each process or project is thoroughly depicted, usually in color. The same procedure is followed for toys.

Vogue Sewing. Rev. ed. New York: Harper, 1982. 510p. $24.95 (646.4)

A standard work, first published in 1970, this is concerned primarily with the style and construction of women's and men's clothing, although the emphasis is on the former. The assumption is that the reader is a novice, and there are detailed instructions at every point. In addition, the guide includes excellent, well-placed illustrations, including color photographs. The step-by-step tailoring procedures are supplemented by instructions and background material about fabrics, various types of needle sizes, sewing techniques, etc. There is even a worthwhile section on removing spots.

SHELLS. *See* Marine Life

SHELVES. *See* Carpentry; Woodworking

SHIPS, MODELS. *See* Models & Modelmaking

SHOPPING. *See* Catalogs; Consumer Education

SHORTHAND. *See* Typing & Shorthand

SHOW WINDOWS

Roth, Laszlo. **Display Design: An Introduction to Window Display, Point-of-Purchase, Posters, Signs and Signage, Sales Environments, and Exhibit Displays.** Englewood Cliffs, NJ: Prentice-Hall, 1983. 168p. $22.95; pap. $12.95 (659.1)

The subtitle explains the scope, but only careful reading demonstrates how well the subject is covered by Roth, an experienced teacher. The author takes a broad look at the numerous possibilities of commercial display and then narrows his discussion to particulars. He moves from an explanation of the countless materials and techniques available to the equal number of tools one can employ. Throughout there are photographs to support the discussion, and current reading lists are appended to most of the chapters. The appendixes include, among other things, a good list of suppliers. While the work is like a textbook, and somewhat esoteric, it is one of the few of its kind presently in print and up-to-date in its coverage. A first choice for those seeking ideas and instruction on everything from posters to window displays.

SILVER. *See* Antiques

SKATING

Fassi, Carlo, and Gregory Smith. **Figure Skating with Carlo Fassi.** New York: Scribner's, 1980. 180p. $17.95 (796.91)

One of the best of the guides to figure skating, this is written by the coach of numerous Olympic winners including Dorothy Hamill. The clear, straightforward explanations are useful for both the beginner and the advanced student. Particularly noteworthy are the large illustrations, which are closely tied to the text. Not only does Fassi show how to train and develop a certain type of skater, but he points out common errors. There are essential jumps and good explanations of free skating.

Fischler, Stan, and Shirley Fischler. **Everybody's Hockey Book.** New York: Scribner's, 1983. 370p. $22.50 (796.96)

One third of this guide is devoted to how-to-do-it information, which is some of the best, most up-to-date available. From equipment to fine points of the game, the authors cover every area of interest for someone trying to learn or improve on ice hockey. There is as much stress on individual exercise and conditioning as there is on the tactics employed. Team play, of course, is demonstrated as vital, and the ins and outs of such action are fully explored. Even the nonplaying fan will profit from and enjoy this part of the book. Less successful, yet interesting, are the early sections on the history of the game and the latter part devoted to rules.

Petkevich, John. **The Skater's Handbook.** New York: Scribner's, 1984. 224p. $14.95 (796.91)

Figure skating is the central focus here, and it is assumed that the reader is a would-be expert. This guide, by a former U.S. men's figure skating champion, is not for the novice. Instead, the author is concerned with what steps the experienced skater can take to become a champion. He is not so much interested in various techniques, liberally covered in other guides, as with steps one must take to ensure expert training. To this end, he discusses how to secure the services of a coach, what basic training programs should be undertaken, and various methods that have proven successful in his career. An added bonus is the considerable information on various skating organizations, equipment, clubs, rinks, journals, and just about anything else to round out the education of the skater.

Stephenson, Richard, and Theodore Clark. **The Ice Skater's Bible.** New York: Doubleday, 1982. 144p. pap. $5.95 (796.91)
   Opening with a short history of skating, the authors then move on to an elementary explanation of what equipment is needed. Next come the basics of instruction, from learning how to stay on one's feet to proper methods of stopping and turning. Once the elementary aspects of the sport have been covered, there follow specific chapters on specialized interests such as speed and figure skating and free skating. The text is clear and easy to follow—made even more so by the illustrations, which are found on almost every page.

Stoll, Sharon. **Roller Skating: Fundamentals and Techniques.** New York: Scribner's, 1983. 191p. pap. $9.95 (793.3)
   Working on the assumption that the reader knows nothing about roller skates, or even how to stay vertical while on them, the author offers a step-by-step approach to self-assurance and enjoyment. There are sections on how to choose the right skates, where to skate, and techniques involved with taking spills, gaining speed, turning, stopping, and even dancing. Useful photographs underline the main points.

SKIING

Abraham, Horst. **Skiing Right.** Boulder, CO: Johnson Books, 1983. 237p. pap. $12.95 (796.93)
   Of the numerous books on how to ski, this is one of the best. Written by an expert (an official of the Professional Ski Instructors of America) it draws on a tested theory that the right hemisphere of the brain can be used to improve skills. There are practical, day-by-day suggestions on how to become better at the sport. All of this is written with style and authority. While hardly for the beginner, it will be of great value for individuals who want to improve their skills. There are sections, too, on the history of the sport and on various teaching methods, and a directory of North American ski resorts.

Berry, William. **The Great North American Ski Book.** Rev. ed. New York: Scribner's, 1982. 471p. $24.95 (796.93)
   One of the more comprehensive books on the fine art of the slopes, this is in a second edition and is an updated version of the *America's Ski Book* (1973). The author used to be with *Ski* magazine, and he writes well as he thoroughly covers the topic. There seems to be absolutely nothing left out, and whether one is a beginner or an expert this would be a first place to turn for information and advice. After a discussion of equipment and its maintenance and various techniques of skiing, Berry considers (and informally grades) various resorts and slopes. He then turns to the subject of keeping fit for the sport, and even considers how to take care

of your car in the snow, explaining what to do in case of an accident, etc. There is a good index and numerous illustrations.

Caldwell, John. **Cross Country Skiing Today.** Brattleboro, VT: Stephen Greene Pr., 1977. 176p. $8.95; pap. $4.95 (796.9)

Covering all the basics from exercise, fitness, and nutrition to types of equipment and techniques of skiing, this is one of the best of numerous guides on the subject. (The "today" in the title is as descriptive now as when the book was published in 1977, and little of the information is dated.) Caldwell is an experienced writer who knows how and where to illustrate the text as well as how to explain things clearly and with enthusiasm. He gives detailed instructions on the best approaches to waxing, how to engage in day trips, things to avoid doing, and scores of other points, which cause some people to refer to this book as the "bible" of cross-country skiing.

Crawford-Currie, Ronald. **Cross Country Skiing.** New York: Van Nostrand, 1982. 160p. $19.95 (796.93)

A complete guide to the sport of cross-country skiing, this excels in the number of illustrations it provides—many in color—and the carefully written text. As fitness is the key to successful cross-country skiing, the book opens with an exercise schedule. Then comes the bad news about the cost of equipment and clothing—although the latter can be held to a minimum. The heart of the book is how to do cross-country skiing, and here the author assumes that the average beginner wants to see each move illustrated. That is literally accomplished by the line drawings and photographs accompanying the clearly written instructions. The book then considers related matters such as where to go, day trips, ideal tours, etc.

Flemmen, Asbjorn, and Olav Grosvold. **Teaching Children to Ski.** New York: Scribner's, 1983. 175p. pap. $9.95 (796.93)

Two experts explain why it is necessary to be extremely careful in teaching children how to ski. The basic message is to give the child as much space as is needed, and to limit the early instruction to essentials. The authors believe that too much emphasis on skills reduces the fun for the child and turns pleasure into a task. In the early part of the book, they explain how to teach the essentials. They then shift to actual cases and suggest what is to be done when a child refuses to do this or that, or simply cannot seem to master a maneuver. Each step is illustrated with line drawings of children skiing.

Masia, Seth. **The Ski Maintenance and Repair Handbook.** Chicago: Contemporary, 1982. 192p. pap. $7.95 (796.9)

How to do everything from taking care of your ski boots to general troubleshooting will be found in this book. The style is direct and the facts are accurate. Photographs illustrate the various types of alpine ski equipment discussed. Some of the material appeared earlier in *Ski* magazine, where the author is editor.

Shedden, John. **Skillful Skiing.** New York: Sterling, 1983. 126p. $12.95 (796.9)

The emphasis here is on illustration, and particularly the stop-motion shots of particular movements. These are accompanied by equally excellent diagrams showing the fundamentals of the downhill sport. The illustration-by-illustration technique seems particularly suited for someone who is not familiar with skiing. It is helpful, too, for the would-be expert who wishes to improve his or her style. In addition, there are the usual sections on equipment and a part devoted to exercise.

SOCCER

Hollander, Zander, ed. **American Encyclopedia of Soccer.** New York: Everest House, 1980. 540p. $29.95 (796.33)

An exhaustive work, this focuses primarily on the United States. Only limited space is given to the sections on world soccer. Aside from this fault, there is little to criticize. Players and fans will appreciate the rules of the game, but the primary interest of the editor and contributors is on history, prominent players, and detailed records. Most of the emphasis is on professional soccer, although there is a good history (and records) of the college scene. A particular strength: biographies of over 2,000 players. There are excellent illustrations.

Widdows, Richard. **The Arco Book of Soccer Techniques and Tactics.** New York: Arco, 1984. 192p. $16.95 (796.33)

The frustration and the natural loneliness of the goalkeeper are not considered, but the author does have an excellent section on the finer points of the goalkeeper's art. In fact, he insists that this is the pivotal point of a good defense, and requires more than an individual effort—it requires a team in full support. It is this attention to detail that makes Widdows such a good guide to the sport. While it is assumed that the reader has some knowledge of soccer, nothing is really left to chance. Each player's responsibility and major schemes of attack and defense are explained. There are numerous photographs, many in color, as well as line drawings to underline the comments and suggestions. Some of it looks easier than it is, e.g., heading and various forms of dribbling. While written for would-be players, the book will be of almost equal interest to fans, who may gain a new appreciation of the goalkeeper as well as the problems of a corner kick.

Yannis, Alex. **Inside Soccer: The Complete Book of Soccer for Spectators, Players and Coaches.** New York: McGraw-Hill, 1980. 305p. $9.95 (796.3)

For anyone who wants to learn basic soccer principles, this well-illustrated guide should be a first choice. The opening sections discuss the history of the game and the status of both professional and amateur teams in the United States. The heart of the manual is the four chapters explaining steps in mastering the game, how soccer is coached, and what to look for as a spectator. The writing style is good, and all terms are clearly defined. While not for the player with experience, this is a fine guide for the beginner.

SOFTBALL. See Baseball

SOFTWARE. See Computers—Programming & Software

SOLAR & WIND POWER
  See also Homes—Energy Conservation

Carter, Joe, ed. **Solarizing Your Present Home: Practical Solar Heating Systems You Can Build.** Emmaus, PA: Rodale, 1981. 671p. $24.95 (643.1)

This is an encyclopedic approach to solar heating for the individual home. Enough information is given for anyone to decide whether to go ahead with the project, its probable cost, and what it is likely to do in the way of saving energy. The explanations are clear and precise, and often detailed enough to allow the near expert to carry out the project without much outside help. Almost all areas are covered, including greenhouses. The various types of heating units described range from standard hot water systems to space heaters. The author establishes formulas and methods that the reader can use to determine whether solar heat is practical for a given situation. There are helpful tables and charts that compare different methods and procedures. Instructions concentrate on remodeling an existing home, but most of the information is applicable to new home construction.

Keisling, Bill. **The Homeowner's Handbook of Solar Water Heating Systems.** Emmaus, PA: Rodale, 1983. 256p. $16.95; pap. $12.95 (696.6)

Most books on solar water heating concentrate on the home. This certainly does that, including as it does good descriptions of various simple-to-complex systems of great variety in cost. There are useful instructions on how to figure what is best for a given situation. While more briefly treated, the distinctive element of the guide, and one that sets it off from others, is its guidance in building or buying systems to heat water in a swimming pool, hot tub, or spa. The author develops economical ways of cutting costs by choosing the proper approach for a given situation. There is nothing particularly new here, but the scope is wider than that in most titles of this type, and the illustrations are much above average. This would be a good secondary title, and a first for someone with more than home heating in mind.

Marier, Donald. **Wind Power for the Homeowner.** Emmaus, PA: Rodale, 1981. 368p. $16.95; pap. $10.95 (621.31)

The editor of the periodical *Alternative Sources of Energy* gives all the basic information a beginner will need when he or she contemplates conversion to wind energy. Here is accurate data on types of equipment, how they are installed, probable costs, maintenance, and possible legal problems. The author is particularly good in his analysis of different parts of the average wind power operation. The illustrations suit the text.

Park, Jack. **The Wind Power Book.** New York: Van Nostrand, 1981. 254p. $19.95; pap. $11.95 (621.4)

How much does it cost to set up a wind power system for an average home or a larger type of structure? What kinds of materials are available? What are the problems of construction, site selection, and maintenance? These and scores of other questions are answered clearly, and in detail, in this, the best of the how-to-do-it books for wind power. It is the best because the author explains the difficulties involved and then makes concrete suggestions for trying one approach, and then another, until the particular problem is resolved. There is, for example, a list of average wind speeds in various parts of the United States. Whether the reader is concerned with generating electricity or pumping water by wind power, the information is all here. There are numerous illustrations, as well as an introduction by Robert Redford.

Reif, Daniel. **Passive Solar Water Heaters: How to Design and Build a Batch System.** Andover, MA: Brick House, 1983. 190p. $17.95; pap. $12.95 (696.6)

One of the best books available on the subject, this is detailed and relatively easy to follow (easy, that is, if the reader has some experience in construction; it is not for the beginner). The author opens with a short history of the batch system, and then explains how to choose the best site to ensure the maximum amount of heat and, of course, sun. There are numerous tables that support and explain the author's theory that the water tank itself should be a part of the system and placed in the path of the sun, not off to one side. The book includes illustrations, detailed plans, and exceptionally clear instructions.

U.S. Department of Health. **Wind Power and Windmills.** Washington, DC: GPO, 1980. 12p. $1.25 (A1.68:1256)

A quick overview of wind power, this pamphlet explains the benefits and drawbacks of one of the world's oldest power sources. Written for the layperson, it includes data on research up to 1980.

U.S. Department of Housing and Urban Development. **Hot Water from the Sun.** Washington, DC: GPO, 1980. 125p. $4.75 (HH1.6/3:Su7)

A good overview of solar water heating, this offers the consumer various plans and methods of capturing solar energy. The systems are explained, and there is a step-by-step method of figuring costs and potential savings. Methods of installation, in new or existing structures, are outlined.

U.S. National Aeronautics and Space Administration. **Capturing Energy from the Wind.** Washington, DC: GPO, 1982. 84p. pap. $6 (NASI21:455)

While not a how-to-do-it guide, this can be useful for anyone interested in windmill construction. The compilers offer a color-illustrated panorama of current (as of 1982) developments in the use of wind-turned power stations. There is also a brief history of the subject.

SOUPS. *See* Cooking

SPELUNKING. *See* Caving

SPORTS
   See also Baseball; Basketball; Bodybuilding; Bowling; Caving; Falconry; Fencing; Gambling & Betting; Games; Golf; Gymnastics; Judo & Karate & Aikido; Mountaineering; Scuba Diving; Skating; Skiing; Soccer; Tennis

Arnot, Robert, and Charles Gaines. **Sportselection.** New York: Viking, 1984. 288p. $17.95 (613.1)

Dr. Arnot, a specialist in sports medicine, believes everyone has the physical and psychological makeup to fit comfortably into some sport. The point of the book is to match the reader with the proper sport. Seven sports are covered—tennis, windsurfing, swimming, running, skiing (downhill and cross-country), and cycling. There are illustrated physical tests the reader can take to find the ideal sport. In addition, the authors offer background material to aid in making a choice. Some sports, such as cycling and swimming, are for "virtually everyone." Others, such as skiing, require a high degree of agility. The book ends with a discussion of how to start a child out in the right sport. All of this is objective and scientifically accurate, but it does not answer the question about the person who is simply too lazy to exercise. Still, for those who are looking for the ideal sport/exercise, this is the book.

Bell, Keith. **Championship Thinking: The Athlete's Guide to Winning Performance in All Sports.** Englewood Cliffs, NJ: Prentice-Hall, 1983. 188p. $17.95; pap. $8.95 (796.01)

The power of positive thought is a cliché, yet the author believes that it is all-important, as the subtitle states. Of course, he goes considerably beyond that well-known phrase to demonstrate precisely what steps an athlete must take to prepare for a contest. An athlete himself, as well as a psychologist, Bell knows the various approaches one can use to steady the nerves, kill anxiety, and build self-confidence. Each of these steps is explained, but in general the author is concerned with the ability of the individual to control and channel thought. This allows for relaxation and a realistic appraisal of oneself. Bell is wise enough not to promise complete success for every reader, and he avoids technical terms and jargon. The result is a valuable and intelligent guide.

Bennett, James, and James Pravitz. **The Miracle of Sports Psychology.** Englewood Cliffs, NJ: Prentice-Hall, 1982. 165p. $16.95; pap. $7.95 (796.01)

The psychological factors are as important, if not more important, as the physical factors in producing a winning team or individual. So argue these authors, who then offer a step-by-step program for the average athlete who wishes to be in top mental form for any sport. The various procedures and exercises range from simple relaxation techniques to more involved training of the subconscious. All of this is presented in an authoritative yet easy-to-understand way. Many of the lessons are as applicable to the layperson as to the sports figure.

Brancazio, Peter. **Sportscience: Physical Laws and Optimum Performance.** New York: Simon & Schuster, 1984. 400p. $17.95 (612.76)

According to the author, an astrophysicist, there are laws governing sports that one can master to win. It is not simply chance, or even physical skill, but natural laws or physics at play. The book is divided by these laws, from velocity to inertia, and under each large division there are hints and subdivisions that consider individual effort. If one believes in the adaptation of physical forces to sports, the book may be valuable. Others can simply enjoy it for the new twist and quite good tips on, for example, improving running and jogging.

Diagram Group. **The Rule Book.** New York: St. Martin's, 1983. 430p. $9.95 (796.03)

This offers a capsule listing of rules and regulations for the world's basic sports. Arranged alphabetically by name of the sport or game, each entry includes a number of line drawings that underline and clarify the points. Coverage is worldwide and includes such basics as the playing area or space needed, types of equipment, number of players, methods of scoring, etc. While the information is often too brief for sticky situations, it is sufficient to give the reader an excellent notion of what is involved. *Note:* An earlier version of this, and still quite suitable, is *Rules of the Game* (1974); *The Official World Encyclopedia of Sports and Games* (1979) is also useful.

Dolan, Edward. **Calling the Play: A Beginner's Guide to Amateur Sports Officiating.** New York: Atheneum, 1982. 232p. $14.95 (796)

Examining the rules of 15 major sports, the author points out the necessity for the beginning official not only to appreciate the rules but to develop a sense of control and authority. Written for the novice, the guide clearly explains the basics, from how and where to stand to various techniques of calling a particular move. This combination of intuition, mechanics, and common sense sets the guide apart from many of its type. It will help anyone develop into a good and knowledgeable official.

Haas, Robert. **Eat to Win: The Sports Nutrition Bible.** New York: Rawson Wade, 1983. 267p. $14.95 (613.2)

A best-seller, this is by a nutritionist who has worked with some of the world's leading athletes. As might be expected, Haas believes the key to success in sports is a well-balanced diet with a particular emphasis on complex carbohydrates. These carbohydrates are quickly converted into energy, which helps the active athlete. The precise rules for the diet depend on individual blood chemistry, and the author recommends that the reader get a blood test before starting on this diet. There are recipes and menus as well. The important point is that the diet is for people who are exceptionally active. The less active might find it accomplishes the opposite effect, i.e., they would put on weight.

Menke, Frank. **The Encyclopedia of Sports.** San Diego: Barnes, 1939–   . Irreg. 6th ed., 1978. 1,132p. $30 (796.03)

Considered a standard work in the field of sports, this is outstanding on several counts. First, it has numerous illustrations and clear descriptions of the world's sports. Second, it has over 100 pages devoted to records and statistics. Third, there is precise information on the rules, history, and methods of play in numerous sports. The drawback is that it does not cover some modern activities, so it is in need of a further revision. Still, for basic data over a wide area, this cannot be beat.

Schrier, Eric, and William Allman, eds. **The Science in Sports.** New York: Scribner's, 1984. 190p. $14.95 (613.7)

Not a how-to-do-it book, but a how-it-is-done guide that may, if only indirectly, help someone play better in various sports. Taken from *Science 84* magazine, there are close to 40 explanations about peculiar aspects of play. Under four broad subject headings, the authors consider such matters as how to make a knuckleball dance and how, when firing a gun, one can fire with the heartbeat, thus ensuring more accuracy. There are numerous other discussions of such things as diet, drink, panic, and various skills required for particular athletic efforts. Highly readable, and, if nothing else, quite entertaining.

Smith, Nathan, et al. **Kid Sports: A Survival Guide for Parents.** Reading, MA: Addison-Wesley, 1983. 229p. $16; pap. $8.25 (796.01)

Sports for children pose a number of health problems and sometimes result in an overly developed competitive spirit. Questions about such things, along with sound suggestions, are offered by the author, a doctor, and his coauthors, who are experts in sports. The writers give specific advice on how to keep the child active, but safe and well. They carry the child from early sports to the time when a college may be bidding for his or her services. Motives of both children and parents are analyzed in the early chapters, followed by advice on the natural kinds of sports for children at different ages and stages of physical development. There are sections and chapters on nutrition, training, injuries, and stress. For teen-agers, parents, and coaches, there is a fine discussion of drugs, recruiting, natural competitive spirit, and the like.

Syer, John, and Christopher Connolly. **Sporting Body, Sporting Mind: An Athlete's Guide to Mental Training.** New York: Cambridge University Pr., 1984. 160p. $13.95; pap. $5.95 (796)

What is the best mental state to be in to win at a sport? How does one develop and maintain such a state? To answer these and related questions, the authors offer a practical guide to mental training for anyone in any type of competitive sports. They put great stress on the individual's recognizing strengths and weaknesses, and developing the former while learning to repress the latter. There are exercises in each chapter to deal with such things as relaxation and concentration, anxiety and depression, building the will to win, etc. There are good photographs to support the argument.

U.S. Department of Health. **Children and Youth in Action: Physical Activities and Sports.** Washington, DC: GPO, 1980. 51p. $3.50 (HE23.1002:C43/2)

How can we encourage and help a child in sports and other physical activities? The answer is here. Suggestions are made (for different ages from five into the teens) involving the child in various physical activities. Both general fitness and recreational aspects are considered. There are good sections on how to overcome sex stereotypes, and on methods of judging various sports.

STAMPS

Mackay, James. **Stamp Collecting.** New York: Van Nostrand, 1983. 80p. $13.95 (769.56)

Although written from a British standpoint (the author was formerly curator of the British Museum's philatelic collections), this is a solid, basic guide for the beginner. It assumes that the reader knows little or nothing about collecting. After a short history of stamps, Mackay shows how to approach both a specific and a general type of collection. Tips on everything from purchasing stamps to placing them in an album are given in a clear, precise style. The illustrations are excellent, and most are in color.

Schwarz, Ted. **Beginner's Guide to Stamp Collecting.** New York: Arco, 1983. 188p. $14.95; pap. $8.95 (769.56)

An expert on stamps explains that the only real requirement in becoming a collector is enthusiasm and a generous capacity for learning. With that, he discusses the variations in evaluating, purchasing, and selling stamps. There is a good and necessary section on the various methods of mounting and storing them. The coverage is international, although many of the examples are drawn from the

United States. The need to concentrate on a given subject area, country, or time period is stressed, and there are sections on organizations devoted to the hobby. The historical aspect of stamps is less well treated, but there is a useful list of publications to aid the collector. Suitable for all ages.

Scott Standard Postage Stamp Catalogue. New York: Scott, 1868–   . Annual. 1984 ed., 4 vols. $20 ea. (769)

First published over 100 years ago, this is by far the most important, the most basic of the numerous stamp catalogs. It is the first place to turn in order to identify and learn about the stamps of the world. Each entry briefly indicates the color, shape, and dimensions of the stamp, and the listings are illustrated. This four-volume annual guide is also used to gain an idea of a stamp's estimated value, even though values differ wildly and it should be stressed that the price given is only an estimate based on previous sales. The coverage is international. Another much-used annual from the same publisher is *Scott Specialized Catalogue of United States Stamps* (1923–   , annual).

U.S. Postal Service. **United States Postage Stamps.** Washington, DC: GPO, 1970. 287p. $8.50. Supplements, 1972–1984, 40–60p., $4–$5 ea. (P4.10:970)

This basic guide is an illustrated description of all U.S. postage and special services stamps issued to 1970. The supplements carry the guide through 1983. All are in loose-leaf pages with three-ring punch.

Young, Walter. **Stamp Collecting A to Z.** San Diego: Barnes, 1981. 216p. $15 (737)

Just about everything you ever wanted to know about stamp collecting is included in this basic guide. In five sections, the author discusses such things as topics for collecting stamps, definitions of terms, historical studies, and philatelic agencies in various countries. There are about 400 different essays and articles in the reader section, and here the author explores various aspects of collecting. There is, for example, background on stamps as well as material on purchasing and selling stamps, preservation, insurance, and the like. There are numerous, useful illustrations and a section on collecting stamps by topics and subjects as opposed to the normal procedure of building around a country or a time frame. There is a slight English bias, but not enough to matter. While most of this is much too basic for the experienced collector, it is an excellent starting point for the beginner.

STAMPS, RUBBER

Thomson, George L. **Rubber Stamps and How to Make Them.** New York: Pantheon, 1982. 95p. pap. $5.95 (681.6)

Rubber stamps are both a collecting mania and an art medium. Here Thomson devotes himself to the artistic side, and gives general directions for making rubber stamps. On the whole, he is more concerned with how to use the stamps in an artistic, decorative way and less involved with their construction. His examples are almost exclusively from medieval sources such as the *Book of Kells* and natural designs of the tenth through fourteenth centuries. More detail on the construction of stamps would have been useful, but this is at least a beginning.

STOVES. *See* Fireplaces & Stoves

SURVIVAL TECHNIQUES (WILDERNESS)

Brown, Tom, and Brandt Morgan. **Tom Brown's Field Guide to Wilderness Survival.** New York: Berkley, 1983. 287p. pap. $6.95 (613.6)
   What can you do when you are lost in the woods? What steps should you take if you are injured out-of-doors and no help is immediately available? These and countless other emergencies are discussed in this excellent guide to survival in the wilderness. The approach is to start with general possibilities and move to particular behaviors. Each section is concerned with attitude, food, equipment, etc. The author instructs the reader in the necessary skills required for such activities as trapping animals and fighting the cold. The book is well written and based on Brown's extensive knowledge of, and respect for, the wilderness.

Simer, Peter, and John Sullivan. **The National Outdoor Leadership School's Wilderness Guide.** New York: Simon & Schuster, 1983. 345p. $16.95; pap. $8.95 (796.51)
   This guide shows the reader how to survive and enjoy life in the backwoods. It is modeled after courses taught in this famous Wyoming school, and, reading along, one understands why the school has such a good reputation. The advice is as reliable as it is comprehensive, and nothing is left to chance. If you want to know the best type of clothing for certain conditions, or the good and bad points about boots, this is the place to turn. In addition to an intelligent discussion of equipment, there are words of wisdom on everything from reading a compass to cooking over a fire.

U.S. Department of Defense. **Survival, Evasion and Escape.** Washington, DC: GPO, 1976. 431p. $9 (D101.20:21-76/2)
   This is an army technical and field manual designed for military personnel, but it is extremely useful for anyone who might be lost in a desolate area. Included are discussions of how to obtain food, how to protect oneself against extreme heat or cold, how to find one's way to civilization by the stars, how to build rafts and fires, and even what to do in case of an attack by a shark. As a survival manual this is hard to beat, and it is in no way dated. It not only instructs, but should delight almost anyone interested in the outdoors.

TAILORING. *See* Sewing

TAXIDERMY

McFall, Waddy. **Taxidermy Step by Step.** Piscataway, NJ: Winchester Pr., 1975. 230p. $12.95 (579)
   For the beginner, this is a step-by-step journey through the basics of taxidermy. The author begins with specimen collection, turns to the tools and methods employed in the profession, and then considers the steps in the preparation of the specimen. There is a section devoted to tanning. Mounting is always a problem for beginners, and this is explained in some detail. The author introduces simple

projects, but then gradually turns to more involved work. Explanations are clear and the illustrations adequate.

TEA

Sen, Soshitsu. **Tea Life, Tea Mind.** New York: Weatherhill, 1979. 95p. pap. $7.50 (394.1)

The best brief book available on the Japanese tea ceremony, this offers both directions as to how it is carried out and an idea of the philosophical-religious importance of the event. The author is a famous tea master who offers just enough biographical information to set the ceremony in proper context. The book is well and carefully written.

TELEPHONE

Clifford, Martin. **Your Telephone: Operation, Selection and Installation.** Indianapolis, IN: Sams, 1983. 336p. pap. $13.95 (621.386)

Everything anyone would want to know about the telephone—and more—is found in this well-organized guide. Published at the time of the AT&T breakup, the book begins with an explanation of why users can now own their telephones. What does one get from the purchase? Clifford shows precisely, with a clear explanation of the average phone's basic parts, and goes on to explain the many different types of phones. There are sections on home installation, accompanied by useful drawings and photographs. The remainder of the guide may not be as useful to most people, covering such things as how to ensure privacy, the use of phones in cars and boats, and the newer technologies.

Cox, Wesley. **Kiss Ma Bell Good-Bye: How to Install Your Own Telephones, Extensions & Accessories.** New York: Crown, 1983. 128p. pap. $4.95 (621.38)

By now almost everyone knows that Ma Bell no longer has a monopoly on telephones and that anyone can own his or her telephone. The question remains: How can these phones and other related equipment be safely installed? The answer, even for the most physically awkward, is contained in this manual. Here, the author lists precisely what is needed, down to the specific tools (which are minimal). He explains how to install the phone and considers numerous accessories such as answering machines and connections to a computer. There is a good concluding section on what to look for when the phone stops functioning. The illustrations are helpful and augment the text, which is easy to follow.

TELESCOPES. *See* Astronomy

TELEVISION

Cohen, Henry, and Bruce Apar. **The Home Video Survival Guide.** New York: Amphoto, 1983. 192p. pap. $9.95 (621.38)

The authors' own *Video* magazine as well as *Consumer Reports* give current buying information on video equipment, but this is a summary (as of early 1983) of the best on the market. Where the book excels, and where it remains timeless, is in the good advice on what to look for (and what to avoid) in a typical video equipment safari. There are sections, too, on getting everything possible out of existing equipment. Well written and easy to follow, this is a book for almost anyone with a video investment.

David, Ed. **The Intelligent Idiot's Guide to Getting the Most Out of Your Home Video.** Philadelphia, PA: Running Pr., 1983. 219p. $19.50; pap. $8.95 (621.38)

The obvious flaw 'in any book that describes, explains, and advises on home electronic equipment is that it soon becomes dated. The problem exists here, but in a limited way. The primary focus is on the broad application of video in the home, and what it can or cannot do for the average nonelectronic whiz. Most of the advice will be applicable for years. The author deals with such basics as the best places to shop for equipment, what types of firms to avoid, and tips on basic technical matters. Among the topics considered are the advantages and disadvantages of VHS and Beta, connecting television to cable, the basics of video photography and equipment, cleaning tips, videotapes and accessories, etc. A concluding section lists addresses and phone numbers of major equipment suppliers. This kind of advice, which is offered in a relaxed, easy-to-understand fashion, is laced with personal opinions about various kinds of equipment. Granted, data on specific brand names may change, but the good-neighbor approach of the author and the wide scope of his treatment should ensure a long and useful life for this manual.

Dunton, Mark, and David Owen. **The Complete Video Handbook.** New York: Random House, 1982. 224p. $19.95 (621.38)

While particulars of this guide will quickly date, the general overview and historical and technical explanations are likely to be of value for many years. The authors offer a thorough survey of videocassette recorders. Each model, component, and related piece of equipment is discussed, explained, and analyzed. Of particular value are the sections devoted to home video production, camera and television functions, and video skills. All of the main points are well illustrated.

Easton, Anthony. **The Home Satellite TV Book: How to Put the World in Your Backyard.** New York: Harper, 1982. 380p. $16.95; pap. $10.95 (621.38)

How do you put together a home satellite TV system? The answer is given here, at least for anyone with about $3,000 to spend on the necessary equipment. The author also presupposes on the part of the reader at least some knowledge of electronics. With that, one may proceed to follow his specific instructions and recommendations for everything from selecting the proper-size dish to antenna placement. Less useful are the suggestions on how to establish a dealership. The book includes current (as of 1982) Federal Communications Commission (FCC) regulations and a list of suppliers and transmitting signals. This field changes rapidly, and technical developments should be double-checked in current periodicals and at a dealer's outlet.

Goodman, Robert. **Maintaining and Repairing Videocassette Recorders.** Blue Ridge Summit, PA: TAB, 1983. 406p. $21.95; pap. $14.95 (621.38)

Thanks to good illustrations and direct, easy-to-follow instructions, a person with mechanical aptitude will be able to repair any of the basic brand-name VCRs by using this guide. (Actually, it will be of most value to the trained expert, although the explanations are at such a level that even an amateur with patience will be able to carry out the needed repairs.) Both Beta and VHS formats are considered. The author gives the necessary background on each type of machine and then explains the various types of tests needed to arrive at conclusions about the difficulties. The separate parts are analyzed in terms of what happens when a component does not function and how it can be repaired. The last chapters consider specific brand names, section by section.

Jolly, Brad. **Videotaping Local History.** Nashville, TN: American Association for State and Local History, 1982. 160p. pap. $11.95 (791.4)

Thanks to videotape, it is now possible to both see and hear individuals who can provide a wealth of information on local history. How to set up such an interview, and how to purchase, service, and use the right equipment are discussed in detail. Jolly also considers the ins and outs of actually capturing local history on tape and even how to establish a video library. There are good illustrations, and the writing is clear.

U.S. Federal Communications Commission. **How to Identify and Resolve Radio-TV Interference Problems.** Washington, DC: GPO, 1982. 31p. $5 (CC1.74/-In 8)

An illustrated guide, this shows various problems of reception and then suggests methods of improving the broadcast or cutting out the interference completely. Some knowledge of electronics on the reader's part is taken for granted, but generally the guide will be useful for the amateur.

Utz, Peter. **The Complete Home Video Book: A Source of Information Essential to the Video Enthusiast.** Englewood Cliffs, NJ: Spectrum/Prentice-Hall, 1983. 608p. $29.95 set; also available in paper (778.59)

The title is correct. This is the most "complete" book available on home video as of early 1984, and it promises to remain such for some time to come. Granted, the information on specific technologies and products will change, but the general introduction and the background data so necessary for an appreciation of the subject will remain fairly constant. The book is divided into two sections. The first explains in considerable detail the variations in the different types of video, and how to select and evaluate each for a particular need. There is specific information on how to set up the equipment and then how to operate it efficiently. The second part, which is more technical, has information on the care and maintenance of the various units. There is also material on the artistic use of the machines. Few people will want to read both sections in full, but the index allows rapid consultation, and the work is more of an encyclopedia than a basic how-to-do-it guide.

TELEVISION PHOTOGRAPHY. See Photography—Motion Pictures & Television

TENNIS

Cath, Stanley H., et al. **Love and Hate on the Tennis Court.** New York: Scribner's, 1977. 192p. $7.95 (796.3)

While issued in 1977, this remains a tennis classic and is one of the best of many works written on winning through a psychological appreciation of oneself and one's opponent. The authors (several players and psychiatrists) suggest that tennis play reveals the true personality of the players. The authors show how the game is played by different types who stress aggression, humor, or even cheating. They write in a friendly, informative, relaxed style and most players could not help but gain from reading the various essays. Not all action, of course, is thought to be a psychological extension of the player's personality, and sensible advice is given on the other aspects of the game. See also John McPhee's *Levels of the Game* (Farrar, 1969).

MacCurdy, Doug, and Shawn Tully. **Sports Illustrated Tennis.** New York: Lippincott, 1980. 155p. $8.95; pap. $5.95 (796.34)

This is a typical *Sports Illustrated* guide, with abundant illustrations and step-by-step instructions on the fundamentals of tennis. The strength of the manual is in the advice it gives on various types of serves and strokes. There are the usual instructions and rules for both singles and doubles.

Richmond, Barrie, and Jane Carley. **Total Tennis: The Mind Body Method.** New York: Macmillan, 1980. 180p. $9.95 (796.34)

Among scores of books on tennis, this is one of the best because it takes into consideration all aspects of the game, from mind set to physical training. It differs from a book on tennis psychology such as Cath's (q.v.) in that there is considerable time spent on teaching the essentials of the game. What is more, the instructions are as applicable to children and young people as they are to adults. There are two added bonuses: One part analyzes different basic types of instruction by a set of experts; another part considers the psychological makeup of relatively famous tennis stars.

Seixas, Vic. **Prime Time Tennis.** New York: Scribner's, 1983. 256p. $14.95 (796.34)

By "prime time" the author means tennis players over 40. He correctly assumes that the game is different for this group than it is for youngsters. He pays particular attention to compensating for lost muscle and reflex actions. The secret is style, or a modification of style. Various approaches are considered and the reader is left to take what specific path seems best. There are the usual basic suggestions on how to play the game, what equipment to use, exercise, etc. In addition, the player-author counterpoints his advice with stories of great matches and tennis stars, and general comments. The illustrations are good.

Shannon, Bill. **United States Tennis Association Official Encyclopedia of Tennis.** 3rd ed. New York: Harper, 1981. 558p. $25 (796.34)

The United States Tennis Association sponsors this authoritative and comprehensive encyclopedia, which is updated every two or three years. Here is almost everything anyone would want to know about tennis, e.g., biographies, history, notes on equipment, rules, records of major players, championship matches, and much more. While the focus is on U.S. tennis, there is some attention given to the sport in other countries, particularly in the biographical sketches and in reports on major matches. This is adequately illustrated, and there is a good index.

Talbert, William, and Bruce Old. **Tennis Tactics: Singles and Doubles.** New York: Harper, 1983. 192p. $16.95 (796.34)

The authors believe strongly in the psychological aspects of tennis, and while not discounting the importance of physical skills, claim that all things being equal, the better player will be the one who understands the subtleties of the serve or an angle shot. It is knowing when and where as much as how to do it, and knowing, too, one's own limitations and strengths. Along the way there are some basic tennis lessons, but primarily this book is for the experienced player who wants to improve his or her game. As the U.S. Open chairman (not champion) at the time of the book's publication, Talbert knows of what he writes.

THEATER

Cook, Philip. **How to Enjoy Theatre.** Topsfield, MA: Merrimack, 1984. 192p. $15 (792)

As with any art form, familiarity is the key to appreciation of theater. Cook grants this but goes much further. He provides an easy-to-follow, extremely well-written capsule history of the theater. The emphasis is on England, where this book was first published. He covers the United States and the continent too, but more briefly. Cook's major contribution is his step-by-step approach to going to a play. He explains what the reader should know about basics such as the play itself, acting, and set design. He even dares to offer suggestions about what constitutes good and bad acting. There are many excellent illustrations throughout this extremely useful and intelligent guide. A first choice for beginners, it will also be of help to veterans, although not all will necessarily agree with Cook's points about acting and direction.

Corson, Richard. **Stage Makeup.** Englewood Cliffs, NJ: Prentice-Hall, 1981. 1942– . Irreg. 1981 ed., 420p. $28.95 (792)

Written for both the actor and the makeup person, this is a basic guide to the subject, and one that is often updated. While published as a textbook, it can be used by nonprofessionals and amateur actors who may be interested only in various parts of the book. Essentially, it explains the different steps in routine makeup procedures, and then moves into various creative innovations. Techniques and materials are carefully considered, and there are numerous illustrations.

Gillette, A. S. **Stage Scenery.** New York: Harper, 1959– . Irreg. 1981 ed., 440p. $21.95 (792)

A detailed, professional guide, this can be used by amateurs and experts alike. Often updated, it includes basic information on all aspects of scenery, including construction and rigging. The focus is on making and manipulating scenery, not on its design. In fact, there is a section dealing with how the person in charge of stage scenery interacts with the set designer. Other parts consider the relationship of stagehands and supervisors with the director and with one another. Still, most of the emphasis (and, ultimately, the value) is on the actual construction of sets. The guide is well illustrated and the directions, although technical at times, are relatively easy to follow.

Green, Joann. **The Small Theatre Handbook: A Guide to Management and Production.** Cambridge, MA: Harvard Common Pr., 1981. 163p. $11.95; pap. $8.95 (792)

How do you establish, maintain, and develop a theater company? The answers are given here, at least for the small company, defined as one with a budget of less than $100,000 a year. (Much of the advice is applicable to amateurs as well as to professionals with limited funding.) The best sections of this book, written by a former small theater artistic director, are those concerned with the basics of management, organization, and tours. There are numerous illustrations and sample documents. The writing style is excellent and the advice realistic.

Ingham, Rosemary, and Liz Covey. **The Costume Designer's Handbook.** Englewood Cliffs, NJ: Prentice-Hall, 1983. 264p. $24.95; pap. $12.95 (792.02)

A comprehensive guide "for amateurs and professionals," this is a basic explanation of what is needed to produce costumes. The reader is carried step by step from the original script to early sketches and to the final costume. There are profuse illustrations with line drawings and superior photographs. How to achieve the best costume for the particular production is discussed in detail. Useful additions are the guide to major sources of supplies in large cities and suggested readings. The eight chapters are among the best written on the subject and serve as an excellent introduction to costume design.

Loeschke, Maravene. **All about Mime: Understanding and Performing the Expressive Silence.** Englewood Cliffs, NJ: Prentice-Hall, 1982. 208p. $17.95; pap. $8.95 (792.3)

One of the best books on learning mime, this offers step-by-step instructions for the beginner, as well as a good history of the acting form. The various approaches, from the French, which is most familiar to Americans, to the Asian are explored and explained. The author considers basics such as the proper way to walk, use of the hands, and facial expressions. Various types of mime solos are discussed, as well. In fact, almost every conceivable aspect of the form is considered, and it is all done in a clear, comprehensible fashion.

TOOLS
See also Carpentry; Woodworking

Geary, Don. **How to Sharpen Anything.** Blue Ridge Summit, PA: TAB, 1983. 213p. $19.95; pap. $12.95 (621.9)

The title explains it all—and here one finds instructions on sharpening knives, lawn mowers, axes, saws, pruning equipment, and even fish hooks, to pick out a few of the scores of items covered. Specific advice is given for each, along with what is needed by way of equipment, from the usual grindstone to machines found in the average home workshop. Illustrations are included, as well as the usual cautionary notes on avoiding accidents.

Watson, Aldren. **Hand Tools: Their Ways & Workings.** New York: Norton, 1982. 424p. $29.95 (684.08)

Before you can properly learn how to use a tool, you should understand precisely what it will and will not do—or so believes the author of this fascinating guide. Using his own accurate illustrations, he carefully describes each tool and tells how it is employed. There are precise directions on what to do with each tool, as well as tricks of the trade that make the work much easier. The book ends with information on toolmakers and suppliers, and even a plan for a compact workbench.

TOYS

See also Antiques; Handicrafts

Bialosky, Peggy. **The Teddy Bear Catalog.** New York: Workman, 1981. 223p. pap. $4.95 (688.7)

Both a price list and a catalog of teddy bears manufactured from the turn of the century to 1980, this is as much fun to look through as to use. There are numerous photographs, and while not always as good as they might be, they at least show the variety in the friendly bear's bearing. Each type of animal is described, and there are sections on collecting and repair and even a history of the beast.

Bialosky, Peggy, et al. **How to Make Your Own Teddy Bear.** New York: Workman, 1983. 111p. $14.95; pap. $7.95 (688.72)

Here are full-size patterns, with precise instructions on construction and materials, for making various types and sizes of teddy bears. The basic interest is in papa, mama, and baby girl bears. The guidelines are accompanied by black-and-white photographs. All of this requires more than a passing affection for the stuffed animals because, in addition to instructions, there are numerous sections on everything from naming a bear to casting a bear horoscope. This is not everyone's idea of a choice interest, but for those captured by the animal, this guide, along with Bialosky's *Teddy Bear Catalog* (q.v.), is required reading.

Blizzard, Richard. **Blizzard's Wonderful Wooden Toys.** New York: Sterling, 1983. 224p. pap. $9.95 (745.592)

From sandboxes to models, Blizzard offers the reader excellent verbal and illustrated plans for the construction of children's toys. He is particularly good at the out-of-the-ordinary, e.g., a rocking dog. While some of these can be constructed by the beginner, most presuppose a knowledge of woodworking and carpentry. The book was originally issued in England, but it offers no difficulty for American users.

Brann, Donald. **Toymaking: Children's Furniture Simplified.** Rev. ed. Briarcliff Manor, NY: Easi Bild Directions, 1982. 226p. pap. $6.95 (745.59)

Full-size, detailed patterns are featured in this extremely clear and easy-to-follow guide to constructing scores of wooden toys and some furniture. The projects vary in difficulty, but most can be completed by high school students and adults. The patterns may not always be imaginative, but they are certainly among the best around in terms of total detail.

Burtt, Kent, and Karen Kalkstein. **Smart Toys: For Babies from Birth to Two.** New York: Harper, 1981. 166p. pap. $8.95 (649.55)

Safe, inexpensive, and sure to enchant the child—that is the promise of these 77 different toys and play items that can be made by almost anyone. The materials are things found around the home, although here and there one may have to purchase something. The instructions, accompanied by illustrations, show how to make the toys. The arrangement is by age group, and there is an explanation of what types of playthings a child is likely to enjoy within that age group.

Fraser, Peter. **Puppets and Puppetry.** New York: Stein & Day, 1982. 168p. $16.95 (745.59)

While many people consider puppets and puppetry to be an art form as much for adults as for children, here the focus is on the basics without too much consideration of the age argument. Fraser shows how to design and construct simple puppets. These vary in size and type, although most of the emphasis is on the standard marionette. With that, he turns to other aspects—the theater, clothing, lighting, sound and stage effects, use of the voice, etc. First published in England, this is equally useful in America. *Note:* The brief but excellent bibliography suggests more reading on puppets.

Hall, Carolyn. **The Teddy Bear Craft Book.** New York: Van Nostrand, 1984. 158p. $19.95 (745.59)

An expert with a needle offers 25 patterns for making a wide variety of teddy bears. First and foremost is the bear as a bear, which comes in a number of shapes and sizes. Each pattern is full size and one can simply trace it from the book. With the pattern the author offers easy-to-follow instructions about materials and the steps necessary to make the bear. (Not all projects feature the full-size patterns, but there are references to sections where the reader is told what to do to achieve the same end.) In addition to the bears as bears, one finds designs for the animal in bean bags and decorations—some of which are a bit much, even for the most dedicated bear lover. Still, on balance the author shows much good taste.

Johnson, Doris. **Children's Toys and Books: Choosing the Best for All Ages from Infancy to Adolescence.** New York: Scribner's, 1982. 196p. $12.95 (649.5)

A commonsense checklist of things to look for when purchasing a toy for a child (up to age 12), this is written by a concerned parent and psychologist. There are good sections on different types of toys (in terms of shapes, sizes, and uses) for various age groups, and a useful, although hardly exciting, chapter on book selection. The best part of the book is the description of toys by specific manufacturers. Here the author points out what is good and bad about each. Unfortunately, the details are skimpy and there is little or no comparison, but at least the listing is accurate and one has a good idea of the purpose of the toy. There is a quick overview of toys for the handicapped and sick child and a useful discussion of toy safety and the use by toy companies of television commercials.

Stearns, Philip. **How to Make Model Soldiers.** New York: Arco, 1974. 80p. o.p. (745.59)

Basic topics from the assembly to the painting of model soldiers are handled here in a clear, lucid fashion. Step-by-step photographs accompany the directions and techniques, and even the most awkward person will have no difficulty in following them. The drawback, at least for some, is that this was first published in England, and many of the examples assume a British orientation. Still, U.S. institutions are included in the lists of manufacturers, societies, and museums. A useful feature is the comparison of metal, plastic, and mixed-media figures. There is a good section on making a diorama.

Studley, Vance. **The Wood Worker's Book of Wooden Toys: How to Make Toys That Whirr, Bob, and Make Musical Sounds.** New York: Van Nostrand, 1980. 112p. $15.95 (745.5)

The author explains how to make classic children's toys in enough detail, and with enough illustrations, that a novice should have little difficulty. There is the usual introductory material on tools and materials, as well as a list of suppliers and a glossary.

TRACK ATHLETICS. *See* Sports

TRAVEL

Devine, Elizabeth, and Nancy Braganti. **The Traveler's Guide to European Customs and Manners.** Deephaven, MN: Meadowbrook, 1984. 216p. pap. $5.95 (914.04)

While most guidebooks offer basic suggestions on how to cope with foreign customs, none goes into the detail found here. Actually, the guide is for the individual who feels ill at ease under the best of circumstances, and needs more help than common sense and a quick look through a general guide will offer. It may be of use, too, to business people, but anyone who has gotten to the stage where serious money is involved knows all the hints given here, and then some. (Then, too, learning about customs is fun even for the person who stays at home.) The authors suggest what to do in all kinds of situations, from using the telephone to renting a room. In all, 25 countries are explored.

Griffith, Susan. **Work Your Way around the World.** Cincinnati: Writer's Digest, 1983. 292p. pap. $10.95 (650.14)

An ideal way to get around the world is to work from time to time in different countries. This is not as easy as it sounds because nations sometimes have restrictive laws that prevent such employment. Conversely, there are legitimate ways around those laws. There are, as well, countries where the problem is not the law, but simply finding work. The author explains the restrictions that will be found, what type of labor is needed, and the opportunities, problems, and language requirements in each of the nations considered. A helpful addition is the comments from people who have worked abroad. A less helpful part of the book concerns basic information on travel. While this is primarily for young people, more adventuresome older travelers will find the book of great interest.

Johnson, Daniel. **Just in Case: A Passenger's Guide to Airplane Safety and Survival.** New York: Plenum, 1984. 298p. $16.95 (613.6)

Depending on the reader's psychological state of mind, this will either be a reassuring guide to flight or a nightmare. The author sets out to explain, in rather a matter-of-fact, routine fashion, what to do in an airplane in case of an emergency. He explains various devices and procedures, from the face masks that pop down when the plane loses altitude to getting out an emergency door. The idea is that the well-educated traveler will be able to act effectively when instructions are not all that clear. The catch, of course, is that people tend not to act rationally in an emergency situation. How many, for example, will recall the steps to take in operating an oxygen mask when the plane seems to be falling out of the sky? True, the author addresses himself to stress reactions, but the words, while intellectually correct, do not necessarily lead to appropriate action. No matter, the book is a splendid introduction to the subject for those who fly.

Kepler, John, et al. **Americans Abroad: A Handbook for Living and Working Overseas.** New York: Praeger, 1983. 570p. $29.95 (910.2)

What do you do when an overseas job becomes available? What are the advantages and disadvantages of working outside the United States? These and hundreds of other practical questions are answered in a guide that takes into consideration the average (not only highly paid executive) jobs abroad. The author and a group of experts who write on the various topics covered in the book speak from experience and no little research. Particularly useful are the considerations about the education of children, finance, health, adjusting to a different social and cultural climate, etc. Illustrations and more specific information focus on seven major urban centers. There is useful information about local conditions and an application of some of the advice given earlier in the book.

Kowet, Don. **The Jet Lag Book.** New York: Crown, 1983. 140p. pap. $4.95 (613.6)

There are numerous theories and ideas about how to overcome jet lag, yet this appears to be one of the most authoritative and certainly the most clearly stated. The author sets forth various steps the traveler can take to defeat the effect of going through a number of time zones. There is nothing particularly new in the information about meals, when and when not to sleep, or internal clocks, but it is nicely put.

Portnoy, Sanford, and Joan Portnoy. **How to Take Great Trips with Your Kids.** Cambridge, MA: Harvard Common Pr., 1984. 180p. $14.95; pap. $7.95 (910.2)

Is it possible to travel with young children and retain one's sanity? These two authors think so. They explain how to avoid such things as car sickness, restless children, and emergencies of both the common and uncommon sort. It is not an accident that the authors are experienced in psychology and in family travel. That combination ensures that they give practical advice that will convince the parent either to cancel the trip and leave the child at home, or to take the trip (and this book) along with the kids. There are some excellent sections on how to tame the child's natural energy in a closed space such as a car or plane. Good games and other lines of attack are offered.

Simony, Maggy, ed. **Traveler's Reading Guides.** Bayport, NY: Freelance, 1981–1983. 3 vols. 260–285p. ea. pap. $12.95 ea. (016.9)

When trying to decide which book is suitable for planning a trip to Paris or Panama, this is a fine point of departure. The three volumes list and describe background books on travel. In addition to the normal travel guides, there are related works such as novels about Paris and Panama, for example, and magazine articles about various places. One volume covers North America, another Europe, and a third the rest of the world.

U.S. Department of Health. **Health Information for International Travel.** Washington, DC: GPO, 1974–   . Annual. 1983 ed., 119p. pap. $4.25 (HE20.7009/3:31)

This publication lists the necessary and advisable health shots for foreign travel. Also included is a standard number of points about health and travel that are of value to those going abroad.

U.S. Department of State. **Your Trip Abroad.** Washington, DC: GPO, 1982. 30p. $3.75 (S1.69:155)

Ideal for the person who has never been abroad before, this covers everything one needs to know about how to obtain a passport, visas, and possibly other documents; what to expect at various points of entry in other countries; and the rules of U.S. customs and what can or cannot be brought back from abroad. There are additional readings and passport agencies listed. *Note:* This is frequently updated, so look for the latest edition.

TRAVEL—GUIDES & DIRECTORIES

The American Express International Traveler's Pocket Dictionary and Phrase Books. New York: Simon & Schuster, 1984. 4 vols., 238p. ea. pap. $5.95 ea. French (448.3); German (438.3); Italian (458.3); Spanish (468.3)

Designed specifically for the person who knows little or none of the language of a foreign country, these guides follow the standard key word and phrase approach. There are sections covering hotels, eating, shopping, illness, etc. For each, the words are in English with the French, German, etc., translation. The guides go beyond the ordinary because they concentrate on bilingual keywords, about 10,000, in both English and in the foreign language. What one has, in effect, is a brilliantly conceived, easy-to-use, portable foreign language dictionary. More are planned by the publisher in cooperation with the compilers of *Webster's New World Dictionary.* As of 1984, they are the best of their type available, both in terms of easy use and price.

The American Express Pocket Guide to. . . . New York: Simon & Schuster, 1983–   . 200–250p. $7.95 ea.

The series, as of mid-1984, includes 12 guides, among them *Florence* (1983), *Spain* (1984), *Mexico* (1984), and *Venice* (1984). These guides are useful for three reasons: (1) they tend to be kept current and the information is accurate; (2) they are slim, and can be carried with ease; and (3) the organization is such that they can be easily consulted for information, e.g., about half of each guide is an alphabetical list of sights to see in the country or the city (the other half includes a detailed list of various types of hotels and restaurants, as well as information on such things as basic words and phrases and what to do with the children). Neither as detailed nor as wide in scope as Michelin or Frommer (q.v.), they are useful for day-to-day consultation when the traveler is on the go.

American Youth Hostels. **Hosteling U.S.A.: The Official American Youth Hostels Handbook.** Rev. ed. Charlotte, NC: East Woods, 1983. 205p. pap. $7.95 (647.94)

Essentially this is a directory, organized by state, with basic information on some 270 specific hostels, including their fees and proximity to sights of interest. Accommodations are rated by a fixed set of measurements such as the type of cooking facilities. Maps appear on almost every page. In addition, there is a history of hosteling and a clear explanation of the types of units involved. There are also accounts by young people who have participated in the movement. Nicely organized, clearly written, and frequently updated, this is a basic guide for any person considering the use of hostels.

Baedeker's. . . . Englewood Cliffs, NJ: Prentice-Hall. Various dates, paging, prices. (914–916)

The name "Baedeker," which goes back to the nineteenth century, is almost synonymous with travel guides. The present series is translated into English and follows the basic pattern established by the original publisher. Most of the focus is on what to see, and there is detailed information on when a museum, church, or public building is open and what it contains. All of this is arranged by cities and areas of the particular country that is covered. Photographs, maps, and plans of urban centers are included. The beginning of each volume offers a general overview of the country, its culture and history, while the volume concludes with basic information on currency, accommodations, appropriate clothing, etc. The Baedeker guides are not as detailed as the Michelin (q.v.). Currently, most of the western European countries are covered by Baedeker guides in English translation, although many of them are dated (i.e., published before 1980). *Note:* Large usedbook stores often have sections of the familiar red-covered guides, sometimes dating back to early in the twentieth century or even earlier. These can be quite useful to the dedicated traveler who may want to study particular buildings and monuments that are covered in more detail in the earlier guides.

Cohen, Marjorie. **Work, Study, Travel Abroad 1984–1985.** 7th ed. New York: St. Martin's, 1984. 310p. pap. $6.95 (910.202)

Updated every two years, this basic guide is the first place to turn when considering work or study outside the United States. Published under the guidance of the International Education Exchange, the guide is reliable, current, and filled with precisely the type of information young people (and some older ones) are seeking. There is brief information on what is offered, what is paid (or how much the tuition is), facilities, work and study conditions, and various programs, tours, etc. Coverage is worldwide, although most of the focus is on Europe. The various study programs are arranged by types of sponsoring groups, from private organizations to U.S. academic institutions.

Fielding's. . . . New York: Morrow. Various dates, paging, prices. 1984 ed. of *Fielding's Europe,* 853p. pap. $12.95 (914)

This differs from Fodor's guides (q.v.) in that of the 25 or so published, most are broader in nature, so that they include Europe, the Far East, etc., as a whole and not country by country. There are, too, "selective shopping guides" to Europe. In those, the text is geographically arranged with a product breakdown by country or area. Fielding excels in finding acceptable yet less than luxury-priced hotels, restaurants, and shopping places. Each book opens with general advice about the region, and then is divided by country and city. There is good practical advice on everything from tipping to how to bargain or make a phone call. There is less information in these guides on historical and tourist sites than there is in the others, although major points of interest are covered. The guides are usually updated annually, and the information is relatively reliable.

Fodor's Modern Guides. New York: McKay. Various dates, paging, prices. *Budget Europe,* 1984. 688p. $11.95 (910.2)

In sheer number, there are more Fodor guides than those in any other series produced by domestic publishers—by 1984 about 120 to 150. (Michelin, q.v., has about 110 guides, but not all are in English.) Prepared for middle-class travelers, the Fodor Guides are a familiar sight to anyone abroad. Like most travel guides, they are updated annually, and the information tends to be slightly erratic, depending often on quoted rather than real prices for hotels, meals, etc. The standard material on the history of the country rarely changes, nor does the useful information on what to see—although changes in admission hours and charges will be noted as necessary. The guide offers the standard pattern of explaining something about the country and how to get there. This is followed by the body of the book, which is a city-by-city, region-by-region description plus information on everything from shopping to art galleries. The series includes separate books for all major countries of the world, although it tends to avoid third world nations. There are also guides to large U.S. cities from Los Angeles to New York, as well as some states.

Frommer's Europe on $25 a Day. New York: Pasmantier, 1983. 738p. pap. $9.25 (914)

This is the basic guide, but the same firm offers 14 others to European countries and cities as well as some Latin American countries. They all follow the same general pattern. At one time the European guide was the bible for young travelers, particularly when the title read *Europe on $5 a Day.* Now that prices have gone up, and there are other guides that are equally useful (for example, the Fielding series, q.v.), some of the glamour has worn off the work. Still, they are seen throughout Europe in the hands of those who are looking for inexpensive lodgings or meals, and they are filled with highly practical tips (many from readers) on all elements of travel. Less useful, and sometimes quite scanty, is the information on sights and museums. The guide excels in its carefree writing style and it will give the traveler complete confidence. Guides are revised annually.

Harvard Student Agencies. **Let's Go: The Budget Guide to Europe.** New York: St. Martin's, 1960– . Annual. Various paging. pap. $8.95 (914)

This is the informal replacement for *Europe on $5 a Day* (Frommer, q.v.) in that it attempts to do what Frommer did earlier. Here the emphasis remains on inexpensive transport and lodgings, with particular attention to the needs of students and young people. It differs from the earlier Frommer in that coverage is not only of western Europe, but extends to some of the Middle East and Russia. While this is a superb guide for the average young person, it may be of little benefit to others. The total focus is on cost, not on such things as noise, size of the room, cleanliness, courtesy, and other amenities sought by the average traveler. At the same time, it has a major benefit in that the writers often discuss out-of-the-way places the average tourist rarely visits. Updated annually, it is a first choice for many, and even those who do not use it for lodgings will find the suggestions for travel exciting. *Note:* Let's Go guides are published for France; Greece, Israel, and Egypt; and Italy.

Heise, Jon, and Dennis O'Reilly. **The Travel Book: Guide to the Travel Guides.** New York: Bowker, 1981. 319p. $26.95 (016.91)

Which is the best travel guide to Europe? What is the best guide to restaurants? These and scores of other questions are answered in this discussion of some 600 English-language travel books, many of which are updated each year. Each guide is carefully described in a well-written annotation. The organization is by continent and by country, although the book opens with guides that attempt to cover the whole world. Included, too, are works written for specialized groups such as the handicapped and students, and for special-interest groups such as music and art lovers. A basic place to turn for help in selecting a travel guide.

Hotel & Motel Red Book. New York: American Hotel Association Directory, 1886– . Annual. Various paging, prices (647)

When one is looking for a hotel or motel with an eye on cost, location, facilities, etc., this is a place to turn. While this guide is limited in scope to members of the sponsoring organization, most medium- to large-size hotels and motels do belong, so few are overlooked. The United States and Canada are the primary areas covered, but other countries are included as well. There are advertisements and numerous illustrations. Another useful source of information, although limited in coverage to members of the American Automobile Association, is the AAA tour books and travel guides, which list, state by state, community by community, hotels and motels acceptable to AAA. Updated annually, the books give full information on costs, facilities, check-in and checkout times, etc. The guides may be had from any AAA office if you are a member. AAA covers the United States, North and South America, and many European countries.

Michelin Red [Green] Guides. New York: French & European; Michelin. 1900– . Irreg. Various paging, prices (914)

The best-known guides in Europe, the French Michelin is divided into two basic series, and usually is published in two to four languages, often including English. At any one time there are some 110 to 130 guides available in the United States. Michelin is only slightly behind Fodor (q.v.) in terms of areas covered. The *red* books list hotels and restaurants by cities and towns for particular countries. Other facilities, including garages, are noted. The hotels are ranked in terms of price, location, and general comfort and quiet. Restaurants are ranked in terms of quality and price. There are frequent and useful maps to guide the tourist. The *green* books, of which there are a majority in English, are concerned with sights and places of interest, again arranged by city or community or region. The editors rank museums, etc., by importance—a rating that many find a trifle less than appropriate to the quiet aesthetic style, but, nevertheless useful. The Michelin guides are updated frequently and most of the information is current and reliable.

Mobil Travel Guides. Chicago: Rand McNally. Various dates, paging, prices. 1983 ed., ea. vol. 235–300p. $7.95 (917)

The seven volumes in this often updated set cover seven areas in the United States, from *Mobil Travel Guide: California and the West* to *Mobil Travel Guide: Northeastern States*. Each follows a definite pattern. They are divided by states and by cities and communities. The user finds information on places to stay, restaurants, primary attractions, and events that occur throughout the year in a particular area. All of these are rated in such a way that one can immediately determine their importance as well as their price. Each volume opens with road maps of states in the region covered. One may not always agree with the ratings, but the editors include a generous selection of price categories so there is a wide area of choice. Throughout the years, these guides have proven reliable and relatively accurate.

Look, of course, for the latest edition. *Note:* An eighth volume is *Mobil Travel Guide: Major Cities,* which takes information from the guides for some 50 urban centers in the United States. Not really needed, but a good reference source.

Rundback, Betty. **Bed & Breakfast USA: A Guide to Tourist Homes and Guest Houses.** New York: Dutton, 1982. 221p. $5.95 (917.3)

While most Americans consider it routine to stay at a hotel or motel, this is not the case in Europe, where bed and breakfast is a long tradition. Here one finds accommodation in someone's home, usually expanded to include space for several guests. Traditionally breakfast is included in the low-cost charge. The appeal of such places is that they are more personal and less costly than other types of lodging. The author has listed, state by state, the best such places in the United States and Canada. Full descriptions of facilities along with details on services, prices, phone numbers, etc. are included. This is an extremely useful guide, and while the rates may change, the general information remains basically the same.

U.S. Department of Defense. **Guides to the Spoken Language.** Washington, DC: GPO, 1979–1980. 64–85p. ea. $4.25 ea. (D101.11:30-3)

Published as army technical and field manuals, these guides are designed for personnel stationed abroad. They are equally useful for travelers, and while not designed to make one fluent in the language, they do provide basic conversational words and phrases. The booklets include the English phrase and the translation in both phonetic style and written form. They are excellent for understanding directions, menus, signs, etc. The series includes a separate manual for each of the following languages: French, German, Greek, Italian, Japanese, Norwegian, Portuguese, Russian, Spanish, Tagalog, and Turkish.

U.S. Department of Education. **Opportunities Abroad for Educators.** Washington, DC: GPO, 1984. 31p. $4.25 (Ed1.1984)

Usually updated each year, this covers opportunities for teaching abroad, and gives information on how to find such openings. There is a list of seminars, exchange programs, and related opportunities in postsecondary education.

Weintz, Caroline, and Walter Weintz. **The Discount Guide for Travelers over 55.** Rev. ed. New York: Dutton, 1983. 256p. pap. $5.95 (910)

How you can travel for less than the average price if you are 55 or over is the subject of this handy guide. Since it is geographically arranged, it is easy to quickly locate hotels, car rentals firms, airlines, museums, and other institutions where you can get special rates—often from 10 to 50 percent off or more. The coverage is primarily of the United States and Canada, but does include Europe and Central and South America. Full information is given for each bargain.

TREES & SHRUBS

Beckett, Kenneth. **The Complete Book of Evergreens.** New York: Van Nostrand, 1981. 160p. $16.95 (635.9)

Focusing on the primary evergreens of North America, the author gives the reader basic information necessary to choose the best for any garden or lawn situation. The primary attributes of each evergreen are stated, and there are black-and-white illustrations as well as colored photographs of the evergreens in full bloom. The text is easy to follow, and complete directions are given on how to plant, cultivate, and care for the individual tree or shrub. Particularly useful are data on where to put each evergreen for a special purpose, and the amount of light and shade required by different varieties.

Chamberlin, Susan. **Hedges, Screens & Espaliers: How to Select, Grow & Enjoy.** Tucson, AZ: HP Books, 1982. 176p. pap. $7.95 (635.9)

While there is always the fence to provide privacy, the author suggests that a more effective and aesthetic approach is to depend on nature, i.e., hedges and natural screens. After a general discussion she offers specific advice on the best type of natural growth to muffle sound, keep in (or out) children and animals, aid in security, etc. Types of plants are considered for each situation. There is a section, too, on espaliers (plants that grow in various shapes against a flat surface, usually a wall). Illustrations are used throughout, and for such protective planting, this is a fine guide.

Elias, Thomas. **The Complete Trees of North America: Field Guide and Natural History.** New York: Van Nostrand, 1980. 948p. $19.95 (582.16)

The title is correct. This is truly "complete," and as such is a basic guide to the identification of 800 trees that grow north of Mexico. After a general introduction there are descriptions of major groups, families, genera, and species. All of this is keyed in such a way that one can move from the large family to the specific tree with ease. The 200 illustrations are photographs, maps, and line drawings, and there is a ruler at the bottom of each page that is a handy guide to size. In addition to the illustrations, there is a map showing distribution of the tree. Flowers and/or fruits are considered, too. Thanks to the handy arrangement, the lack of technical terms, and the clear writing and illustrations, this is the basic book for anyone interested in trees.

Hora, Bayard, ed. **The Oxford Encyclopedia of Trees of the World.** New York: Oxford University Pr., 1981. 288p. $24.95 (582.16)

One or two pages are given to each major genus, and each description includes a photograph and/or a painting of the tree. Where there are different species, there is an illustration of the more common types. An expert is responsible for each major section, which explains the characteristics of the tree, where it may be found, its importance to the economy of the country, and other fascinating facts. Considerable attention is given to trees of North America, and this is one of the best guides available for not only common but also unusual trees. Opening sections consider the basic structure of the tree and its place in the world. Clearly written, carefully illustrated, this is an exceptionally good work of its kind.

Huxley, Anthony, ed. **Evergreen Garden Trees and Shrubs.** Rev. ed. New York: Sterling, 1984. 181p. pap. $6.95 (635.97)

Complete with illustrations and specific tips and directions, this is a manual that shows how to use some 300 varieties of trees and shrubs to improve a garden, make a hedge, or simply set off a house. There are beautiful colored illustrations and scale drawings that show the ultimate size of the specimen. The latter feature prevents the unsuspecting gardener from planting a small tree that may grow to dominate and shade the whole yard. There are entries explaining problems (disease, pests, bad weather) and others that relate such basics as feeding, soil, and climatic requirements. All of this is done with verve and style by a British author who thoroughly understands the subject.

Line, Les. **The Audubon Society Book of Trees.** New York: Abrams, 1981. 263p. $50 (582.16)

Here the color photograph is the thing, and the book is outstanding for the marvelous illustrations of individual trees or trees in a landscape. Beyond that there is a full text that not only describes the trees and their habitat, but considers allied things such as mosses, plants of the forest, and even related birds and animal life.

Loewer, H. Peter. **Evergreens: A Guide to Landscape, Lawn and Garden.** New York: Walker, 1981. 132p. $14.95 (635.9)

This expert gardener and author of numerous books offers some easy-to-follow advice on evergreens. His relaxed, cheerful style is in evidence once again, and he presents rather technical data in a carefully thought out manner. The book opens with necessary background information on evergreens and their place in the average garden or lawn. If one skips to the third chapter, there is an informative discussion of the genera of evergreens, followed by information on flower-bearing varieties. In between is basic information on planting, propagation, and general care. A section on pruning may prove particularly helpful. The book concludes with a list of sources of supplies and organizations and societies involved with the subject of this guide.

Ortho Books Editors. **All about Trees.** San Francisco: Ortho, 1982. 112p. pap. $5.95 (635.97)

This follows the Ortho format of generous numbers of colored illustrations and an emphasis on the type of information the average person wants to have when considering trees. Here considerable attention is devoted to helping the homeowner decide on the best kind of tree, not only for the climate but for such things as color, use as a barrier against noise and neighbors, or for fruits and berries. Arrangement is by botanical name, but there are generous cross-references in the index from common names. In addition to useful notes on appearance and use, there are judicious warnings about possible difficulties, such as weaknesses to drastic weather changes.

U.S. Department of Agriculture. **Important Forest Trees of the United States.** Washington, DC: GPO, 1979. 70p. $5 (A1.76:519)

An inexpensive, well-illustrated guide, this focuses on about 200 trees likely to be found in U.S. forests and wildlife preserves. The descriptions are concise, and the drawings fit nicely with the text. Of considerable use to beginners are the range maps, which indicate what grows where.

TRICKS. *See* Magic; Puzzles

TYPING & SHORTHAND

Gregg Shorthand. Boston: Gregg, 1949–   . Irreg. 1983 ed., $10.95 (653)

In the latter part of the nineteenth century, the Englishman John Gregg devised his by-now-famous approach to shorthand. This is a version of his first manual, although with considerable revision and with specific guides for the modern student. After a good presentation of basic principles, there follows a methodical plan of learning the system. This is well-illustrated and includes numerous practice programs.

Hutchison, Howard. **The Typewriter Repair Manual.** Blue Ridge Summit, PA: TAB, 1981. 350p. $17.95; pap. $10.95 (652.3)

While this is addressed to someone who is learning typewriter repair, and not necessarily the layperson, it can be useful for the latter. There is a basic explanation, with good illustrations each step of the way, of the workings of both manual and electric typewriters. There are useful parts on how to keep the machine operating at top efficiency through careful maintenance, which is equally carefully explained. Less helpful is the last part of the book, which includes specific information on the repair of several models.

Leslie, Louis, et al. **Gregg Shorthand, Functional Method.** New York: McGraw-Hill, 1963–   . Irreg. 1983 ed., $12.95 (653)

This follows the pattern of John Gregg's system, but with important modifications. The book is really a basic text, and as such is arranged for classroom use. There is an introductory explanation of the method, and then entire reliance on the use of the shorthand system. In fact, there is little written text. The emphasis is on rapid mastery of symbols, and on spelling and punctuation.

Lessenberry, D. D., et al. **Century 21 Typewriting.** Cincinnati: South-Western, 1927–   . Irreg. 1983 ed., $9.50 (652.3)

This is a complete course in typing. Various aspects are discussed but the focus is on exercises, methodically presented and graded according to skill. The emphasis is on both business and personal typing. *Note:* This is one volume of a well-illustrated series that is frequently updated. Other titles in the series include *Century 21 Typewriting: First Year Course* and *Century 21 Typewriting: Advanced Course.* They are all time tested, often employed in professional schools, and considered tops in the field.

Levine, Nathan. **Typing for Everyone.** New York: Arco, 1971–   . Irreg. 1983 ed., $10; pap. $6.95 (652.3)

This is a useful guide for anyone who wishes to learn touch-typing and does not know the first thing about how to begin. The author shows the basic mechanics of the typical typewriter and what must be known to use it with maximum efficiency. At the heart of the guide are time typing sheets and direct step-by-step instructions. The manual is particularly useful for its various drills, which help the reader to master accuracy and speed. The illustrations are adequate.

UPHOLSTERY. *See* Furniture

VEGETABLE & FRUIT GARDENING
See also Gardening

Bubel, Nancy. **The Country Journal Book of Vegetable Gardening.** Brattleboro, VT: Country Journal, 1983. 244p. pap. $10.95 (635)

A columnist for the magazine the Country Journal explains the easiest, best, and most efficient ways to grow vegetables in a typical home garden. True, the basic information will be found in scores of books, but this differs in that instruction is month by month with specific information on what to do at each crucial time of the year, and the advice is wide ranging from specifics on the best soil and conditions for a given type of vegetable to how to keep birds and animals from eating up the whole crop. Finally, the author has a pleasing, conversational style that makes it all easy to read and fun to browse in. The illustrations are numerous and good.

Consumer Guide Editors. **Vegetable Gardening Encyclopedia.** New York: Galahad, 1982. 384p. pap. $4.98 (635)

Written in an informal style and illustrated with line drawings, this guide is perfect for the novice gardener and for those who just want a reference guide to vegetables. It is divided into four parts—the garden, the plants, the kitchen, and a reference section. It takes the reader chronologically from a garden's planning stages to how to dry, can, store, and freeze the harvest. The authors concentrate on those with a small (5' x 10') backyard plot and advocate the style of gardening now known as "intensive backyard farming." After instructing the reader on choosing a site, making a plan on paper, and deciding what to grow and where to grow it, the authors move to gardening tools and the practical side of gardening. They then turn to soil conditions and improving them, and provide an alphabetized list of herbs and vegetables with their individual characteristics. The reader must keep in mind, however, that he or she may not have the time or money to provide these ideal conditions in a backyard setting. The same is true for the section on pest control—it is unlikely that one would be beset by all these problems or able to cure them all. Part three concentrates on the kitchen aspects of gardening. There is a wealth of information here on preserving—in whatever form—the harvest, including how to sprout vegetables for use in salads and cooking. The reference section contains a glossary of gardening terms, a list of cooperative extension services, and a list of major seed companies.

Creasy, Rosalind. **The Complete Book of Edible Landscaping.** New York: Sierra/ Random House, 1982. 379p. $25; pap. $14.95 (635)

Published by the Sierra Club, this is another sumptuously illustrated guide to a particular aspect of gardening. As the title suggests, the author believes a yard can be landscaped with items one can turn into food. Specifically explained for various climatic zones, the plan considers vegetables, fruit trees, herbs, and related natural delights. The landscaping directions are augmented by over 160 pages listing, with explanations, 140 different edible varieties. As beautiful as it is practical, this unusual book is for the more imaginative gardener. Note: Unfortunately, most of the varieties are for a mild climate and will not be suitable for areas with winters below freezing.

Gessert, Kate. **The Beautiful Food & Garden Encyclopedia of Attractive Food Plants.** New York: Van Nostrand, 1983. 264p. $24.95 (635)

A recurrent problem for the gardener is whether to grow vegetables or flowers. Why not grow food plants that are as attractive as flowers, asks the author. She then proceeds to give practical advice on how you can have flowers and vegetables for both aesthetic and gourmet delight. What to grow and how to grow it is covered, but, more important, Gessert explains what serves to tempt both the stomach and the eye. Small to more elaborate garden designs are suggested, and these are accompanied by photographs and drawings—as are discussions of individual plants. Each of the entries includes a full description of the vegetable, herb, or plant as well as its minuses and pluses as a feature in the overall garden design.

Halpin, Anne. **The Organic Gardener's Complete Guide to Vegetables and Fruits.** Emmaus, PA: Rodale, 1982. 512p. $19.95 (635.04)

Expert advice on the natural, organic growth of about 50 fruits and slightly more vegetables is given here in enough detail, and with enough illustrations, so that even the beginner can produce a bumper crop. The emphasis, of course, is how to develop a rich soil without using fertilizers and chemicals. The book covers the basics from planning the garden, preparing the soil, cultivating the crop, and dealing with insects to harvesting and storage. Numerous illustrations are provided.

Harrington, Geri. **Cash Crops for Thrifty Gardeners.** New York: Perigee, 1984. 197p. pap. $10.95 (635)

There are crops a gardener can grow to sell and thereby gain—at least to a degree—a measure of economic security. Harrington, who has had experience in such matters, goes about explaining what types of vegetables or flowers should be profitable. Most of the items are off the beaten garden path, and, for that reason, seem to ensure success in sales. According to the author, people buy what they cannot easily find elsewhere, or, for that matter, grow themselves. Once the crop or flowers are decided on, the next step is to start growing things—and this is explained, although not always in the detail found in more specialized gardening books. The real strength of this guide is in its basic suggestion of turning gardening into a profit-making activity and its step-by-step instructions on how to sell what is grown.

Hendrickson, Robert. **The Berry Book: The Illustrated Home Gardener's Guide to Growing and Using over 50 Kinds and 500 Varieties of Berries.** New York: Doubleday, 1981. 259p. $14.95 (637.7)

Almost everything there is to know about berries is included in this sweeping survey of 50 types and 500 varieties. Each kind is illustrated with drawings. The text ranges from where and how to plant berries, to cultivating, pruning, harvesting, canning, freezing, and eating them. Both the popular types (strawberries, raspberries, huckleberries) and the less well known varieties are discussed. Unfortunately, the discussion of wild berries is not very clear, e.g., can they or can they not be domesticated? Still, for most domestic berries the author provides everything, including directions of what to grow on small plots or large areas of ground. There are recipes and a list of sources of berry plants.

Jabs, Carolyn. **The Heirloom Gardener.** Sierra Club/Random House, 1984. 310p. $17.95; pap. $9.95 (635)

By "heirloom" this writer for the *New York Times* means rare and endangered fruits and vegetables. The task the author sets for herself is to explore these rarities, explain their nature, and show methods by which they can be saved as part of the heritage of the nation. The descriptions and prose are illustrated by nineteenth-century drawings, usually from catalogs. In addition to information on how one acquires and cultivates such rarities, there is information on museums and farms where they are an important part of the presentation. An exceptional book that can be enjoyed by both the dedicated gardener and the casual reader.

London, Sheryl. **Anything Grows! Ingenious Ways to Grow More Food in Front Yards, Backyards, Side Yards, in the Suburbs, in the City, on Rooftops, Even Parking Lots.** Emmaus, PA: Rodale, 1984. 255p. $17.95; pap. $11.95 (635)

The book lives up to its subtitle, and there is a clear explanation of how to grow vegetables just about anywhere that has a minimum amount of soil and light. The catch is that the really difficult places take special preparation—from added soil to climate controls. This, in turn, means work; but if one is willing to apply oneself, then a carrot can grow on a rooftop in Brooklyn. The author provides a special set of exercises to help the gardener build the body for hauling and plowing. While aside from the exercises there is nothing new here, it does collect the problem areas in one book and give practical solutions.

Lorenz, Oscar, and Donald Maynard. **Knott's Handbook for Vegetable Growers.** 2nd ed. New York: Wiley, 1980. 390p. $17.50 (635)

While primarily for the farmer or the gardener with an above-average seed plot, this guide will be of value, at least for ready-reference purposes, to the average vegetable gardener. The reason is that the emphasis on charts, diagrams, tables, and illustrations, plus an excellent index, makes it possible to find answers to numerous questions quickly. Here the authors are concerned with basics of planting, growing, fertilization, insect and weed control, harvesting, and other related matters. True, the tractor speed charts are not going to be of much interest to the average gardener, but if one wants to find out the nutritional composition of a vegetable it can be had with the flip of the page. Not for everyone, yet certainly a valuable source of information for the involved grower.

Minnich, Jerry. **Gardening for Maximum Nutrition.** Emmaus, PA: Rodale, 1983. 220p. $15.95 (635)

This guide quite fulfills the promise of its subtitle: "easy ways to double the nutritional value of your backyard garden." The author begins by explaining that farmer's market and supermarket vegetables are not really fresh and that, indeed, the only real assurance of complete nutritional value comes from growing your own food. The next question is what to grow, and here Minnich lists the more nutritious vegetables, including such things as cowpeas and dandelion greens. He then goes on to explain how to prepare the garden, plant it, and care for it until the harvest. There are good sections on cooking, storage, and general preparation of vegetables. This is not everyone's book—some prefer taste and aesthetic appearance to top nutrition, after all. Those who are first interested in health, and in do-it-yourself in gardening will find this is an important manual.

Raymond, Dick. **Garden Way's Joy of Gardening.** Pownal, VT: Garden Way, 1983. 365p. $17.95; pap. $14.95 (635.2)

Here the popular television gardener directs his talents to the growing of vegetables, and while some of the tips are for the climate in and around Vermont, they are general enough to be applicable almost anywhere. As might be expected, there are the usual good descriptions of what to grow, how difficult various plants are to grow, and when to harvest them. Specific directions are given as to planting, care of the garden, and problems that may arise. Illustrations are good, and there are numerous color photographs. What sets this apart from other books is the relaxed yet accurate text and the general joy of gardening Raymond manages to communicate. He takes great delight in being first with the best advice, and many of his instructions for such things as growing tomatoes rely on secrets that will make the reader's garden the envy of the neighborhood.

Sunset Editors. **How to Grow Vegetables and Berries.** Menlo Park, CA: Lane, 1982. 112p. $5.95 (635)

Although published in California, this guide can be used throughout the United States. In fact, there are handy climate maps that show what plants can be grown where and when. The assumption is that the gardener knows little or nothing, so all of the basic steps are covered, including how to plant. The heart of the book is close to 70 pages of alphabetically arranged vegetables and berries. Each is illustrated. There is necessary information on climatic and soil conditions as well as when to water and when to harvest. The book ends with general instructions on the maintenance and care of the garden.

U.S. Department of Agriculture. **Growing Tomatoes in the Home Garden.** Washington, DC: GPO, 1981. 13p. $2 (A1.77:180/4)

From various types of tomatoes, to their ability to grow in certain kinds of soil and different lighting conditions, to what to do when disease strikes—all are covered in this handy pamphlet. Complete instructions help make an expert out of the beginner.

U.S. Department of Agriculture. **Growing Vegetables in the Home Garden.** Washington, DC: GPO, 1978. 49p. $3.25 (A1.77:202/2)

This is a basic, easy-to-follow set of instructions for the beginner who wants to know precisely how to grow vegetables. The manual covers the types of vegetables one should consider growing, the proper place to plant them, and how to care for them. A useful table of safe planting dates for different parts of the country is included.

VEGETABLES. See Cooking—Vegetables; Food

VETERINARY MEDICINE. See Horses; Pets; and specific pets, e.g., Cats, Dogs, etc.

VIDEO. See Games; Photography—Motion Pictures & Television; Radio; Television

WALLPAPERING. See Painting & Wallpapering

WALLS. See Fences & Walls

WATCHES. *See* Clocks & Watches

WATER CONSERVATION

Addkison, Roy. **Running Dry: How to Conserve Water Indoors and Out.** New York: Stein & Day, 1983. 160p. $16.95; pap. $9.95 (644.6)

While water in most areas seems as abundant and free as the air, this is hardly the case. Addkison documents the development of water shortages and major droughts, and speculates on various theories concerning the furture of the water supply. The heart of his book is devoted to ways that the individual can conserve water in and out of the house. Many suggestions are simple, e.g., tips on the use of rainwater. Others are complex, such as the use of various methods to recycle water. There is a shorter section on conservation beyond the individual home.

WATERCOLORS. *See* Painting (Art)

WEATHER

Battan, Louis. **Weather in Your Life.** San Francisco: Freeman, 1983. 230p. $19.95; pap. $10.95 (551.6)

Here is an unusual, highly readable, and informative book that is the beginning of any how-to-do-it approach to the weather. The author relates a considerable amount of information about weather—so much, in fact, that it may make it easier for you to appreciate dramatic weather changes. A meteorologist whose writing style is as good as his research reputation, Battan explains almost every aspect of weather, from its origins to its relationship to comfort and the arts. He is strongest when he discusses, usually in separate chapters, just how weather affects a given human situation, and when he points out the various ways of coping with extremes. One can move to a more agreeable clime, of course, or consider modifications in living structures that will make them more comfortable.

Dabbert, Walter. **Weather for Outdoorsmen: A Complete Guide to Understanding and Predicting Weather in Mountains and Valleys, on the Water, and in the Woods.** New York: Scribner's, 1981. 240p. $14.95 (551.63)

Good to his promise, the author literally explains how one can predict the weather in a number of places and under a variety of circumstances. There is no magic formula, and the individual is likely to be no better or worse in forecasting than the ubiquitous television weatherperson. Dabbert sets off by explaining what causes weather conditions and changes, and the elements involved in a sunny or a rainy day. He then moves on to how various and obvious conditions foreshadow certain types of weather. There are a few tricks, but on the whole most of the information depends on a thorough grounding in meteorology. (Dabbert happens to be a meteorologist, and a good one at that.) While the text is geared to the outdoor person, there is absolutely no reason it will not be equally fascinating to the person who rarely puts his or her head out of the front door.

Dunlop, S., and F. Wilson. **The Larousse Guide to Weather Forecasting.** New York: Larousse, 1982. 160p. $17.95; pap. $8.95 (551.6)

Here is a simple, easy-to-follow guide that will help the average person predict the weather. One may wonder why that should be necessary, particularly with so many weather reports readily at hand in newspapers and on television and radio. But that is not the point. The point is that the individual with an interest in the subject can soon learn to master it, and often be as accurate as the official weatherperson, if not more so. There are numerous colored photographs with supplemental maps and diagrams. The reliance is primarily on visual observation (of everything from cloud formations to the color of the sky), and little depends on the use of expensive instruments, although these are considered. This book is of value to both adults and young people.

Hardy, Ralph, et al. **The Weather Book.** Boston: Little, 1982. 224p. $24.95 (551.6)
This will not help the how-to-do-it or self-help fan change the weather, but it will do much to explain what constitutes weather. Hardy and his coauthors are English meteorologists who explain the difference between weather and climate, and then proceed to analyze various manifestations from clouds and rain to tornadoes and smog. There is an intriguing discussion of possible climatic changes brought about by excess amounts of carbon dioxide in the atmosphere. A final section considers how the familiar television weatherperson got there in the first place, i.e., the authors trace the development of weather prediction from early history to the present. An added joy is the many illustrations, from color photographs to well-placed charts and maps.

Ludlum, David. **The American Weather Book.** Boston: Houghton, 1982. 296p. $14.95; pap. $8.95 (551.69)
Each month the weather varies, and the interested observer can turn the pages of this guide, month by month, to see what to expect. Of course, it is not a daily guide to the weather, but it does indicate such things as average weather patterns, as well as the hottest, coldest, wettest days and the like. Various sections of the country are considered so that one gets an overall view.

Ramsey, Dan. **How to Forecast Weather.** Blue Ridge Summit, PA: TAB, 1983. 213p. $16.95; pap. $10.95 (551.63)
This guide will not make the average reader a better weatherperson than the star of the evening news, but enough good information is given to at least allow the reader a better understanding of weather forecasting. Of most interest is the section on the various weather instruments that can be purchased to collect data. (The manufacturers are duly listed.) There is a brief description of these scientific instruments, as well as quite detailed data on what constitutes weather and climate. The section on forecasting is a small but important part of the book.

Schaefer, Vincent, and John Day. **A Field Guide to the Atmosphere.** Boston: Houghton, 1981. 359p. $13.95 (551.52)
Answers to questions regarding the names of cloud formations, the meanings of atmospheric disturbances, and other common queries are found in this handy guide. It is an ideal field manual for someone who wants help in understanding and appreciating what goes on in the heavens, both day and night. The text is as clear and precise as the more than 300 color photographs. Written particularly for the

layperson, the guide is among the best available. *Note:* There is a section on basic experiments, primarily for younger people.

WEAVING

Beveridge, June. **Warp/Weft/Sett: A Reference Manual for Handweavers.** New York: Van Nostrand, 1980. 176p. $22.95 (746.1)

Written for the experienced weaver, this is a handy, well-organized manual that carefully explains the intricacies of weaving. With each set of instructions there are photographs and specific descriptions covering such things as the number of picks per inch and warp size. The yarn suppliers list may be dated, but the instructions are as timeless as weaving itself.

Chadwick, Eileen. **The Craft of Hand Spinning.** New York: Scribner's, 1980. 167p. $14.95 (746.1)

While written from the English point of view, the information here is about as basic as you can get, and very useful for beginners. Those a bit further along with spinning will discover it offers useful information on English fleeces not covered in other books.

Gilmurray, Susan. **Weaving Tricks.** New York: Van Nostrand, 1981.189p. $12.95 (746.1)

Tailored for the experienced weaver, this guide offers numerous techniques and methods of solving common problems connected with the craft. There are numerous line drawings to support the author's straightforward suggestions. Most of the material is not covered in standard books on weaving.

Jackson, Constance, and Judith Plowman. **The Woolcraft Book: Spinning, Dyeing and Weaving.** New York: Scribner's, 1982. 192p. $24.95 (746.1)

Although written by New Zealand authors, this guide offers useful advice to anyone anywhere on the basics of spinning, dyeing, and weaving. The particular focus is on spinning, and while not many readers are likely to have access to fleece, those who do will appreciate the coverage. Beyond that there are extremely useful charts on differences in wool from various parts of the world. Such things as breeds of sheep and the best use of the wool from each breed are emphasized. The section on chemical and plant dyeing is good, as is the part of the book devoted to weaving. The authors teach the subject, and they have illustrated the text with numerous photographs and drawings. There are projects and details on differences between various types of tools, spinning wheels, and looms.

Meltzer, Marilyn. **Weave It.** New York: Van Nostrand, 1981. 96p. $14.95 (746.1)

Subtitled "28 projects for your home," this includes everything from hammocks and rugs to wall hangings. What is different about this book is that the designs are the work of some of America's leading weavers. The result is step-by-step instructions for well-designed and functional objects. The illustrations are good, and the level of skill required varies from that of the near beginner to the expert.

Regensteiner, Else. **The Art of Weaving.** New York: Van Nostrand, 1970. 184p. o.p. (746.1)

Although published over a decade ago, this remains one of the best books on the fundamentals of weaving. Directed to beginners, it takes the reader through each and every essential step. As a teacher, the author is aware of the need for clear explanations, and she begins with a discussion of equipment needed. From there, she moves to types of yarns, weaves, and various kinds of weaving. Each of the descriptions and explanations is fully illustrated, often with color photographs. Possibly the most effective part of the book is the author's discussion of design and how she is inspired by nature to come up with startling colors and shapes.

WEIGHT LIFTING. *See* Bodybuilding

WELDING

Althouse, Andrew, et al. **Modern Welding.** South Holland, IL: Goodheart-Willcox, 1980. 752p. $17.50 (671.5)
A much-used textbook, this is too involved for the average layperson, but it does offer valuable how-to-do-it tips for the individual with some knowledge of welding. There are good chapters on the fundamentals of the craft and the various metals involved. Projects in the sections on various types of welding require sophisticated equipment, but here and there are ideas that will help someone solve a difficult problem.

Geary, Don. **The Welder's Bible.** Blue Ridge Summit, PA: TAB, 1980. 408p. $18.95; pap. $12.95 (671.5)
Primarily written and illustrated for the beginner, this puts special emphasis on oxyacetylene welding. The author thinks it the best and the safest kind, but more to the point, it is the kind for which equipment is likely to be available to the average reader. The basic techniques, from brazing to soldering, are considered in detail. There are good sections on how welding can be used in the typical home situation. The author's enthusiasm for the craft is carried over into a less successful treatment of how the reader may turn his or her skills into a commercial business.

WILDLIFE
See also Animals—Field Guides; Nature Study

Davids, Richard. **How to Talk to Birds and Other Uncommon Ways of Enjoying Nature the Year Round.** New York: Knopf, 1972. 242p. $6.95 (500.9)
The good life is outside the front door—at least according to Davids, who is an avid nature fan and firmly believes that the key to happiness is to enjoy nature. Here he tells how it is done, and in a delightful way. No effort is made to construct a field guide to this or that, but there are scores of suggestions and tips on how to enjoy everything from looking at birds to walking with children. The author's enthusiasm is contagious and winning.

Jordan, W. J., and John Hughes. **Care of the Wild: Family First Aid for All Wild Creatures.** New York: Rawson, 1982. 223p. $14.95; pap. $8.95 (636.08)
What is to be done when a bird breaks a wing, a small animal a leg, or a toad or bat is caught in such a way as to inflict minor damage? The two authors come up with reliable, easy-to-follow answers, and the result is a truly remarkable book. It is one most people will want to carry with them when camping, and others will wish

to have around the house for emergencies. The authors have a way of explaining even the most difficult operation simply and with the kind of self-confidence that communicates itself to the reader. A vast number of mammals, birds, and types of wildlife are considered. First aid is supplemented by preventive measures, such as what to do when an animal is captured—particularly how to handle it without damage to the animal or oneself—as well as feeding procedures and eventual releasing methods. There are, to the surprise of many, numerous animal rehabilitation centers about the United States, and these are duly listed.

Landi, Val. **The Great American Countryside.** New York: Macmillan, 1982. 440p. $24.95; pap. $12.95 (917.3)

A sweeping guide to the flora, fauna, and sites of interest in the United States, this is a region-by-region, state-by-state examination of what the observant traveler can discover. Whether the topic is a geyser, a redwood, or a fox, the author has a brief note, usually accompanied by a line drawing or a black-and-white photograph. A combination travel guide and naturalist's delight, this will be of interest to almost anyone. It beautifully augments traditional guides that concentrate on man-made and historic sites.

Reader's Digest North American Wildlife. New York: Random House, 1982. 559p. $20.50 (574.9)

Prepared for the amateur, this wildlife guide briefly explains and illustrates over 2,000 plants and animals found in North America. Among the entries: 278 birds, 110 fish, 54 amphibians, 91 mammals. There are also close to 200 trees and some 700 wild flowers considered, as well as mushrooms and plants. The material is arranged under nine broad subject headings from mammals and birds to wild flowers. For most entries, there is the common name, the scientific name, a description, comments on different and interesting features, and a map showing approximate location. Each has a color illustration. The book is thoroughly indexed, and it is fairly easy to find a mysterious item. As with all *Reader's Digest* titles, this has a handsome format, is written with verve and clarity, and can be used by almost anyone.

Roth, Charles. **The Wildlife Observer's Guidebook.** Englewood Cliffs, NJ: Prentice-Hall, 1982. 239p. $15.95; pap. $7.95 (590.72)

For those who know nothing about how to observe wildlife, including younger people, this is a good introduction. The author gives precise directions on how to look and what to note. He covers everything from the creatures' environment and behavioral patterns to their eating habits. There are instructions on how the observer should dress, when to hide, and emergency procedures for bites, as well as stimulating background material on the various animals. Readings are numerous; illustrations are good. While not for the expert, this is a suitable beginning guide for the amateur.

WIND POWER. *See* Solar & Wind Power

WINE
See also Drinks

Broadbent, Michael. **The Great Vintage Wine Book.** New York: Knopf, 1980. 432p. $25 (641.2)

This British wine critic is not interested in average wine. He examines great vintages (at often great cost) from 1653 to 1979 and banters about such familiar descriptive terms as bouquet, taste, well-defined, etc. For each wine, he supplies a one-to-five star rating, although here and there he thinks the wine not worth even a single star. In terms of coverage, most of the attention is given to French wines, with several nods to Europe and hardly a mention of California. While of limited use to people who do not have a well-stocked wine store about (or a large income), the guide is useful in that it offers basic instruction in evaluation, if only by example, and supplies the reader with a massive list of descriptive phrases to amaze and confuse friends.

Broadbent, Michael. **Michael Broadbent's Pocket Guide to Wine Tasting.** New York: Simon & Schuster, 1982. 144p. $5.95 (641.2)

First published in England in the late 1960s, this is a classic and enormously helpful book for anyone who wants to gain an appreciation of wine. Now updated, the guide is a convincing demonstration that taste is rarely wrong, that with a little practice and an open mind one can learn to identify not only good wines, but those that satisfy individual requirements. While Broadbent can place a wine's age, place or origin, and type quickly, this is not likely to come easily to others. Still, there is solid advice on how to go about the process, even down to the proper descriptive terms to employ. There are fine color photographs showing variations in color of the reds and whites. A good reading list is appended.

Johnson, Frank. **The Professional Wine Reference.** Rev. ed. New York: Harper, 1983. 401p. pap. $8.95 (641.2)

The focus is on the various wine-producing areas of the world. There are numerous facts and opinions about many wine production processes, as well as tips on the best of the crops. The material varies in length from essays to brief entries, and the author is careful about defining and explaining foreign terminology. This book nicely complements other titles, but is not a required item.

Johnson, Hugh. **Hugh Johnson's Modern Encyclopedia of Wine.** New York: Simon & Schuster, 1983. 544p. $29.95 (641.2)

Well known as a writer on wine, Johnson sets out here to cover every aspect of wine for the interested layperson. He succeeds, and this is one of the best of many such works now available. The principal 70 or so wine-producing countries of the world are covered—about one-third is devoted to France, another third to the rest of Europe and the United States, and one-third to the rest of the world. These sections are of interest to both the investor in wines and the taster, particularly as the author answers many common questions about practical problems. Certain top wines are featured, with information on how they are made. There are good sections on storing, purchasing, and tasting wine, and related topics. The normal problem about what wine to serve with what dish is considered in great detail, and with common sense. There are excellent illustrations, the writing style is pleasant, and the material is accurate. It is a superior reference work for answering questions about wines, as well as a fine place to browse.

Johnson, Hugh. **World Atlas of Wine.** Rev. ed. New York: Simon & Schuster, 1978. 288p. $29.95; pap. $8.95 (641.22)

This is a delightful guide, both for browsing in and for pinpointing specific wine areas of the world. The maps and photographs are beautiful, and the numerous diagrams and tables help even the uninitiated find the path to the best wines. Johnson covers every major wine-growing part of the world, but tends to concentrate on France and the better-known wine sections. He considers, in geographical order, the various regions and their best wines. (This latter recommendation is, of course, by now dated, but many of the wines are still available.) There is a good explanation and a detailed history of the whole wine-making process.

Lichine, Alexis. **Alexis Lichine's Guide to the Wines and Vineyards of France.** Rev. ed. New York: Knopf, 1982. 483p. $18.50; pap. $9.95 (641.2)

A standard guide, first published in 1979, this offers information about and appreciation of the numerous French wines. Arrangement is by area or château from the Loire to Bordeaux, and for each section the author notes the particular characteristics of the wines. There are useful parts devoted to tasting, how to determine a good wine from a bad (including black-and-white illustrations of labels), and the use of wine with foods. Note that this is updated about every three years, and the reader should look for the latest edition, particularly as the author considers wines of the preceding year or so in some detail.

Price, Pamela. **Enjoying Wine: A Taster's Companion.** North Pomfret, VT: David & Charles, 1983. 202p. $18.95; pap. $12.95 (641.22)

How can you learn to test wine by taste and judge its worth? Some claim it is an inborn trait that cannot be learned, but wine expert Price argues this is not the case. Wine-tasting techniques, which she considers in much detail, can be mastered by anyone with patience and an appreciation for detail. After a general discussion of the whole process, there are individual sections on different types of wines. In addition, there is advice on what types of wines to serve with what foods, the various types of glassware and equipment needed, etc. Although published in England, the book's approach can be appreciated by anyone, anywhere. If you think the art can be learned, this is for you.

Robards, Terry. **Terry Robards' New Book of Wine: The Ultimate Guide to Wines throughout the World.** New York: Putnam's, 1984. 512p. $19.95 (641.2)

A current, thorough coverage of wines for both beginner and expert, this is a revision of the popular New York Times Book of Wine (1976). Almost all aspects of the world wine scene are covered. Robards moves with ease from a thorough study and listing of California wineries to a consideration of the best in French and Italian wines. Along the way are sections dedicated to tasting, the use of wines with certain types of foods, the storage and the aging of wine, and the kinds of glassware to use for varieties of wine. Scores of other points are covered. It is difficult to imagine a question on current practices that is not answered somewhere in these pages.

Spurrier, Steven, and Michael Dovaz. **Academie du Vin Complete Wine Course.** New York: Putnam's, 1983. 224p. $19.95 (641.2)

Set out in a series of four courses, or study areas, this is a kind of textbook for the dedicated would-be wine expert. It is, as the subtitle says, "a comprehensive course in wine appreciation, tasting and study." The emphasis, of course, is on France and French wines. The guide opens with explanations of such things as different types of wines and their storage. The second part is involved with more advanced types of wines and wine growing, and here a nod is given to wines outside France. Next comes a full course on wine tasting, including various vintages. Finally there is a section on how to appreciate wine when served with food or in other situations. Most of this is much too detailed and advanced for the amateur, but it is a fine guide for the serious wine taster.

Sutcliffe, Serena, ed. **Andre Simon's Wines of the World.** 2nd ed. New York: McGraw-Hill, 1981. 639p. $35 (641.2)

Here the focus is on the principal wine-producing areas of the world. Each country or region is described by an expert. The articles, which may be only a few pages or well over 120 pages, depending on the importance of the area, cover such things as producers, premiere wines, growing conditions, and just about anything the dedicated wine lover would wish to know. There are excellent colored illustrations and adequate maps, although the latter are not as good as those found in other books of this type. *Note:* This was first published in 1967, revised in 1972, and is now an almost totally new book.

WOODCARVING

Tangerman, E. J. **Capturing Personality in Woodcarving.** New York: Sterling, 1981. 128p. pap. $5.95 (731.4)

Here are simple, easy-to-follow instructions for carving small wooden figures and masks. The emphasis, as the title suggests, is on methods of bringing the faces to life. The author considers both humans and animals, as well as some inanimate objects. The book is well illustrated.

Tangerman, E. J. **Tangerman's Basic Whittling and Woodcarving.** New York: Sterling, 1984. 128p. pap. $6.95 (731.4)

Take up a knife and a piece of wood and begin to carve and whittle. There is, however, more to it than that, at least according to Tangerman, who is an expert in such things. Here he shows how whittling can shape a piece of wood into a winning object. Along the way, he demonstrates the various types of knives one should use, as well as their care and sharpening. The illustrations are passable, but not up to the specific instructions.

WOODWORKING
See also Carpentry; Homes—Maintenance & Repair; Tools

Adams, J. T. **Arco's Complete Woodworking Handbook.** Rev. ed. New York: Arco, 1981. 700p. $19.95 (684)

Whether it is a question of the right kind of wood or the proper type of tool, this is a good place to turn for help and information. Among the most complete of the general woodworking guides, it covers every conceivable area of interest to both the beginner and the expert. There are the usual chapters on fundamentals of woodworking, plus detailed and illustrated sections on painting, wood finishes and finishing, building materials, shop safety, etc. The style is easy to follow and the step-by-step instructions are sensible.

Better Homes and Gardens Woodworking Projects You Can Build. Des Moines, IA: Meredith, 1980. 96p. pap. $4.95 (684.1)

"You can build" are the key words, and here even the beginner will find encouragement and help in constructing items for use around the house. Some 60 detailed plans and descriptions are offered for such things as tables, shelves, dividers, and uncomplicated cabinets. The designs are good, if not imaginative, and for each project one finds a photograph of how it should look when completed. There are the usual diagrams and adequate instruction. The short sections on basic carpentry are of little real value to anyone who is familiar with woodworking.

Burch, Monte. **The Home Cabinetmaker: Woodworking Techniques, Furniture Building, and Installing Millwork.** New York: Harper, 1981. 543p. $27.95 (684)

One of the best overall books on cabinetmaking, this is written for both the beginner and the near expert. The author, who has had years of experience in woodworking, begins with basics (how to select various types of woods, tools, etc.) and moves on to plans for eight projects. The sections on what is needed for a good shop are excellent, and there is even a nod to the individual who is looking for information on how to establish a business. The parts on installation are detailed and will save readers much time, trouble, and commotion. There are equally good instructions on the maintenance of tools. The writer supplements his precise, clear directions with illustrations, both line drawings and photographs. While the plans for various projects are too advanced for beginners, the rest of the book is an excellent introduction to the whole subject.

Capotosto, Rosario. **Capotosto's Woodworking Techniques and Projects.** New York: Van Nostrand, 1982. 410p. $29.95 (684.1)

Assuming the reader knows little or nothing about woodworking, the author divides this useful manual into four sections. The first part explains basics from tools and techniques to methods of laying out plans. The second and third parts are plans for close to 50 projects of varying difficulty. Each project demonstrates a different technique, a different set of learning processes that help to develop the user's skills. The book ends with a discussion of special problems and how to use common equipment for complex jobs. Along the way everything is defined and explained with extreme care. This, coupled with numerous and excellent illustrations, makes the book an ideal beginner's guide for both adults and young people.

Feirer, John. **The Woodworker's Reference Guide and Sourcebook.** New York: Scribner's, 1983. 332p. $35 (684.08)

This is not a how-to-do-it book, but a guide to places where the reader will find information about wood and woodworking. Divided into several primary categories, the book opens with a thorough discussion of the various types of woods, including man-made products. As a reference, it is suitable for anyone working with wood, whether they are carpenters, cabinetmakers, or furniture designers. There are then detailed lists of suppliers of wood, tools, plans, and even organizations, colleges, and schools with an interest in the subject. Throughout one finds references to key magazines and books as well as documents, and the work particularly is valuable for its up-to-date bibliographies. It is truly encyclopedic in scope, and a valuable reference guide.

Hand, Jackson. **How to Do Your Own Wood Finishing.** 2nd ed. New York: Harper, 1976. 170p. pap. $3.95 (698.3)

Written for both the amateur craftsperson and the individual who simply wants to refinish a single piece of furniture, this gives explicit, easy-to-follow instructions. The illustrations are useful, and there is full information on equipment and wood products, and even a glossary of terms.

Oberrecht, Ken. **Plywood Projects.** New York: Scribner's, 1984. 241p. $24.95 (684.08)

In objects from cabinets to furniture to simple devices, the author demonstrates the advantages of working with plywood. Each of the 50 or so projects is outlined in considerable detail and with numerous photographs, drawings, and charts. Tools and materials needed for each project are explained in an easy-to-understand chart format. A basic problem with plywood is that it lacks the refinement of other woods, and often looks cheap. Oberrecht explains what can be done to bring out the best in the material to make it look glorious.

Ortho Books Editors. **How to Design & Build Storage Projects.** San Francisco: Ortho, 1983. 96p. pap. $5.95 (643.7)

Following the standard pattern of numerous illustrations and precise instructions, this is another of the worthwhile guides in the Ortho Home Improvement Series. The book opens with suggestions on how to find and expand existing storage space in the average home. Once a space is located, the challenge is to construct something that will make the most of the area. To this end, there are instructions on various types of storage units. Another part of the book is devoted to a variety of tools and working techniques. Useful as the guide is, it is not for the beginner. The supposition is that the reader has a basic understanding of carpentry and the language of design and construction.

St. Michel, Jean Paul, ed. **201 Woodworking Projects for Indoors and Outdoors.** Lonqueuil, Canada: Deco-Plans, 1982. 359p. pap. $15.95 (684)

In an oversized format with numerous plans and illustrations, the author sets out 201 projects. These range from children's toys and furniture to bookcases and kitchen planning. Precise measurements and details are given for each of the projects. The focus is on items around the average home. While the brief text is clear enough, there is a strong supposition that the reader is familiar with basic woodworking. A useful aid in any home workshop.

Scott, Ernest. **Working in Wood: The Illustrated Manual of Tools, Methods, Materials and Classic Construction.** New York: Putnam's, 1980. 272p. $25 (684)

Directed to both the beginner and the expert, this is the best all-around encyclopedic approach to woodworking. It is divided into six sections: classic constructions, tools, design, methods, materials, and fixtures and fittings. Each has a good introduction and extremely specific advice and instructions. Each, too, has abundant illustrations, many in color. The explanations are clear and straightforward, and the scope is such that all conceivable aspects of woodworking are considered. There are numerous cross-references and a good index. The oversized volume may not be ideal for having at the workbench, but it certainly is ideal for its handsome appearance.

Studley, Vance. **The Woodworker's Book of Wooden Kitchen Utensils.** New York: Van Nostrand, 1981. 128p. $14.95 (674.88)

An unusual book about an unusual subject, this is welcomed by anyone who deplores the general horror associated with kitchen utensil design. Some kitchen tools are handsome, but decidedly expensive. Others are reasonable, but decidedly ugly. So why not make your own? Here the author details 39 different utensils that can be turned out by the amateur and near expert, with emphasis on the latter. The utensils range from a simple wine rack and bamboo tea whisk to more complicated items. Each is accompanied by black-and-white line drawings and extremely clear directions. For beginners, there are basics of woodworking. Still, the most fascinating section concerns the history of cooks' tools, as well as a good bibliography on the subject.

Underhill, Roy. **The Woodwright's Companion: Exploring Traditional Woodcraft.** Chapel Hill: University of North Carolina Pr., 1983. 184p. $19.95; pap. $12.95 (684.08)

This is dedicated to the individual who loves to find, repair, and work with traditional woodworking equipment such as hand saws and whetstones. After giving the reader encouragement in locating and using traditional tools, the author goes on to explain various projects such as shingled roofs, or less awesome tasks such as making stands. There are numerous illustrations, but the unique feature is the author's enthusiasm and dedication. Even the power-tool expert may be won over—as, of course, are viewers of Underhill's television show on PBS. *Note:* This is a companion to the author's somewhat similar *The Woodwright's Shop* (1981).

WORD GAMES

Moore, Thurston. **The Original Word Game Dictionary.** New York: Stein & Day, 1983. 360p. $16.95; pap. $8.95 (793.73)

Here are the words needed to play such popular games as Scrabble and Boggle, as well as nine new ones introduced by the author. The dictionary, stripped down to essentials, includes only words with two to nine letters. The arrangement allows for rapid use, although the dictionary is of little value for anything but word games. There are only simple definitions after each word. Still, for what it does, this book does it well enough. Included are some extraneous materials on such things as a word game party.

WORD PROCESSING. *See* Computers—Word Processing

AUTHOR INDEX

This is a combined author index for *How-To: 1400 Best Books on Doing Almost Everything* and *Self-Help: 1400 Best Books on Personal Growth*, both by Bill Katz and Linda Sternberg Katz (Bowker, 1985). Numbers printed in regular type refer to page numbers in *How-To;* numbers printed in **boldface** refer to page numbers in *Self-Help*.

Note: Multiple authorship of titles is indicated as follows: All entries for second (or third) authors show a *See* or *See also* reference to the primary author, for example, *Smith, Jane. See Jones, William*. If all entries for Jones are coauthored by Smith, the primary entry will appear as *Jones, William, 84, 123, 224*. If Smith is not a coauthor on all entries for Jones, the primary entry will appear as *Jones, William, 84, 123 (Smith, jt. auth.), 224*, or, perhaps, *Jones, William, 84, 123 (Smith, jt. auth.), 224 (Brown, jt. auth.)*.

TITLE INDEX

This is a combined title index for *How-To: 1400 Best Books on Doing Almost Everything* and *Self-Help: 1400 Best Books on Personal Growth*, both by Bill Katz and Linda Sternberg Katz (Bowker, 1985). Numbers printed in regular type refer to page numbers in *How-To;* numbers printed in **boldface** refer to page numbers in *Self-Help.*

SUBJECT INDEX

This is a combined subject index for *How-To: 1400 Best Books on Doing Almost Everything* and *Self-Help: 1400 Best Books on Personal Growth*, both by Bill Katz and Linda Sternberg Katz (Bowker, 1985). Numbers printed in regular type refer to page numbers in *How-To;* numbers printed in **boldface** refer to page numbers in *Self-Help.*